TOWER HAMLETS COLLEGE
Learning Centre

||||||||||||||||||||||||||||||||||
074237

£18·95

WITHDRAWN FROM HAVERING COLLEGES
SIXTH FORM LIBRARY

This book is to be returned on or before the last date stamped below or you will be charged a fine

DRIVING VISIONS

D1336194

EXPLORING THE ROAD MOVIE

DRIVING VISIONS

by *DAVID LADERMAN*

THE LIBRARY
TOWER HAMLETS COLLEGE
POPLAR HIGH STREET
LONDON E14 0AF
Tel: 0207 510 7763

UNIVERSITY OF TEXAS PRESS, AUSTIN

Order No·
Class: 791·436 LAD
Accession No: 074237
Type: L

Copyright © 2002 by the University of Texas Press
All rights reserved
Printed in the United States of America
First edition, 2002

Requests for permission to reproduce material from this work
should be sent to Permissions, University of Texas Press, P.O.
Box 7819, Austin, TX 78713-7819.

⊗ The paper used in this book meets the minimum require-
ments of ANSI/NISO Z39.48-1992 (R1997) (Permanence of
Paper).

Library of Congress Cataloging-in-Publication Data

Laderman, David.
Driving visions : exploring the road movie / by David Laderman.
    p.   cm.
ISBN 0-292-74731-4 (alk. paper) —
ISBN 0-292-74732-2 (pbk. : alk. paper)
1. Road films—History and criticism.   I. Title.
PN1995.9.R63 L33   2002
791.43′6—dc21   2001008417

To Mom, Dad, and Gary,
for giving me the journey

And to Claudia,
for making the road especially sweet

CONTENTS

ACKNOWLEDGMENTS

I would like to thank Scott Simmon and Jim Kitses for their extremely helpful comments on earlier drafts of this book. Thanks also to Pete Bateman of Larry Edmonds Bookshop in Los Angeles, Sam Sanchez at College of San Mateo, and Mark Bowen of San Francisco's Le Video for assisting with illustrations. And a big thank you to Jim Burr.

DRIVING VISIONS

The road of excess leads to the palace of wisdom.
—William Blake

Outside of society, that's where I wanna be.
—Patti Smith

Chapter 1 . . . .

PAVING THE WAY

Sources and Features of the Road Movie

They have been driving for days through the desert, with little sleep. They want to get to Mexico. The police have been relentlessly pursuing them. Yet they are more desperately fleeing their own oppressive society: hard labor at cheap wages, a prisonlike domestic life, verbal and physical abuse, a legal system that presumes them guilty. Crossing numerous state lines, they have likewise crossed into an altered state of perception. Driving, they have re-discovered themselves; they have been reborn, aided by the midwife of their desperate journey. Transcending mere friendship or romance, they are now buddies, comrades, soul mates.

But they will not get to Mexico. A different kind of freedom awaits them. They are trapped. Behind, they are surrounded by a veritable army of law enforcement; before them stretches the Grand Canyon. Having truly lived for a few brief days on the road, they embrace for the last time. Revelation and liberation taste too sweet; the abyss beckons. Suddenly the car speeds over the edge—into a glorious white light.

Sketched in such archetypal terms, these final moments from *Thelma and Louise* (Ridley Scott, 1991) invoke a vast parade of other road movies, crys-tallizing many of the essential features of the genre. The film's infamous end-ing dramatizes the fundamental core impulse of the road movie: rebellion against conservative social norms.

The driving force propelling most road movies, in other words, is an em-brace of the journey as a means of cultural critique. Road movies generally aim beyond the borders of cultural familiarity, seeking the unfamiliar for revelation, or at least for the thrill of the unknown. Such traveling, coded as defamiliarization, likewise suggests a mobile refuge from social circumstances felt to be lacking or oppressive in some way. This broadly conceived notion of cultural critique functions in road movies on many levels: cinematically, in terms of innovative traveling camera work, montage, and soundtrack; narratively, in terms of an open-ended, rambling plot structure; thematically, in terms of frustrated, often desperate characters lighting out for something better, someplace else. Thus the road movie celebrates subversion as a literal venturing outside of society. This book charts the historical evolution of such modernist, visionary rebellion as the engine driving the genre—to be sure, in a variety of directions.

But before considering the road movie, let us consider the road: an essential element of American society and history, but also a universal symbol of the course of life, the movement of desire, and the lure of both freedom and destiny. Like the wheel, the road expresses our distinction as humans, embodying the essential stuff that makes human civilization possible. Conjuring an array of utopian connotations (most generally, "possibility" itself), the road secures us with direction and purpose. And yet, the road also can provoke anxiety: We take the road, but it also takes us. Will we survive the upcoming hairpin turn? Are we on an extended detour, full of delusions? Do we need to turn onto a new road? Often the road provides an outlet for our excesses, enticing our desire for thrill and mystery. The horizon beckons both auspiciously and ominously. Exceeding the borders of the culture it makes possible, for better or for worse, the road represents the unknown.

The Road Movie's Modernist Engine

The road movie appears as a dynamic manifestation of American society's fascination with the road. Comprised of an intricate matrix of cultural predilections, the genre of the road movie explores the "borders" (the status quo conventions) of American society. Often from a culturally critical perspective, the road movie asks, What does it mean to exceed the boundaries, to transgress the limits, of American society? The genre insists that not merely excess, but *"the road* of excess," leads to special insight (a "palace," true—but one need not *stay* there . . .). Mapping the excessive experiences—whether physical, spiritual, emotional—of those making the journey, road movies also portray a road of excess instead of a practical or functional road: travel for travel's sake, travel as an "end" in itself. In representing such excessive motion through compelling film style and narrative, the road movie constitutes a significant if often overlooked strain of film history. Overlooked because the genre enjoys a uniquely elusive status. During the classical Hollywood era, various traditional genres generated road movie elements; then the road movie emerges with distinction through the New American cinema of the late 1960s, as an "independent" film genre, vehicle of antigenre sensibilities and countercultural rebellion.

Before road movies took off as a distinct genre in the late 1960s, cars and movies had long been sharing the twentieth-century highway of American technology. As consumer objects, cars and films seemed to evolve hand in hand, providing mobility (literally, or in the form of "escapist" narrative entertainment) for Americans in transition, first from rural to urban, then from urban to suburban lifestyles. Both cars and movies promised to express the idealized uniqueness of the individual consumer; it is therefore perhaps no coincidence that both industries became, at approximately the same time (late 1920s), mass production, assembly-line institutions, more or less homogenizing their respective commodities (Hey, 194). Conceived together, automobiles and films dynamically reflect our culture as it becomes transformed by transportational and representational technologies.[1] As Michael Atkinson puts it, "Few cultural developments outside the first atomic bomb test at Los Alamos have had such a decisive impact on movies. The structure of the car, designed both to conform to our bodies' shortcomings and powerfully extend them, has become how we regard the world (through the screen-like, Panavision-shaped lens of the windscreen and, like a miniature movie within a movie, the rear view mirror)" (16).

This historical relationship between cars and films has more specific parameters. Cars assisted in the making of films, and in the early development of film narrative. Directors like D. W. Griffith used them for effective traveling shots. "Whereas motion had been confined to the objects within the image, it was now transferred to the spectator, thrusting him into the action and making him a participant in the drama" (Brougher, 171). But films too assisted in the "making" of cars, which have since the earliest silent films enjoyed "prop star" status. The automobile as icon and driving as action were incorporated in film narratives as early as Biograph's *Runaway Match* (1903) and *The Gentlemen Highwaymen* (1905). The former deploys the car to help a couple elope; the latter uses a car to terrorize a couple. A bit later, Griffith's *The Drive for a Life* (1909) introduces the "saved by an auto" theme (J. Smith, 179–92). Certainly the silent comedians, then the gangsters of the thirties, depended in various ways on their automobiles to keep the story going.[2] The popular classical genres of the 1930s and 1940s continued to develop more sophisticated representations of driving. Then, on the cusp of classical Hollywood's demise, the 1960s counterculture infused the cinematic act of driving with a politically rebellious spirit, best exemplified by *Bonnie and Clyde* (1967) and *Easy Rider* (1969). Both films integrate road travel (in cars or on motorcycles) more centrally into the narrative. Since then, the road movie has flourished.

Some critics have suggested that the road movie's contemporary proliferation is symptomatic of postmodern anxiety and restlessness. As an "ideogram of human desire and last-ditch search for self," contemporary road movies, according to Atkinson, reflect the crisis in meaning evoked by the end of the millennium for "a generation raised on television and the open-ended roadlike format of the weekly serial" (14–16). Timothy Corrigan, in one of the first extended writings on the genre, similarly considers the road movie a prime example of "generic hysteria": "a historical body in trouble with its representation of itself and its historical place" (143). Corrigan's cursory but insightful description of the road movie's evolution echoes signatures of the postmodern condition:

> The historical journey of the road movie might consequently be described through an obsessive itinerary that moves through the prophetic tales of Ulmer and Lang, prototypical road movies that were not yet generic, through the postwar formulation of the genre, characterized by amnesia, hallucinations and theatrical crisis. In the mid-seventies and eighties, the genre has made its very action and subject its own historical hysteria: if genre is the prototype of classification and interpretation, it now becomes the *mise-en-abyme* reflection of an audience that can no longer imagine a naturalized history. The environment, conditions and actions of the road movie have become a borderless refuse bin. (152–53)

My own historical framework for exploring the genre is an elaboration of what Corrigan here suggests, comprising generally a movement from classical predecessors ("prototypical road movies that were not yet generic"), through a crucial, genre-defining modernist phase ("hallucinations and theatrical crisis"), to the contemporary postmodern period ("borderless refuse bin").

In using the broad, often slippery term "modernist" to characterize the road movie's engine of visionary rebellion and cultural critique, a few preliminary comments are in order. First, modernism as a broad cultural and industrial phenomenon characterizing early- to mid-twentieth-century America. The road movie's love affair with driving—with cars and motorcycles as mechanically developed vehicles of transport and exploration—seems generally driven by this modernist sensibility, which celebrates technology as a liberating force that can lead us into the future. Second, modernism as an aesthetic practice, where romanticism gets modernized. While the great examples of modernism of the early twentieth century—Brecht, Joyce, Woolf, Picasso, the Surrealists—are typically considered reactions *against* the romanticism and realism dominating nineteenth-century arts and letters, it is important to appreciate the legacy of both romanticism and realism *within* modernist art and literature. This legacy revolves around the modernist conception of art as visionary, and as capable of social criticism. Despite—and, perhaps, because of—their emphasis on obscure psychological introspection and subversion of the classical realist text, many early-twentieth-century modernist works suggest some romantic sense of liberation, as well as some progressive vision of truth.

In other words, modernist art expands the representational limits of both the realist trend of physical description and the romantic trend of celebrating the imaginary realm. The modernism that inspires the road movie more directly than early-twentieth-century industrial and aesthetic trends would be the films of Bergman, Fellini, Resnais, and the French New Wave. Beyond making self-conscious use of advances in film technology (fast film stock, location shooting, lightweight cameras, etc.), the American road movie of the New Hollywood imports the following from postwar European film modernism: elliptical narrative structure and self-reflexive devices; elusive development of alienated characters; bold traveling shots and montage sequences. Combining the legacies of classical Hollywood and the 1950s highway boom, the road movie offers a distinctly American version of these European modernist influences.

Perhaps the most important and immediate formative feature of the road movie's modernist engine is the countercultural unrest of late-1960s America —a historical moment that may be characterized as modernism's last gasp as it transforms into postmodern culture.[3] John Orr makes this point specifically in relation to what he terms the "neomodern" cinema between 1958 and 1978, a "critical and subversive rendering of modernity" that breaks with Hollywood narratives by returning to high modernism. Focusing on "the political revolts of 1968" (the precise countercultural context of the road movie's emergence), Orr describes how modernism and romanticism were "effectively combined": "The political style of Parisian contestation, its street revolts, its existential powers of invention, its self-conscious theatricality and obsession with cultural signs, all were modernist in their inspired dissonance. Yet the apocalyptic dream of a global industrial society based on equal participation of all was utopian and at times romantic." The "neomodern" cinema informing the road movie "uses both the narrative fragment and the play with the camera," but also "needs the linear movement of cinema-as-technique which *enhances* the mimetic power of the image" (2–4). The road movie's overt concern with rebellion, social criticism, and liberating thrills derives from this modernist sensibility.

Yet historically modernism possesses a conformist streak. Modernist works sometimes reek of elitist reflexivity (allusions to previous master-pieces), perpetuating the politically conservative elevation of the artist as a mystically gifted individual.[4] In many road movies, modernist rebellion con-tinually works itself through such inflections of conformity—inflections de-rived from classical Hollywood formula, from postmodern aesthetics, from gender and race subtexts, and from modernism itself.[5] Yet the genre's pri-mary modernist drive articulates a suspicious disillusionment with dominant cinematic, cultural, and political institutions—as well as a vision, quite lit-erally, beyond them.

The Journey in Literature

Let us begin our exploration of what makes a road movie with a detour, through the journey narrative in literature. The road movie grows out of this long-standing literary tradition, which in turn reflects the history of Western culture at large. Especially important in the historical continuity between journey literature and road movies is the thematic impulse of cultural cri-tique. However, another purpose here is to distinguish American cinematic versions of the journey from these literary predecessors.

Not all journey literature revolves around cultural critique, but an over-view of some major works reveals a general use of the journey narrative struc-ture as a vehicle for some kind of social commentary. We might begin with the beginning, so to speak: Homer's *Odyssey*. The tale of Odysseus's ram-bling trajectory to Ithaca after the Trojan War is framed by his imprison-ment as the novel begins, and his home, to which he longs to return. The journey itself, fantastic and often grotesque, stages a series of episodes and "detours" that lure him from his goal of returning home. There is a sense in which Homer is perpetually postponing the end of the journey, by distract-ing Odysseus from his desire to reclaim his identity as King of Ithaca. This emphasizes the journey over the destination, questioning the presumed va-lidity of the latter. Once he finally arrives, he still must struggle to reassert his identity: he has to prove who he is. This dramatizes the difficulty—shared by the Prodigal Son and, more recently, Thomas Wolfe's George Webber—of ever being able to "go home again."

In many ways Homer's *Odyssey* lays out the basic narrative formula of many later classic works of journey literature. Chaucer's medieval master-piece *The Canterbury Tales* weaves a rich diversity of voices, all narrating various adventures during the April pilgrimage to Becket's shrine. Two clas-sic Renaissance works, Rabelais's *Gargantua and Pantagruel* (1564) and Cer-vantes's *Don Quixote* (1615), are similarly structured as travel adventures. Both works use fanciful, often fantastical episodes during the protagonist's journey as a means of social satire. Through the journey structure, Pantagruel and Don Quixote become relatively disconnected from any stable social con-text; thus, they become more able to critically observe social mores. Both works are considered classics of Renaissance literature because they critique the religious medieval order Western culture was about to move away from. While Don Quixote, for example, is on one level blinded to reality by the romances he has read and his overexcited imagination, the narrative of his journey contains a veiled attack on the relationship between the Catholic Church and Spanish politics.

The use of the journey narrative as a means of social satire is developed further in several classics of the Enlightenment era, especially through the emerging picaresque novel. Voltaire's *Candide* (1759) parodies idealist politi-cal philosophy through a rambunctious series of adventures for the epony-mous main character. This journey novel dramatizes the overwhelming chaos of the emerging mercantile, materialistic culture, as well as the brutal hypoc-risy of the Spanish Inquisition (and politics in general). In England, Daniel Defoe's *Moll Flanders* (1722) and Henry Fielding's *Tom Jones* (1749) use the picaresque novel to scrutinize the social customs of the day. Through its sym-pathetic realism, *Moll Flanders* is especially striking for its suggestion that the main character's traveling mishaps are in fact *not* mishaps, but the results of an exploitative society that forces her from situation to situation.

Moll Flanders eventually comes to America, where the European literary tradition of the journey narrative is given particular nuance and character. The very birth and adolescence of America seems crucially founded upon the notion of the journey, which thus becomes an essential feature of American cultural identity. Janis P. Stout contends that the journey narrative character-izes much American literature because the journey is so essentially embedded in American national history, a history that "begins with voyages, of explo-ration or escape or migration." Whether as classic westerly movement, or as return to the East, "spatial movement has been the characteristic expres-sion of our sense of life" (4–5). The first European expeditions of conquest, then the flight of persecuted Europeans coming to colonize the New World; the ensuing frontier expansion and homesteading migrations, then continu-ous immigration waves throughout the nineteenth and twentieth centuries;

all these historical chapters constitute America's national self-definition in terms of movement and expansion.[6]

In fact, the sense of the journey at the heart of American cultural identity embodies a romanticized vision of the wilderness (Nash, 67). However, as American journey narratives reveal, the reified, romanticized image of the wilderness bears within it the contradiction between nature and culture; that is, the need to both conquer and celebrate the wilderness. James Fenimore Cooper's *Leatherstocking Tales* (1823–41) plays out many of these themes, with Natty Bumppo expressing his love for the native beauty and traditions of the land, even as he heralds the encroaching preindustrial culture.[7]

More significant would be Mark Twain's *Adventures of Huckleberry Finn* (1884), where the title character, after escaping from his brutal father, drifts on a raft down the Mississippi River with a runaway slave named Jim. The story of their journey downstream becomes a penetrating commentary on the society they travel past and through, revealing corruption, moral decay, and intellectual impoverishment. Huck learns the dignity of human life by virtue of being on the road ("on the river"); he helps Jim escape at the end, symbolically repudiating the moral blindness of the "respectable" slaveholding culture. Moreover, the novel implies that living with nature (represented by the journey downriver) is more pure and authentic than the culture observed from a fluid distance.[8]

Across the Atlantic in England some years later, another journey downriver would further develop this type of social criticism leveled at cultural modernization. Joseph Conrad's *Heart of Darkness* (1902) describes cruel colonial exploitation in the Belgian Congo through the device of Marlowe's journey in search of the powerful white trader Kurtz, who has abandoned cultural imperialism for his own brand of despotism among the natives. *Heart of Darkness* is especially significant for the way it engages a powerful political critique through the journey, yet also explores the dark underside of Western cultural expansion on a psychological level. Along these lines, D. H. Lawrence's *Women in Love* (1920) provides some notable imagery of travel and mobility, within a modernist political context similar to Conrad's. In a crucial chapter titled "Excurse," Birkin and Ursula take a drive through the country; a violent roadside argument ensues, which eventually brings them into a deep bond of love. To realize this love, they decide they must depart their familiar surroundings and journey aimlessly (308). Anticipating countless road movies, the kind of travel they aim to fulfill is without destination, charged with rebellion against a choking industrialized stability.

Early-twentieth-century American journey literature offers its own brand of such British modernism.[9] While still deploying the journey as cultural critique, contemporary American road novels generally devote more romantic attention to the highway and automobile.[10] Yet the automobile bears within it an ambivalence, around whether it frees or imprisons us. In his discussion of the automobile in modern American fiction, David Laird claims that "cars run through literature in defiantly paradoxical and contradictory ways," as both a means of realizing the "romance impulse" of freedom, exploration and escape, as well as a menacing incarnation of our culture's destructive addiction to technology (245).

One important classic American writer whose work forcefully embodies these tensions is John Steinbeck. Mobility in Steinbeck's work usually functions to examine the depressed economic classes, and the sociopolitical causes that produce them. Modernizing the journey narrative, his writings still echo Whitman and Twain by suggesting that spiritual salvation from a corrupt culture is found in the transcendence of nature. *The Grapes of Wrath* (1939) is Steinbeck's best and most famous treatment of these themes, where a mystical affirmation of all life as holy is interwoven with a family's brutal struggle for survival on the road during the Depression.[11] The source for John Ford's classic Hollywood precursor to the road movie (discussed below), it has been described as "America's best-known proletarian road saga" and "the strongest political test of the redemptive powers of Whitmanesque Transcendentalism in our highway literature" (Lackey, 83).

Janis P. Stout considers *The Grapes of Wrath* an example of "the home-founding journey"; other classical American journey categories or "patterns" she postulates are the "exploration and escape" (*The Pioneers*), the "return to Europe" (*The Ambassadors*), and "the quest" (*Moby Dick*). Her last category, "lost and wandering," focuses on the twentieth-century journey as one "of uncertain destination or duration, the journey to no end" (105). This American postwar literary landscape more dramatically influences the road movie. An exemplary starting point is Henry Miller's 1947 *The Air-Conditioned Nightmare*, not discussed by Stout, presumably because it is nonfiction. Yet the work forcefully conveys the spirit of frustrated meandering that precedes and informs the road movie. After returning from a trip to Europe, the author rambles on a cross-country trek, observing with acerbic disgust America's headlong spiral into rampant materialism, leaving behind its more substantial European roots.

Miller's mood of restless wandering gets harnessed and taken for a more glorious ride by Jack Kerouac in *On the Road* (1955), discussed at length in Stout's "lost and wandering" chapter. Like some of Kerouac's later novels (*The Subterraneans, The Dharma Bums, Desolation Angels*), *On the Road* combines spiritual and sensual exploration through the journey motif; but this journey has little direction or destination, and celebrates pure movement as moving purity. Kerouac's watershed novel can be understood, in retrospect, as a "master narrative" for the road movie, especially the distinctive modernist/rebel version that emerges in the late 1960s. It reflects the affluence of American postwar society, which spawns leisure travel (even though the novel's protagonist is often down and out). More importantly, it articulates the alternative social values of the Beat movement that later blossom into the 1960s counterculture. Several of the novel's more specific thematic and stylistic preoccupations prove useful both in describing the road movie as a genre and in outlining its ideological contours and contradictions.

On the Road tells the rambling tale of two young male buddies, Sal Paradise and Dean Moriarty, who trek back and forth across America to reawaken their souls by rediscovering the landscape. The somewhat cyclical, meandering quality of the narrative, and Sal's whimsical first-person narration—neither in the classical realist vein—both contribute to the novel's celebration of quest and transience over destination and stability. *On the Road* quickly became a countercultural manifesto through its articulation of a bohemian lifestyle that rejected traditional, conservative "family values," the Protestant work ethic, and middle-class materialism (all of which, of course, "the 1950s" became shorthand for).

On the Road's strategic mode for expressing this cultural critique is to glorify the automobile, not only as the primary means for traveling, but also as a figurative vehicle of transformation. Many lengthy, poetic descriptions of riding in cars and driving cars suggest even a certain mystical fusion between Sal and Dean, and the car.[12] The road itself is another overinvested motif in the novel, romanticized as a sort of wilderness beyond urban and suburban enclaves. This sense of road travel as outside of and opposed to mainstream urban culture is bolstered in *On the Road* by the dominant frontier imagery of the American Wild West. Several passages express Sal and Dean's spiritual and sensual awakenings in terms of retrieving a mythical cowboy identity: early on, Sal describes Dean as a "Western kinsman of the sun" (11). A related figure comprising the novel's frame of reference is the hobo, symbol of the Depression era who is idealized by Sal and Dean for his unattached, rambling lifestyle, and for the implicit critique of materialism he represents. They embrace the hobo lifestyle as the debris of a failed economic system—thus as holding special spiritual secrets for them. Many road movies blend the cowboy and hobo figures into the road outlaw, crystallizing the notion of being both morally and literally outside the law and society.

Another landmark work of American fiction first published in 1955 likewise uses road travel to challenge traditional moral and cultural authority, but through a sardonic European perspective full of irony. Vladimir Nabokov's *Lolita* does not embrace road travel as primary narrative design in the way *On the Road* does; in fact, for the most part the novel elaborates its sardonic and incisive critique of middle American conformity while Humbert and Lo are stationary (at her mother's house, or later while he is teaching and she is in school). But *Lolita* does periodically put this most unlikely outlaw couple on the road and on the run. During these passages, Humbert vents his disdain for American mass commercial culture (which Lolita so loves, and in fact embodies), trenchantly observing the various provincial towns, motels, roadside amusements and restaurants they pass through. In many ways, Humbert is the ultimate road-traveler-as-American-outsider: his violation of the sacrosanct incest taboo (perhaps the ultimate law) seems a reflection of his bitterly superior (European) deconstruction of American society. His fugitive status as anti-American intellectual criminal becomes symbolically expressed through his often aimless, yet always evasive cross-country journeys with Lolita.

Initially, when Humbert finally has Lolita to himself and they become lovers, the open road signifies freedom and the pursuit of (his) sensual delights. Gradually though, being on the road becomes a nightmarish prison as he becomes paranoid about being pursued. His perpetual mobility likewise renders his control over Lolita ineffective: she finally escapes from him while on the road. Indeed, Humbert is finally captured when, after killing Quilty, he deliberately drives on the wrong side of the road: "The road now stretched across open country, and it occurred to me—not by way of protest, not as a symbol, or anything like that, but merely as a novel experience—that since I had disregarded all laws of humanity, I might as well disregard the rules of traffic. So I crossed to the left side of the highway and checked the feeling, and the feeling was good" (Nabokov, 278–79). While Humbert may not see this act of rebellious driving as symbolic, we certainly are entitled to (I think he insidiously encourages us to, by disavowing any significance to this "novel experience"). In terms of future road movies, we should note the purely aesthetic thrill he derives from reckless driving. This last thrill he will enjoy before going to prison is in fact another incarnation of the core impulse, intolerable to conventional society, that drives him to the nymphet: an amoral sensuality.

But *Lolita* is more interested in Humbert's relationship with Lolita (and America) than it is with being on the road. It also shares little of Kerouac's celebration of the American landscape. Thus, for the road movie, *On the Road* is the more formative work, precisely because it both celebrates and criticizes America by driving through it. It also forged quite a literary legacy that continues today, and that very much feeds off the simultaneous film genre. The 1960s and 1970s saw the popularity of novels descending directly from the spirit of *On the Road,* such as *Rabbit Run* (John Updike, 1960), *Fear and Loathing in Las Vegas* (Hunter S. Thompson, 1971), *Zen and the Art of Motorcycle Maintenance* (Robert Pirsig, 1974), and *The Eden Express* (Mark Vonnegut, 1975). In a postmodern vein, *Americana* (1971), Don DeLillo's first novel, seems remarkably ahead of its time. Inflecting the journey novel with tongue-in-cheek irony (perhaps harking back to the picaresque travel satires mentioned above, as well as *Lolita*), it foresees Reagan's America of the 1980s, focusing its cultural critique around the omnipresent impact of mass media. All these use the cross-country journey as a means of achieving extreme experiences, conceived as therapeutic relief from stable, repressive domestic American culture.

A more violent critique of American culture is found in two influential road-crime novels, Jim Thompson's *The Getaway* (1958) and Truman Capote's *In Cold Blood* (1965). Thompson's novel (which was made into two mediocre road movies) follows Doc and Carol across country as they flee a bank heist, and one murder after another. Notable here is the mutual paranoia that binds the greedy outlaw couple; the perpetual detouring of their escape route; and the nightmarish haven in Mexico they get away to. *In Cold Blood* is a "true crime" novel that uses the apparently senseless murder by two ex-convicts of a midwestern family to explore the alienation lurking beneath the surface of both conformist and outlaw America. The novel achieves a critical mosaic by "crosscutting" between the two killers on the road, and the disturbing quirks of the small-town investigation. With short stories such as "Christine" and "Breakdown" (both made into films), and his recent novel *Desperation* (1997), Stephen King has contributed significantly to the road novel as horror story (which parallels the contemporary road movie trend that foists terror and violence on naive drivers).[13] Two other compelling nightmare-on-the-road novels are Stephen Wright's *Going Native* (1994) and Steven Dixon's *Interstate* (1995), both possessing a keen cinematic sensibility.

Despite a predominant obsession with violence, modern road novels still serve the yearning for discovery and social commentary, as reflected in works like William Least Heat Moon's *Blue Highways* (1982), Cynthia Kadohata's *The Floating World* (1989), Jonathan Lethem's *Amnesia Moon* (1995), Chelsea Cain's *Dharma Girl* (1996), and Steve Erickson's *American Nomad* (1997). *Blue Highways* provides a powerful Native American perspective on the meaning of America, from within a van named "Ghost Dancing."[14] *Ameri-*

can Nomad is proffered by the inner sleeve book jacket notes as "part memoir, part road movie." Assigned by *Rolling Stone* to cover the last election of the millennium, the author gets fired early on, but drives on, impelled by wanderlust, to discover and reveal the contradictions of an America characterized by "memory without history."

Iconography and Style

By emphasizing the imagery and activity of the car (or motorcycle) as the foundation of the narrative, road movies reimagine the journey literature described above in a distinctly American and industrialized context. While often preserving from this literary tradition a focus on the learning experiences of the traveling hero in an unfamiliar setting, road movies rearticulate the quest motif in the "increasingly mechanized" framework of automobile modernity. "Cars and motorcycles represent a mechanized extension of the body, through which that body could move farther and faster than ever before and quite literally evade the trajectory of classical narrative" (Corrigan, 144–46). Car travel in road movies becomes not merely a means of transportation to a destination; rather, the traveling itself becomes the narrative's primary focus. The notion of travel as cultural critique becomes both modernized and modernist, as reinvented by the road movie.

Let us first recognize that road movies depend for their generic distinction on the utter centrality of the combustion engine (automobile or motorcycle) in terms of the movement of the story and characters. "Driving" thus becomes an essential term to clarify. While some very important road movies involve motorcycles, trains, busses, bicycles, or even walking, the most common and most generically privileged vehicle is the automobile. This is due probably to the fact that cars, especially in the postwar era, became so much more popular than motorcycles, trains, or busses. In this respect, we should emphasize the individualized nature of such traveling, in contrast to the popularity of prewar America's collective train and trolley transportation. Mass automobile culture—that is, individual automobiles available to the mass population—invokes the rugged individualist mythology of the Old West, yet extends this mythology as a compelling expression of postwar mobility. But also we should note how the interior space of a car makes for more dramatic possibilities of character interaction.[15] Throughout this study, "driving" therefore designates the road movie's particular motion and motivation. Very often behind the wheel, but also as passenger or hitcher or whatever, road movie characters usually move on the road in a high-speed motorized vehicle. If not literally driving, they "drive" by hitting the road.

In this respect, we should think of road movie protagonists as occupying the mobile site that negotiates the motorized vehicle with the highway. On a basic iconographic and narrative level, road movies are about driving.[16]

A second but equally fundamental aspect of the road movie's distinctive iconic features is the interstate highway system—in other words, the specific component of the setting traveled by the cars, motorbikes, and their drivers. According to Daniel Lopez's "road movie" entry in his genre catalog *Films by Genre*, "the open road is the environment in which the central action takes place" (256). The road movie therefore gains much of its generic material from the accelerated development in the mid-1950s of the interstate highway system (discussed below). Cohan and Hark begin their introduction to *The Road Movie Book* by observing that, in expressing "liberation" from "hegemonic norms, road movies project American Western mythology onto the landscape traversed and bound by the nation's highways" (1). Configured as visual grounding and context for the genre's primary action of driving, these highways symbolize the potential of venturing beyond the familiarity of home, whether on a whim or as a planned excursion. The ability to cross borders via these highways becomes the central feature of the genre's mise en scène. To cross a state or county line is to leave the familiar behind, to venture into the new and unknown. From this perspective, we can distinguish the road movie from other car-oriented subgenres, such as the racing film of the mid-1960s. In their obsession with destination and winning, films like *The Great Race* (1965) or *Grand Prix* (1966) possess little of the road movie's independent spirit (nothing much rebellious about following a race course). Likewise, city driving films like *American Graffiti* (1973), *Taxi Driver* (1976), *Crash* (1996), and *The Cruise* (1999) displace the border crossings and distances crucial to the road movie with confined urban settings and more circular routes going basically nowhere.[17]

Another aspect of the road movie's iconography related to these highways is the vast, open landscape bordered by seductive horizons. These expansive spaces obviously recall the Western's compelling articulation of the frontier, and more generally the shifting nature/culture divide. However, the road movie reinvents the Western's preindustrial iconography of slow-paced horse treks as motorized motion and speed. Important here is not so much the crossing of borders as the traversal of space. These open spaces serve as context and setting for the highways (just as the highways do for the traveling car or motorbike). Sargeant and Watson lucidly convey the privileged road movie space of the desert, "a void in which long-established meanings vanish, the insane heat drives images to haze and nothing is as it once seemed"; with their "vision of the open road eternally vanishing into the horizon," road movies "offer audiences a glimpse at an ecstatic freedom" (13–14). From this angle we can appreciate the road movie's repeated venture beyond familiar culture as a rejuvenating hegira through some emptiness imagined as more primal. Freedom becomes rediscovered as movement across open space.

However, we should emphasize that most road movies do not take place entirely in a so-called wilderness. In fact, road movies exaggerate cultural isolation with vestiges—like the car itself—of that culture. Most often the sense of some wilderness beyond culture becomes heightened in road movies with sundry detours, motels, diners, and gas stations. These various pit stops are often exploited for significant narrative developments. First of all, logic necessitates the drivers must stop somewhere temporarily to meet various rudimentary needs (rest, food, fuel). Second, the journey narrative can gain dramatic intrigue from unexpected plot twists resulting from such intermissions (meeting some new character, committing a crime), or from simply developing the travelers' relationship. Discussing road movies after *Easy Rider,* Lee Hill relates these "diversions and sidetracks" to the genre's overall portrayal of the journey as aimless and fragmented (43). Put differently, these periodic stationary pauses usually serve to enhance the main narrative and thematic thrust: the journey itself.

Still another important component of the road movie's distinctive look and style are various film techniques. One technique road movies tend to mobilize with a certain verve is the traveling shot. Let us first distinguish the road movie traveling shot from the more conventional tracking shot. The latter is usually more "grounded" and slow, related to running or walking (*Touch of Evil*'s opening shot; *Last Year at Marienbad*'s hallway sequences; the final running shot of *The 400 Blows*). Road movie traveling shots by contrast attempt to convey a visceral sense of traveling at a hyperhuman, modernized speed. As such, the point of view of these traveling shots is usually located with the driver, or the car itself (though aerial shots and parallel "side-by-side" traveling shots are fairly common). In *Cinema and Modernity* John Orr describes such road movie aesthetics accordingly:

> The studio perennial of talking heads framed against a process screen is dropped in favour of car mounts placed at any number of angles, high angle chopper shots and following shots from other automobiles. The camera moves with the moving object in its lens, as part of the process of movement in general. This reflexive fix is part of what gives the car its spectator appeal, making it an ecstatic version of the body extended in space and time. (130)

Moreover, these traveling shots are often freely and creatively intercut, an expression of the multiple and shifting perspectives of the car and/or the driver. Especially during actual driving sequences, a montage-style editing often predominates. In the legacy of Eisenstein, this montage approach sublimates car travel to an idea or sensibility, in contrast with the linear, destination-oriented concept of travel, where one action leads to another—and which continuity editing expresses more effectively. Road movies of course possess much continuity editing, but they tend to integrate significant montage sequences so as to emphasize "traveling for traveling's sake." Not unlike science fiction's fetishizing of technology, whether from a utopian or dystopian perspective, road movies valorize a certain aesthetic thrill related to high-speed car travel, regardless of plot or message.

Beyond the mise en scène described earlier related to iconography and setting, road movies generally use frame compositions that incorporate the front or side windshields and rearview mirrors. To be sure, this is due largely to driver point of view shots; but these frame compositions also function reflexively, exaggerating or enhancing the camera's presence. Unlike interior domestic scenes that use doorways and windows to create a sense of entrapment and enclosure, the road movie makes use of the formalistic frame-within-a-frame so as to foreground the crucial act of looking and seeing while driving. Additionally, the reflection of characters in glass and mirrors, commonly exploited in road movies, serves often as a literal projection of character onto the car, and into the space being traveled. This framing/reflection technique helps visualize aesthetically the theme of self-exploration as a projection of self through space.

We should mention a last, yet prominent aspect of road movie aesthetics, one that typically complements these framing and editing techniques: a vigorous music soundtrack. The distinctive emergence of the road movie in the late 1960s is culturally interwoven with the advent of rock and popular music, and the genre usually deploys the former as another aesthetic expression of the visceral and sensual thrill of driving, of moving at high speed. "Road movies have become ineluctably tied to the cheap-and-nasty aesthetics of rock 'n' roll (with Chuck Berry's 'Route 66' as the first unofficial anthem), rebel youth culture and the no-future potential of crazed automobile use" (Atkinson, 16). The car radio and tape deck figure commonly here, providing narrative pretext and synchronous source for an overinvested music track during driving scenes. Yet equally prevalent is the more formalistic nonsynchronous music soundtrack, which is less motivated by narrative logic but which aurally enhances the mood of the on-screen driving experience.[18]

Subject Matter and Themes

Turning now to the road movie's general thematic preoccupations, we can begin with its basic plot and character structure. In his concise definition of the genre, Lopez postulates that "the protagonists in this type of film are either rugged individualists who make the road their home and use it for some daredevil purpose or challenge, or they are solitary individuals who embrace the road as a way of life" (256–57). More recently Cohan and Hark expand this basic plot premise by linking the genre's "potential for romanticizing alienation" with its ability to challenge "the uniform identity of the nation's culture" (1). Yet this notion of individuals at odds with social conventions should be further refined to acknowledge that most road movies put a couple behind the wheel. This couple character structure appears mostly in two versions, romance or friendship; yet often it furnishes narrative tension between the two people traveling together. Cohan and Hark situate the prevalence of road movie couples within that of Hollywood movies generally, noting that "two people in the front seat of a vehicle make for easy classical framing and keep the dialogue going," developing "intimacy and plot conflict quickly" (8).

While the couple as narrative focus is fairly typical of classical and popular Hollywood, the road movie's open-ended narrative structure tends to venture beyond typical Hollywood terrain. Because road movie heroes are driven "to seek the freedom of the road as a refuge from a harrowing past, or to search for its exhilarating, liberating strength" (Lopez, 257), the genre's plot often carves out a rambling, picaresque narrative path. As a result, the road movie may not possess a clear-cut beginning, middle, or end; likewise, the genre often shifts gears regarding mood and plot with a certain disorienting, open-air free will. Generally it distances itself from the Aristotelian dramatic unities, in favor of the episodic style of Cervantes or Brecht. By foregrounding the journey in a nomadic vein, the road movie evokes a countercinema in relation to classical narrative (just as its themes generally tend to be countercultural).

Before exploring in more detail these countercultural themes, we should address the genre's articulation of a human-machine interface. Using Buscombe's terms, this theme is the "inner form" to the genre's "outer form" emphasis on driving described above. That is, traveling in a motorized vehicle is what road movie characters do, and the fundamental action and mise en scène convey this. But on a more thematic level, road movie characters bond with their vehicles. Cars and motorbikes often evolve in the narrative as a kind of prosthetic limb or "buddy" for the driver. Road movies may develop character by showing some kind of interaction between car and driver, the latter channeling desire or anger through the former. Cars and their promise of high-speed freedom possess characters, aid them, or destroy them.[19] At times this sense of human-machine interface suggests that the vehicle itself is a character in the film, through special close-ups of the car's machinery "working" to race down the road, for example. Sometimes this interface configuration expresses technophobic criticism of how humans can become overtaken by the automobile. Yet equally common is an affirmative celebration of the thrill of industrial speed, in the spirit of the Italian futurists.[20] Here car travel is conceived as progressive liberation—humans joining forces with machinery, propelled into space. In any case, the road movie often portrays the postindustrial convergence between human and machine as a manic will-to-drive. Though road movies such as *Death Race 2000*, *The Road Warrior*, and *Crash* most literally dramatize a hyperindustrialized, precybernetic fusion of car and driver, all road movies involve some meditation on the human relation to technology.[21]

The flip side to such reflection on technology within the genre is what Leo Marx has described as the "pastoral ideal." As Marx demonstrates, pastoralism is essential to the American literary and cultural tradition, deriving especially from the transcendentalist veneration of nature in the works of Emerson, Thoreau, and Whitman. Rooted in the romantic spirit of the eighteenth and nineteenth centuries, pastoralism appears throughout the road movie canon as both motivation and goal: a longing to escape America's congested, confining urban centers; a compulsion to rediscover nature and taste the unpredictable wilderness; a burning need to withdraw from culture, sometimes from humanity itself. In distinguishing between a "popular and sentimental" pastoralism, and one that is "imaginative and complex" (5), Marx's discussion becomes specially relevant to the road movie, since he focuses on literature that idealizes the garden but that also takes account of the ineluctable presence of technology. This pastoralism becomes "complex" through the "sudden appearance in the landscape" of the very industrial technology being rejected and fled (16). This more compelling form of pastoralism is not naive, but rather incorporates cynicism into its romanticism, addressing the impossibility of escaping culture, and the contradictions inherent in the very longing to do so. The road movie dramatizes Marx's "machine in the garden," not only because it is cinematic (industrial reproduction of the garden), but more so because it paradoxically fetishizes the automobile as the vehicle for fulfilling the pastoral longing. The road movie's romantic vision beyond an oppressive society is often propelled by the pastoralist critique of industrial culture; yet this romantic spirit is always already coded through the automachine as industrial vestige.

While clearly contributing to the road movie's drive, pastoralism as a term seems too timid, even anachronistic, to fully characterize the heart of the genre's engine. I contend rather that the more precise and most fundamental theme expressed by the road movie is postwar youth culture rebellion.[22] The postwar suburban boredom of the young and the restless, portrayed in films like *Rebel without a Cause* and *Blackboard Jungle* (both 1955), evolves into pointed rebellion and even attempted revolution in the 1960s. The road movie emerges distinctively as this decade's mood of social protest and alternative lifestyle reached a heated apex. Sargeant and Watson underline this point by linking the birth of the road movie with the drug culture of the 1960s, which "fed into the transgression of boundaries, both physical, social, and personal" (11). A mind-altered state ("tripping" or "speeding") resonates with the road movie's "high"-speed road trip: to escape reality, or to find a more authentic reality, both break beyond conventional states. The rock music sensibility mentioned above also contributes to the road movie's essential youth rebellion drive. An illuminating road movie subcategory in this respect is the "rock 'n' road" movie: road movies about rock musicians or fans on tour, or merely on the road. Rock 'n' road movies bring into clear focus the truly formative link between rock music and the road movie, both cultural offspring of 1950s youth culture and the 1960s counterculture. Thus the generic definition of the road movie is crucially bound up with the antiestablishment counterculture of the late 1960s (which, let us recall, included the neopastoralist environmental movement and "back to nature" trends).[23]

At the same time, the general mood here is disenchantment. Robin Wood has explained that the fundamental feature of the post–*Easy Rider* buddy road movie is the "disintegration of the concept of home." These journeys have "no goal," or a goal "that proves illusory" (*Hollywood from Vietnam to Reagan*, 227–28). A utopian vision of social reform drives the road movie beyond society's limits; but the inability to realize such a vision often turns the journey in an aimless, forlorn, and somewhat bitter direction. The road movie is born as a genre in and through the early-1970s souring of the counterculture: moody visionaries roam the highways, searching for a freedom that is both liberating and frightening. Putting it rather succinctly at the start of her essay "Revitalizing the Road Genre," Katie Mills observes, "If we find nothing else unanimous about adventure road films, we might agree that they appeal to that darker side of people's psyches where rebellion thrives, wild and free" (307).

However, the argument driving this book is that the road movie's generic core is constituted more precisely by a *tension* between rebellion and conformity. That is, just as the road movie's machine is always present in its garden, so too more broadly the road movie's overt concern with rebellion against traditional social norms is consistently undermined, diluted, or at least haunted by the very conservative cultural codes the genre so desperately takes flight from. This book explores how the road movie's historical evolution as genre reconfigures and redefines rebellion in the context of the perpetually shifting specter of conformity.

The genre's deliberate rebellious impulse is conveyed primarily through two narrative pretexts: the quest road movie (descending from *Easy Rider*) and the outlaw road movie (descending from *Bonnie and Clyde*). Quest road movies emphasize roaming itself, usually in terms of some discovery; the tone suggests a movement *toward* something (life's meaning, the true America, Mexico, etc.). Outlaw road movies emphasize a more desperate, fugitive flight *from* the scene of a crime or the pursuit of the law. Most road movies incline toward one or the other of these two narrative directions.[24] Yet ensuing chapters discussing specific films will demonstrate that often one type possesses elements of the other (i.e., *Easy Rider* involves some crime, *Bonnie and Clyde* involves some sense of discovery), and that *both* types link transgression and liberation with mobility.

Despite these two narrative modes driven by rebellion, the road movie's conservative subtext is never far behind. As Julian Stringer notes, the road movie's promise of freedom and escape is constantly circumscribed by the culture it flees so furiously, "because setting off onto the highway necessarily entails the transportation of significant amounts of cultural baggage." In his discussion, the genre's ostensible drive to get away from society usually involves a focus on interpersonal intimacy between characters within the car, which undermines such escape (165–66). Another example of such "cultural baggage" or conservative subtext would be the genre's overall attitudes regarding race and gender. Most road movies, for example, retain a traditional sexist hierarchy that privileges the white heterosexual male, in terms of narrative and visual point of view. As in typical Hollywood films, the road movie tends to define the active impulse (here, to drive) as male, relegating women characters to passive passengers and/or erotic distractions. We get a vivid representation of the urge to drive as male in *On the Road* (as already suggested, perhaps the literary prototype for the road movie). Sal and Dean basically treat women with adolescent disdain or fascination, seeing them as obstacles to their road travels. In fact, *On the Road* clearly posits the car as the preferred subservient object, when compared with women—a comparison the novel repeatedly makes.[25]

Certainly *Easy Rider, Two-Lane Blacktop,* and most other buddy road movies of the 1970s and 1980s marginalize women along similar lines. Robin Wood has suggested a homophobic underside to the sexism of these films. By marginalizing women to such a degree, Wood argues, these films (perhaps unconsciously) raise the possibility of a male love story, which must then be fervently disavowed. This disavowal of the "surreptitious gay subtext" often takes the form of demeaning both women and gay characters, as a guarantee of the heroes' heterosexuality (*Hollywood from Vietnam to Reagan,* 227–30). As Marsha Kinder puts it in the introduction to her essay "The Return of the Outlaw Couple": "Of course, the heroes aren't really 'fags,' and to prove this the film will usually include a scene ridiculing homosexuals. . . . Women may be included, but they are always restricted to minor roles" (2). Kinder proceeds to explain how even road movies possessing well-developed women characters nevertheless keep them strapped to the passenger seat. The heroines of *Bonnie and Clyde, Badlands, The Sugarland Express,* and *Thieves like Us* are strong, but their "strength is ambiguous" (6). That is, though they often survive their male counterparts and contribute substantially to the plot, these outlaw road movie heroines are characterized within stereotypical bounds. Naive, irrational, passive, and secondary to the male, they are "appendages to masculinist fantasies" (Roberts, 62). Whether in traditional exaltation of machismo, or as an exploration of masculine identity crisis, the bulk of the road movie genre seems to presuppose a focus on masculinity.[26] This presupposition often bears patriarchal baggage, which both the feminist and gay road movies of the 1990s explicitly challenge.

Beyond this traditional patriarchal configuration, a certain exoticism regarding race pervades many road movies. This exoticism generally appears in the visionary longings of the protagonists, who idealize "primitive" cultures as a kind of "dark continent" destination, an antidote to the materialistic Western industrial culture they are rebelling against. Cameron Bailey has described the prevalence of this tendency to exoticize the racial Other in the New York independent film movement of the 1980s—a movement that furnished many postmodern road movies, such as *Stranger than Paradise, Wild at Heart, Something Wild* (1988), and *True Stories* (1986) (30). Once again Kerouac's *On the Road* is instructive and instrumental here; Bailey himself connects the New York indie films with the Beat sensibility (32). Throughout the novel Sal and Dean idealize and romanticize black jazz musicians, and people of color in general; one section in particular quite unapologetically articulates Sal's white middle-class male frustration: "wishing I were a Negro, feeling that the best the white world had offered was not enough ecstasy for me, not enough life, joy, kicks, darkness, music, not enough night.

. . . I wished I were a Denver Mexican, or even a poor overworked Jap, anything but what I was so drearily, a 'white man' disillusioned" (148).

But it is during the novel's extended climax, where they journey into Mexico, that this exoticism becomes most pronounced. In literally leaving behind their national identity, Sal and Dean glorify Mexicans and Native Americans as possessing special magical qualities that provide a cure for their spiritual ills. While there is nothing inherently wrong with rejecting dominant American cultural values in favor of those of a non-Western or developing nation, such an attitude plays out a simplified dichotomy where the racial Other is fetishized from a white point of view. Often insidiously, sometimes inadvertently, these conservative attitudes toward both people of color and women have been incorporated into many contemporary road movies. Beyond Bailey's discussion of Lulu as the racial and sexual Other of *Something Wild* (that is, as the "something wild"), Sharon Willis has shown how Lynch's *Wild at Heart* likewise relies upon traditional Orientalist versions of people of color ("Special Effects," 288–93).[27] More recently, Pamela Robertson demonstrates that this conservative patriarchal framework stubbornly operates in the gay road movie *The Adventures of Priscilla, Queen of the Desert* (277–85). Other examples of this racial exoticism that come to mind are the black Rasta bicyclist in *Thelma and Louise,* the Native American cop in *My Own Private Idaho,* and the Native American shaman of *Natural Born Killers.*

These conservative subtextual attitudes regarding race and gender should be understood within the more ubiquitous political subtext underlying the road movie's white line fever: American expansionism and imperialism. A sense of conquest through traveling, of asserting one's self by venturing elsewhere, often accompanies the genre's rebellious drive to get beyond society —by covertly reiterating that very society's intrinsic need to exploit and colonize. The road movie's ambivalence around critiquing and/or extending the imperialist facet of American cultural history comes into sharper focus if we consider the prevalence of violence in road movies. The genre tends to treat violence as a progressive gesture, an instrument of liberation (violence against "the system"). This political conception of violence as liberation fits within the genre's more general suggestion about violence: that to venture outside society and against culture is to tread where the rules of the game no longer apply, and where the ominous, unpredictable violence of the wilderness prevails. Thus violence becomes a fantasized, exhilarating component of the genre's countercultural topography and attitude.

Yet violence is integral to the establishment of American political and cultural identity, as Richard Slotkin's *Gunfighter Nation* has persuasively illustrated. That is, the nation "regenerates" itself through violence associated with "the myth of the Frontier"—for Slotkin, "our oldest and most characteristic myth." As Slotkin puts it, "Violence is central to both the historical development of the Frontier and its mythic representation" (10–11). To the extent that it mobilizes and modernizes frontier mythology, the road movie's ostensibly rebellious and socially critical violence—stabbings, gunfights, torture, car chases, crashes, and explosions—often becomes a *repetition* of the materialistic and patriotic violence Slotkin describes. From this perspective, the road movie's rather furious attempt to achieve subversion seems proportional to an impervious, almost compulsive reassertion of traditional American values.

Classical Hollywood Predecessors

Despite being an independent, postmodernist genre, the road movie should be understood in relation to classical genres. Upon closer inspection, the road movie reveals itself to be not only a "new" independent genre of the New American cinema but also an amalgam of certain classical Hollywood elements. Reviewing these genre precursors helps us gain an appreciation of the classical roots of the road movie, and to illuminate some of the nuances of the road movie's core tension between rebellion and conformity.

The Western, for example, is a classical genre of substantial formative significance for the road movie.[28] With its emphasis on the precarious, ambiguous border between nature and culture, and its prevalent use of the journey as narrative structure, the Western functions in a sense as the road movie's grandparent. The frontier America of the Western's preindustrial mythology becomes rearticulated as industrial Americana in the road movie. More significantly, both genres explore wandering and/or migration in narrative and aesthetic terms. With its lone rider of the vast open plains trekking through the romanticized but ominous wilderness, the Western anticipates the road movie both visually and thematically. The films of John Ford, such as *Stagecoach* (1939), *She Wore a Yellow Ribbon* (1949), and *The Searchers* (1956), are especially potent examples of how the genre aesthetically valorizes the journey as a form of social criticism, revelation, and redemption.[29] Slotkin, for example, sees the journey structuring *Stagecoach* as enacting both a cultural critique of civilization's so-called progressive institutions and a need to "project a further Frontier, a mythic space outside American space and American history" (311). Other Westerns with pronounced road movie sensibilities are those organized around a wagon/cattle "drive," such as *The Covered Wagon* (James Cruze, 1923), *The Big Trail* (Raoul Walsh, 1930), and *Red River* (Howard Hawks, 1948).

More directly influential on road movies—more "parental"—are Depression-era social conscience films, such as *I Am a Fugitive from a Chain Gang* (1932), *Wild Boys of the Road* (1933), *You Only Live Once* (1937), and *The Grapes of Wrath* (1940), as well as screwball comedies like *It Happened One Night* (1934) and *Sullivan's Travels* (1942). In varying ways and to varying degrees, all these films use mobility to express a rebellious response to the social crisis of the Depression. The facts of unemployment and severe economic instability lead to a general sense of rootlessness, which Depression films exploited for story and character focus. These Hollywood films are full of wandering and flight. Belonging at least partially to other genres (prison film, screwball, gangster), these Depression films are not road movies in any deliberate or self-conscious sense. But they do sketch out in embryonic form some of the traits and concerns that are used more deliberately after 1967. Most importantly, these films link road travel with social isolation and social criticism.[30]

Mervyn LeRoy's classic *I Am a Fugitive from a Chain Gang* serves well to illustrate the tonal and thematic influence of Depression-era Hollywood on the road movie. Though this film is set after World War I, it follows the main character James Allen (Paul Muni) up through the beginning of the Depression; it has thus been read as delineating certain causes for the Depression, while also reflecting that period's dismal, bitter mood.[31] More relevant to our discussion is how the issue and imagery of mobility is at the heart of the film's relatively severe social and political commentary. On the ship home from the war, James Allen explains to his army buddies that he wants to become an architect, specifically to build bridges. One soldier's response can later be reread as ironic foreshadowing of Allen's dark fate: "We'll be reading about you in the papers." Notable is how the film's opening invokes mobility in two ways: Allen's vision of climbing the social and economic ladder (figurative, vertical mobility); and also his visionary desire to build bridges, a motif that runs throughout the film as a romanticized celebration of travel (literal, horizontal mobility).

This double-faceted ideal of mobility is contrasted almost immediately upon his arrival home, where a harsh mood of confinement reigns, coding stability as paralysis. Though the family priest has secured a job for him, Allen sees it as "leading nowhere"; he equates the factory whistle with the military bugle. His mother and the priest both represent the conformity he wants to break out of: he needs to travel so as to build the bridges. Beyond intuiting the link between horizontal mobility and upward socioeconomic mobility, Allen sees his own creative fulfillment, even the expression of his very individuality, in terms of movement. Stability and domesticity are coded in the mise en scène as a kind of prison, as he stares out the factory window, visually restrained. The frame-within-the-frame exaggerates his desire for escape through movement.

Once he does embark on a job hunt, the film initiates an aesthetic approach it will repeat throughout: a montage of maps documenting his movements, often overlapping with close-ups of his feet or face. These brief segments of punctuation overinvest the idea of his travels as a descent into joblessness and homelessness, with their nonnarrative, documentary slant. The narrative proper starts up again just before the "crime" that lands him in prison. He is forced to assist in a robbery, then is arrested and convicted as an accomplice. These two sequences—his unsuccessful job hunt, and his unfair conviction—emphasize how his status as "fugitive" is thrust upon him by social circumstances.

Like the home life he returned to earlier, prison life in the chain gang becomes another confining stability he will have to escape from. This is underlined by the powerful metaphoric crosscutting of shots of horses reined in the stables with the men in chains. More significantly, these shots (and many later sequences of the chain gang) portray confined movement as in- or subhuman, implying that movement and travel embody an essential humane freedom. But the ideal of travel becomes complicated by his own moral outrage, and the higher stakes involved: the price of freedom will cost more than fugitive status. After escaping, he has to change his name and identity in order to reenter society. Eventually and temporarily, this works: "Allen James" becomes a successful businessman who builds bridges. During this brief idyllic section of the film, the literal, horizontal trajectory of movement has been translated into a vertical "travel" up the socioeconomic ladder, fulfilling his original dream.

In fact, as the plot continues to unfold, *I Am a Fugitive* foresees the future road movie in its suspicion, or at least undermining, of the stability intrinsic to his fulfilled dream. His identity change was a recipe for his success, but it also precipitates his downfall, specifically through the woman who blackmails him into marriage once she discovers his true "fugitive" identity. When this marriage becomes intolerable to him, he reveals his secret and agrees to go back and serve proper time, so as to clear his record and finally start a normal life with the woman he truly loves. But the justice and prison systems abuse him once again. For his second, more desperate escape, he steals a truck, and in a final bitter irony has to blow up a bridge to evade his pursuers.

1.1. An ominous image of stability: James Allen (Paul Muni) will seek refuge on the road.

From then on, indefinitely, he is forced to live on the run in an underground world, outside "normal" society. Though he does find true love, this romance and its promise of authentic domesticity is beyond his reach, as the film ends with the grim shot of him fading away into the darkness. Here the road becomes coded as a brutal necessity for survival and escape from oppression; it is not glorified as an alternative lifestyle or freedom from society's conventions (as it shall be in the countercultural Depression road movie *Bonnie and Clyde*).

The film's dark ending, with Allen on the run in the black night, points toward the cycle of films that in many ways grew out of such Depression films, and that more directly influence the road movie: film noir. Films such as *Detour* (1945), *Desperate* (1947), *They Live by Night* (1949), *Gun Crazy* (1950), and *Plunder Road* (1957) might thus be considered the road movie's elder siblings, for their expression of postwar cultural anxiety and paranoia through the trope of the automobile. With their dark, often fatal destinies awaiting their protagonists as punishment for venturing beyond conservative culture, these noir road films anticipate the cynical tone of many post-1960s road movies. Phil Patton credits film noir with consolidating and exaggerating people's anxieties about the open road as the refuge of criminals and thus a site of potential, unpredictable violence (248–49). Jim Kitses has recently described *Gun Crazy*'s road travel structure, for example, as essential to the lead couple's sense of isolation from society: "The high-speed get-aways, together with the scenes of the couple in transit, shape *Gun Crazy* as a road movie, the constant movement and furious action a graphic expres-sion of their nomadic life together and its illicit pursuit of happiness" (43). Ed Dimendberg has likewise suggested how an obscure noir road movie like *Plunder Road* delivers "a melancholy verdict about the promise of the open road," in its fatalistic portrayal of highways and traffic jams (132–34).[32]

In contrast to its Depression-era predecessors, the noir road film exag-gerates the criminal or outlaw element, in desperate psychological (rather than sociopolitical) terms. Future road movies in fact will neatly combine the psychological identity crisis derived from noir with the social and politi-cal critique derived from Depression films. However, we more clearly recog-nize film noir in the road movie: *Bonnie and Clyde*'s indebted affinity to *Gun Crazy* is more palpable than to, say, a Western like *Stagecoach*, or even to a Depression film like *Wild Boys of the Road*. In other words, film noir pro-vides the most immediate link between the road movie and the classical era— which makes a certain sense, since noir films were mostly low-budget, inde-pendent B-movies. Thus, noir road films anticipate both the ensuing decline of the Hollywood institution, and the new independent American cinema that would foster the road movie.

As an elaboration upon the above discussion of *I Am a Fugitive*, let us consider in some detail two classic Hollywood predecessors to the road movie: *The Grapes of Wrath* and *Detour*. Boasting star Henry Fonda and a somewhat grand, epic scale, the Ford film deals with the Depression era, yet invokes the sensibility of the Western, primarily through Ford's directorial signature. *Detour* on the other hand is a low-budget B-movie with a meager if concise structure, thus foreshadowing the road movie's production context and feel. Additionally, each film effectively outlines the two predominant road movie tendencies, described above as quest and outlaw narratives. *The Grapes of Wrath* is a romantic, politically progressive film with much social critique (Henry Fonda's Tom Joad is father in more than one way to Peter Fonda's Captain America); the family's quest for a home is bound up with the quest for social justice. *Detour* is more psychologically and criminally oriented, coding road travel as an ominous threat to identity. While the main character starts out on the quest of getting across country to join his girl, he quickly becomes driven to desperately flee the harrowing circumstances he himself has inadvertently created on the road.

The Grapes of Wrath marks an important transition toward the contem-porary road movie. Expanding upon *I Am a Fugitive*'s notion of bitter escape

1.2. The Godfather of the road movie's visionary driver: Tom Joad (Henry Fonda).

from oppression, it suggests that road travel has the potential for revelation. With typical Fordian hope and faith, the film balances the dystopian associations of Depression mobility with a utopian sensibility promising transcendence. At the start of *The Grapes of Wrath,* Tom Joad has just been released from prison, where he served time for killing a man in self-defense (so he claims—and we believe him). Recalling James Allen's unfair time spent in prison, Joad's character is depicted from the start as unjustly imprisoned by society, which confers upon him a certain dignified, outsider/rebel status.[33] After a brief opening montage of long shots of Joad walking alone on the road, Joad's first act is to talk a truck driver into breaking company rules and giving him a ride home. This opening suggests the road movie's association of righteous rebellion against society's rules—especially those of emerging corporate America—with road travel.

Once he arrives, he finds that his home and family are gone, initiating the theme of mobility in dystopian, melancholic terms. Like in *I Am a Fugitive,* mobility and instability are not chosen here, as they are in many post-Kerouac road movies. Yet what *The Grapes of Wrath* anticipates in those films—and what distinguishes it from *I Am a Fugitive*—is the sense of road travel as a means of revelation. After Joad joins up with his family, who are migrating west to California with hopes of livelihood, he is forced to view society from the enlightening distance instability affords (a luxury that feels to the Joads like a disease). This becomes dramatically clear if we consider Joad's encounter, upon arriving home, with Muley. After Joad discovers Muley dwelling half-crazed in the abandoned Joad home, we see in flashback how Muley's family was helpless against the company bulldozers that crushed his home. Muley's stability, underlined by his having physically remained on the Joad place, as well as by the flashback, seems both cause and effect of his deranged, confused (if incisive) state of mind. Moreover, this segment's extreme low key lighting and oblique camera angles exemplify what Mike Cormack describes as a visual translation of the Depression's "crisis of explanation" (48).

Joad on the other hand keeps moving, unattached, developing a critical distance through the distances he travels. On the road the Joads are instructed about corporate and government corruption, as well as human cruelty and greed. Additionally, their forced transience permits them to move away from one bad situation to another. By the film's end, Joad has seen and learned so much that he is morally compelled to continue on the road, to keep learning and keep fighting. Joad is no longer a captive of the road, as James Allen was at the end of *I Am a Fugitive;* he has had a revelation, and

1.3. The Joads learn hard lessons about American culture on the road.

embraces the road from a politicized perspective. Like James Allen, he must disappear into the night and the underground; but unlike James Allen, he is following a calling to discover the truth, and fight for its discovery by others. This difference in attitude is reflected in different visual styles: an eye-level medium/close shot of Allen withdrawing from the camera into pure black, versus a low-angle medium/full shot of Joad straddling a fence, gazing up into a predawn glow.

Beyond Gregg Toland's remarkable pre–film noir cinematography, the aesthetics of *The Grapes of Wrath* are also quite significant in terms of the development of the road movie genre. For example, the film uses periodic nonnarrative road travel montages, which romanticize the flow of cars and trucks with slightly low angles; accompanied by patriotic music, these montage sequences dignify the populist texture of the Okie migration, emphasizing it as social rather than individual. Another important road movie technique in the film is the use of faces reflected in the glass windshield and rearview mirrors of the car. This not only connects the characters with the car, but also plays on mobility as reflection. We see the characters framed by moving screens within the framed screen of the film itself, imagery suggesting how the characters (and we the audience) become integrated into the moving vehicle (and the moving image). Yet another more celebrated road movie technique appears in the scene where the Joads enter one of the migrant camps, and the camera is mounted on the car, giving us a compelling traveling point of view shot. Here the traveling shot and its "vehicle" are self-consciously combined, putting the viewer in the perspective of the traveling car. (Such road film techniques become prominent in, for example, *The Sugarland Express, Kings of the Road,* and *Thelma and Louise.*)

The film ends with Ma Joad making her final speech to Pa as they drive on, about how the real people like themselves "keep coming." They have been told throughout the film that they have to keep moving, but here a politically subversive reversal occurs, inspired by her son's good-bye speech the previous night, as she embraces rootless wandering (perhaps only for the moment, and in the abstract). This notion of road travel as affirmation rehabilitates Depression mobility, underlined by the film's closing low-angle shot of traveling cars. Like *I Am a Fugitive*'s ending, it also suggests the openended nonclosure of many later road movies: the story ends with more movement and new destinations. Road movie protagonists often choose perpetual movement even as the film's discourse ends (see, for example, the endings of *Five Easy Pieces* and *Paris, Texas*).

Five years later, Edgar G. Ulmer's brilliant 1945 film noir *Detour* would integrate road travel more self-consciously into its narrative framework. Yet

1.4. Moving forward, looking backward, haunted by the road: *Detour*'s credit sequence.

this film's use of the road harks back in mood and theme to *I Am a Fugitive,* but goes far beyond the latter in its nihilism and paranoia. Whereas the road in *The Grapes of Wrath* at times represents hope and enlightenment, *Detour*'s road offers no such utopian possibilities. The film almost lasciviously (even for a film noir) writhes in its own dismal dead end, exemplified immediately by the first shots of the credit sequence: a series of traveling shots that, though traveling forward, look backward down the highway at a bleak desert landscape. Aside from announcing the narrative significance of the road (and in fact framing the narrative with road imagery), the credit sequence foreshadows the story's fatalistic sense of entrapment. In a few moments, Al Roberts (Tom Neal) shall begin his flashback, the story beginning at its ending in typical noir fashion, looking backward and going nowhere. Viscerally awkward and disorienting, since we cannot see where we are going, these prenarrative images emphasize how the road (the journey) haunts destination, just as the past in noir haunts the future.

Detour's opening credit sequence crystallizes the film's overall synthesis of film noir with road travel. As a second framing device, the film shifts to night, inscribing our protagonist into more ominous road imagery: first walking alone on the highway, then riding in a car, finally disembarking at a roadside diner, where he displays the almost brutal antisocial behavior so typical of noir antiheroes. By locating its narration at night in a roadside diner, *Detour* emphasizes transience—as opposed to *Double Indemnity*'s insurance office, or *Murder, My Sweet*'s police station, for example. Then the film bitterly mocks the conventional ideal of romantic stability, as we watch Al become tormented by the song on the jukebox, a song he cannot bear to hear, since it will force him to recall (and tell) his story. This song, "I Can't Believe That You're in Love with Me," embodies the idealized facade of romance and stability that originally had lured him on his self-destructive, nightmarish path out west, to Hollywood, to marry his true love Sue.[34]

When he starts out on this journey, destination and stability are foremost in his mind, as fulfillment of the romantic ideal that he desires; but the road, the journey itself, will soon derail not only these motives, but his very identity. The dissolution of Al's identity is prefigured visually in an initial montage sequence that begins with a map, then a series of collaged images of him walking, hitchhiking, and riding in cars. While recalling similar sequences in *I Am a Fugitive*, Al's voice-over inflects the travel montage with paranoia and peril, linking moral uncertainties and a fear of fate with the dangers of the road.[35] At the same time, Al expresses his worries about money; the film as a whole reflects much economic anxiety (characters driven by greed or financial hardship; but also the film's "Poverty Row" production values). The hard-boiled, dime novel philosophizing of Al's "inner" (nonsynchronous) voice-over combines with the road montage to convey dramatically how the journey provokes both critical introspection and a risk of everything familiar—including his own self. When Al gets his fateful ride in Arizona (so close to his California goal!) with Mr. Haskell, the film personifies in the latter the menaces of the road Al has just been describing. Haskell is a shady character involved in illegal gambling activities, who mysteriously pops pills; later, his inexplicable death profoundly accelerates Al's perpetual detour. Al decides he must adopt Haskell's identity to save his own.

Not only is the road full of menace in *Detour;* driving itself becomes the activity that seems to seal Al's fate. Riding as a passenger at night, Al dozes off, coding much of the journey as a nightmare, a journey in between reality and the imaginary realm. When Al starts driving, two aspects of the mise en scène suggest the moment's special significance. First, while Haskell sleeps, Al gazes into the rearview mirror, envisioning Sue singing in a nightclub, fantasizing his union with her, but also his destination in general (the ideal of stability). The ironic placement of this fantasy just before Haskell's death emphasizes what he will *not* attain, and where he will *not* be going (thus the film's title). More importantly, this fantasy literally emerges out of the rearview mirror, a frame-within-a-frame that reflects both himself and the road. The second aspect of the mise en scène that seems to punish Al for driving has to do with the rain—another staple of the noir world, once again nicely integrated here into the notion of danger on the road. By forcing Al to stop to put up the top, the rain is the narrative catalyst for Al to either discover Haskell dead or accidentally kill him—the film never clarifies which.

Detour further weaves paranoia into its narrative fabric of road travel with the ensuing consecutive appearances of authority figures. Just after hiding Haskell's body, Al is about to get into the car, when a policeman rides up. He reprimands Al for reckless highway parking, speaking through one rolled-down door window, as Al listens through the other (more road travel framing devices). Soon after, Al arrives at the California border checkpoint, where two officers question him about his cargo. But the scene climaxes ironically when one of the officers asks for Al's "identification," querying him point-blank whether he is in fact Charles Haskell. Significant here for the road movie genre is how the protagonist's figurative crossing into a new identity (that of a dead man, and as a fugitive) is symbolically expressed through a topographical border crossing. The presence of government authority makes this crossing of borders all the more harrowing. Like Humbert's manic driving in *Lolita,* Al is transgressing society's law. Typical of the noir formula, Al's crossing into the state of California—his destination, the land of his personal romantic dreams, as well as the nation's collective dreams (the West, Hollywood)—now suddenly becomes haunted by an ambiguous crime and punishment. He must paradoxically and hopelessly flee his previous actions and former true self.

While resting in a motel, Al learns the empty, sleazy truth about Haskell: he was pretending to be a hymnal salesman to his long-estranged father, so as to get money from him for gambling. Then Al takes, or is taken by, the ultimate bad turn: the film's hitchhiking femme fatale. Al picks up Vera (Ann Savage) as he leaves the motel, a stupid or at least perplexing gesture, given his desperate circumstances.[36] We should note that, though Al calls to her offering a ride, Ulmer focuses a tight and lengthy traveling shot on her legs as she moves toward his car, foreshadowing of course her sexual assertiveness, but also her power to take control of Al's mobility. After his voice-over sizes her up (equivocating about whether sexual attraction or pity has aroused his interest), she suddenly turns on him with vicious insight. Her diatribe against him, in which she claims to know his entire "scheme" (murdering Haskell, stealing his car and identity), derives from her status as road traveler; she met Haskell on the road, in much the same way she came to be sitting across from Al. As a road femme fatale, she is able to perceive beneath Al's facade; yet she also possesses an excessive imagination laced with cynical paranoia, another result of her wandering road experiences. She emerges from the road landscape as a demonic prophetess, to further embroil Al in his own loss of identity, perhaps to punish him with the excesses of his own impulses—and those of the patriarchal capitalist culture at large.[37] Let us recall that Vera's reputation has preceded her, through Haskell's description of her as a vicious sexual beast (the scars on his arm). If Haskell's bizarre death suggests the hazards of the road, Vera embodies its anarchic menace and allure. Whereas Al and Haskell are pitted against Vera in the traditionally patriarchal portrayal of the femme fatale, we should also note how *Detour* aligns Al and Vera as hitchhikers. The noir genre's moral ambiguities and doppelgänger effects suggest that Al himself belongs to the very highway landscape from which Vera emerges.

Though they only travel together a short time before arriving in Los Angeles, Al and Vera form a grotesquely ironic glimpse of the outlaw romantic couple (as earlier Al and Haskell appear as unlikely progenitors of the buddy road pair). Their snappy repartee, full of cutting innuendo, plays like screwball comedy turned inside out, a perverse reworking of *It Happened One Night.* Unlike the young lovers on the run at the end of *You Only Live Once* or *Gun Crazy,* who are murdered as victims and romanticized as martyrs, *Detour*'s outlaw couple is forced together by the car they travel in, as well as bizarre coincidence. After she "traps" him in the car with her knowledge of the situation, the drive ends; the journey is over. The stable domesticity Al had longed for with Sue soon becomes brutally parodied with Vera's incarceration of Al in a hotel room (he opens the window, she slams it shut). Her physical entrapment of him in turn parallels her insanely far-fetched intention to incarcerate his true identity within Haskell's, so as to extort more money from Haskell's dying father. In surprising anticipation of a nihilistic AIDS road movie like *The Living End,* Vera seems to be sick and dying, her wildly irreverent schemes and visions driven by bitter vengeance against a death sentence unjustly handed to her.

Trapped by a blackmailing "wife" in a domestic prison (like James Allen in *I Am a Fugitive*), Al now must escape from Vera. After accidentally strangling her, Al is consigned to return to the road, again like James Allen, with no identity, no future. In contrast to Allen's open-ended disappearance into the black night, Al's voice-over tells us he knows "a car will stop," and we see the highway patrolman pull up beside him.[38] The fate that has put its finger on him "for no good reason" begins and ends within an image of road travel as a transgression, not only of society's laws, but of one's very identity.

The Road Movie and Genre Criticism

These classical Hollywood precursors to the road movie offer a compelling glimpse of where and how the independent road movie will take off. Yet to further elaborate the formative classical influences on the genre, and to further elucidate my sense of the road movie's modernist engine of visionary rebellion, let us turn briefly here to a few key concepts from classical genre criticism.

First, the core dialectic between rebellion and conformity I focus on is not unique to the road movie. In *Hollywood from Vietnam to Reagan,* Wood suggests that the broad institution of the classical Hollywood cinema and its compulsion toward formula (genre) is predicated upon a balanced interplay between romanticism and classicism (or rebellion and conformity). Here, romantic rebellion undergoes a process of repressive, "classical" codification reflective of dominant ideology (48). Certainly the Western's conflict between nature and culture (a strong influence on the road movie) articulates a tension between rebellion and conformity: the lone gunman rejects the encroaching Eastern cultural values in favor of the ways of the rough wilderness. This "home/wandering antinomy" has likewise been identified (again by Wood) as the "basic ideological tension" of both film noir and the screwball comedy ("Ideology, Genre, Auteur," 63). It also appears to be the distilled core of the family melodrama, as well as the musical. In the former, the repressive social conventions of 1950s family ideology choke off illicit sensuality (Schatz, 226–28); in the latter, the spontaneous, authentic individuality of performance struggles to overcome the cold organization of showbiz productions (Feuer, 331–35). Finally, let us not forget the overexcited entrepreneur gone overboard, the gangster, ruthlessly rebelling against legal and moral boundaries to amass his fortune and power (E. Mitchell, 206–8). There is a clear sense in which the road movie's formulation of the rebellion/conformity duality extends a bedrock thematic concern familiar to most classical genres: the negotiation between individual impulse and social organization.

Yet I will suggest here, and demonstrate throughout this book, that the road movie distinguishes itself from all these classical genres by virtue of its literal (as opposed to figurative) portrayal of rebellion. This literal quality derives from the genre's explicit modernist narrative approach—itself directly shaped and inspired by the 1960s counterculture. While road movies incorporate, to a degree, the kind of timid social criticism derivative of Hollywood genres, they also more emphatically offer an overt, politicized image of subversion. That is, the road movie's modernist portrayal of rebellion pushes countercinema strategies to the foreground, where the narration along with the narrative challenges typically passive viewer reception. The classically phrased rebellion of the Western, gangster, screwball comedy, or family melodrama, in contrast, is portrayed more figuratively. Embedded or submerged in the "closed," artificial context of classical genre formula, such rebellion often erupts through indirect symbolism, quickly contained catharsis, or subtextual innuendo. The commercial institution of the classical studio system itself underlies this enclosed "artificial paradise" feel—escapist, to be sure, but not much like the escape often driving road movies, with their traveling locations, low budget, and narrative "on the run." The forces of conformity dominate the stage of classical genres, whereas in the road movie they take the backseat, so to speak.

In many ways, what I am proposing about the road movie as genre relates to Barbara Klinger's critical identification of the "progressive" Hollywood genre. Taking issue with the notion that there is such a thing as a "progressive" Hollywood genre, she links various utopian readings of film noir, 1950s melodrama, exploitation films, and 1970s horror films through the emphasis in such readings on the way these genres ideologically subvert Hollywood "from within," through "rupture" and "excess." Other attributes of her "progressive" genre apply quite accurately to the road movie: a "pessimistic world view," where "the overall atmosphere . . . is bleak, cynical, apocalyptic, and/or highly ironic"; resistance to the law and family (for the road movie, "stability"—geographic, social, and moral); a narrative structure emphasizing ambiguity and ideological contradiction; the refusal of narrative closure (for the road movie, the journey continuing beyond the film); stylistic self-consciousness (versus Hollywood's more typical realistic illusionism) ("'Cinema/Ideology/Criticism' Revisited," 80–83). Quite rightly, Klinger is suspicious of readings that valorize such trademarks as subversive; she argues instead that rupture, irony, and excess have always been constitutive features of the classical Hollywood genre. These "subversive" qualities operate not against but *for* the ultimately stabilizing classical genre system. Classical genres foster such "rebellion" as a temporary titillation, destined finally to be contained and corrected by the status quo.

As I have suggested above, and as future chapters will detail, the road movie possesses many of these "progressive" characteristics, and Klinger's suspicion about them resonates with my own focus on the rebellion/conformity dialectic that operates insidiously beneath the genre's surface of wild adventure. On the other hand, what distinguishes the road movie, I believe, from her "progressive" genres is precisely this *surface* of rebellion—a crucial defining aspect of the road movie genre. The progressive Hollywood genres she discusses all work within the Hollywood system (including, in their own weird ways, the exploitation and 1970s horror films). In contrast, the road movie is born and bred through the independent American film movement that arose from Hollywood's ashes. In the independent film context that renders it generically distinctive, the road movie often makes rebellion and cultural critique its explicit content, through modernist and postmodern aesthetics.

Most significantly, the tension between rebellion and conformity in classical genres—even in Klinger's "progressive" genres—usually resolves itself in the appearance of restored order, if not harmonious integration, which ultimately celebrates conformity. In contrast, the road movie tends to resolve itself with more ambiguity, and certainly often attempts to preserve and re-iterate the rebellious spirit of its initial departure. We might consider as emblematic the nonclosure ending of *Five Easy Pieces* (Bob Rafelson, 1970), where Bobby (Jack Nicholson) suddenly abandons his girlfriend at a gas station and drives away—in the opposite direction from which they were originally traveling. "Whereas the classical odyssey ended in a homecoming, the attainment of a hard-won goal or a reconciliation of sorts, the post-*Easy Rider* road movie deals with characters who are orphaned in some fashion, and confronted by the elusiveness or futility of their dreams and various manifestations of alienation" (L. Hill, 43).

This sense of restless wandering, foregrounded throughout, lingering at the end, distinguishes the road movie's rebellion against conformity from that of classical Hollywood. Thus, I submit that the road movie is *more authentically progressive* than Klinger's examples, yet still bears within it the ideological give-and-take derived from the classical genre system, between anarchy and order, rebellion and conformity. Beyond reflecting the influence of classical genres, this dialectic likewise expresses an American society historically torn between the two sides—inside and outside—of the frontier. In other words, what makes the genre so provocative is its distinctively modernist staging of a rather classical, perhaps timeless and universal struggle between two primal drives: the dynamic and the static. As Hamlet may have put it: to move on, or not to move on; that is the question.

In posing the question, the road movie—like Hamlet—has already chosen.

1950s Highway Culture

Detour's westward journey has been described as a "derouting of narrative" itself, as well as "a kind of debased farcical version of the American pioneer venture" (Polan, 215, 270). Along these lines, another critic sees the film finally as a bitter deconstruction of the American "ideological connection between individualism and democracy," in that the film's "use of the road metaphor turns the mythic American ideals on their head" (Britton, 182). While this dystopian version of road travel pervades many films noir throughout the 1950s, a more optimistic and utopian version dominates the mainstream public imagination. Beyond the classical genres discussed above, the broader cultural developments of the 1950s had a significant formative influence on the road movie. This decade is in fact somewhat anomalous for the road movie, since no road movies of note were produced during this period.[39] And yet the literary and cultural developments of this decade are essential to a lucid comprehension of the genre. It is my feeling that no road movies were produced during this period precisely *because* the penultimate conditions of its articulation were being produced (not unlike, say, the appearance of the Vietnam War film genre *years after* the Vietnam War). In this respect we might envision an embryonic trajectory where the classical genre tendencies suggested above "pass through" the 1950s, then emerge in the late 1960s as a distinct genre.

Generally speaking, these new conditions revolve around the advent of the automobile as a popular commodity on a mass scale, desired by and available to most of the public. Let us first recall that this is the era of highly stylized and diversified automobiles, so as to accommodate—it was presumed—the multifarious individual tastes of consumers (MacMinn, 237–39). As they become more accessible to more Americans than ever, 1950s automobiles become treated to the concepts of total design influencing much of commodity culture. Out of this context emerges hot rod culture and customization—a marginal but telling manifestation of how the 1950s automobile comes to signify not just socioeconomic status but personality. Beginning as a fad in Southern California, customization had gone national by mid-decade (Robert, 191). One writer even suggests that the flamboyant styles, garish colors, and overall excessive attention to cosmetics characteristic of 1950s automobiles run parallel to these same tendencies in 1950s Hollywood film style (Hey, 198). This increase in stylization and accessibility reflects the intensification of the automobile's perceived (as opposed to real) ability to express the individuality of consumers—an important notion for the road movie's fusion of character and car. Yet another aspect of the visual popularization of the car that foresees the road movie is the automobile's increased prevalence as motif in the British and American pop art painting movement of the late 50s and early 60s (Silk, 120–21; Klinger, "Road to Dystopia," 194–97).

More significant than the proliferation of the automobile as stylized commodity is the construction of the *actual* interstate highway system—so crucial, as suggested earlier, to the road movie's iconography and narrative. The intensified interstate highway development of the 1950s bolsters both the suburban culture boom (especially with respect to commuting) and the burgeoning recreational activity of tourism. We can further appreciate the social and historical significance of such family-oriented connotations with a brief digression on the man primarily responsible for the new highways, President Dwight D. Eisenhower. Eisenhower, in fact, was a low-ranking soldier on assignment in 1919 with the U.S. Army's first transcontinental trip by car and truck, from Washington, D.C., to San Francisco. Riddled with accidents and delays, the much-publicized trip left a lasting impression—on young Ike, and the nation at large—of how poor American roads were. Thus Eisenhower first nurtured his vision (one he would take with him to the White House) of the improvement and expansion of American roads as an obligation that, when fulfilled, would unify and strengthen the nation. Before being elected president in 1952 and fashioning his highway development program, Eisenhower's attitude toward road construction was further fostered by a second military experience, this time at the end of World War II. When the Allied forces captured Germany, Eisenhower toured Hitler's Autobahn, and was given a more specific idea of how roads could increase national identity and security. He was so impressed by the wide lanes and high-speed flow, he vowed to have something like it in America (Lewis, 89–91).

Riding the wave of postwar economic strength and prosperity, Eisenhower initiated a huge expansion of the interstates. The commission he appointed to oversee the project was composed primarily of auto industry insiders; they not surprisingly recommended massive investment. The new interstate highway project, they claimed, would fuel the economy (especially the automobile and auto-related industries, including gasoline, construction, motels, and real estate), create jobs, and further enhance suburban growth by connecting more fluidly the suburbs with urban employment areas. Another more intriguing way the president and his commission sold the new interstate highway project to the American public was by linking it with Cold War ideology. According to this ideology, the plausible threats of atomic warfare and Communist invasion necessitated these new highways, so as to facilitate the mass evacuations and military mobilizations required to defend the country (Lewis, 107–8). Eisenhower probably picked up this notion of linking militarized nationalism with mobility from Hitler and his Autobahn.[40] After an unexpected protracted political struggle (unexpected, yet familiar from the Civil War, over whether the states or the federal government should have authority over the proposed roadways), the Federal Aid Highway Act was signed into law in 1956, the year of Eisenhower's reelection. It earmarked $25 billion for the construction of 40,000 miles of highway over the next twelve years.

The highway surge of the 1950s promotes an image of America as a healthy body whose lifeblood flows through a network of road arteries. It also presents itself as a bold step forward into the modernized future, exaggerating both the entrepreneurial spirit of individualized freedom and the community spirit of transportation as communication. The new highways would reconstitute the nation's identity as a unity, while reinventing the American pioneer spirit with evocative frontier imagery. A faith in governmental authority likewise underlies much of the general meaning of these new highways for American drivers. The road movie emerges through the forceful prism of what we might call Eisenhower's Road, a road that celebrates the search for the meaning of America on the highway.

At the same time, the interstate highway boom of the 1950s had profound cultural consequences for America, beyond and in many ways contrary to the conformist ideological boosterism of Eisenhower's vision. Many of the negative consequences of this accelerated highway construction—appreciated after the fact—revolve around the displacement of minority communities and farmers. Environmental damage likewise was barely a concept when the project got under way.[41] Yet the new highways also engendered more subtle cultural tremors related to the transformation of spatial orientation for Americans. This transformation began before World War II, shifting the car from satisfying a basic human need (transportation) to becoming an instrument of a burgeoning "metropolitan consumerism." Both cause and effect of suburban expansion, this new consumerism created new transportation dependencies on the automobile (Interrante, 91). Metropolitan consumerism accelerated and intensified after the war into "consumption communities" that "flourished in the suburban culture" of the 1950s. Kenneth Hey makes some provocative observations regarding the experiences of automobility and film as mutually interdependent articulations of this new suburban culture:

> Both the automobile experience and the film experience put barriers between their users and the social world which existed outside. Both experiences involved movement, and both permitted the consumer to select desirable settings for themes, offering an ecstatic experience potentially devoid of depressing connections to reality. . . . Both movies and automobiles increasingly reinforced personal isolation, whether in a commuter traffic jam or behind 3-D glasses, and thus they both served as sanctuaries of individualism in a world of corporate conformity. (199)

These similarities between car and film are symptomatic of the new sense of movement and space—and movement in space—that emerges in the 1950s, and that becomes crucial to the tone and theme of road movies.

More recently, Edward Dimendberg has described how "[t]he highway provides a controlled visual experience analogous to the montage and multiplicity of perspectives afforded by cinema" (107). To account for this postwar fusion of the cinematic with highway driving, he proposes the notion of "centrifugal space," a broad phenomenal and cultural effect of modernity that goes beyond architectural design trends. Rather, it involves perception and behavior, "new experiences of time, speed and distance" that emphasize "dispersed settlements" and "horizontal sprawl" rather than "urban verticality" (92). He considers the highway the best and most compelling example of centrifugal space, and analyzes it in three cultural texts: Germany's Autobahn (as portrayed in a documentary film); GM's and Norman Bel Geddes's Futurama show of 1939; and the road film noir *Plunder Road* (1957). The first two texts articulate centrifugal space—high-speed, open-road travel—in terms of national unity and power, an optimistic movement into the future, and a celebration of mobility as spectacle. On the other hand, *Plunder Road* reflects a dystopian, paranoid version of centrifugal space (not unlike *Detour* and *Gun Crazy*). Anticipating the suspicion of governmental and corporate authority to emerge in the 1960s, *Plunder Road*'s centrifugal space suggests the overtaking and stifling of human potential, engulfing mobility in congestion and paralysis.

Yet another undercurrent to the dominant conservative road travel imagery of the 1950s is bohemian more than paranoid. Tina Olsin Lent has described how American mobility's acceleration during the 1950s goes in two different directions, at once contradictory and complementary, which we might label mainstream and subversive. On the one hand, as we have seen, the new interstate highway system makes possible the tourism and leisure travel industries, which appeal primarily to a wide spectrum of working- and middle-class families. Tina Lent shows how various spreads in *Life* magazine, as well as Hollywood road movies like *The Long, Long Trailer* (Minnelli, 1954), produced road imagery that "helped define and reinforce the hegemonic view of America as a white, middle-class, consumer-based society" (1).[42] She then discusses works by Henry Miller, Kerouac, and Simone de Beauvoir, as well as road photographs by Cartier-Bresson and Robert Frank, that give "voice to alternative views of America that challenged the hegemonic view of a populace united in harmony and affluence" (5). These road texts are equally enthusiastic about American road travel, but from a dissenting perspective of alienation. In fact, both the mainstream and subversive, or suburban and bohemian, tendencies are interrelated: the Beats, as products of this affluent society, had the luxury to wander underground. More importantly, both perspectives, as opposed as they appear, descend from a Whitmanesque search for the true America.

The historical factors described above that contribute to the road movie's formation are themselves inflected by the tension between rebellion and conformity at the heart of the genre. Hollywood's rambling social criticism is confined by the conventional roadblocks of classical genre formula. Likewise, the mass automobile culture and interstate highways of the 1950s beckon both suburbia and bohemia. These two tendencies provide a social and cinematic parentage for the birth of the road movie. The restless 1950s youth culture, epitomized by the Beats, steals the automobile from its drab 9-to-5 or weekend leisure routine, paving the way for the rebellious countercultural driving of the late 1960s. Tom Joad's son comes of age as a hippie on a motorcycle, and recrosses America.

The Wild One
The Wild Angels
Bonnie and Clyde
Easy Rider

Chapter 2 . . . .

BLAZING THE TRAIL
Visionary Rebellion and the Late-1960s Road Movie

In many ways, the road movie lights out for its own territory, forging its own distinct generic identity, through the critical and commercial success of two New American independent trailblazers: *Bonnie and Clyde* (1967) and *Easy Rider* (1969). Propelled in spirit and theme by the visionary rebellion of the counterculture, both films remake the classical into the New Hollywood by embracing the liberation of life on the road. *Bonnie and Clyde* celebrates fugitive mobility as a sensual and subversive thrill. At the same time, Clyde's entrepreneurial gangsterism and Bonnie's domestic yearnings illustrate the genre's intrinsic process of heading off such subversive rambling. The ideological pull of work and home is too strong, and contributes to their doom. *Easy Rider* articulates more literally the 1960s countercultural political critique that *Bonnie and Clyde* allegorizes. Going beyond Roger Corman's biker flicks, this landmark American independent film "almost single-handedly created the road movie as a vital post-60s genre" (L. Hill, 72). The film dynamically affirms transience as an alternative lifestyle and a critical weapon against conservative America. Yet Captain America can never fully leave behind his own breeding and name, and the film's own "search for America" becomes insidiously conservative. As Lee Hill puts it, "[T]he film juxtaposes its antiheroes' attraction to idealism and commitment with their tendency towards self-interest and hedonism" (44).[1] The ideological containment of rebellion built into both *Bonnie and Clyde* and *Easy Rider* converges with the end of each film's road: reactionary rednecks crucify both pairs of outlaws. Additionally, each film's tragic ending suggests an almost mystical correspondence between the human spirit, the combustion engine, and camera technology. *Bonnie and Clyde*'s outlaw couple and *Easy Rider*'s buddy vision quest lay out the basic features of the genre, features reflective of late-1960s counterculture.

Both films are historical landmarks of the New American cinema, exemplary of the "radical visions" Glenn Man explores in the period of institutional and aesthetic transition, 1967–76 (2–5). Both films enthusiastically embody the characteristics of the New Hollywood—auteurism, generic revisionism, narrative and ideological deconstruction, reflexivity. Yet the present discussion shall emphasize how they filter these characteristics through the narrative and thematic prism of road travel—specifically, the popular postwar road travel of driving cars and/or riding motorcycles. As the classical road movie-esque genres previously discussed wind down in the 1950s, the dominant transportation mode of driving accelerates its permeation of early-1960s consumer culture. By the late sixties, the cultural phenomenon of driving—inflected by Beat literature, highway tourism, and more broadly a prosperous economy—achieves a certain apex by being represented in what Timothy Corrigan calls the "*real* road movie": "movies about cars, trucks, motorcycles," in which "the quest motif becomes increasingly mechanized" (144–45; emphasis added). While Corrigan's frame of reference encompasses the entire postwar period (perhaps beginning, as he suggests, with *Detour*), he historically situates the birth of this new genre in "the mid-sixties," when "the protagonist's identity is almost fully displaced onto the mechanized vehicle," and where "the perspective of the camera . . . adopts the framed perspective of the vehicle itself" (145–46).[2]

Bonnie and Clyde and *Easy Rider* are emblematic of this "real" road movie, and constitute its starting point. These two films embrace driving as the foundational crux of the plot; likewise, the journey becomes their essential structuring framework to an extent beyond the classical Hollywood films discussed above. This explicit emphasis on driving, energized by the broader context of the New American cinema, is what is "new" (or "real") about these contemporary road movies (though of course this "newness" bears within it classical genre and archetypal literary influences).

Bridge to the Road Movie:
The Wild One and *The Wild Angels*

But before delving into these two trailblazing road movies, let me sketch a bridge between them and the classical precursors previously discussed, by briefly acknowledging two biker films that, though not road movies, provide a kind of threshold through which the road movie shall appear.[3] *The Wild One* (Laslo Benedek, 1954) is historically significant as a youth culture film that deals with the "juvenile delinquency" theme, as do other youth melodramas from the same period, such as *Rebel without a Cause, The Man with the Golden Arm,* and *Blackboard Jungle.* But unlike those films, *The Wild One* represents its rebellious youth through the narrative trope of restless mobility, in a way more pronounced than even *Rebel without a Cause.* In their discussion of *Easy Rider* as exemplary of the "subversive currents" of 1960s Hollywood, Cagin and Dray cite *Rebel without a Cause* and *The Wild One* as "anticipating the counterculture"; but they emphasize the influence of *The Wild One* as "the first bona fide motorcycle movie" for its reinforcing of "the image of motorcycles as dangerous and vaguely nihilistic" (42). *The Wild One* thus anticipates the road movie by furnishing crucial generic material.

The film's contribution to the formation of the future road movie begins, in fact, with its opening shot (perhaps its most compelling shot, given the rest of the film's fairly conventional direction). Recalling a Ford composition, the camera is placed close to the ground, at a slight low angle, in the center of a highway, looking far down the empty open road toward the vanishing point where sky and land meet. As the voice-over and credits begin, the shot holds firm with almost forced patience, building suspense by virtue of watching and waiting: the audience knows something will come down this road. Eventually we hear the faint hum that gradually becomes a furious collective roar, as tiny specks come into view, finally emerging as motorcycles, racing right into and right past the camera.[4]

This opening is important for its suggestion of the feel and look of future road movies. Though the film's story more or less stays put within the topographical boundaries of the town of Wrightsville, we should note how various narrative elements follow this first shot's suggestion. The film's main character, Johnny (Marlon Brando), "the wild one," is largely defined by his motorbike and the lifestyle it represents. His motorbike is the vehicle of his potency, his very "wildness": he expresses his bike, and the bike expresses him. At one point he explains to Kathie (Mary Murphy), daughter of the town sheriff, that he and his gang "just like to go," without knowing where; that "it's cool" to not know where you're going, but to go anyway. As a cipher of the social phenomenon the film intends to explore (based on a *Harper's* magazine story about a real event in Hollister, California, on July 4, 1947), he is "the wild one" precisely because he is impelled to keep moving, purely for thrills. Regardless of the social damage done, Johnny celebrates the private anarchy of driving around, breaking society's conventions and laws (not only traffic laws, but also the conventional values of stability: do-

2.1. *The Wild One*'s iconography of rebellion: Johnny's (Marlon Brando) motorbike subculture both threatens and attracts small-town, conservative Kathie (Mary Murphy).

mesticity, marriage, employment, etc.). Though we rarely see this rambling in the film (which is why it is not a road movie), it is referred to beyond the confines of the town, especially in the opening sequences as they head toward Wrightsville. More important than these limited and indirect references to wanderlust is the film's iconography, replete with motorcycle fetishism. The bikes and the clothes that go with them (leather jackets, gloves, etc.) occupy a good deal of the film's mise en scène, receiving substantial attention from the characters (infatuation from the gang members, paranoia from the townspeople).[5] *Bonnie and Clyde* and *Easy Rider* will dynamically expand upon such iconic and thematic elements.

Roger Corman's *The Wild Angels* (1966) is a second biker film that more dramatically opened up the generic road movie space through which *Bonnie and Clyde* and *Easy Rider* would pass. Appearing just one year before *Bonnie and Clyde,* it possesses none of the narrative or stylistic sophistication of Penn's film. Rather, it is an "exploitation" biker flick with minimal production values or plot. But this aspect of the film proves important to the road movie: the low-budget, independently produced, on-the-run filmmaking style that Corman initiated in American film in the late 1950s vividly suggests the tone of the future road movie. Corman's lucrative B-movie independent film company, American International Pictures (AIP), was symptomatic of the collapsing and reformulating Hollywood system. Like the old Hollywood, AIP productions were based primarily on speed and profit; yet the independent, low-budget context surrounding Corman, along with the countercultural influence, yielded some experimentation with film form (Cagin and Dray, 38–39). Thus, *The Wild Angels* suggests some important narrative qualities that concretely anticipate the road movie genre just around the bend.

Like *The Wild One, The Wild Angels* offers an iconography and attitude of rebellion through the narrative trope of the roving motorcycle gang, here in the context of the 1960s counterculture—specifically the Hell's Angels phenomenon. The film feverishly articulates subversion of conventional American institutions (such as church, work, family, etc.) through the aimless mobility of the Angels' motorcycle subculture, insisting on the equation of perpetual movement with moral, political, and spiritual freedom. While *The Wild One*'s youth become contained (if not rehabilitated) as the film ends, here the linking of social outcasts with motorcycle transience is more extreme, less romanticized, and less recuperable by society (Cagin and Dray, 45). Reflective of the bohemian hippie spirit of the 1960s counterculture, these "wild angels" form a kind of alternative, underground society that plays by its own rules—the foremost of which seems to be that their "home" is the open road.

All of the above thematic elements become essential to the road movie. But *The Wild Angels,* like *The Wild One,* is not a road movie: most of the film, in fact, takes place in specific locations where, perhaps ironically, the stability—the lack of movement—is emphasized. While the story does move from location to location, the film does not; most scenes occur after arrival or before departure. Thus, the film's articulation of traveling is more implied than explicit. Yet a few scenes are worth reviewing as seeds that will blossom more fully in soon-to-emerge road movies.

The film's opening segments seem to envision lucidly the future road movie. The first scene shows a young child on a tricycle, escaping from his suburban prison (as Corman has filmed it, through the "bars" of the proverbial "white picket fence") as well as his mother's punitive wrath: she shouts "no, no, no" as she chases him down. The child runs into the parked front tire of the motorcycle chopper belonging to Heavenly Blues (Peter Fonda); as the mom pulls her child away, Blues peels out of the neighborhood, onto the open road of America's highways. Then, during the film's credits, we get a montage of traveling shots celebrating Blues riding. This type of "driving montage" reappears throughout *Easy Rider* (and other future road movies), not as mere overture but as narrative punctuation. Other approaches to film technique in *The Wild Angels* that are significant for the road movie genre are the rearview mirror shot, where we look out through the windshield into the future but also into the mirror at the road behind (the past); a variation of *The Wild One*'s opening shot, with the camera low to the ground waiting for the eventual arrival of the motorbikes; and a sequence where Blues, alone at night, hiding from the police, becomes fragmented by a bizarre montage sequence as he approaches and mounts his bike. Such editing emphasizes his mystical (and perhaps sensual) connection with his bike (on the soundtrack we hear the strange erotic howls of alley cats).

The film's first narrative segment proper is likewise telling of how the road movie will unfold. Blues rides up to the oil rig where his buddy Loser (Bruce Dern) works. Blues tells him they have found his bike in Mexico, and liberates Loser from his job (i.e., from stability, stagnation, digging into the land for profit rather than traveling across it). The two ride off to retrieve the bike, his vehicle of freedom and pleasure. We should note that the second obstacle to retrieving this vehicle of freedom (the first being his job) is his wife, who does not want him to go. The woman as wife is forced here (and in most road movies) to represent home, and thus often confinement. Then, while in Mexico, they encounter a third obstacle: they have to fight off a Mexican gang to get back the bike. Both these obstacles anticipate the road movie's conservative subtextual attitude toward the sexual and racial Other. Despite the supposed counter- or subcultural context of the road movie, this lingering white patriarchal perspective, reductively demonizing women and people of color, links the genre with conservative society (and conservative, conventional movies). Other symbolic gestures during this sequence that suggest the generic road movie sensibility include freeing a horse from being tied up, and stealing a cop's motorcycle to escape.

From a different angle, some of the film's dialogue laconically articulates the crucial notion of traveling as cultural critique so central to the road movie. Developed as dramatic structure in later films, this notion revolves around driving as freedom from, and subversion of, conventional cultural authority. When the Angels are riding through a small town, a policeman rides up alongside one of the Angels asking, "Where do you think you're going?," to which he replies, "Anywhere but here, man." Beyond recollecting Johnny's famous "What d'ya got?" reply in *The Wild One* to the question "What are you rebelling against?" the Angel's rejoinder here rather poignantly underlines how society's exertion of authority depends upon the regulation of mobility. The policeman's sarcastic reference to mobility becomes subverted when the Angel responds literally to the repression of mobility built into the idiom the cop uses. Moreover, the Angel refutes this control with a refutation of destination itself, and a celebration of mobility for its own sake, which society (signified by the policeman) cannot tolerate. Along these lines, another less subtle verbal articulation of road movie genre thematics occurs near the film's end, when Blues confronts the minister speaking in the church at Loser's funeral: "We want to be free. Free to ride our machines, without being hassled by The Man."

Like the opening credit sequence, the film's ending engenders important generic road movie material. In road movies, being on the road must come to some kind of an end, so that the film can end; *The Wild Angels* accurately foretells the ending tone of most road movies as one of loss and disenchantment. After a fight breaks out at Loser's burial, between the Angels and the local townspeople of Sequoia Groves (Loser's hometown), the police arrive. The Angels take off, but Blues stays, despite his girlfriend Mike (Nancy Sinatra) imploring that he come along. He explains, "There's nowhere to go." The film ends with a long high-angle shot of the graveyard, Blues left alone to face the encroaching police. This framing seems to graphically convey his surprising choice to stay put—visually small and trapped by the present situation, trapped too by the harsh empty reality beneath the Angels' ideal of constant movement. Despite the compulsion to go, there is no place to go, there is always the disenchantment of destination, of having to arrive some place, only to have to move on again. The bitter, open-ended tone here, of moving on aimlessly and not going anywhere, is a strong characteristic of many road movie endings (it will pervade both *Bonnie and Clyde* and *Easy Rider*). Even when the outlaw drivers are not shot down at the end (as they are in *Bonnie and Clyde* and *Easy Rider*), they are often shown continuing in their movement, in a kind of forlorn uncertainty, a melancholy spirit of unending, unfulfilled longing. Most important road movies—certainly those emerging in the early 1970s, in the wake of *Bonnie and Clyde* and *Easy Rider*—do not have Hollywood "happy endings," a quality that testifies to the genre's European connection, its status as independent film, and its critique of dominant cultural and narrative conventions.

Beyond the features mentioned above, *The Wild Angels* also serves as an appropriate preface to *Bonnie and Clyde* and *Easy Rider* because of Peter Fonda's star presence and participation in both *Easy Rider* and *The Wild Angels* (though we might acknowledge actor Michael J. Pollard as Pigmy in *The Wild Angels* and C. W. Moss in *Bonnie and Clyde*). Cagin and Dray contextualize *Easy Rider*'s genesis in terms of Peter Fonda's rebound from a two-year acting absence to appear in the irreverent and controversial Corman film (37); supposedly, Fonda got the idea for *Easy Rider* while observing a still from *The Wild Angels*, envisioning a "really good movie about motorcycles and drugs" (47). *The Wild Angels* made him an icon of the counterculture, establishing the persona he would develop further in *The Trip* (1967) and *Easy Rider*.

Mobility as Narrative in *Bonnie and Clyde*

Since *Bonnie and Clyde* appears two years before *Easy Rider*, let us consider it the first part of a two-part emergence. One could argue that *Easy Rider* had more popular impact, and possessed more social relevance, upon its release. In retrospect, *Easy Rider* feels more like the "origin" for the road movie, due to its mythological status as emblem of the 1960s counterculture. Yet few would deny that *Bonnie and Clyde* is the superior film. It seems to have aged better, due to its more artistically striking direction—"an infinitely more intelligent and eloquent film than the more popular *Easy Rider*," according to Corrigan (150).

Though *Bonnie and Clyde* is set during the Depression and recounts the tale of the infamous gangster couple, it is usually considered a film "about" the countercultural political activism of the 1960s. Director Arthur Penn has discussed his film as a deliberate and self-conscious attempt to politically galvanize the counterculture.[6] Ryan and Kellner claim that the film, in juxtaposing nature (mobile freedom) with culture (confinement), "evokes the romanticism that was prevalent in the late sixties" (21). Glenn Man likewise sees the film as directly reflecting the "upheavals of the mid sixties" through its incorporation of the modernist, French New Wave style, which "disturbed the establishment" (7–8). Corrigan sees the film as presenting "a historical account of modern perception, perception that in the sixties is already beginning to reduce history to the material of images" (150). Taking a more complicated view of the film's reflection upon the late 1960s, Leong, Sell, and Thomas trace the film to both the counterculture and the dominant consumer culture. Ambivalently expressing the political tensions of late-capitalist culture, *Bonnie and Clyde* "purposefully attempted to consolidate popular political and cultural fantasy after the immobilization of the New Left" (77). Below we shall explore this quality in terms of the genre's core dialectical tension: how the film's "radical" politics become reinscribed in a framework of social conformity. But first we shall bring into sharper focus *Bonnie and Clyde*'s road movie characteristics: the various ways the film integrates automobility into its iconography, narrative, and themes; and its specific strategies for deploying mobility as a vehicle of cultural critique.

Bonnie and Clyde greatly expands upon American classical road movie precursors by deploying road travel extensively and self-consciously. The countercultural critique of big business and conservative values becomes allegorized largely through the film's elaboration of automobility. The latter proves an important element of this outlaw couple's mystique, as well as their visionary, sensual lifestyle. But perhaps most importantly—distinguishing the film as perhaps the first true contemporary road movie—the story itself is told through the narrative fabric of automobility. The first few moments of the film establish the crucial role driving will play throughout, setting up the dichotomy of mobility versus stability, so as to privilege the former.

The film opens with Bonnie (Faye Dunaway) seemingly trapped inside her room, conveyed through a series of carefully framed jump cuts, most notably one using the bars of her bed as the visual equivalent of a prison. She is bored, restless, and confined. She spots Clyde (Warren Beatty) outside, who is planning to steal her mother's car. It is significant that she comes outside to confront him lingering around her mother's car: she literally moves, she is the narrative catalyst. She also moves in the direction the road movie shall take her—toward the car, leaving her home and all its oppressive stability behind. This foreshadows the film's association of freedom with the road and stolen cars. Even though she is also moving toward Clyde, as a romantic/sexual object of desire, he is visually and narratively linked with the parked car: he hovers around it, not to meet Bonnie, but to get the car. One could surmise—especially in light of her later character development—that she is attracted to him partially because of his association with the car, and the liberation the two together signify for her. The car and its potential mobility are thus set up as the causal vortex of their meeting, and the start of the story.

Driving and movement away from home soon take on more narrative importance. Though Clyde has invited Bonnie to accompany him into town, it is *she* who keeps moving, leading along both Clyde and the camera. Eventually Clyde sees he will have to impress her by using his gun to rob a store. But the real thrill comes when they steal a car, to drive away from the crime. The soundtrack's notorious banjo music, "Foggie Mountain Breakdown," is heard for the first time as they "formally" introduce themselves to each other while hopping into the car, then laugh wildly while driving away. Eye-level traveling shots from the backseat, intercut with various high-angle shots, encourage viewer identification with the spectacle of their getaway, but also reflect the perspective of the car itself.

Once parked in the woods, as if to perpetuate the rush, Bonnie starts kissing him passionately. After realizing he is not interested in (or not capable of) sex, she moves away from the car in embarrassed frustration, demanding to be taken home. But he lures her back toward him (and toward the car) by explaining how "different" she is, and how he can help her get the "different things" she wants. This "difference" he sees in her foreshadows their ensuing status as both social outcasts and "star" celebrities. In what will become a staple feature of many future road movies, first articulated here, they achieve their outlaw/star status by realizing their social difference through mobility. In the next scene in a diner, he continues to tell her with prophetic insight and certainty about who she has been, and who she can become, culminating with the question, according to him, she asks herself: "When and how am I ever gonna get away from this?" He provides his own answer: "Now you know," implying that the promise of mobility he offers her is the key to her freedom.

The film develops further its distinctive road movie narrative design by rendering the moving car essential to their criminal lifestyle. They steal a new car as they leave the diner (upbeat banjo music accompanying the theft); stealing cars makes driving even more exciting; it also ensures their survival at several points throughout the film. Small road movie details quickly proliferate: for their first night together, he sleeps "out by the car," while she sleeps on a car seat in an abandoned house. More important, the car fosters the transient space within which their relationship develops. A frontal medium shot frames them together, driving toward their first robbery: Clyde's nervous fear is glaring, whereas ironically she is cool and ready. On both a visual and narrative level, the film's early segments establish the automobile as a third party to their dynamic duo. During their first few robberies (which go badly), Bonnie waits in the car with the engine running, an expression of her impatient, restless energy.

2.2. A publicity still for *Bonnie and Clyde* emphasizes the automobile as third party to their romantic, rambling life of crime.

An important turn of events occurs when they enlist C. W. Moss (Michael J. Pollard) to join their travels. Significantly, C. W. works at a gas station, suggestive of stability and employment, but in a sense on the fringes of the *stationary*: a place where cars stop on their way. Being literally on the road*side*, he is susceptible to the lure of being on the road, and is easily seduced by Bonnie and Clyde when they pull in. Of course, C. W. becomes a kind of adopted son, the first member of the extended, decidedly unconventional family Bonnie and Clyde shall spawn. But I would emphasize his narrative significance in terms of his contribution to the mobility theme: as an auto mechanic, as someone who knows car engines and who learns to drive Bonnie and Clyde around. His first lesson, in fact, is rather hard-earned, even disastrous. By parking during their first bank job as a threesome, C. W. "causes" Clyde to kill a man. In severely restricting their mobility by parking the car, C. W. has committed a crime that infuriates Clyde, who scolds his new "son" later in a movie theater during a rather ironic screening of *Goldiggers of 1933* (specifically during the "We're in the Money" musical number, which mesmerizes Bonnie). Yet throughout the film—even during his betrayal of them at the end—C. W. serves the couple (and the narrative) by helping make cars go.

In the spirit of *On the Road*, the film continues to dramatize the association of liberation with motion, though things become more complicated when Clyde's brother Buck (Gene Hackman) and his wife Blanche (Estelle Parsons) join the trio. As the film earlier contrasted Bonnie's home-as-prison with Clyde's wanderlust-as-freedom, so here their alternative mobile lifestyle is rendered attractive largely through contrast with Blanche, who embodies the dull perils of domesticity and stability. When she first meets Bonnie and Clyde, her awkward movements and inhibited posture seem antithetical to Bonnie's lithe sensuality, as well as Clyde and Buck's boyish enthusiasm. Verbally too Blanche expresses anxiety about moving around, longing for a traditional home with Buck. In fact, the tables turn in her favor at the rented house in Missouri, where she blossoms in her element; carried over the threshold by Buck, she is happy to be in a "home." Bonnie on the other hand becomes bored and irritable; her frustration with Clyde and their diluted romance mirrors her frustration with being stuck inside.

This sequence culminates by driving home the point that mobility is more desirable than stability. While holed up in their "home," they become careless, giving themselves away by ordering out for groceries. The police arrive, and a violent shoot-out ensues, where the Barrow gang have to escape using their cars as cover, blasting their way out. Though the ostensible weapons of the confrontation are guns, it is really the cars that engage in battle. The police cars are blocking the driveway, but the Barrow gang drive more aggressively and cleverly, pushing the cop cars out of the way. The mise en scène suggests that inside the motel room they are eventually doomed to be captured; but once driving in their cars they gain the upper hand. Not coincidentally, Blanche is almost left behind; she gets in the way, fouls things up, unable to move (or think) like the others. They are forced to sweep her up as she runs hysterically down the street. Perhaps because she has no choice, Blanche eventually settles into the mobile lifestyle. One scene in particular illustrates this, where Buck reads aloud from a newspaper (swiped from a mailbox while driving by). Basking in an ominous limelight, she laughs with the others about how the police and newspapers have exaggerated and distorted their crimes. We should note that this scene takes place while driving, associating their mobility with the "truth," in contrast to the newspapers' falsehoods. Throughout the film, whenever the Barrow gang is stationary and enclosed, they become irritable and vulnerable to attack; on the road, they become free and happy—or at least they enjoy some kind of refuge.

Gradually, however, the film complicates its utopian promise of mobility by developing a dark shadow. A turning point along these lines occurs approximately midway through the film, when the gang steals a car belonging to Eugene Grizzard (Gene Wilder). Just previously, Bonnie had been complaining to Clyde about how her mother needs some of the money they have amassed; C. W. interrupts with bad news about their current car, and how they will have to steal another one. Eugene witnesses the theft, then goes after them with his fiancée Velma (Evans Evans). She reminds him of the potential danger in going after them, so they turn back for the police. In a carnivalesque gesture that subverts their own subversive identity as outlaws, the Barrow gang go after them for kicks, and pull them over. They force Eugene and Velma into their car, Bonnie reassuring them that they are "folks just like us." Now that they are all driving along in the same car, they gradually form a happy group. Framed by the front windshield, their good time and intimacy derive from being inside the moving car; the driving helps them transcend their differences, and brings out their personalities, integrated here as a joyful community.[7]

Beyond creating community, driving also yields revelation. As dusk descends and they drive on, sharing a meal together, Eugene learns the truth about Velma's age. A second darker revelation is intolerable for Bonnie, which she herself provokes, by asking Eugene his line of work. He casually remarks that he is an undertaker. Whether superstitious or visionary (or both), Bonnie becomes upset, ordering them out of the car, in the middle of the night, in the middle of nowhere. She alone seems to sense how the presence of the death that (she knows) inevitably awaits them now has prematurely tainted their journey.

After this point, Bonnie develops an attitude toward mobility that transcends that of Clyde and the gang. Though apparently couched in a nostalgia for home, she possesses a visionary impulse to move in a direction more meaningful than Clyde's fugitive aimlessness. After they abandon Eugene and Velma, the film cuts abruptly to the next day, where she is running through a corn field, desperately fleeing the car: she wants to see her mother. While this emotionally intense scene plays partially as a pretext for Clyde to demonstrate his loving devotion to her, it also intimates more of Bonnie's restlessness, developed during the latter sections of the film in terms of the darker side of mobility. This becomes vividly dramatized when the gang visit Bonnie's mother and family in a neutral no-man's-land. Celebrated for its use of filters and subtle slow-motion photography, the sequence achieves a startling dark mood in glaring sunlight, rendering this "family reunion" eerie and a little surreal. Moreover, the fragmented snippets of conversation, edited in a kind of drunken montage, underline the alienating gulf between Bonnie and her former life (of stability). Earlier she longed to get away from home; now, she seems to half-heartedly long to return home, the magic of mobility having worn thin. She can't go home again, but she can't go on either. This scene, like Bonnie herself, seems to foretell their doom.

This disenchantment with mobility, revealed through Bonnie's perspective, taints the film's few remaining episodes. In a tourist court in Platte City, Iowa, she orders the others back to their own cabin so she can be alone with Clyde. She laments that she's "got the blues so bad." Then she delivers what I consider to be a crucial line in the genesis of the contemporary road movie: "At first, when we started, I thought we were really goin' somewhere; but this is it, we're just goin'." This sentiment echoes what her mother had said to them earlier: seeing right through Clyde's tall tales about settling down, she solemnly advises that they "had best keep runnin'." Especially in its latter segments, *Bonnie and Clyde* articulates the dialectical ambivalence toward mobility that appears in most future road movies. As the seductive sheen of mobility fades, life on the road wavers between two tonalities: freedom from futility, and the futility of freedom.

Bonnie's melancholy seems born out a while later, when the police again corner them in their very stability, this time while they sleep. As earlier, the basic domestic survival chore of acquiring food gives away their hideout; and in a more dismal revision of the earlier escape scene, they bust out using their cars, but this time Buck and Blanche are both shot. They make it to

2.3. Disenchanted visionaries: wounded on the road, Clyde looks for another car to steal, as Bonnie laments in pain.

temporary safety, their cars parked at night in a forest, like hunted, wounded animals, effectively emphasizing just how far outside of society they have gone. With the fade to dawn, the police have them surrounded, and open fire. They try to escape, using their cars as shields, their mobility as evasion; but their cars limp in circles, taunted like bulls in a ring, headed off in every direction by a barrage of bullets. Bonnie and Clyde manage to crawl away through the tall grass; but in a symbolic coup the frenzied police and bounty hunters slaughter their cars, exploding them in a cathartic, banshee-wailing rage. Such furious glee suggests how the automobile—and mobility in general, since they never possess the same car—has become an extension of the outlaws, exemplary of the road movie's romantic human-car fusion. Like their cars, Buck and Blanche cannot escape: he dies surrounded like a wild howling beast. Her capture leads eventually to Bonnie and Clyde's own capture, when Sheriff Hamer (Forest Pyle) tricks her into revealing C. W.'s last name. As for Bonnie and Clyde, once again it is the mobility of cars that saves them. After both have been shot, and have dragged themselves away with

C. W.'s loyal help, Clyde lumbers over to steal another car. The banjo music returns at a slower, more weary pace, connoting perhaps that this cannot go on, that they cannot keep going.

As it winds toward its bloody, climactic roadside conclusion, *Bonnie and Clyde* further shadows the notion of mobility as liberation and rebellion with a dystopian mood emanating primarily from Bonnie.[8] Penn's treatment of Bonnie's published poem, ostensibly an affirmative expression of Bonnie's artistic voice, is laced with darkly ambiguous details. While recovering and hiding out at C. W.'s father's house, she reads "The Story of Bonnie and Clyde" to Clyde in the car; but it is raining outside. Then, as the poem continues through her voice-over, the film dissolves to their eventual killer, Sheriff Frank Hamer, observing the poem published in a newspaper. A public relations coup, such success for the poet Bonnie is received by the sheriff as mockery, further fueling his determination to murder them. She concludes the recitation after a second dissolve back to her and Clyde lounging in the sunlight on the grass. The published poem has such inspirational impact on Clyde that finally he can perform sexually. But this sunny moment of artistic success, fame, and lovemaking offers only fleeting respite: the newspaper she reads from is blown away, as two sheets tumbling in the wind, suggesting that even fame cannot save them from the bitter fruition of their fugitive rambling.

Appropriately, this bitter fruition is dramatized in the context of driving cars. During a routine, banal visit into town, a series of subtly symbolic gestures do not bode well: a police car parks next to Clyde waiting in his parked car; one of his sunglass lenses pops out, but he wears them anyway; and Bonnie props a little doll up on the dashboard, a poignant emblem of the innocence she will never return to. They manage to drive away, but this is no getaway. We get our last driving montage of them as she bites into an apple and shares it with him, before pulling over to help C. W.'s father Malcolm (Dub Taylor) with his own "car trouble." When Malcolm dives under his car because another car unexpectedly drives up, the firestorm begins: a rapid-fire montage of slow-motion shots of their bodies and their car, annihilated by bullets. The remarkable scene culminates Bonnie and Clyde's rebellious automobility as a fusion with their car in death. It also creates a tragic catharsis of grandiose visual and narrative proportions that seems to fulfill the film's eventual disenchantment with mobility. In fact, driving figures in almost every aspect of their death, and the film's closure: the fake breakdown, their approach in the car, the unexpected car, and perhaps most powerfully, the film's final shot. When the Sheriff, his men, Malcolm, and the two black farmhands all walk up to survey the carnage, the camera recedes back behind the car, looking out through the windshield shattered with gunshots. Robert Kolker suggests that the camera here "cowers in reaction to what has happened," and that the film's point of view has been destroyed (43). But I see this last image of the film as being from the car's point of view, bringing together the camera, the car, and the audience in a vision of the killers that seems to condemn them.

Visionary Ambition and Restless Sensuality in *Bonnie and Clyde*

Bonnie and Clyde utilizes driving on the open road as its primary narrative structure. But the film also articulates rebellion and liberation through a mobility that transgresses social and legal (as well as state) borders. In this regard, the film elaborates two notions, touched upon above, that descend directly from *On the Road* and that become essential road movie themes: visionary ambition and restless sensuality. Visionary ambition often gets played out in the road movie—as it does in *Bonnie and Clyde*—as a longing to be elsewhere, a frustration with the present (stabilized) situation, a dream of a better destiny. Likewise frustrated with the stable present, restless sensuality suggests more of a primal urge to keep moving, located in and expressed through the body (rather than the mind). This bodily energy in turn expresses itself through a compulsion to drive, and more generally a fetishism of cars and driving. As we shall see, these two road movie notions are often mutually interdependent.

Let us return to the early scene at the diner, where Clyde lures Bonnie to run away with him. Here, Clyde clearly represents visionary ambition, while Bonnie embodies restless sensuality. Besides the exciting life of crime he offers, Clyde "sees" into her past and her very identity. However inarticulate and clumsy he is, Clyde displays this visionary quality throughout most of the film. He has plans, he is always moving toward them, envisioning a life more compelling than common. He follows his intuition, driven to go elsewhere. Even at the end, after agreeing reluctantly to betray them, C. W. believes that the "laws" can never catch Clyde, that "he's got a sense." This visionary quality proves complementary to Bonnie's overt erotic impulses. Her mostly unfulfilled sexual appetite seems a traditionally sexist characterization, in that she signifies sexuality. Moreover, one could read the film's ending through the prism of the film noir tradition, where she is punished with death for finally achieving the object of her excessive sexual desire:

Clyde's finally aroused body (though they are *both* punished with death for their criminal, mobile, alternative lifestyle). Her sexual desire is coded as excessive, her restless sensuality made all the more pronounced in relation to Clyde's gimpy foot and sexual impotence.

And yet, Bonnie is no femme fatale; in fact, she turns out to be the true visionary in the film. Her sensuality eventually becomes visionary, suggesting through her characterization an almost Blakean link between Eros and insight. Glenn Man rightly sees the film as told from her perspective (9); but beyond this, we certainly sense a deeper visionary quality from her than from Clyde. Though she has less testosterone urge to go, she more deeply appreciates the satisfaction of mobility. Being on the road inspires her to create. First of all, she is a storyteller and a poet. The fact that her first reading early in the film is mocked with interruptions by Buck, then interrupted by the arrival of the police and the shoot-out, suggests her artistic vision as a transcendence of both sides of the law. She is truly visionary and radical. Also, in the spirit of Dada and Warhol, she comes up with the idea to take the photograph with Sheriff Hamer and send it to the news media, displaying a keen sense of how to subversively appropriate the news media's sensationalism. Then she writes the poem that is the story of their life: she, not Clyde, turns life into art, envisions the narrative potential of their travels, and becomes the public voice of their adventures. Moreover, as we have seen, the publication of her mythologizing poem is what finally triggers Clyde's dormant sexuality.

Despite, or perhaps because of, her deeper appreciation of mobility, Bonnie also understands the ultimate futility in continual movement. In the "family reunion" scene, and in other scenes toward the end of the film, Bonnie sees beneath the facade of "going somewhere": she comes to learn that the promise of some useful gain upon arrival is an illusion. A parallel suggestion is that she has a vision of a life beyond crime, which Clyde is too blind to see. Just before they are killed, and after their sexual union, Clyde proposes marriage. As if to test his authenticity, she asks Clyde what he would do differently if he could do it all over again; he replies, to her dismay, that they would rob banks in one state and live in another. His limited vision, banal in its pragmatism, causes her to silently turn away, with a caustic grin barely visible on her face. The restless sensuality that initially propelled her onto the road becomes visionary ambition, which in turn now renders the road full of perpetual longing. This sense of disenchantment related to constant movement—the downside to the thrill—recalls the somber ending of *The Wild Angels*, and anticipates the overall tone of many road movies of the early 1970s.

Cultural Critique in *Bonnie and Clyde*

Bonnie and Clyde celebrates driving as the expression of this visionary ambition and restless sensuality; yet the film gains its sociopolitical dimension
as rebellious cultural critique partially from its historical setting of Depression America. Beyond self-consciously revising the gangster genre, the film
also incorporates elements of the social conscience films discussed in the
previous chapter (both genres originating during the Depression). This re-
visionary use of Depression America films serves as an allegorical veil for
the film's countercultural attitude and relevance. Thus, the film's articulation
of the distinct road movie genre through Depression America seems hardly
arbitrary. The Depression setting furnishes the essential political critique,
roughly liberal and progressive, that will pervade the genre as a whole (even
during its postmodern phase). Overall the mobile social criticism of the road
movie has substantial roots in the social crisis of the Depression.

Bonnie and Clyde configures this political critique, first of all, through a
sympathy with the average working person, over and against the conservative authority figures (the banks, the police, etc.). Bonnie and Clyde's chosen
homelessness mirrors that of the victims of a cruel economic system, but
turns the dismal effects of the Depression into affirmation. The morning after
their first night in the abandoned house, the ousted family suddenly appears,
surprising the outlaw couple; but when Clyde learns how the bank has appropriated their house, he allows them to shoot the sign the bank has put up. The
father calls over his black "helper" to join in the shooting. We should note
how the scene emphasizes not the glaring traces of slavery still active in the
South, but the inclusion of the black minority/victim by the working-class
white minority/victim into the ritual of rebellion, which Clyde oversees. Significantly, the scene ends—to Bonnie's surprise—with Clyde spontaneously
defining their identity as a couple in terms of this political critique of big
business: "We rob banks." An exchange of knowing grins ends the scene.

At the same time, the film complicates Clyde's rather simplistic identification with working folk as victims of the Depression. In one of their first
robberies, a grocer attacks Clyde with an ax; shocked by the murderous assault, Clyde exclaims, "He tried to kill me!" and "I'm not against him!" Of
course, Clyde is no political analyst, and does not see how, from the grocer's
point of view, being robbed by the banks or by a dapper gangster produces
the same suffering and rage. Likewise, at a later bank heist, Clyde distinguishes rather naively between "the bank's money" and one of the patrons'
money, allowing the latter to keep his. Clyde wants to represent the interests
of the "common folk," but does not see how he contributes to their prob-

lems. He scolds and humiliates Sheriff Hamer for bounty hunting instead of staying home to protect the people who pay his salary. With respect to the film's working-class sympathy, the most poignant moment occurs near the end, when C. W. drives an injured Bonnie and Clyde into a makeshift grouping of homeless families, who share food and water with their folk heroes; the children surround the car, peering into the backseat whispering, "Is that really Bonnie Parker?"

As I believe this last example illustrates, *Bonnie and Clyde* integrates social criticism into its narrative scheme of road travel, but in a rather different way than films made during the Depression. Somehow the political references cited above seem rather fleeting and tepid in contrast to the more thorough development of political critique in *I Am a Fugitive from a Chain Gang* and *The Grapes of Wrath*. Highly critical of this aspect of the film, Kolker views its flimsy political landscape in terms of, on the one hand, the overinvested bond created between spectator and the two antiheroes; and consequently an overall derogatory, flippant portrayal of everyone else (34–40). Additionally, in contrast to *Bonnie and Clyde*'s countercultural lens on Depression America, the film's somewhat superficial political references also reflect the dominant celebrity/consumer culture of the 1960s. In other words, many of these scenes of politicized rebellion seem a pretext for glorifying the two main characters as heroes. They become celebrities as much as champions of the working-class cause.[9] As countless commentators have noted, Penn's direction seems hyperaware of how the mass media use them, and how they use the mass media. Bonnie and Clyde are turned into stars by the media, exploited for their exploits; yet they also embrace their star status, which inevitably leads to their downfall. For Kolker, "[T]he myth-making that occurs within the narrative is doubled by the myth-making that is carried on by the narrative itself" (30); for Man, "the most insistent form of the film's reflexivity is its commentary on its own mythmaking nature" (18). Coding the road trip as a spectacle or performance becomes a consistent aspect of future road movies.

This tension between stardom and politics becomes more clear if we reconsider the film's upbeat banjo music, as well as its high key lighting. In offering an aural equivalent to the thrill of driving, the banjo music subverts the traditional gangster tone of urban darkness (and seriousness) with a light, rural comedic tone. Likewise, the film's predominant high key lighting and daylight scenes, mostly in outdoor rural settings, depart from (and figuratively lighten) the gangster genre. Often accompanied by fast editing during the getaway scenes, this music and lighting seem to express the optimistic vitality of the gangsters' individualized personalities. We should distinguish

2.4. The Barrow Gang: countercultural "family," self-made stars.

this approach from Ford's low angles and patriotic music, which convey the social and political integrity of the Joad family (they are no celebrities—at least not *within* the film); or from *I Am a Fugitive*'s low key lighting, the darkness James Allen can never escape (Allen becomes a celebrity of sorts, but this quickly leads to his downfall, reincarceration, and endless desperation on the road). Yet *Bonnie and Clyde* is distinctly post-Kerouac in its almost sensual passion for mobility and its romantic use of the Depression as a time of rebellious liberation.

Ending the Road Movie:
Bonnie and Clyde's Political Tensions

The film's celebrated ending is perhaps the best site for discussing the political tensions within the film as a whole. Setting the tone for the narrative fate and closure of many road movies to follow, this visually stunning ending, on the surface, insists upon its political critique of authority; beneath the surface, it vacillates ideologically between rebellion and conformity. *Bonnie and Clyde* strongly suggests that an alternative, rebellious journey is doomed to defeat by the fascistic trappings of a conservative society. This sense of doom is one way in which the film exposes (if not judges) the extremes of conservative, traditional social boundaries. After almost two hours of attractive and interesting character development, their slow-motion contortions in death contrast severely with the harshly distant final medium shot of the killers, accomplices, and onlookers. From this perspective, the ending seems to indict the traditional conservative authority figures of the police, while sympathizing with Bonnie and Clyde as victims of a brutal murder.

But where does the road of rebellion and alternative vision lead finally? Their final punishment allows the film to come to an end, arresting their mobility with utter finality.[10] Despite director Arthur Penn's specific intentions or broader political views, the conventional demands of classical narrative closure seem to join hands insidiously with those of conservative society, not only putting a stop to their journey, but also lashing out with an ideological comeuppance typical of the gangster genre (and Hollywood films in general).[11] Perhaps an unconscious sigh of relief emerges—from the text and the audience—somewhere in the silent aftermath of the deed, the cut to a black screen, and the gradual fade-in of red letters spelling out "The End." There is a sense that they are getting what they deserved, that their "alternative" fugitive criminal lifestyle must ultimately lead to their destruction by the forces of society. Regardless of how attractive and sympathetic they are, and regardless of how shocking and disturbing their deaths therefore appear, ideological safety and conformity prevail.

From a slightly different angle, Bonnie and Clyde seem to carry the seeds of their own inability to prevail because their "alternative" is itself politically limited and naive. The conservative values Bonnie and Clyde intend to flee are internalized by them, especially Clyde, whose lust for money and success mirrors the drive within the capitalist society he battles. For example, in the early scene where Bonnie wants to go back home, Clyde persuades her to go with him. Upon closer scrutiny (beyond its emphasis on mobility), this scene reveals the contradiction within the genre between rebellion and conformity. Clyde, that is, articulates the utterly conformist American archetypal link between horizontal mobility and economic upward mobility: let's go, and in going, make money. This socially conventional Horatio Alger myth of individual success underpins Clyde's own socially unconventional ambition to realize their "difference." As Edward Mitchell has shown, the cultural contradiction of the "perverted Horatio Alger pattern" (208) pervades the classic gangster genre, thus illustrating how *Bonnie and Clyde* is clearly a gangster film constructed as a road movie. Throughout the film, Clyde will see himself as rebelling against capitalist society, yet upon second glance—as his words to Bonnie here reveal—he embodies the fundamental tenets of that society. What distinguishes this contradiction in the road movie from that of the classic gangster is precisely Clyde's visionary desire, as well as the film's overall theme of rebellious social criticism. *Bonnie and Clyde* the road movie is more self-consciously political than a classic gangster film (just as it more self-consciously articulates social criticism through road travel than a road movie–esque gangster film like *Gun Crazy*). Yet we should appreciate here how the film's dual generic structure is provocatively caught between the past and the future, following the gangster formula (tradition) as much as inventing the independent road movie (rebellion).

Another way the conservative haunts the alternative in *Bonnie and Clyde* is through its portrayal of blacks. Since the film takes place in the Deep South, we know blacks populate the landscape Bonnie and Clyde traverse; in fact, given the film's ostensible political attitude, we would expect some substantial interaction between our outlaw couple and the victims of institutionalized racism. Instead, their appearance feels rather contrived, mostly as token, passive spectators to the picaresque adventures of our attractive white antiheroes. A black man sits in the background as Bonnie and Clyde first stroll through town (note their active movement, versus his passive stasis); later, a few blacks watch as C. W. desperately unparks the car. At the film's end, two blacks unexpectedly approach the planned ambush, precipitating the bloodletting. Whether Penn intends to sketch an implicit bond between the outlaw couple and the region's ex-slaves, the black characters are mostly voiceless ciphers, static, watching rather than participating in the action. This black spectatorship built into the film reveals an awkwardly racialized and conservative facet of the celebrity emphasis discussed earlier: Bonnie and Clyde are the stars within the fiction, blacks (and the working poor) their adoring audience. Such generic and thematic traces of the conservative within the alternative suggest the ideological complexity of narrativizing political rebellion, as the road movie often attempts to do.

In this respect, the film articulates a limited, ambivalent political critique. Ryan and Kellner, for example, contend that the film's "social vision . . . confines itself to thumbing its nose at the 'Establishment' and complaining" (23). The film thus harks back to the road film noir approach described above: a doomed fate for the criminals, in a relatively apolitical narrative context. But what *Bonnie and Clyde* adds to the noir approach is precisely its (relatively limited) sociopolitical emphasis, which derives from its Depression setting and the influence of the Depression road film precursor of classical Hollywood. Let us here recall that *Bonnie and Clyde* spawned a whole series of Depression road movies into the 1970s (*Boxcar Bertha, Paper Moon, Thieves like Us, Bound for Glory*), all of which nostalgically harness the social crisis associated with the Depression, so as to express countercultural critique.

Easy Rider: Mobilizing the Road Movie

Most of the road movie elements mobilized by *Bonnie and Clyde*—glorified transience, fugitive/alternative lifestyle, cultural critique, visionary ambition, and restless sensuality—were further molded in 1969 into what remains arguably the quintessential, genre-defining road movie, Dennis Hopper's *Easy Rider*.[12] Aesthetically, *Easy Rider* pushes *Bonnie and Clyde*'s modernist New Wave style in a more generically distinctive direction (though today the film's exaggerated jump-cut editing and hyperzoom shots seem more dated than *Bonnie and Clyde*'s stylistic restraint). Bearing out Corrigan's opinion that *Bonnie and Clyde* is the superior film, the American Film Institute's controversial "100 Greatest American Movies List" of 1998 judges *Bonnie and Clyde* at number 27, *Easy Rider* at number 88. Yet *Easy Rider* was instrumental in launching the American independent narrative film as a successful and profitable reflection of the counterculture. More significant for our discussion, it also offers the most pristine delineation, from within this independent, countercultural context, of the road movie as a distinct genre.[13]

By setting two men out "in search of America" who "couldn't find it anywhere" (though in fact the tag line refers to a single "man"), *Easy Rider* establishes the quest as its basic plot structure. The film distinguishes itself from the gangster/outlaw emphasis of *Bonnie and Clyde*—and from the entire classical genre precursor trajectory—by creating a new genre centered more around the quest for spiritual and cultural identity. While *Bonnie and Clyde* possesses some of these elements, the couple remains partially disguised by both the Depression setting and the gangster genre. The quest as spiritual and cultural in *Easy Rider*, however, appears explicitly on the surface of the film's narrative. In this sense *Easy Rider* has strong affinities with *On the Road*, and may be seen as a loose film version of the novel. With its meandering plot and mild lawlessness (usually related to drugs), the film attempts like that novel to integrate the search for self with a rediscovery of America by traveling across (and into) it.

Despite its surface differences from *Bonnie and Clyde*, *Easy Rider* develops many of the former film's basic road movie characteristics (which is why *taken together* they form a formidable and persuasive origin for the road movie). Let us begin with the readily apparent narrative and character focus on a traveling couple. Peter Fonda plays Wyatt, better known as "Captain America," the detached, visionary observer, while Dennis Hopper plays

2.5. *Easy Rider*'s uneasy rider: Peter Fonda as Wyatt, the man on the road who couldn't find America.

Billy, his earthy, impatient partner. Binding two conflicting character types (active/passive, intellectual/sensual, straight/wild, etc.), this variation on the Sal/Dean and Clyde/Bonnie personality duo forms the film's central character tension. This personality pairing, more or less consistent in the genre, distills and reflects the central themes of visionary ambition and restless sensuality. In the context of *Easy Rider,* we might further elaborate these two themes as a compulsive thrill-seeking drive on the one hand, and a reflective, spiritual search on the other. Additionally, *Easy Rider* uniquely contributes to the road movie couple by pairing *two men* together (again, similar to *On the Road,* as well as the Western film genre), setting in motion what will become a prevalent road movie subset, the "buddy" road movie. But even the buddy couple seems to work within the more general personality pairing suggested above.[14]

Secondly, like *Bonnie and Clyde, Easy Rider* immediately sets up the hierarchy that privileges mobility over stability. We saw how *Bonnie and Clyde* opened with a scene contrasting domestic imprisonment (Bonnie in her room) with the promise of liberation through mobility (Clyde outside admiring the car). Though *Easy Rider* opens rather differently, it makes a similar point. A static, eye-level shot of a run-down wrecking shop in Mexico becomes gradually "invaded" by the offscreen sound of approaching motorcycles (reminiscent of *The Wild One*'s first shot). The sound of approaching bikes creates a certain suspense, signaling the arrival of character into the lifeless mise en scène. But let us appreciate how the film's first narrative gesture introduces mobility as an aesthetic and narrative element, in contrast to—or at least in tension with—the static shot and the static setting (wrecked cars in a junkyard). Finally Wyatt and Billy ride into the shot and park. Another similarity with *Bonnie and Clyde* is the first instance of the mobile camera. In *Bonnie and Clyde*, it tracked along with them walking into town; here in *Easy Rider*, as Wyatt and Billy go behind some wreckage to make their dope deal, the camera seems to have adopted the mobility of their bikes, as it rather fluidly follows them through the junkyard. Viewed in the context of each film's mobility/stability hierarchy, these first uses of the mobile camera foreshadow movement as narrative force.

Beyond initiating the mobility/stability hierarchy, *Easy Rider*'s first few moments deploy other various symbolic devices that establish the film's (and the genre's) direction. After they sell their cocaine in a bizarre scene at the end of an airport runway in Los Angeles, the film explicitly prepares us for their imminent journey by lovingly gliding over Wyatt's infamous motorcycle, in close-up, drifting in and out of focus in a sort of rhapsodic, rapturous gaze. As he inserts the money from the deal into the gas tank, then puts on his helmet, the nonsynchronous rock music of Steppenwolf's "Pusher" assists in creating excitement about the bike, and the ensuing road trip. In the final preparatory gesture before their actual journey begins, Captain America and Billy pull into a static shot of the open road (replaying the composition and movement of the opening shot), where Wyatt removes his watch, observes it pointedly, then chucks it. The gesture is stylistically underlined by a combination quick zoom/montage, as it hits the ground. A bit heavy-handed, the gesture is important for the road movie, signaling an urge to move beyond not only social and narrative conventions, but temporal and spatial ones.

But the film's distinctive sense of glorified road travel, and its explicit narrative emphasis on the journey, is most powerfully suggested by the credit sequence, which stands as a kind of overture to the rest of the film's narrative. Directly influenced by the credit sequence of *The Wild Angels* discussed above, this montage sequence of the two buddies riding their bikes is energized with the song most associated with the film, the hard-driving "Born to Be Wild" by Steppenwolf. The song seems to viscerally express the thrill of riding we see on the screen. The lyrics too are essential to the sequence's articulation of the road movie genre:

> Head out on the highway,
> Lookin' for adventure,
> And whatever comes my way,
> Born to be wild . . .

Unlike *Bonnie and Clyde*'s mood-mixing, controversial banjo music, *Easy Rider*'s rock music soundtrack enjoys more narrative significance, since it clearly celebrates mobility: many driving sequences seem designed by and for the song playing, in anticipation of the music video.[15] The collected popular rock songs also give the film contemporary political relevance, exploiting the social impact of rock music and its ability to convey the thrill of road travel for the counterculture. From just these first few moments of the film we can glean some crucial generic features of the road movie: rock music, drugs, the thrill of riding/driving itself, the search as journey, the journey as discovery, and alternative social values.

Uneasy Riding Counter to the Culture

The film immediately follows its credit sequence glorifying road travel with a brief dramatic episode emphasizing society's rejection of their alternative values and mobile lifestyle. In the evening, presumably after riding all day, Billy and Wyatt pull into a motel parking lot, and ask for a room. The manager takes one look at them, retreats inside, and locks the door. Billy yells, "You asshole!" and they both pull away. The scene sketches how their bikes are *a part of* the two riders (they never get off their bikes, their motors still running), but also how the bikes symbolize something "different" and threatening for mainstream America. Appropriated subversively from conventional car use (commuting, tourism, etc.), the mobility they embrace all too clearly expresses their cultural critique and chosen outsider status. Not coincidentally, this first dramatic scene also invokes the film's overall political attitude, developed more fully in later scenes: that conservative society rejects them more than they reject it; that they seek acceptance in their very difference, but that society cannot tolerate such difference. Thus Billy's angry curse is contextualized as a response to being silently snubbed.

The end of this scene is marked by one of the film's more distinctive aesthetic devices. Though rarely used in future road movies, it helped dis-

2.6. *Easy Rider* glorifies mobility with dynamic traveling shots and montages.

tinguish a new genre with something like a new film language, one deriving specifically from the thematic focus on driving. I am referring to the flash-forward scene transitions, here a rapid-fire back-and-forth montage, of the shot of them camping out in the wilderness, with the shot of the motel they have just left. This flash-forward montage renders more pronounced the causal relationship between the motel owner's rejection of them as outsiders, and their having to camp out in the wilderness, on the fringes of society. Used throughout the film, this technique translates the excitement of their tripping (physical and mental) with Eisensteinian energy. Moreover, it visually conveys the sense that their traveling transcends not merely cultural, but temporal and spatial limits (connecting with Wyatt chucking his watch earlier).[16] Overall the film is filled with striking tracking shots, zoom shots, and montage sequences; combined with the pervasive rock music soundtrack, these aim to aesthetically convey the unleashing of spiritual energy through a politicized driving. Thus *Easy Rider* moves beyond *Bonnie and Clyde* as a rebel road movie: its narrative and style celebrate road travel more explicitly. Set in its own politically contentious present, squarely addressing the cultural tensions of the day, less reliant on traditional generic formula (such as the gangster film), *Easy Rider* more lucidly creates the road movie as distinct genre.

Other sequences in the film equate transient mobility with rebellious liberation, further "defining" the road movie genre. Whereas the driving montage of *The Wild Angels* was used specifically as credit sequence, *Easy Rider* reuses the driving montage throughout the film as narrative substance. One of these driving montages occurs early in their journey, when Wyatt picks up a hitchhiker (Luke Askew). As the Byrds' quietly lyrical song "Wasn't Born to Follow" plays on the soundtrack (a kind of mellow flip side to "Born to Be Wild"), we observe a dynamic series of shots of them riding through a lush forest area. Comprising jump cuts, zooms, traveling point of view shots, low-angle, frontal, and rear shots, the montage does not tell a story, or even follow the action of their movement (as traditional continuity cutting would). Rather, it conveys the sensation of freewheeling mobility, as well as the notion that mobility facilitates an appreciation of natural beauty. After a brief pause to fuel up, another driving montage begins (this time to a song by The Band, "The Weight"): a series of gorgeous desert evening shots, mostly in Monument Valley, with the hitchhiker on Wyatt's bike pointing to the landscape and describing it. Though we never hear his words, we can presume he is helping Wyatt to rediscover America's beauty. With night descending toward the end of the sequence, several shots seem clearly to allude to the cinema of John Ford, with the vast sky hanging over a low horizon line, and with mountain and rock formations in majestic silhouette against a glorious twilight. Just one significant way we can distinguish the road movie from Ford's Western is in *Easy Rider*'s self-conscious moving camera (versus Ford's mostly static compositions). In one of this sequence's last and most visually stunning shots, the camera begins panning in a wide arc at a rather brisk pace, continuing for quite some time, eventually stopping where the three are climbing up on some rocks. No doubt admiring the scenery, the moving camera (here and throughout) also celebrates movement itself. The scanning motion imitates the look (omniscient here), but a look *that moves,* a look that precipitates a body in motion (riding the motorbike).

Typically one passes through the landscape, as a means, toward destination; but in *Easy Rider* movement through the landscape becomes an end in itself, specifically in terms of appreciating the landscape. Moreover, such appreciation of the environment becomes a way to rediscover one's self. Barbara Klinger argues that the film's romanticized imagery of the American landscape participates in a traditional tourist discourse (discussed more below). Yet the film, I think, sees its own portrayal of the American landscape *in opposition to* the mainstream middle-class tourism Klinger invokes, in that this portrayal is more "authentic," transforming or at least deeply affecting our easy riders. The safe, objectifying distance of mainstream tourism is what the film attempts to transgress. Driving/riding, that is, not only reacquaints one with the majestic landscape (as conventional tourism does); it also possesses the redemptive power of personal rejuvenation. In yet another driving montage later in the film, on their way to Mardi Gras, Wyatt, Billy, and George (Jack Nicholson) engage in silly acrobatics, pretending to be flying, suggesting a return to childhood innocence.

Such personal rejuvenation through mobility is also reflected on the roadside; the feverish joy of mobility becomes a contagious spectacle for those not riding. In other words, another facet of the film's glorification of mobility is its focus on various "spectators" throughout the rambling narrative. Driving as a mobile spectacle attracts the fawning attention of the stationary "passers-by." This notion is first invoked at the commune, where Wyatt and Billy bring the hitchhiker. While there, Wyatt becomes the object of female desire, due partially (we are meant to infer) from his status as wanderer, as ephemeral man-on-the-move. As we saw with the motel owner in the beginning of the film (and as we shall discuss below), the spectacle of their mobility can provoke fear and rage for some spectators within the film; yet it often seems to elicit admiration from those they pass by or fleetingly meet.[17] This becomes especially pronounced when they ride through the South, and poor blacks wave to them from their shantytown shacks. Like *Bonnie and Clyde*'s problematic "use" of blacks as silent, passive, and symbolic, *Easy Rider* attempts to portray an affinity between hippie outsiders and oppressed blacks. However, this well-intended but tokenistic portrayal creates another kind of oppression. Lee Hill rightly describes the film's treatment of blacks as "a missed opportunity to expand the film's critique of the American Dream" (54).[18] In any case, part of the film's spectacular appeal to its audience is to fictionalize an "audience" for the easy riders within the narrative.

Another layer of *Easy Rider*'s celebration of mobility is the narrative motif of the campfire scene, conversations that quietly articulate much of the film's rebellious, culturally critical attitude. Usually fairly brief, these campfire scenes serve as effective moments of punctuation, for reflection upon the journey. At one such scene, Wyatt asks the hitchhiker if he ever wanted "to be somebody else." While Wyatt seems in earnest, the hitchhiker's response sounds more like Billy, mocking that once he "wanted to be Porky Pig." Wyatt responds to his own question more seriously, that he himself "never wanted to be anyone else." The dialogue is significant for how it suggests that the process of road travel provokes an internal, psychological process (or journey), thus implying a causal bridge between quest and questioning.

2.7. *Easy Rider*'s campfire scenes: pauses in mobility create a space for reflection, but also tension. Director Dennis Hopper (*right*) as Billy and Peter Fonda as Wyatt.

Additionally, the question of being "somebody else" puts identity itself into question, into a possible state of crisis (let us recall *Detour* and *I Am a Fugitive* in this respect). On the other hand, Wyatt's response underlines that he is not truly outside of society's definition of identity: he still clings to who he is.[19] Perhaps in a Zen sort of way he is content with himself, in opposition to the dominant consumer culture that fosters the forever unfulfilled desire to be somebody else (or to possess something else). After Wyatt and Billy hook up with George, these conversation scenes become more politically incisive, articulating the racist and fascist dimensions of the American cultural landscape.

In *Easy Rider*, references to stability come to signify the shackles of conservative society, problematizing the film's overt rebellion. In a scene that expands upon their rejection by the motel owner, they visit a small southern town and end up in prison. Here their punishment is slightly more justified, since they had joined a parade without a permit. Actually, they roll into the parade, mocking a sanitized version of their own bohemian mobility. The prison they are put in too seems an exaggerated microcosm of the town (which, in fact, we see little of; the prison seems to *be* the town). After a montage of wall scrawlings in their cell, the frame-within-a-frame compositions suggest the thematic link between home/town/stability and imprisonment, invoking the classical road movie tradition of *I Am a Fugitive* (as well as paving the generic way for a feminist road movie like *Thelma and Louise*). It is no coincidence that lawyer George Hansen, whom they have just met, refers to "scissors-happy" citizens outside on a kick to "beautify America," in the context of generally rampant racism. The three of them hit the road for a brief respite of freedom and joy, before George's description proves brutally accurate.

The film's most intense critique of conformist America through the trope of stability occurs shortly afterward, in two parts. The first part is when they pull into a diner in the heart of the South. A group of redneck men sitting at one table immediately react to them, assuming they are "troublemakers." They express their repulsion for these hippies with a litany of repulsive racist and homophobic remarks, deliberately loud and provocative. At the same time, our trio of uneasy riders become the object of another gaze from another table: a group of teenage girls, who start fawning over them and flirting with them. Here we have a powerful dramatization of the spectacle of mobility they represent (discussed earlier), and two contesting spectatorial reactions. The film cuts back and forth between the two groups, emphasizing how two different looks converge on them—one look eroticizes them, the other degrades them. Yet we should note how both looks are fascinated by them as exotic, as Other, from a voyeuristic distance. The female gaze expresses desire, the male gaze expresses hatred: by juxtaposing the two looks, the film suggests that they are two aspects of the *same* look.[20] The diner setting represents stability, but it also fosters the enactment of an objectifying gaze that—as this scene so clearly suggests—further imprisons and oppresses them. Unlike at the close of the commune sequence, where they choose to move on, here they are forced to move on—to pay, in a sense, for the mobile life they have chosen, with endless, forced mobility. Their difference from society—whether fetishized or vilified—is marked by the reciprocity of their mobility and their exoticized otherness.

But this scene in the diner is a relatively timid prelude to a more horrifying image of conformist America. Once again they are camped out, forced outside of society. Around the campfire, George makes his infamous speech —perhaps the film's "message," if it has one—about how America used to be a great country, but that people have become scared of freedom. Thus, people fear Wyatt and Billy because they represent true freedom by being "different" (though as we have seen, and will see below, the difference and freedom they represent turns out to be not so different or free). People can talk about freedom, George goes on, but when it comes to actually being free, that is another story. Bought and sold in the marketplace, conformist Americans will kill to prove they are free, even if they kill what they fear. Of course, George has prophesied his own death. As they sleep, the rednecks brutally attack them with clubs and hammers, fatally wounding George. Even though they are camped out in the forest, the seemingly peaceful refuge of nature, their stasis renders them prey to the wrath of culture's bigots (who, we see, are willing to venture outside of society, into the wilderness, to mete out their judgment).

"We Blew It": Disenchantment on the Road

At the end of the film, their last campfire discussion questions the meaning and validity of their quest (thus the very premise of the film), as Wyatt insists on the failure, even futility, not of America, but of their own journey. The ambiguity and dejection of Wyatt's "We blew it" line, in fact, gives full expression to a creeping uneasiness within all the campfire scenes. While they do articulate a visionary, critical potential through mobility, these scenes also possess "disturbing portents of things to come" (L. Hill, 48). Not unlike similar stationary scenes in *Bonnie and Clyde* discussed above, these scenes expose the tension between Billy and Wyatt, who get on each other's nerves when they stop; Billy especially often becomes restless and paranoid. We sense this tension the first night with the hitchhiker, where Billy is in a rush to get to Mardi Gras, and is a little peeved that they are going out of their way to bring the hitchhiker to the commune. When Wyatt says "I think I'll crash," Billy retorts, "I think you've already crashed." When Billy proceeds to question the hitchhiker about where he is from, the latter explains that "it's hard to say," that he is from some city, and that it does not matter which, since all cities are alike. That is why he is "out here." Note how the hitchhiker articulates the film's celebration of wanderlust as antidote to urban oppression, yet the tension between the three is equally thick and oppressive as they sit together; it is as if they cannot help embodying that which they rebel against.

The hitchhiker's (and the film's) preference for being outside of society, out in the wilderness, comes to relative fruition in the commune. But the relativity of this fruition is key here: as during other scenes of stability, the film's political tensions around mobility and rebellion come to the surface. Though an alternative to city living, and to mainstream America in general, the commune seems plagued by many of the same fundamental problems related to "stable" society: securing food, domesticity as prison, cleaning house, possessing versus sharing, privacy. When Wyatt muses that "they're gonna make it," we are not so sure: in the context of what we have seen, his prediction rings fragile if not false. Wyatt's somewhat arrogant solitude during the latter part of the commune segment—positioned above Billy and the two girls in the water, or alone in a field picking blades of grass—conveys how for him the mobile alternative is preferable to this stable one. He later explains to the hitchhiker who lives there that he is "hip about time," but that he has "just gotta go." Thus their journey, and its eventual lack of fulfillment, comes to mirror ironically the unfulfilled desires proffered by the consumer/materialist culture they take flight from. Though he admires both the commune and the farmer for their realization of agrarian/naturalist utopian alternatives recalling preindustrial America (Whitman meets the Old West), he himself, spurned on by Billy, has to keep moving.

In line with *Bonnie and Clyde* and the road movie generally, the initial promise and thrill of mobility gradually turns sour. At a certain point down the road, the road movie's glorified mobility seems to yield a disillusioned attitude in the protagonists, who have been unable truly to escape, and who have internalized (brought with them) the pressures of conformist society.

After George's murder, the film becomes increasingly dark in mood, developing a bitter tone of disenchantment. It is as though the oppressive conventions of stable society are ultimately inescapable, contaminating their easy riding on a variety of levels. The sense that stability, and all of its pitfalls, clings to their wanderlust is most pronounced during the film's first climax (the second being their deaths, discussed below): the LSD trip. After arriving at Madame Tinkertoy's, the legendary New Orleans brothel George had been guiding them to, Wyatt administers the LSD to Billy and their two lady friends. The scene at the whorehouse suggests that Wyatt cannot shake his melancholia regarding George's death. Overcome by malaise about their trip, he nevertheless remains typically aloof. The turning toward psychedelia in their journey thus betrays a certain frustration with literal, horizontal movement. The "content" of the acid trip itself seems a kind of negative catharsis, an internal journey that reveals what their external wanderings attempted (unsuccessfully) to alleviate. Interspersed with psychedelic special effects, a collage/montage of bizarre religious imagery and naked bodies writhing and moaning in pain flash on screen, while the unhinged soundtrack reveals industrial pumping noises, and confessional agony: one of the prostitutes rants about not being beautiful; Wyatt discourses feverishly on his alienation from his parents, and about death.

On one level, for Wyatt and Billy the acid adventure is a complementary extension of their travels. But given the narrative context preceding the acid trip (George's murder, the inescapable oppression of society), and the trip's overall dark tone (it is a bummer), I see the sequence more as a displacement than a development of their mobility. The retreat from their literal journey into a confined space (the cemetery, within Mardi Gras, within the city of New Orleans) reflects the unfulfilled promise of journeying, and the withdrawal of mobility into purely imaginary terms. It is notable that once again—for the third time—the presence of women is made by the film to represent romantic/sexual desire within the context of the stable society they attempt to reject through their mobility. First at the commune, then in the diner, and now in the cemetery, the desire of women for them is embedded in the landscape of oppressive stability. Perhaps inadvertently but no less systematically, the film aligns women with stability, with the setting that must be left behind, thus setting the road movie stage as a male fantasy.[21]

After the acid trip sequence, there is one last campfire scene—perhaps the most crucial one—where Wyatt expresses the realization: "We blew it." Despite Billy's naive optimism, Wyatt sees that they have failed. Precisely *what* they have failed at is deliberately left unclear, open to speculation. Then, as if to drive a nail in the coffin of this confessed failure of the counterculture, the conservative forces of stability haunting them throughout much of the second half of the film again have taken to the road themselves, to assassinate our easy riders. The last riding montage is quite distinct from all those previous, setting a dismal tone for this assassination. It is comprised mainly of ugly industrial landscape imagery, suggestive of technology's debris: factories, smoke, telephone wires, harsh glare on water, cross-traffic. After Wyatt's pronouncement that they have failed, the landscape they pass through—and, more significantly, the passing through it—no longer seems so attractive. If they have failed to be truly countercultural, the road now mirrors their failure with images of technology's own failure to fulfill its ideological promise of improving society: here, it seems more like a contamination. Perhaps the countercultural drive of our rambling protagonists has become infected by conservative society's misguided technology fetishism, fostering their failure. In any case, the end of this montage subtly suggests that the failure of the journey is also interpersonal: full shots of them riding show them separating, moving apart from each other, as well as moving backward within the frame as they literally move forward.[22] It is the end of the road; it is the end of being on the road; and it is the end of wanting to be on the road.

The End of the Road:
Political Tensions in *Easy Rider*

Like *Bonnie and Clyde*, *Easy Rider* ends on a brutal note where conservative authority figures fatally punish the road rebels. Wyatt and Billy are not gunned down in a police ambush, but are gunned down, apparently, for simply being on the road. But let us appreciate their "crime": a bohemian mobile lifestyle, one intolerable to American society's more reactionary forces, who claim the same road and refuse to share it. First Billy is "accidentally" shot by the two rednecks who pull up beside him. We should note the sharp visual contrast between the motorcycle—incarnation of the extreme, nonconformist individuality they represent—and the huge pickup truck, a traveling fortress symbolic of ultraconformist, backwoods America. Clutching his rifle, the one in the passenger seat gibes Billy, "Why don't you get a haircut?" Billy gives them the finger, and the gun goes off: we then see Billy and his bike go flying. When Wyatt arrives, after turning back, Billy is heard groaning that he wants to "get them"; the rednecks, meanwhile, having passed them, say "We gotta go back." As Wyatt pulls away to go for help, he thinks they might be coming back to help;[23] but no, they kill Wyatt too. Echoing the strikingly stylistic machine gun–fire montage concluding Penn's film, here camera technology, travel imagery, and death converge: Wyatt's gas tank is exploded with one shot, impact and explosion portrayed with a quick montage, followed by a slow-motion shot of the crashing bike, which leads into the final aerial shot lifting away from the wreckage.

As has been widely noted about this infamous ending, there is no view of Wyatt being killed, no body in death is revealed: all we need see, according to this road movie, is the death of the vehicle. On the one hand, this approach derives from the pyrotechnic fetishism within cinema that prefers large, more-than-human spectacles of explosion and disaster. In this sense the road movie in general should be understood for how it fulfills this mainstream cinematic interest in grand (often special effects–laden) spectacles of technological fireworks. On the other hand, and more in the specific context of the film, this ending dramatizes how Wyatt and Billy have "become" their bikes. This last aerial shot suggests Wyatt's spirit rising up toward the heavens, rendering the human-bike fusion especially poetic.

Recalling our discussion above of *Bonnie and Clyde*'s ending, this ending seems a cynical indictment of society as vicious and repressive. Yet it also reasserts society and its stable conventions, which prevail in narrative closure. These two possible readings are not necessarily mutually exclusive; but the residual ambivalence built into the film's ending may be unpacked to reveal the ideological contradiction lurking beneath the surface of *Easy Rider*. This contradiction revolves around the return of the repressed: the insidious presence of the very thing the road movie protagonists criticize by leaving behind. Put differently, the ambitious drive to go outside American society celebrated by *Easy Rider* becomes recuperated to the traditional American culture it seeks to critique. We have touched upon this contradiction above, but because this contradiction is so powerfully built into the road movie genre, we shall delve into it further in concluding our discussion of *Easy Rider*.

The film's slippery rebellion/conformity dialectic is perhaps most readily accessible in terms of its relationship to the Western film genre. While it is true that *Easy Rider* "reverses the premise of most Westerns" (L. Hill, 34), a reading against the grain reveals the film's *affinities* with the Western, affinities that in turn reveal a conformist subtext. For example, the scene early in the film at the rancher's home suggesting a bond between the motorcycle and the horse is viewed by Ryan and Kellner as indicative of an "ideal of freedom that is highly traditional," marking their journey as "into the past" as much as across the country (23–24). Later, as Wyatt and Billy eat with the rancher's family, Wyatt expresses his admiration for the rugged individualism of the old-world rancher: "It's not every man who can live off the land." While the film ostensibly contrasts Wyatt's earnest respect with Billy's self-absorption (he starts to eat before the family prayer, and fails to remove his hat at the table), I would emphasize the (subtextual) conformity regarding gender in this scene. Just preceding Wyatt's comments of admiration, the rancher asks his dutifully subservient and silent Mexican wife to serve more coffee. The lifestyle Wyatt admires—and that he himself embodies, to a degree—bears within it cultural and historical baggage full of patriarchal and imperialist oppression.[24]

We have also remarked upon *Easy Rider*'s visual affinity with the Western. On the one hand, the film's (countercultural) attitude toward the landscape and nature is quite distinct from that of the Western. But it also rearticulates the Western's nostalgia for the frontier, and the more general American pastoralist tradition of fondness for the wilderness. Barbara Klinger provides a compelling critique of such romantic use of landscape in *Easy Rider*. She situates the film's "picturesque road montages" within mainstream America's celebration in the mid-sixties of the national landscape (the nation-as-landscape), a celebration vividly legible in the conventional magazine spreads of *National Geographic* (184–88). Klinger reminds us that such a "vision of the wilderness. . . . has been immortalized in images from the classic Western," interpreting the long panning shot discussed earlier as communicating the scenery's "grandeur reverently and

2.8. A solemn Wyatt searches for America: ironically, it's on his back—and inside him.

completely" (189). Yet Klinger argues that the film's use of landscape is dialectical. Its conservative invocations of American scenery are offset (or challenged) by landscape imagery influenced by the counterculture—specifically pop art's apocalyptic and ironic vision of technology's invasion of "America the Beautiful." Even Ryan and Kellner—who see both *Bonnie and Clyde*'s and *Easy Rider*'s underlying conservatism in terms of idealizing nature—concede that "[w]hile hippie romanticism can be conservative, it also helped spawn the ecology movement, legislation to protect the environment, and the rediscovery of natural agriculture and foods" (26).

Thus, on a variety of levels, *Easy Rider*'s rebellion and conservatism always play off each other, haunt each other—though the former is overt and the latter covert. From this perspective, Wyatt's nickname Captain America suddenly expresses the militant patriotism and "manifest destiny" it also mocks. Ryan and Kellner elaborate the ideological contradiction encapsulated in the nickname "Captain America"—itself an expression of the film's overall dialectical tension between rebellion and conformity—as such: "It [the film] is critical of a certain America, but it can also be read as merely enacting the fundamental principle of capitalist America—the freedom of the market, which is in some respects metaphorized as the freedom of the open road. The primary complaint against America in the film is that it is not American enough" (25).

As suggested earlier, this ideological tension also operates quite dramatically in the film's ending, where the road rebels are martyred by the forces of conservative society, but where the latter ensure ideological containment in narrative closure.[25] This residual political ambivalence becomes further complicated by the ending's suggestion of transcendence and martyrdom. That is, the cultural dominance of the redneck Captain America (expressed through his phallic gunblast) becomes mirrored by the countercultural dominance of the radical Captain America (expressed through his assassination/crucifixion, and ensuing spiritual sublimation). Captain America and the killer redneck may be flip sides of the same coin. We might therefore view the exploding gas tank as ironically symbolizing a certain nemesis, the vengeful return of all Wyatt and Billy supposedly reject, since their money is stashed there. Granting more critical self-consciousness to the filmmakers regarding these contradictions, Hill surmises that they "seemed to have known instinctively that the notion of the 60s as a decade of idealism, progress and hope for the future was as fragile and delicate as a strip of celluloid" (33).

In any case, the film's modernist perspective vacillates between utopian social critique and, more insidiously, a reiteration of elitism and imperialism. *Easy Rider* and *Bonnie and Clyde* are politicized, rebellious road movies, but their doomed endings seem to (1) reveal each film's overall subtextual ideological contradictions; and (2) foretell the co-opted and/or nullified fate of progressive, countercultural politics into the seventies. The next chapter will show how the road movie's initial modernist, visionary confidence begins rather quickly to doubt itself in the early 1970s. Still modernist, the road movie's proliferation during this period is characterized by a movement away from the idea(l) of social rebellion, toward exaggerated cynicism, irony, and nihilism.

The Rain People   Vanishing Point
Five Easy Pieces   Badlands
Two-Lane Blacktop   The Sugarland Express

. . . .

Chapter 3

DRIFTING ON EMPTY

Existential Irony and the Early-1970s Road Movie

Bonnie and Clyde and *Easy Rider* should be viewed as the genre-defining origin of the contemporary road movie, not only for the various ways they elaborate road travel, and not only for the way this elaboration reflects the countercultural, New American independent film sensibility. They also are truly watershed films, to which can be traced most road movies comprising the genre's first wave, roughly between 1967 and 1975. That is, *Bonnie and Clyde* and *Easy Rider* constitute what Schatz calls a genre's "experimental stage," where the road movie's "conventions are isolated and established." The early-70s road movies appearing in their wake constitute the genre's "classic stage, in which the conventions reach their 'equilibrium' and are mutually understood by artist and audience" (37). However, we should keep in mind that Schatz's evolutionary schema applies, historically and aesthetically, to the classical Hollywood era; being postclassical and countercultural, the road movie's historical and aesthetic context is characterized even initially by the "self-consciousness" he situates *at the end* of a genre's cycle.[1] Most of these road movies—counterculturally inflected, independently produced, medium-to-low budget—fall more or less into either of the two categories *Easy Rider* and *Bonnie and Clyde* delineate: the quest road movie and the outlaw road movie. Bearing in mind that quest and outlaw road movies often overlap, let us list an overture of the most important early-70s examples. Quest road movies would include *The Rain People* (Coppola, 1969), *Five Easy Pieces* (Rafelson, 1970), *Two-Lane Blacktop* (Hellman, 1971), *Duel* (Spielberg, 1971), *Vanishing Point* (Sarafian, 1971), *The Last Detail* (Ashby, 1973), *Scarecrow* (Schatzberg, 1973), *Paper Moon* (Bogdanovich,

1973), *Harry and Tonto* (Mazursky, 1974), *Bring Me the Head of Alfredo Garcia* (Peckinpah, 1974), and *Road Movie* (Strick, 1975); key outlaw road movies would be *Boxcar Bertha* (Scorsese, 1972), *The Getaway* (Peckinpah, 1972), *The Sugarland Express* (Spielberg, 1973), *Badlands* (Malick, 1973), *Slither* (Zieff, 1973), *Thieves like Us* (Altman, 1974), *Thunderbolt and Lightfoot* (Cimino, 1974), *Dirty Mary, Crazy Larry* (Hough, 1974), and *Crazy Mama* (Demme, 1975).

While most of these films bear overt influences from *Easy Rider* and *Bonnie and Clyde,* they also distinguish themselves from those two films in ways important to the evolution of the genre. The defeated tone on which *Bonnie and Clyde* and *Easy Rider* end ("We blew it"), where the road closes in on the protagonists, seems to pervade the early-1970s road movie proliferation. Rather than leading to freedom and exploration, the early-70s road often leads nowhere in particular, sometimes in circles, invoking a forlorn mood of wandering. The sense of purpose, direction, and excitement that characterizes the previous road journeys—even when there is no specific destination—is distinctly minimized on the cinematic highway of the early 1970s. Moreover, such lack of drive is deployed rather consistently as an aesthetic and thematic strategy. While *Bonnie and Clyde* and *Easy Rider* are clearly informed by romanticism, visionary rebellion, and a modernist critique of conformist society, the early-70s road movie conveys a cynicism about being on the road, and an ironic withdrawal from the pretense that roaming actually does take the driver outside of society.[2]

Laden with psychological confusion and wayward angst, these road movies adopt a nomadic narrative structure, focusing on existential loss more than social critique. Developing a psychological more than sociopolitical emphasis, these films thus more intensely reflect the influence of postwar European cinema, where auteurism, modernism, and existentialism merge. Driving on the open road becomes an allegory of a personal search through life's meaningless landscape. Road movie modernism here has turned inward, away from cultural critique. Consequently, we observe in these films a general tendency to depoliticize the genre, as well as a more ironic attitude toward the journey (little of Kerouac's indulgence or Fonda's earnestness here).

In most early-70s road movies, the tension between rebellion and tradition operates, but has been softened and muted: character and narrative drive often appear through a murky lens, or not at all. In this more existential focus, the genre's core conflict with conformist society has been internalized, "rebellion" thus becoming an amorphous anxiety about self. While pushing the fusion of human and car more to the foreground, *Two-Lane Blacktop*

(1971), *Vanishing Point* (1971), *Badlands* (1973), and other early-1970s road movies also emphasize individual psychology more than social criticism, often conveying a deep sense of alienation characterized by Thomas Elsaesser as a "pathos of failure" and by Robert Kolker as a "cinema of loneliness." *Two-Lane Blacktop* best crystallizes these tendencies, with nearly no dialogue or character motivation. In terms of plot, the quest (a race across country) gradually loses coherence, literally disintegrating at the film's infamous ending. Arguably one of the most influential films of the last forty years, *Badlands* delineates the outlaw couple in near-mythic proportions. While the film bears traces of *Bonnie and Clyde*'s social criticism and romanticism, its overall tone is detached and ironic, a spellbinding portrait of gothic Midwestern Americana. Whereas *Bonnie and Clyde*'s and *Easy Rider*'s modernism reflects the spirit of Brecht (a visionary, "revolutionary" modernism), the modernism here suggests Joyce and Beckett, what Susan Sontag calls the "aesthetics of silence" (obscure introspection, psychological dissolution). More specific aspects of this subtle shift in gears include (1) a more pronounced dramatization of the genre's fusion of the human and automobile; (2) consequently, a more "mechanized" (dehumanized, "empty") development of character; (3) a more fragmented, aleatory narrative structure; and generally (4) a road trip symbolic of emotional malaise. Often exuding a deeply antisocial mood, these films nevertheless *minimize* overtly rebellious gestures against society; that is, the rebellion here is filtered through an enigmatic dramaturgy of apathy. This apathy in turn inflects both the movement of the narrative and the development of characters, producing a paradoxical sense of "standstill" while moving, the inverse of running in place: going without making oneself go. In other words, a sense of drift.[3]

Not surprisingly, the shift we are describing in road movie sensibility reflects and articulates the broader cultural sensibility of early-1970s America, which may be described as a time of bitter confusion about American political institutions and the overall direction of American society. For the counterculture, it was a hard-nosed come-down, as the Woodstock generation's hopes for deep social change failed to blossom, mostly thwarted by entrenched conservative forces (Kent State emblematic here). Moving into the 1970s, the country seemed torn apart by the Vietnam War, the civil rights struggle, feminism, and other socially and politically divisive issues. This mood perhaps culminates with the Watergate crisis, which spawned widespread cynicism toward political authority.[4] In the introduction to his discussion of *Two-Lane Blacktop*, Adam Webb muses on the social climate of the film's reception in 1971:

Collectively Woodstock, Monterey, Free Love and LSD had achieved little of what they promised. Altamont and Manson had exposed the fraudulent Hippy Dream, LBJ's "War On Poverty" had failed, conflict in Vietnam had escalated, and arch conservative Richard Nixon was secure (for a while) in the White House. The optimism and hopes so intrinsic to our images of the previous decade had seemingly evaporated, replaced by the traditional values of the Silent Majority. . . . The Voices that called for change in 1967 were now questioning their very identity. (82–83)

A similar conclusion is reached regarding the sociopolitical resonance of *Vanishing Point*, also from 1971. The film's nihilism reflects the fact that "any remaining fantasy of sixties optimism had been ruthlessly dissipated" by the political violence of 1968–1970 (Sargeant, "'Vanishing Point': Speed Kills," 94). Beyond—and perhaps because of—such general disillusionment pervading the aftermath of the counterculture, American culture simultaneously witnesses the advent of the Me generation, predecessors of the 1980s yuppie, marked by a guiltless embrace of personal (often economic) gain and a focus on personal psychological and emotional "realization" (self-help movements, etc.).

While not explicitly reactionary, most early-70s road movies do reflect a shift away from (and sometimes against) the "activist" visionary spirit of *Bonnie and Clyde* and *Easy Rider*. More precisely, these films are most intriguing for how they *retain* elements of cultural critique and visionary rebellion (always in some way part of the genre), yet within a generally cynical and existential framework. Marsha Kinder, for example, sees the nostalgic settings prevalent in the "return of the outlaw couple" during the early 70s as a means of making a "connection with earlier periods when people felt similarly powerless" (3). Elsaesser more deeply probes this sense of existential crisis, charting it through several important early-70s road movies, in terms of a "pathos of failure." For Elsaesser, the American maverick directors of the 1970s, in contrast to those of the 1950s—such as Ray, Mann, and Fuller—no longer express "goal-oriented moral trajectories." Such lack of direction derives from "a post-rebellious lassitude," a cynicism about the American virtues of "ambition, vision, drive" (13–15). Emphasizing their experimental and self-reflexive European qualities, he sees the fundamental feature of these films as the unmotivated hero on a journey—a feature that renders storytelling itself "unmotivated" and therefore self-conscious. Here, "taking to the road stands for the very quality of contingency" (14). More importantly, he sees such narrative lack of direction as "codifying the ex-

perience of a rebellion whose impulse towards change aborted, and which
. . . is now somehow transfixed in stunned moments of inconsequentiality"
(18). Whether portraying flight from a crime (outlaw) or search for meaning (quest), these films are characterized generally by "cool mockery," which
eventually "fades out on a wave of self-pity." Acknowledging the depoliticized surface of these films, films that "reflect the moral and emotional gestures of a defeated generation," Elsaesser nevertheless suggests that a deeper,
more formalistic political challenge occurs in their subversion of both the
ideology of American enterprise and the dominant "affirmative" classical
narrative (17–19).

In anticipation of the road movies to be discussed, we should note how
Elsaesser's interpretation suggests that this pessimistic and cynical "Watergate" mood provokes—at least in American films, if not elsewhere in American culture—a personalizing of social conflict. That is, political frustration
and disillusionment get internalized by characters, dramatized as individual
psychological and emotional conflicts. Robin Wood relates such individual
alienation (or "pathos of failure") to a broader political "incoherence." "Society appeared to be in a state of advanced disintegration, yet there was
no serious possibility of the emergence of a coherent and comprehensive
alternative." Focusing on *Taxi Driver* as exemplary, Wood shows how "this
quandary" is "habitually rendered . . . in terms of personal drama and individual interaction, and not necessarily consciously registered" (*Hollywood
from Vietnam to Reagan*, 50). In other words, Wood's "incoherent text"—
which characterizes many contemporaneous road movies—makes some attempt to address social and political issues, but cannot decide what it wants
to say, ultimately retreating into solipsistic anxiety and confusion (in the
fragmented modernist tradition of Joyce and Eliot). With no sense of home,
disillusioned with both the idealistic counterculture and a corrupt conservative government, these lonely film protagonists drive around and around, no
place to go and no place to leave behind, their lackluster wanderlust driven
by emotional and psychological scars.

(E)motion as Drift: *The Rain People* and *Five Easy Pieces*

In their attempt to challenge classical Hollywood narrative and to establish
a more European auteur identity, many maverick American directors emerging during the late-1960s shake-up of the old studio system often employed
the road movie early in their careers.[5] The early-70s road movie is a crucial component of not only the general New American film scene with its

"buddy road movies" (Wood), "outlaw couples" (Kinder), and "pathos of failure" (Elsaesser) but also the "film school generation" — Coppola, Scorsese, Spielberg, Lucas. Launching their careers "on the road," most would take a conservative turn a few years later in the blockbuster/"high concept" reinvention of Hollywood. As I will suggest at the end of this chapter, this conservative turn had already begun in their post–*Easy Rider*, Watergate-era road movies.

The subtle shift in the road movie's theme, structure, and tone — where spiritual angst and wayward emotional confusion become more pronounced — is recognizable in a quiet film released the same year as *Easy Rider* by the "godfather" of the film school generation: Francis Coppola's *The Rain People*. Though at the time attracting much less attention than Hopper's film, in retrospect *The Rain People* seems to have possessed more prescience about the road movie's immediate future route. With some striking experimental camera work by Bill Butler, the film overall has a European feel; here, future American movie giant Coppola begins seriously developing his own distinctive auteurist signature.[6] A quest road movie in the spirit of *Easy Rider*, *The Rain People* articulates rebellion and cultural critique in a more introspective framework.

Couched in ambiguity and uncertainty, *The Rain People* focuses on pregnant housewife Natalie Ravenna (Shirley Knight) who suddenly decides to leave her husband and drive aimlessly across country. She does not know why, and neither does the audience: a quarrel with her husband is alluded to, amidst poetic images of water on various surfaces. Before leaving, she visits her parents, where a nasty fight breaks out; she tries to explain to them her feelings of unfulfilled longing, but they do not understand. Intercut with Natalie's flashbacks to her wedding day, this conversation is presented in a highly fragmented, elliptical way, which inhibits articulation of her frustration and, therefore, of her motivation for departure. The camera work in this opening section is visually obscure, an effective aesthetic complement to the obscure, disjunctive plot exposition. The influence of modernist European film is apparent, setting up the film's narrational mode, which calls upon the spectator to participate in "making the meaning" of the film.

A brief driving montage through Pennsylvania helps establish the film as a road movie, with sweeping aerial shots similar to *Easy Rider*'s (though the latter's rock music soundtrack is here replaced with more Hollywood-style romantic strings). The film's journey narrative takes its first major turn when she picks up a hitchhiker, a mentally challenged former high school football star whose name is Jimmie Kilgannon, but who goes by "Killer" (James Caan). More playful than paranoid, Natalie replies with her own fictional identity: "Sara." This name-game seems symbolic of the early-70s road movie search for authenticity on a personal, "internal" level. Killer clings to a past, glorified identity as a football star, while Natalie gropes to escape her past identity as a housewife by inventing a future identity. They travel on together, not exactly an outlaw couple. Neither of the two has a particular sense of direction, Killer's head injury (a neurological "slowness") perhaps an exaggerated version of Natalie's emotional and spiritual confusion. Likewise, the difficulty Natalie has getting information out of Killer—about his past, where he comes from, his family, and so on—mirrors the enigmatic way Natalie herself was introduced by the film. His clipped, elliptical responses to her questions tend to obscure more than divulge, much like the film's visual and narrational mode. Both Natalie and Killer seem to be on the road because of some past personal trauma that is repressed by themselves as well as the film.

At the forefront of this road movie's dramaturgy is an emphasis on familial and romantic melodrama: many long, if fragmented conversations that illustrate a desperate need for interpersonal communication.[7] Any social criticism—what we have called the road movie's essential cultural critique—is obliquely and peripherally referenced as middle-class oppression and ennui. *The Rain People* is driven by a culturally critical journey, but in a substantially different way from *Bonnie and Clyde* and *Easy Rider*. Natalie and Killer embody a certain outcast status; they do not fit in to "normal" society. But "normal" society appears vaguely in the film, more a mood than a real visible force. These road rebels seem adrift in their own malaise, with no clear purpose to their quest. Natalie is looking for something, but it is something inside her, and she does not know what it is; the road trip becomes the metaphor for this hazy, restless intrapsychic longing. Though perhaps overstated, Ryan and Kellner's view of the film as a reactionary "covert attack on feminism" (66) resonates with the point being made here: that in its emphasis on emotional searching, within the framework of romance and family, the film signals a generally conservative shift in the road movie's first generic wave.

Five Easy Pieces, a major release for BBS Productions,[8] is a richer and more historically significant film that goes further in articulating such early-70s road movie angst. Though Michael Dare's liner notes for the Criterion Collection laser disc of *Five Easy Pieces* describe the film as "the ultimate road movie" (and the DVD cover reads: "He rode the fast lane on the road to nowhere"), the film in fact is not much of a road movie in any literal sense. The journey taken halfway through the film takes up approximately 10 minutes of screen time. While this drive may be the film's "spiritual as well as structural center" (Cagin and Dray, 66), its overall journey narrative is rather weak. However, the film is notable for its thematic articulation of the newly emerging road movie sensibility. Its main character, Bobby Dupea (Jack Nicholson), is trying to find *himself* rather than America. He suffers from his own confusion more than from the legal system, or American culture at large (though the latter is implicated as partial cause of his personal confusion). Along these lines, Cagin and Dray note how the film "illuminated the distance between 1969 and 1970" by showing that the crisis of the times was not confined to hippies and the counterculture, but could afflict any American. More significantly, they suggest the film's distinction from *Easy Rider* by stating its central "tension and subject" as "the acute identity crisis of a man who doesn't seem to fit in anywhere" (66).

In *Five Easy Pieces*, the road becomes a metaphor for emotional uncertainty and ambivalent desire. Significantly, and symbolic of the new road movie inflection, the journey Bobby makes is a journey *back home*, with the aim of reconciling with his family and dying father. Similarly, though the film explores Bobby's rootless, unfulfilled life, it actually concentrates on how *stuck* he is—first in Southern California working in an oil field, then back at his wealthy home in Seattle. Gradually we realize that the working-class milieu of the film's first part is a refuge for Bobby from the upper-class family and background he returns to in the second part. Yet both are oppressive and intolerable to him. Bobby is often uncertain about literally where to go; figuratively, he is undecided about how to proceed with his life. Bobby is thus typical of the 1970s road movie driver in that he is on the move but often not moving, driven by a lackadaisical drift, resigned to stay put without desiring stability.

Such weary wanderlust is first suggested in one remarkable scene, where he and his buddy Elton (Billy "Green" Bush) are on their way to work, stuck in a traffic jam on the freeway. Bobby jumps out of the car, climbs up onto a truck carrying a piano, and begins to play. Congested immobility on the freeway is especially frustrating in the road movie; here, Bobby channels this frustration into an absurd, mildly rebellious spectacle of creative expression. Elton takes over the wheel and calls after him, but the truck pulls off the freeway. We then cut to Bobby getting out of the truck much later in the evening, having listlessly allowed himself to be carried by the truck, to wherever. Mobility for him—both journey and destination—does not provoke enthusiasm or commitment, yet he seems to be carried along by a deeply buried yearning to find himself. As he wanders around town, we hear the music he was playing, now as nonsynchronous accompaniment, haunting his wandering with

3.1. Stuck in freeway traffic: the absurd spectacle of frustrated Bobby (Jack Nicholson) on the road.

the aural commentary of his unfulfilled artistic and spiritual potential (later in the film, we learn that years earlier he had abandoned a career as a concert pianist).

This wayward, emotional confusion becomes elaborated more fully in terms of political cynicism during the actual road trip. Though a brief segment, it is highly significant, both within the film, and as a sign of the road movie's departure from the trailblazing films discussed in the previous chapter. First of all, like most road movie protagonists, Bobby does not drive alone: his girlfriend Rayette (Karen Black) accompanies him. But the nature of her role as passenger sheds considerable light on the nature of the drive itself. The first part of the film reveals his unfulfilled life posing as working-class, primarily by concentrating on his unfulfilled and unpleasant relationship with Rayette. That is, the film crystallizes in her all that frustrates Bobby about the blue-collar world in which he does not belong (such "condensation" translates into a grotesque burden she is made to bear). In the trashy pop country songs she sings, she is portrayed as annoying and rather ditzy, and it is hard to figure what he sees in her (throughout the film, the audience is as confused about Bobby's motives and desires as he seems to be).

The film then more dramatically establishes the impetus for his departure, when he learns from Elton that Rayette is pregnant. In a seizure of panic about having to settle down (or even responsibly confront the situation), he decides to quit his job. He then drives to Los Angeles to visit his sister Pantita (Lois Smith), and learns that his father has had a stroke; this in turn "inspires" him to make a visit to his ill father (that is, it is also an excuse to evade his current quagmire). Initially he plans to leave Rayette behind. But while sitting in the car, he goes into a fit of rage, torn apart because he does not really want her to come, but feels too guilty to leave her behind. Let us pause here to note the contours of the film's male point of view: the narrative fact of her pregnancy becomes *his* burden, thus serving as motivation for Bobby's inner turmoil (as well as actor Nicholson's explosive performance). Significantly, the camera is positioned outside the passenger door, looking in on Bobby's thrashing spectacle of rage and confusion, establishing the immediate framework for the drive in terms of his emotional torment over her, and over having to go home at all. Almost by default, he goes back in and asks her to come along. The narrative pretext for the drive is thus set up in terms of his frustration, deriving largely from his screwed-up emotional life.

Beyond this pretext, the subtle shift in the meaning of the road movie's journey becomes most apparent through the two women they pick up soon after they begin driving. Like Bobby, they are also on the road, and thus become invested as symbolic of the state of the genre, as well as the film's general attitude toward mobility. Significantly, Palm (Helena Kallianiotes) and Terry (Toni Basil) are first seen arguing at their stalled vehicle, coding them in terms of interpersonal conflict. They continue arguing in the backseat once Bobby and Ray pick them up. Their conversation clearly suggests a cynical attitude (on the film's part) toward the counterculture. Presented as figures of the counterculture, Palm especially is portrayed as contentious, the more verbal of the two. She and Terry, it comes out, are on their way to Alaska to get away from institutionalized, technologized society; Palm rants about greed and ecological disaster. In contrast to Bobby and Ray's journey, theirs explicitly cites *Easy Rider* in its overt sense of politicized rebellion and cultural critique. But the film sets Palm up so as to tear her down, by coldly trivializing her. This occurs first of all through Terry, who constantly gibes her, at one point saying that despite all her talk of environmental destruction, Palm herself is personally rather sloppy. Additionally, Palm herself fumbles when she cannot remember the word "steam," as she exhorts them about the car companies refusing to make environmentally sensitive cars. Soon Rayette joins in, further embroiling their discussion in petty bickering. All of this renders Palm (and Terry by implication) hypocritical, unreliable, and somewhat ridiculous.

To be sure, only Bobby transcends their foolish attempt at political discussion. Again illustrating the film's male perspective, he views them with aloof irony through his rearview mirror. Moreover, the spectacle of the two bickering passengers is rendered with comic mise en scène, framed between Rayette and Bobby, cramped together in the backseat. It seems the counter-culture—transformed from visionary activism to shallow, petty proselytizing—is not driving anymore, but being driven. This point is further illustrated in Palm's reaction to the film's most famous scene, where in a roadside diner Bobby demands a piece of toast served a certain way. Palm says, "I like what you did back there." She reads a lot into his fit, as the film wants us to do: rebellion against authority, subversion of convention, freedom of expression. But we should note that Bobby's "rebellion" is in fact a rather immature tantrum played largely for humor, over a trivial desire to satisfy his appetite: suddenly he appears less the rebel and more the dissatisfied consumer. Like the spectacle earlier of his thrashing fit in the car before the trip, here a sensationalized and self-centered spectacle dilutes cultural critique, referring it to a symbolic realm (the individual versus commercialism). Bobby himself coolly distances himself from her interpretation of his tantrum.[9] Moreover, her reaction reeks of spectatorial (passive) admiration: she is *attracted* to what he did, as though it were exciting and endearing—which it was. This diner scene has little of the political bite or tension of the diner scenes in *Easy Rider*. Overall, the film's journey suggests that the visionary cultural critique informing *Easy Rider* and *Bonnie and Clyde* has become just another distracting signpost (or passenger) on the highway of internal confusion.

But the film's ending most dramatically signifies the early-70s road movie's mood swing. Rather than the overt disaster and doom of *Bonnie and Clyde* and *Easy Rider*, *Five Easy Pieces* ends on an ambiguous note that leaves Bobby much as the film first found him: lost. He and Rayette are driving back home to California, she still harassing him, to which he responds with silence. When they pull into a gas station, she asks, "You want anything?" He says "No." She has no money, so he gives her his wallet. She asks him *again* if he is sure he does not want anything. Such simple, distilled dialogue and gestures are surely loaded with symbolism: they express his loss of identity, his lack of desire, his lack of involvement. Such symbolism continues in the cinematography: a high-angle extreme long shot of the gas station shows

Bobby, tiny, going into the men's room; meanwhile, a big rig arrives. Suddenly we see the gas station sign clearly: Gulf.

In the men's room, he stares into space, then back at himself in the mirror, supporting himself with his hands on the walls, on either side of the mirror: heavy with emptiness and confusion. He goes out, leaving his jacket behind, shedding the "skin" of his former identity. Once again from extreme long shot, we see that while his car's hood is up (his vehicle not ready to drive), he talks to the big rig truck driver. He gets into the truck (now a medium two-shot), the driver asking if he has a jacket, since it is "colder than hell" up in Canada. Bobby replies that "everything got burned up in the car," and that he will be fine. In another long shot, the truck pulls out going north, in the opposite direction Bobby was driving. As the truck pulls out of the frame, we see Rayette looking for him. Neither he, nor she, nor the audience knows where he is going.[10]

Wherever Bobby is, he is homeless. His confusion drives him, which can be distinguished sharply from Sal's frenetic need to ramble, or from Captain America's clear purpose. A cynical tone prevails, often expressing itself through his ironic, detached dialogue. His attitude toward relationships is equally ironic and detached: psychologically, emotionally, and literally, he is a drifter.

Aimless Racing: *Two-Lane Blacktop*

Released one year after *Five Easy Pieces*, *Two-Lane Blacktop* more clearly articulates this existential road movie sensibility through, ironically enough, a certain nonarticulation, lending new meaning to the phrase "running on empty." Apparently financed with great expectation by Universal to "break into the lucrative youth market" on the heels of *Easy Rider*'s success (Webb, 82), *Two-Lane Blacktop* becomes almost nihilistic in its sense of drift. Running alongside the rebellious, politicized rediscovery of America driving *Easy Rider* and *On the Road*, the film seems a road movie skeleton. Its nihilistic tone harks back to *Detour*, but flattens that film's narrative intensity into a dehumanized, near plotless overvaluation of cars and driving. Taking *Easy Rider*'s fusion between character and car to an extreme, the film possesses little dialogue, story, or character development, focusing instead on driving as an enigmatic ritual. In addition, the blistering, arid landscapes in this film (and in most other early-1970s road movies) invoke Eliot's wasteland more than Kerouac's heartland. Yet *Two-Lane Blacktop* possesses an undeniable potency as a vintage road movie, displacing human and traditional narrative expression with a purer automobile expression.

Two-Lane Blacktop wears the thin guise of a racing film. But this relatively superficial narrative context quickly evaporates, revealing an exploration of the meaning(lessness) of road travel. The film begins with two race car enthusiasts drifting across the country, from race to race. Soon they pick up (rather, they are picked up by) a nomadic young girl. Then a lone, elder driver challenges them at a gas station to race from the Midwest to Washington, D.C. This "race"—and its connotations of goal, competition, and success—gradually transforms into a collective journey without purpose for the unlikely foursome. Along the way, they help each other out while trying to find themselves. Toward the end of the film, the girl's affinity becomes a contentious issue, as she switches from car to car. One would be hard-pressed to say the film "ends": each of the four end up on their own road, in unknown directions.

Notably influenced by the wandering, digressive narrative pacing of European modernist cinema (Antonioni especially comes to mind), *Two-Lane Blacktop* empties itself of any recognizable narrative drive or character development.[11] Moreover, the film treats the theme of rebellion in a highly formalistic, depoliticized fashion. Though there are sparse moments suggesting cultural critique, the rebellion here seems leveled against meaning and coherence itself. Whereas *The Rain People* and *Five Easy Pieces* displace and/or mitigate cultural critique with emotional and psychological searching, *Two-Lane Blacktop* goes one step further with its strikingly dehumanized emphasis on driving, as though the mechanized rumbling of the car engine has saturated the narrative.

Such "carspeak" is first revealed in the opening credits, which name the main characters as "the Driver" (James Taylor), "GTO" (Warren Oates), "the Girl" (Laurie Bird) and "the Mechanic" (Dennis Wilson). These character names signify noncharacters, pared down to a function deriving from the car (with the significant exception of "the girl," to be discussed below). Conversely, the ending credits treat the cars themselves as "characters": "1955 Chevy" and "1970 Pontiac" are listed as members of the cast. Before the opening credits, the film begins with a distinctive road movie nighttime montage of cars revving up and peeling out at a makeshift drag race strip. Quickly the police arrive, and we see the Driver turn around and take off. This introduction's oblique, nonnarrative approach predominates throughout the film, where we drop in inexplicably on a situation already in progress (unlike *Easy Rider*'s opening, which first establishes the story, then goes into its symbolic driving montage). That is, the film does not ease us into a narrative illusion, but rather abruptly confronts us with somewhat obscure images, forcing us to make sense of the beginning of the story (more like *The Rain People*'s introduction). The film's opening also invokes the genre's theme of cultural critique, sketching mobility at odds with society's laws, the drag racing presumably taking place in a remote area beyond any nearby town. But this suggestion of rebellious mobility is faint and ephemeral, recurring only a few times later in the film, similarly fleeting and obscure. After surveying these, we shall address the film's more rigorous driving fetishism.

Two-Lane Blacktop's approach to cultural critique generally seems influenced by *Easy Rider,* but is much less overt. In terms of challenging official authority, there are two other scenes in the film that use the police for heightened tension. Near the start of their "race," GTO is pulled over by a policeman at night; as a joke, the Driver pulls over too, complaining about GTO's driving to the officer. Then, later in the film, the three men are waiting out the early morning hours in a small southern town for a gas station to open; some cops pull up, so they decide to leave. In the first instance, the police function as impediment to literal mobility; in the second instance, they actually instigate mobility, but through intimidation and implied intolerance of a freewheeling, countercultural lifestyle.

Other scenes in the film suggest a challenge, not so much to the official authority of the police, but to the unofficial authority of mainstream, conservative American values. In a scene that recalls *Easy Rider* (but with much less teeth), a young southern redneck tries to intimidate the trio in a diner, first by taunting their racing abilities and knowledge, then by suspiciously asking whether they are "hippies." When the Mechanic says they are "just passing through" (a signature line he uses earlier in the film), the redneck seems displeased with this response, as though it confirms that they *are* in fact hippies. He continues taunting and intimidating them. The scene conveys conservative America's intolerance of difference, specifically the counterculture and its Kerouac-esque mobility. In terms of contrast with *Easy Rider,* we should note that the scene ends with no climax or confrontation; the (political) tensions raised just fizzle away as they finish their meal.

Another type of cultural critique in which the film tepidly engages is a repudiation of domestic stability. Early in the film, GTO begins to explain to the Driver that his family, job, and home all fell apart, implying that his chosen life on the road is the result of the failure of a stable, socially acceptable identity. Revealing in terms of generic shift, however, is the way the Driver cuts GTO off, just after GTO starts opening up, saying, "I don't want to hear about it," and declaring, "it's your problem, not mine" (recalling Natalie's impatience with Killer's needs). The retort intimates not only the Driver's cold, dehumanized alienation (inversely proportional to his enthusiasm for cars), but more importantly the advent of the 70s Me generation. The Driver's blunt disinterest implies that he has got his own tale of woe, his own problems to deal with. Additionally, as the film progresses we realize that GTO "changes his story" with every new listener; nothing he says can be trusted since he is some kind of pathological liar. Though we shall return to GTO below, we should observe here, in sum, how any political critique the film raises becomes mitigated or diluted by a general haze of inarticulateness. Such inability to communicate (Wood's "incoherent text") depoliticizes cultural critique. On the other hand, the film's antinarrative, antihumanism may be read as an aesthetic form of political subversion. In its extreme minimalist narrative, *Two-Lane Blacktop* reconfigures road movie rebellion as existential modernist fragmentation—a "rebellion" not so much against conservative society as against coherence itself.

To illustrate this point, let us consider the various instances of "communication" within the film, all permeated by an emphasis on cars—whether as subject matter, stylistic strategy, or actual vehicle of communication. In the first scene between the Driver and the Mechanic, they do not say anything to each other while the Mechanic changes the tire. A close-up of the Driver shows him thinking, but we have no idea about what: it is a blank stare, inaugurating the extreme understated acting throughout. Finally the Mechanic says something about the engine of one of the other cars at the race. Meanwhile, on the soundtrack a solid wall of industrial noise is blaring, drowning out most of whatever is spoken. The mechanization densely marking this scene is developed on various levels throughout much of the film. Many scenes, including most driving sequences, have virtually no dialogue; and where dialogue does occur, it mostly relates to cars, driving being the all-consuming mental and emotional activity. Just one example among many of such elliptical, enigmatic exchanges would be when GTO asserts, "I go fast enough," to which the Driver responds, "You can never go fast enough."

"You can never go fast enough"—such an aphorism sums up many a road movie. But it also sounds like a line from a rock music song—as well it should. Echoing anthemic song lines (and song titles) from the late 1960s, like the Doors' "Break on through to the other side" and Jimi Hendrix's "Are you experienced?" such dialogue suggests the excessive, visionary lifestyle of rock culture, where exceeding bounds is paramount. The road movie, of course, takes such excess literally, through its representation of perpetual and peripatetic mobility beyond society. As I have suggested earlier, the road movie's affinity with rock music is formative: not only the prevalent motif of the rock music soundtrack while driving, but also the countercultural attitude that distinctively characterizes both forms of expression. *Two-Lane*

Blacktop gives a special twist to the road movie–rock music kinship by casting two rock stars, James Taylor and Dennis Wilson, in the leads. Hellman's use of their rock star personas yields the acting style (or underacting style) largely responsible for the film's cool, restrained, listless tone. Complementing the film's intonations of Antonioni, Bresson, and Camus's Mersault, Taylor and Wilson import their disaffected rock star aura to the performance; in a sense, they are playing themselves as rock stars, relying quite brazenly on the mystique surrounding their extratextual fame. They do not have to say much or do much; their presence alone generates the edgy, decadent rock and roll mood of surviving self-destructive excesses.

The film's integration of this rock star aura into the framework of existential quest becomes effectively enhanced by another allusion, this time to the grungy modernist Westerns of Sam Peckinpah, through the casting of Warren Oates as GTO. In contrast to the film's primary rock star cool, Oates creates GTO as a swaggering if quirky redneck, a man out of time (he refers to himself as an "old-timer"), slightly displaced within both the film's drag-racing subculture and its "sex, drugs and rock 'n' roll" counterculture. Hellman sets the plot in motion, in fact, through the encounter of these two contrasting lifestyles and time periods. Yet the road movie provides a common generic space for the displaced cowboy and touring rock star. What they share is their sometimes lonely, sometimes cool outcast wandering.

Beyond the acting style and actor personas, that is, the film's distinctive "emptiness" regarding plot and character seems most crucially linked to an excessive and pointless automobility.[12] *Two-Lane Blacktop*'s ostensible plot gets going when our Chevy trio (the Driver, the Girl, and the Mechanic) encounters GTO on the road. They have been eyeing each other for a while, the Driver egging GTO on with a smirk, GTO paranoid but ready to meet the challenge, honking reactively at them. At a gas station, they finally confront each other, talking only of what each car can "do," a kind of distilled machismo exchange where, in a way, the cars speak through them. The race they establish seems a half-baked attempt to fill the void of their aimless mobility with an "aim" (the winner gets the loser's car). This geographic and materialistic aim quickly loses its attraction for these road movie anti-heroes, as the bond between them—an obsession with cars and driving—overwhelms the competition, bringing them together in a wandering journey with no purpose.

The race provides the loose narrative framework for this road movie's journey, as well as a pretext for exploring driving as existential errantry. Yet the Girl exerts significant dramatic influence. Indeed, she becomes a crucial counterpoint to the film's dominant male modernist driving fetishism. As we

3.2. Rock star cool on the road: James Taylor as *Two-Lane Blacktop*'s Driver.

shall see, her exclusion from the ritual of the race and the rite of passage is (somewhat stereotypically) predicated upon the threat she poses. Quite unstereotypically, however, *Two-Lane Blacktop* configures this female threat not as a (domestic) lure from the road, but as a mobile loner whose wanderlust proves to be too much for the car-obsessed males. Eventually, her disturbing presence hastens a deconstruction of both the journey and the film itself. Her status as outsider to a "bande à part" (Godard) reveals a good deal about the road movie in general.

Before the race commences, she "enters the picture" by literally entering the image, then the car. While the Driver and Mechanic are in a diner, the Girl gets out of a psychedelic van in the parking lot. Significantly, they do not see her, but we see her through the glass window, as the camera inside the diner pans with her, away from the two men in the foreground. Such camera position and movement suggests audience identification with the two men, but also a critical faculty of observation linked with her, beyond their field of vision and attention. She walks over to their car and gets in. When they come out to their car and find her in the backseat, they just get in and drive

3.3. The Mechanic, played by Beach Boy rock star Dennis Wilson.

away; they have no reaction to her. Initially, that is, she is treated by our two road movie buddies as they treat everything other than the car: no interest, take it or leave it, too cool. She starts up the conversation, asking about who they are and where they are going (the Mechanic replying merely, "Just passing through"). Like Palm in *Five Easy Pieces*, the Girl is made by the film to embody the counterculture: her hippie attire, her references to the zodiac killer and to being stoned, the psychedelic van she emerged from, all suggest a lost Deadhead. Also as in *Five Easy Pieces*, the counterculture here is feminized, suggesting that the alienated, wandering male (the Driver/Bobby) has somehow graduated from political activism or overt cultural critique, entering the more serious realm of existential quest. Put differently, "the Girl"—note only *her* name is gendered—and the counterculture get conflated as this road movie's Other.

Yet at various points throughout the film her character wields a potent critical commentary. Because she is invested by the film as Other (as different and threatening), she is able to provide a more lucid and incisive perspective on these men who drive (and who drive the genre). When the Driver finally speaks after she gets in, he speaks not to her but about the car: "she doesn't seem to be breathing right." Yet the deliberately ambivalent pronoun reference suggests that the men treat their car as they might a woman: a romanticized object to possess and control, source of pleasure and mobile security. Mocking their urge to compete, she teases out this notion by "acting" excited about the prospect of racing GTO (contrasting sharply with the blasé, but earnest demeanor of the men). Just before the race gets going, she calls it "a masculine power trip," wondering why they are not interested in her rear end more than that of the car. On the one hand, here she reinforces the road movie female stereotype by tempting the men from the highway with sex and romance. Yet by representing gender and difference, she also critically exposes the gendered subtext and hierarchy of the genre.[13]

It is somewhat surprising (and refreshing) that, as suggested above, many of the film's significant plot turns revolve around the Girl. Hardly a progressive or politicized feminist portrayal, the film's treatment of her nevertheless creates fissures in its exaggerated male-buddy road movie fabric. In one remarkably revealing scene later in the film, the Driver is trying to teach the Girl how "to drive"—not literally, but how to feel the car running as a sublimated rush. Actually, the scene begins with her abruptly deciding to leave the three men as they wait for the car repair shop to open. Once she disappears, the Driver immediately seeks her out, finding her hitching on the edge of town. This illustrates both her whimsical capacity to wander, and his attachment to her, which runs deeper (more repressed) than he had previously betrayed. He pulls up, she gets in, no words exchanged. We then jump-cut to their "driving" lesson in progress, implying his need to integrate her into his world. In a tightly framed medium shot through the side window, they sit silent in the stationary car, until he finally says, "Let's try it again" (emblematic of the film's overall fragmentary, elliptical discursive approach: try *what* again?). She starts the engine; he tells her to shut her eyes and feel

3.4. The Girl (Laurie Bird), a true woman of the road.

3.5. An incoherent kiss, instead of driving.

the gears, goading her into fusing with the machine. With penetrating, almost transcendent poise, she asks him, "Is this a game?" He replies that he does not know. Finally he gives up; she cannot do it: he stops the engine. Then they kiss, followed by one of the film's many fade-outs: no Hollywood cliché cloaking sexual intimacy here, but rather another instance of the film's disinterest in clarifying itself. The Driver tries to fuse but ends up confusing his two love objects, the Girl and the car; the kiss and the fade-out express in their very evasion of expression the moment's irreconcilability. This bizarre scene of road movie intimacy begins and ends with confusion—for the characters and the audience.

Frustrated and bored with the Driver's obsession with driving, the Girl finally abandons him and the Mechanic at a race, and joins GTO in his car.[14] The Driver, who seems to understand cars much better than people, nevertheless sees this as a betrayal and a loss. Despite his mute, stoic mystique, she has hooked him in some way that he cannot explain, or even acknowledge. In a shot utilizing the rearview mirror, we watch his stone face and steely, vacant eyes watching her pack and leave. As throughout, all pain of separation, all emotion, is repressed, redirected into the drive. The Mechanic tries to talk him out of going after them, but the Driver cannot help himself and follows them: the race (the film's beginning), having first yielded to cooperative wandering (the film's body), now yields to the Driver's pursuit of her (the film's conclusion). The Mechanic warns: "she's gonna burn you." Meanwhile, we see that in GTO's car, she is not much appeased, falling asleep during his odd rambling discourse. All this (male-driven) driving seems for her an unsatisfactory series of distractions from a more real journey, a more authentic mobility.

Indeed, when the Driver and Mechanic catch up with GTO and the Girl at a diner, we observe how, surprisingly, she becomes the most road movie-esque character in the film. The Driver and Mechanic sit down at their table; she and the Driver stare at each other silently. With enigmatic, elliptical mystique rivaling the Driver's, she abruptly says to GTO "It's no good," then gets up and leaves. Through the window of the diner (reminiscent, as in previous scenes, of a car windshield), the three men watch her get onto the back of some guy's motorcycle, leaving her bags on the driveway of the parking lot. On the one hand, this gesture shares some traits with the femme fatale: parasitic, fiercely unaffected, using then disposing of men, leaving a trail of wrecked male identity. Yet it also suggests a disassociation, not merely from society, but from *the cars* of society, and those who drive them: she rides as passenger in a more pure wanderlust. The mise en scène of her disappearance recalls that of her enigmatic appearance earlier: the parking lot of a roadside diner. In a way, her journey as passenger has been cyclical rather than linear, and she embraces it *sans* car fetishism.

In any case, once she is gone, the film "ends" with more perpetual aimless mobility. GTO is off on his own road again, lying to two servicemen he picks up, about how he got his car. The Driver is seen in slow motion, revving up for yet another drag race, the camera positioned with him inside as he stares out the front windshield. The revving sound gradually transforms into an ambient industrial white noise, with eerie, dramatic reverberation on the sound of the shifting stick. He stares out at a ranch, then at "the driver" of the other car, who is anonymous, silhouetted, thus a reflection of the driver himself. The film's final shot is taken from the backseat, looking over his shoulder: the slow motion slows even further as he starts to drive. His hair flies up, intimating an ecstatic bodily surge in response to the heaving car; then the image freeze-frames, then burns up, as if stuck in the projector. Invoking the Mechanic's warning about the Girl "burning" him, this notoriously effective ending perfectly crystallizes the entire film, and the 1970s road movie: no point to the story or journey or image itself: a deeply fragmented dissolution of destination on all levels.[15]

A richly symbolic ending, to be sure. But in many ways the film's road movie theme and sensibility get expressed most vividly through GTO. In contrast to the enigmatic, mechanized nonpersonalities of the Driver, the Girl, and the Mechanic, GTO seems the more humanized and animated; and yet his very accessibility is, like most else in the film, deconstructed. First of all, he is by far the most verbal character in the film, and much of what he speaks resonates as road movie "theory."[16] With the Girl in his car (a sequence bearing faint traces of *Lolita*), he fantasizes about going to Mexico; he also derides the Driver and Mechanic, because all they think about is cars. Here he displays insight into the girl's emotions (an insight the Driver is dispossessed of), sensing her frustration with them. Moreover, he rearticulates the road movie tradition, itself inherited from road literature, of exoticizing Mexico as refuge from American society. Though she is hardly paying attention, he declares (as if reciting a manifesto) that one has to keep moving, and follow one's taste for the "foreign," and that this is how one maintains "balance"; otherwise it all "falls apart." He idealizes their impossible future together on the road: "We'll go on, it doesn't matter where," maybe ending up laying on the beach in Florida to "let the scars heal." When he sees that she is asleep, he keeps talking (to her and/or to himself): "If I'm not grounded pretty soon, I'll go into orbit." His monologue, rambling and fragmented in form and content, suggests a breakdown in communication. Instead of cutting him off, as the Driver does, she lets him ramble without listening. But it likewise suggests an emotional and psychological need to speak and be heard, coloring this road movie journey as therapeutic search.

What gives GTO's search for emotionally satisfying interaction such a compelling edge is the way he keeps "changing his story." There is something of the pathological liar about him. But he also displays a compulsion to indulge the pleasures of spinning tales, of fabricating and fabulating, of perpetually reinventing his past (somewhat in the tradition of picaresque journey novels like *Tristram Shandy* and *Don Quixote*). With each new passenger, he remixes the details of his life, relativizing both what he speaks and the notion of the Truth within the spoken: he is a clownish vehicle of Nietzsche's "perspectivism." "He literally *is* his style which has become an existential means of riding out the tempo and flux of American life. As such he belongs in the tradition of Melville's confidence man" (Seed, 110). In one strangely disconnected episode near the end, GTO is driving an old woman and a girl to the funeral of the latter's "folks," who were killed by a "city car." Perhaps to comfort them, perhaps to endear himself, he starts chattering about buying his mother a house in Florida. His story comes off as sincerely in-

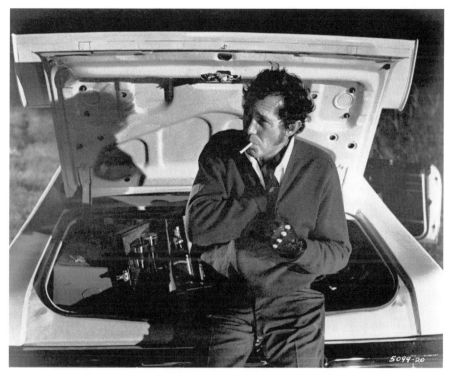

3.6. GTO (Warren Oates): *Two-Lane Blacktop*'s road visionary/fool.

sincere, a "white lie" he seems to justify as a kind of "truth." At the end of the film, with the two servicemen, he cleverly inverts the facts about how he came to own his car, retelling the stakes of the race that started the film, but casting *himself* as the Driver. In compulsively fictionalizing his identity, often through a pastiche of "real" events, GTO embodies crucial characteristics of the 1970s road movie. Gently deranged, lost in his mind as he is lost on the highway, GTO lives out the link between endless (perhaps pointless) road travel and the perpetual reinvention of personal identity. More disturbingly, GTO illustrates how personal identity itself is ultimately fictional. Conjoining somewhat with the film's self-reflexive ending, but also with Sartre's Roquentin, GTO signifies the journey of *Two-Lane Blacktop* as an existential, ultimately futile search. A true road movie hero, GTO nevertheless embraces this state of aimless mobility, yielding an endearing if bizarre figure of redemption.

Manic Driving: *Vanishing Point*

Richard C. Sarafian's *Vanishing Point* (1971) proves to be another vintage road movie, complementary to *Two-Lane Blacktop* for both its similarities and its differences. While *The Rain People, Five Easy Pieces,* and *Two-Lane Blacktop* exemplify fairly clearly the quest road movie, *Vanishing Point* interjects strong elements of the outlaw, though there is no outlaw couple here. In fact, the film is notable partially because Kowalski (Barry Newman), the film's driver, drives alone. He does have a "buddy," but not in the car with him, as will be discussed below. Straddling the two road movie tendencies, *Vanishing Point* provides a nice chronological and generic transition to *Badlands* and other outlaw couple road movies of the 1973–74 season (discussed below).

Vanishing Point focuses on Sandy Kowalski (his name perhaps deliberately invoking *A Streetcar Named Desire*) and his near delirious obsession with winning a wild bet he makes: that he can drive from Denver to San Francisco in a little over 36 hours (a day and a half). Kowalski works as a driver for a car delivery service, and on his way out of town for his next delivery, he pays a visit to his drug dealer. On a busy nighttime boulevard, the wager is made between the two men, appropriately enough, over some speed: if Kowalski wins, the drugs are his for free. Some intriguing points of contact with *Two-Lane Blacktop* are (1) the narrative context of a fetishized car culture, here the car delivery service (he is a professional driver, an ex-racing driver, thus a cousin to *Two-Lane Blacktop*'s "Driver"); (2) the wager, catalyst of the drive, which like *Two-Lane Blacktop*'s "race" becomes a rather superficial pretext for the journey; and (3) most significantly, the sense of incoherence that characterizes the driving journey. While the police figure fleetingly in *Two-Lane Blacktop,* in *Vanishing Point* they provide much more narrative tension as antagonist to Kowalski and his driving. Despite such coding of Kowalski as an outlaw, the film emphasizes his desperate pursuit of some kind of new meaning or sensation. In fact, what makes this a quest more than an outlaw road movie is that no one (including Kowalski, it seems) knows why he is driving so feverishly. Part of the police pursuit involves figuring out the crime he is fleeing; yet the audience knows there has been no crime. Moreover, the wager (like any wager, gamble, or game) possesses a relative and arbitrary significance that makes this journey all the more incoherent. In exceeding the "rules of the game," Kowalski's trip violates all reasonable expectation, becoming a senseless obsession. Along the way, the film makes some attempt to fill in the gaps and "explain," but the overall picture reveals a mysteriously "speeding" driver—driving on speed for the sake of speed, and for the sake of some lost purpose, some Other destination.

One significant and distinguishing feature of *Vanishing Point* is its complex narrational structure, which employs crosscutting and flashbacks extensively. As we have seen, the road movie more typically exaggerates a linear narrative, so as to emphasize the road and journey as a "line" that traverses terrain and crosses borders. In contrast, *Vanishing Point* begins with its ending, structurally and tonally recalling the foregone conclusion of a road film noir like *Detour*.[17] Using bright, blinding light and glaring wide-open space to convey a singular sense of entrapment, *Vanishing Point* looks forward to postmodern road movie/desert noir like *Blood Simple, Delusion, Red Rock West,* and *U Turn*.

Vanishing Point's highly formalistic narrative structure involves a time-space confusion, also in the noir vein, but more ostensibly reflecting a post-hippie, countercultural mysticism. Its high-speed driving seems to shatter the most fundamental barriers of physics as well as logic. As the film begins, a police blockade is being erected at dawn on a deserted highway. This first shot pans left from a gas station to the empty highway; the second shot is low angle, close to the road, as bulldozers arrive. A montage of arriving spectators ensues (more cops, reporters, redneck cowboys, Native American children), revealing a lackadaisical small-town, roadside community that has come to observe the spectacle of capture, of stopping this car that will not stop. As Kowalski comes upon the blockade, he screeches to a halt and spins around, peeling back the way he came (one cowboy spectator turns away, disappointed, or simply bored). When Kowalski sees three cop cars heading toward him, he turns off the road, ripping through a barbed wire fence and racing across the desert, until he comes to an apparently symbolic monument: the wasted debris of a car wreck. He stops, gets out, contemplates the mound with a laugh as though peering into his own absurd destiny, then gets back into his car and starts off again. In contrast to the typical film noir "backward" time structure (or any Hollywood movie beginning with its end), this film's opening segment seems bent on articulating a thematic and narrative incoherence (early-70s, Euro-tinged modernist style rather than classical Hollywood) that will only be partially "explained" later.

To the invigorating accompaniment of a blaring rock music soundtrack, he gets back onto the highway, finally driving head-on toward another car (his white, the other black). Just as they cross each other (no collision), the image freeze-frames, basking in the spectacular frozen blur of the speeding cars. The film's own discourse has "arrested" speed itself for observation

CALIFORNIA- SUNDAY- 10:02 A.M.

3.7. *Vanishing Point*'s vanishing point . . .

more effectively than the fictional cops can arrest him for speeding. During the freeze-frame, the title "California, Sunday, 10:02 A.M." appears — ironically attempting to name and fix time and space in the context of total temporal and spatial disorientation. Then his car "vanishes," after which the image — now of only the black car — starts up again.

A powerful road movie opening, reminiscent of *Two-Lane Blacktop*'s ending: film language and road movie narrative converge in a self-reflexive, generically metacritical dissolution, or "vanishing," due to obsessive, delirious driving. Starting the journey with its end point also creates a more nihilistic sense of fate for the driver, and the narrative as a whole. By revving up with such classic road movie imagery (the desert, the highway, small-town spectators, cop chase, speeding into oblivion), but in the context of the end of the road, the film builds insignificance into the outcome of the narrative and the destination of the journey. Moreover, this flashback structure indicates that Kowalski came to be "vanishing" by virtue of the journey itself, the process of driving. This emphasis, as suggested earlier, renders the film a quest more than an outlaw road movie (the latter typically playing off suspense around "where will this lead?" or "how will this end?"). The audience watches the journey knowing that no matter where or how or why he is driving, he will never arrive at his destination, but only his obscure destiny.

The brilliant twist on all this comes when, at the "real" end of the film, Sarafian gives us a *different* ending from the one we have seen here at the beginning: grinning and glassy-eyed, Kowalski drives full speed into the blockade, blowing himself up. As in *Two-Lane Blacktop*, narrative closure and coherence become dispersed through a spectacle of the film medium's own artifice (two contradictory endings, as well as the first ending's "vanishing"). Also like GTO's tall tales, realism and history — that is, a basic sense of "what happens" — become revealed as self-consciously fictionalized (thus unreliable). The film's two endings "challenge" (his car is a Dodge Challenger) our reliance on logic and perception and memory, as well as our "belief" in the illusionistic realism of film. In the first ending, we do not understand what happened to the car; in the second ending, we "understand" that what we first misunderstood never happened. When the film finally ends, we therefore cannot trust this "real" ending as real, or as an ending.

But let us return to the opening, the film's first ending—after which we cut back in time to an exposé of how it all began two days earlier, in Denver, at 11:30 P.M., at Argo's Car Delivery Service. Kowalski returns from one delivery and maniacally insists on beginning the next, displaying an acute case of road movie fever. Argo pleads with Kowalski to rest, warning prophetically that he is going to kill himself, but Kowalski is addicted to speed and mobility. Further elaborating this notion of driving overdose, the speed he stops to get on his way out of town suggests the symbolic confluence between a chemically induced hyperactive body and mind, and the act of driving as a speed rush. In fact, *Vanishing Point* elaborates upon *Easy Rider*'s LSD sequence: driving as intoxication, the "rush" of driving, driving as "a trip." Instead of Mexicans south of the border, here the drug dealer is a black pimp, a girl on each arm. As elsewhere in the genre, this straight white male driver identifies with people of color: both are outsiders who exceed the conventional bounds of mainstream society.

This brings us to another significant and distinctive aspect of *Vanishing Point*'s journey narrative structure: the use of montage crosscutting, mostly between Kowalski's drive, and the point of view of a blind black small-town disc jockey named "Supersoul" (Cleavon Little). Like many people of color in road movies, Supersoul is made to signify a certain exoticized authenticity. And yet *Vanishing Point* develops his character with more complexity, and more centrality to the narrative, than is typical of blacks in other road movies. After Kowalski starts out on his drive, the film abruptly cuts to early morning the next day, where Supersoul walks down the town's main street to his radio station. A conspicuously white group of townspeople observe him, foreshadowing one of the many affinities that will develop between Supersoul and Kowalski: both are spectacles of difference for Middle America.

When he overhears on the police radio frequency a description of Kowalski's first escape from the police, Supersoul becomes interested in the furiously blazing driver, seeming to feel an instant bond. The film's discourse then develops this transcendent bond by crosscutting between Kowalski pausing for a cigarette after crossing the Nevada state line, and Supersoul eating his lunch. The two loners are figurative buddies, on the same "track," in the same rhythm—more so than they know. As suggested above, Supersoul's blackness marks him as an outsider to white mainstream American society (a kind of equivalent to Kowalski's rebellious speeding). But his blindness

3.8. Kowalski's (Barry Newman)
Challenger rushes like a river and drives
cops over the edge.

doubly marks him as outsider, racially *and physically* Other, invoking the archetypal "seers" of the Old Testament and Greek mythology. Supersoul's visionary function brings to mind *Bonnie and Clyde*'s and *Easy Rider*'s emphasis on visionary roaming. Supersoul can "see" Kowalski, appreciating his strange, manic fury to drive.

In another interesting connection with *Bonnie and Clyde*, Supersoul represents an overlapping of visionary rebellion and the mass media, specifically in terms of Kowalski's "fame" as an outlaw. Let us recall that Bonnie and Clyde become outlaw "stars" by virtue of the mass media's appropriation of them; yet conversely, Bonnie and Clyde learn to use their star image to their advantage (notably Bonnie's orchestration of the photo with the sheriff, as well as her mythologizing poem). *Vanishing Point*'s Supersoul engages in a similar process, transmitting over the airwaves his mystical dialogue with Kowalski, as well as his own prophecies. With apparent empathy and sincerity, he transforms Kowalski into a mythic figure blazing a furious symbolic trail. What Kowalski represents for Supersoul comes from Supersoul's projection more than Kowalski himself, who (not unlike the Driver and Mechanic of *Two-Lane Blacktop*) is mostly mute, vacant, and disinterested. At one point Supersoul starts describing Kowalski over the airwaves as driving a "soul mobile," as "the last American hero with the blue meanies after him," "the last free soul on the planet," the "soul challenger" (punning on the make of his car). While Kowalski seems muted by his existential identity crisis, Supersoul (like GTO) furnishes much of the film's road movie theory (e.g., "speed means freedom of the soul"). Considering the film is set in the early 1970s, it is interesting that the radio—not television—serves as vehicle of their buddy "dialogue" as well as Supersoul's mythologizing message. The radio appears in this context as romantically archaic, decidedly low-tech, verbal instead of visual, thus more evocative of an "underground" and authentic counterculture.

Beyond the symbolism he invests in Kowalski, rendering him a "star,"

3.9. Mystically linked road buddies: Kowalski on the road . . .

3.10. . . . senses Supersoul (Cleavon Little) at his radio station, "listening" to Kowalski's drive.

Supersoul also interacts with Kowalski on a more intimate, mystical level. This is how Supersoul becomes a kind of "buddy" for Kowalski: traveling "with" him as partner, figuratively. The radio station, after all, is KOWL; and Kowalski's car radio seems to magically turn on, carrying Supersoul's voice at significant moments. One scene has Kowalski and Supersoul almost in direct conversation, with Kowalski responding to Supersoul's question on the radio, "How do you feel?" Near the end, when Kowalski is hiding out in the desert, Supersoul displays a brotherly if not parental concern, warning him that he cannot beat the desert like he has the police. At yet another somber moment, Supersoul comments that Kowalski's flight, the police pursuit, and Supersoul's own infatuation all illustrate "the blind leading the blind." Finally, when Kowalski arrives in California to meet his destiny, one last crosscut shows Supersoul sitting silent and alone in his studio, bathed in darkness—seeing, it seems, the end of the road.

Despite Supersoul's buddy role, as well as his visionary powers of insight and mythmaking, it is rather telling that the black man is stationary. Having achieved a certain agency in disseminating his commentary over the airwaves, he is not yet "allowed" (by the genre) to make the journey himself: he can only do so vicariously, mystifying the white man's journey. In other words, ultimately he is a passive observer facilitating the celebration of the white road movie star. From this perspective, he seems a more developed and articulate version of the poor southern blacks who wave at Wyatt and Billy as they pass by, or who observe the rebellious antics of Bonnie and Clyde.

And yet this facet of passivity only partially accounts for Supersoul's role. While the film consigns the black man to a certain "privileged" passivity, it also engages in a potent critique of white racism. This occurs most dramatically at Supersoul's radio station, where he is attacked and beaten up by racist whites, because they know he is "working with" Kowalski. The punishment Kowalski "deserves" (according to those who would punish him) is readily unleashed on the innocent black man, fueled by the fury of racism—a point the film does not shy from making. As if tacitly conspiring with the redneck bigots, the police then try to force Supersoul to lead Kowalski into a trap. But Kowalski is able to detect the lie in Supersoul's voice; an improbable plot turn (to keep Kowalski going), but one that again articulates their mystical, ineffable interface, where the truth of their bond prevails.

The crosscutting structure between Kowalski and Supersoul does not bog down the film's energy or vitality as a road movie. Rather, it serves to heighten the tension of Kowalski's desperate journey, providing distance from it and commentary on it, emphasizing it as a quest, but also a flight from the law. In a way, Supersoul is the link between the audiences *in* the film and audiences *of* the film, negotiating identification with Kowalski, mediating inquiry about him. Certainly he facilitates a glorification of Kowalski as an antihero of speed and rebellion. While Supersoul's role introduces a substantial level of cultural critique, especially regarding racism against blacks, the film's political referencing (like that of *Two-Lane Blacktop*) is overall superficial and vague. *Vanishing Point* is more interested in the mystical fury of driving; Supersoul's "connection" to Kowalski, as well as Kowalski's motivation, remain enigmatic, framed in a deliberate haze. As such, the mystique created by Supersoul's commentary situates the film in the distinctly fragmented and existential road movie mood of the early 70s.

Another narrational strategy complementary to the film's crosscutting is its use of flashbacks. These memories from Kowalski's life punctuate the film with modernist discontinuity, inserted to suggest (not explain) where and what he comes from. In this respect they fill in some of the motivational gap regarding his driving frenzy. And yet, the flashbacks also create new gaps, new questions. Moreover, any insights furnished by these flashbacks reveal (not surprisingly) an emotionally and psychologically distraught character, frustrated with his relationships and his own personal identity. Recalling both *The Rain People* and *Five Easy Pieces*, *Vanishing Point* thus participates in yet another facet of the early-70s road movie sensibility: emotional alienation.

The first flashback occurs after the police start pursuing him. During this chase—which is full of flashy, compelling traveling shots—we suddenly cut to Kowalski crashing a motorcycle during a race on a racetrack. The flashback occurs abruptly, more in the modernist montage style than as a Hollywood dissolve-to-memory. Thus, though we realize we are seeing Kowalski's past, the flashback sequence itself is presented in a somewhat disorienting manner. This first flashback itself continues in a similar modernist vein, cutting to another auto drag race, where he appears unconscious in a crashed car. Despite their obscure presentation (recalling *The Rain People*'s opening sequences), these first flashbacks shed some light on his manic driving compulsion. They also cue us to his superior driving proficiency, born out when he eludes both the police, and a hotshot driver in a red Jaguar, causing both to crash.

The next flashback sequence begins when he is refueling at a gas station, and the young girl working there starts seductively eyeing him. Recalling the scene in *Easy Rider* where the group of girls flirtatiously gawk over Wyatt, Billy, and George, here *Vanishing Point* codes Kowalski as a sex object. Not merely the racing spectacle of rebellious fury that Supersoul mythologizes, he is also sexually enticing to young women, who throughout the film offer themselves to him. (This unlikely gas station attendant does so with her eyes; later a beautiful blonde, first seen riding a horse naked, will verbally offer to "make it" with him.) As the woman at the gas station coyly watches him, the film cuts back in time, revealing that Kowalski used to be a policeman. Thus, in the past Kowalski tried not only to fit into society but to enforce its rules (the rules he presently shows no respect for). Yet this flashback seems more bent on sanctifying him as chivalrous. In the scene, Kowalski uncomfortably observes his brutish partner, who first harasses a girl about the "dope" he thinks she is on, then proceeds to try to rape her in the backseat of the police car. Kowalski intercedes on her behalf. While articulating a very road movie-esque criticism of police authority (as police brutality), the scene also shows Kowalski as a hero of damsels in distress. Considering the moment when this flashback occurs—as Kowalski is being admired—this latter meaning seems the one preferred by the film.

The third flashback occurs when he is out in the desert, off road, just after "telling" Supersoul to "go to hell" for suggesting that he "cannot beat" the desert. Sarafian makes a compelling visual transition to this flashback, with blurry close-ups of Kowalski's glazed eyes, and extreme high long shots of the tracks his car makes racing through the salt flat landscape. Inversely proportional to his current state of desperation and isolation, this most extended flashback is also the most idyllic, taking place first in the snow, then at the beach with his girlfriend (presented, I think, as his one true love). He is still a cop, and the sequence begins with her declaring "I love you" while she rolls a joint, then offers it to him. Sentimental romantic strings play on the soundtrack as the two walk along the beach. This sequence too is stylistically modernist, with conspicuous dissolves and rack focus shots, suggesting a fluid, hazy, and nostalgic memory. Likewise, the synchronous dialogue seems clipped in a stream-of-consciousness style, and disassociated from the images, since we rarely see them talking, but hear them almost too clearly. They discuss his "scar," which we can presumably interpret as symbolic more than literal, since there is no explanation of it; symbolic, that is, of the mysterious frustration eating away at him, driving him. She says she loves his scar, though she knows he hates it; he replies that he only hates "what it means." Soon she goes into the ocean with her surfboard, stating again that she loves him, asking him to "remember me." The shot then dissolves to the surfboard drifting in the surf, implying that she died in a surfing accident. Taken as a whole, this flashback conveys Kowalski's inability to have a healthy romantic relationship: the fragmented modernist film style, disconnected dialogue, and her death all serve to characterize him as a doomed loner.[18]

Some time after this last flashback, the police investigation provides an umbrella of narrative coherence for these snippets from Kowalski's past: wounded in Vietnam (his "scar"?), with an honorable discharge in 1964; worked for the San Diego Police Department, earning two promotions but given a classified discharge; then became a demolition driver in 1968, but disqualified for refusing to take an alcohol test. Yet this factual biographical profile never really clarifies what is driving Kowalski so furiously, and we should assume the film deliberately wants to keep his motives mysterious, perhaps to encourage from the audience what Supersoul engages—a projection onto a blank slate. In the tradition of modernist aesthetics, the film constructs him as divested of obvious meaning, and thus open to interpretation.

On the other hand, we can situate these flashbacks, and the film as a whole, squarely within the early-70s road movie tendency where personal emotional and psychological exploration permeates mobility. All the flashbacks suggest his frustration with jobs and relationships; they portray someone who cannot find himself, and who cannot fit into society. Even the scene ostensibly critiquing police brutality (he himself is the instrument of this critique) seems rather to illustrate yet another instance of him "not belonging"—it *just happens* to be the police department. We sense from these flashbacks that Kowalski is a lost soul; he will never find himself, he will never be content. His speeding driving and *speed*ing body and mind seem nihilistic gestures of escape—mainly from himself. With nothing to lose or gain, with no point to his life, he jumps on the bet as an arbitrary pretext to blaze a trail of his own frustration and futility.

Working hand in hand with its overall nihilistic tone, confusing journey, and confused driver is the film's portrayal of the counterculture. First of all, with uncanny resemblance to *Five Easy Pieces* and *Two-Lane Blacktop*, the film depoliticizes and trivializes the counterculture by locating it in the feminine: pot-smoking hippie women with long blonde hair, sex and romance on their minds; or gay men posing foolishly as highway robbers. The infamous scene involving the latter (cited by Tom Hanks in Epstein and Friedman's 1995 documentary, *The Celluloid Closet*) reveals *Vanishing Point*'s politically regressive and conservative streak. Our first view of them, through Kowalski's approaching windshield, signals their inability on the road (an inability apparently symbolic of a lack of conventional masculinity) and foreshadows their fate. Like Palm and Terry in *Five Easy Pieces,* their car is broken down. After they wave Kowalski down, he offers them a ride. Such a "nice guy," good Samaritan gesture is conspicuously out of character, and we quickly learn the reason for the contrivance: they try to rob him, which becomes a pretext for him to laugh at them, physically overpower them (oh so easily), and throw them out of the car. The fact that Kowalski has thus far driven alone, a truly isolated antihero, renders his only passengers throughout the film (two lascivious gay men) all the more invasive and intolerable (for the film). Criminalized, feminized, they are framed—by the film, within the car—so as to be ridiculed and (r)ejected. Though the ensuing crosscut shows Supersoul being attacked by racist whites, it is unclear whether the film implies a parallel between Supersoul and the gays (i.e., victims of what today are called hate crimes). More likely, the film sees an affinity between the racist whites and gays, since Supersoul and Kowalski are the two buddies under siege.

While I think it is fairly safe to read the two gay men as representative of the counterculture, the film more overtly associates women with the alternative lifestyle and politics of the late 1960s. Beyond the girl at the gas station and his girlfriend in the flashback already discussed (the latter clearly coded as postcounterculture when she states, "Only if you make war on war will you overcome it"), let us consider a bit more closely the naked girl riding the horse near the end. The narrative context of her appearance seems a distillation of the film's arrogant attitude toward the counterculture. First, her boyfriend—a Hell's Angel–type biker, donning military vest and Indian headband—"recognizes" Kowalski, further glamorizing our "star." He agrees to get Kowalski some more speed; upon his return, he provides information to help Kowalski escape a police blockade. But while the boyfriend is gone, the naked woman appears riding her horse as a kind of idyllic hallucination through Kowalski's dazed and druggie point of view. Then these two leftover hippies help Kowalski decipher the true meaning in between Supersoul's "lying" words on the radio. She offers him sex and pot; he turns her down on both counts, preferring cigarettes, speed (no countercultural drugs like pot and LSD for him), and his speeding senseless drive.

Then it comes out that she too "recognizes" him: she has news clippings about him from his demolition/racing days, saying to him, "You haven't changed much." Like the film's elliptical flashback structure, he starts to explain—but it is only a start: "When it came out I . . ." He trails off, unable to express or confront his own (past) identity. As ciphers of the counterculture, they assist him, perhaps support him "politically"; but they are subservient to him, adoring spectators who offer sex and drugs.[19] Moreover, Kowalski clearly stands aloof from them and their "alternative" lifestyle (even though he exploits it for his journey). Wyatt, Bobby, and *Two-Lane Blacktop*'s Driver were likewise possessed of such road movie aloofness, traveling both across *and above* the landscape. But with his conservative attire and haircut, tight-lipped tough-guy stoicism, and overall straight appearance, Kowalski suddenly seems more of a Marlboro Man, a surprising precursor to Dirty Harry.

Vanishing Point's other means of delegitimizing the counterculture is through the filter of religious fanaticism. With echoes of *Easy Rider*'s commune scene, the film serves up a derogatory verdict on the counterculture in the form of a New Christian musical freak show out in the desert. Like Palm in *Five Easy Pieces*, these outcast hippies singing Jesus folk songs are reduced to the lunatic fringe, treated with mockery as misguided if not phony. This cynical attitude is conveyed largely through a cohort Kowalski meets, a "prospector" (Dean Jagger) who has been living out in the desert "since the Depression," and who leads Kowalski to the Jesus freaks to get gas. The prospector becomes a temporary "buddy" for Kowalski, a true seer like Supersoul (and in contrast with the phony Jesus freaks). More survivalist than naturalist (another bond with Kowalski), he catches rattlesnakes, helps Kowalski elude the police by hiding his car, and offers the following parental, conservative advice: "The best way to get away is to root right in." The prospector trades rattlesnakes for gas with the smarmy head preacher, who eyes Kowalski suspiciously, claiming "We don't like strangers." Keeping his distance, Kowalski observes the transaction with a superior smirk. Perhaps the film is engaging in a "cultural critique" of inauthentic religious organizations, more specifically of the born-again Christian phenomenon. But why in the context of hippies? Why not in the context of mainstream conservative America, where it truly thrives? From this perspective, the "sweet Jesus" song that chimes in after Kowalski's death, continuing into the credits, seems truly perplexing, straddling the cynical irony described above but also sincerely suggesting, in the spirit of *Bonnie and Clyde* and *Easy Rider*, some kind of martyrdom at the hands of the law.

More than the early-1970s road movies discussed previously, *Vanishing Point* seems highly self-conscious about being a road movie. It explicitly mo-

3.11. The spectacle of nihilistic explosion: one of *Vanishing Point*'s endings.

bilizes both the outlaw and quest tendencies, using driving as its primary visual and narrative pulse. Full of thrilling, visceral traveling shots and montage sequences of Kowalski's Challenger challenging the road, it also invokes the Western and gangster genres (the loner traversing the wasteland), but in a distinctly modernist, postcountercultural context. Displaying the irony, cynicism, and ineffable identity crisis that characterize the proliferation of road movies in the early 1970s, *Vanishing Point* proves a compelling portrait of the times, and a historically significant example of the genre.

Gothic Irony and the Outlaw Couple: *Badlands*

With its outlaw emphasis on the fugitive pursued by the police, *Vanishing Point* foresees an equally significant, though far more influential film, Terrence Malick's *Badlands* (1973). If *Five Easy Pieces* and *Two-Lane Blacktop* revise and extend the genre-defining *Easy Rider* in an ironic and cynical 1970s context, then certainly *Badlands* does something similar for *Bonnie and Clyde*. As Marsha Kinder has explained, *Badlands* belongs to a crop of films from 1973–74 that descend directly from *Bonnie and Clyde,* constituting what she calls the "outlaw couple" film (and which are all road movies). Based on the real-life murder spree of Charles Starkweather in the late 1950s, *Badlands* remains one of the most influential American films of the postwar era. Of the three films she discusses (the other two being *The Sugarland Express* and *Thieves like Us*), *Badlands* has surely aged the most gracefully, leaving in its wake a crowded legacy of road movies. Much of the film's power derives from its peculiar, compelling tone, which is laced with irony and, not exactly cynicism, but a kind of gothic affectation.

The film follows Kit (Martin Sheen) and Holly (Sissy Spacek) as they roam across the "badlands" of the American Midwest, fleeing the scene of one murder after another (all at Kit's hands). Despite its focus on young lovers as social outcasts on the road, the film's ironic treatment of its "romantic" couple serves generally to dilute the drive behind their rebellion. Throughout the film, Kit seems to be acting out images he has observed, of what an outlaw should say and how one should act. He is sincere in his very insincerity, naively reinventing himself as James Dean.[20] Likewise, Holly's flat, matter-of-fact voice-over forges cool distance between audience and subject matter. Though the film's distancing effects provoke an intriguing viewing experience, they display little Brechtian sociopolitical referencing. *Badlands* can therefore be situated in the more self-conscious, self-reflexive 1970s cultural context. Several features of the film link it with the early-70s road movies previously discussed: ephemeral, ambiguous nods to sociopolitical issues; a minimalist approach to plot, character, and dialogue; an aesthetic rather than political modernism; and a tone more ironic than romantic.

The causes of their departure sketched in the beginning help situate the film in the early-70s road movie mood. While economic hard times contribute to their crime spree, more central catalysts seem to be boredom and a family crisis. As the film opens, we see Kit working as a garbage man, walking alongside the clunky, slow-moving garbage truck; the first few lines of dialogue with his partner establish Kit as quirky if not bizarre and somewhat restless. The peculiar interest he takes in people's garbage perhaps betrays a frustration with such suburban, snail-paced, functional mobility: he belongs in a vocation of higher speed and higher profile. Walking home from his shift, he spots Holly spinning a baton on a quiet, tree-lined neighborhood street, and starts up a conversation. After Holly tells him that her father probably would not approve of her dating a garbage man, Kit quits his job. His visit to the unemployment office is hardly fruitful, and he ends up working at a slaughterhouse. This plot setup locates the impulse to hit the road in young rebellious romance ("star-crossed lovers"), and in reaction to dismal socioeconomic conditions. Contrary to the conventionally bright and booming image of 1950s America, the film portrays a stark and dark version, where an economic recession seems to have paralyzed all opportunity. Not unlike *Bonnie and Clyde*'s substitution of the 1930s for the 1960s, *Badlands* uses the Eisenhower and Kennedy ("New Frontier") era as ironic reflection of the barren, socioeconomic downer of the early 1970s. Kit comes off as a young person without direction, but also without prospects.

The beginning of *Badlands* nicely integrates the romantic, familial, and economic motives for their rebellion, since Kit's inauspicious employment and identity confusion is what forces him and Holly to keep their relationship secret from her father (Warren Oates). In a visually stunning scene, Kit finally approaches her father while he is at work painting a billboard. By virtue of the distilled emptiness of the vast landscape, and the use of extreme long shot, their first encounter is rendered gothic if not mythological. Adding to the scene's rich, archetypal resonance is the encroaching beast of consumerism and advertising towering over them. Holly's father rejects Kit's strangely formal asking for her hand. Kit obliges, receding into the distance while the father shakes his head in dismay. Yet we sense that Kit will be back to take matters into his own hands.

While Kit shares some traits with Bobby (e.g., confused rambling), he also is less educated and analytical, more driven by forces he does not comprehend. And yet he possesses little of Kowalski's furious overdrive. Unlike either road movie driver, he makes a concrete reactive decision to hit the road. He enters Holly's house with a gun (nonchalantly revealed to us in Kit's back pocket when he happens to turn around) and starts packing Holly's clothes: he is going to take her away. When father and daughter come home, Kit states his intentions, but the father does not take him seriously, insisting that Kit leave immediately or he will call the police. Whereas previously the father had been poised above Kit at the billboard, judging Kit inadequate and refusing his request, here Kit has become King of their house, usurping the father's role, towering above the latter on the stairway. When the father makes a move, Kit shoots him in the stomach, pummeling down the stairs toward him afterward, as if to verify the murder he just committed by observing its effect. While economic need clearly participates in this violent ignition of their journey, this theme of cultural critique rarely comes up again once they are on the road. Instead, the film launches their flight more in reaction to the Oedipal conflict between son and father over daughter/mother.[21]

In one of the more poetic and generically potent gestures in the history of the road movie, the catalyst of their departure climaxes, after murdering the father, with setting fire to home. In Kit's mind, such a blaze will hide evidence as well as make it look like an accident. To ensure the latter, adding fuel to the fire of his guilt, he makes a recording of his (falsified, fictional) explanation of what took place, leaving the record playing on a phonograph outside the burning house. Yet the film, here and throughout, cues the audience to his faulty logic, setting him up to be observed through an ironic lens for his misguided if not demented charm. Moreover, the gorgeous montage cinematography and haunting choral music create a gothic, mystical, almost surreal inferno, one that signifies ignition, and that both laments and sublimates the destruction of suburban stability and domesticity.

Once they hit the road, they embrace the life of the outlaw couple with ingenuous panache, driving aimlessly and dreaming of elsewhere. In one of the first episodes on the road, they set up a makeshift camp in the woods, which suggests that they still cling to the idea of security in physical stability, even though here the setting is explicitly outcast and antisocial. Like Kit's James Dean posturing, and like Holly's movie star infatuation, their "tree house" camp seems molded from the imagery of childhood storybooks: Tarzan, Robinson Crusoe, Tom Sawyer.[22] Rather than conveying a new stable environment, this "home" appears tensely tenuous, a primeval wonderland where these enfants terribles live more like animals than humans—not, however, in the "back to nature" hippie-harmony vein, but more evocative of the rugged wilderness of the preindustrial frontier. The ensuing narrative turn emphasizes this connotation, when their camp is invaded by gun-toting modern cowboys. Oddly suggestive now of the Vietnam War, Kit hides in a foxhole, then surprises them from behind and kills them. Forced back onto the road, they come to realize that their life as outlaws shall never know stability or rest. We should also note how Holly's voice-over informs us that Kit had told her the intruders were bounty hunters: he overheard them discussing reward money, and therefore deserved to get shot (echoes of *Bonnie and Clyde*'s Sheriff Hamer). Though she believes him (or at least seems to accept his explanation), we know that either he made this up, or really did hear voices—but in his head. Indeed, Kit strikingly resembles GTO: a spinner of tales, pathologically lying, displaying bizarre, mentally unstable reasoning.

As Kit and Holly drive from place to place, the film looks more and more like *Bonnie and Clyde,* in many ways remaking or revising it. At the same time, *Badlands* establishes its own distinct vision, which comes into focus if we consider more carefully the nature of its outlaw couple's roaming. The sense of purpose or direction that drove Bonnie and Clyde (and, for that matter, Wyatt and Billy) seems lacking here, very much in the spirit of the early-70s road movie. Kit's most entrepreneurial notion is to drive to Canada so he can get a job on an oil rig—more a fantasized speculation than a practical plan. Even his murders seem oddly casual, as though he is posing as a killer, following the code of the fugitive. As a result, he seems uninspired, going through the motions, an empty shell. Holly herself expresses confusion about why he has killed this or that person. Indeed, Holly's bizarre passivity mirrors Kit's subtle dementia: though she acutely observes Kit, Holly remains emotionally divested of the adventure, coolly removed in the passenger seat, often in her own world (parallel with Kit's "voices"). As Kinder puts it, "[H]er passivity is as pathological as his aggression; they are equally callous to the murders" (7). Her unmotivated and unemotional persona recalls the characters of *Two-Lane Blacktop;* likewise, Kit's confusion about himself and his journey brings to mind *Five Easy Pieces* (both Bobby and Kit

3.12. The outlaw couple of *Badlands*: Kit (Martin Sheen) and Holly (Sissy Spacek), restless in the backseat.

look to Canada rather than Mexico for refuge). In their dispossessed mental imbalance, both characters may be linked with *The Rain People*'s Natalie.

One scene among many that illustrates this aimless, removed aspect of their mobility is when Kit spins a bottle below an overpass out in the middle of nowhere, to decide what direction they should take. When the bottle points back the way they came (a symbolic reference to the relativity—thus futility—of any direction they choose), Kit complains that the ground is uneven, then arbitrarily chooses a direction himself claiming, "If I can't decide, I ain't worth nothin', so it doesn't matter anyway." Here he ingenuously verbalizes the nature of their journey (and, in many ways, the road movie's generic journey): going without going anywhere, going to be going. The mise en scène too emphasizes this road movie theme, portraying an empty, disorienting landscape with no landmarks or sense of direction. In her stoic aloofness (looking down at him from the overpass), Holly in fact most dramatically embodies this quality, by going along for the ride that is going nowhere in particular. Somewhat like the Girl in *Two-Lane Blacktop*, Holly is strangely removed from this road movie's (male) drive to drive; as a relatively disinterested passenger, she interjects critical commentary (exaggerated in Holly's case by her voice-over). Kit moves the story while Holly straddles the dividing line between story and discourse, participating but also commenting, both inside and outside the film and the genre, thus elucidating its contours.

And yet, this road movie is more character-oriented than others previously discussed in this chapter. This derives largely I think from its focus on the romantic couple, which here is not melodramatic or sentimental, but does hark back to Hollywood fare (precursors like the screwball *It Happened One Night* and the gangster/noir *Gun Crazy* come to mind). Its modernist irony is thus not so much related to plot (like in the road movies discussed above) as it is, more subtly, to tone and aesthetics. For example, the film beautifully balances romance with irony, and classicism with modernism, in another gloriously road movie–esque scene where they dance at night to Nat King Cole's "A Blossom Fell." When Kit hears the song come on the radio as they drive through the black desert night, he decides to pull over to honor the song with a dance. As the song plays crisply from the car radio, the camera glides in close-up along the headlight beam until the dancing couple slowly enter the frame. It is a stylishly compelling moment, with dynamic high-contrast lighting, suggesting their "star" status in the spotlight, but also foreshadowing their impending separation, as well as their fate of capture (song lyric: "The dream has ended, for true love dies . . ."). In addition, the romantic sentimentality of the song contrasts with their vacant, slightly deranged personalities, as well as with their fugitive status. Lastly, though they dance together, they are not passionate: Kit seems once again ingenuously self-conscious, thus "acting" more than "being"; while Holly is typically unmoved, stiffly following Kit's lead. Malick constructs this pathetically romantic moment through a mannerist, even baroque lens. The scene is classical, yet aesthetically and tonally modernist, invoking Ginger and Fred but also questioning the ideological pretenses of the romantic (outlaw) couple.

Put differently, their relationship seems a pretext for the film's aesthetic approach, which brings everything together under the codes of ironic distance and gothic minimalism. According to Kinder, the film emphasizes the aesthetic over the political, undercutting its mythmaking on a narrative level (they are rather banal "heroes") by glorifying them stylistically. About the house-burning sequence, Kinder explains, "The visuals encourage us to be fascinated with the spectacle, but at the same time we are aware that the nostalgia and ritual are slightly overdone, almost reaching an exaggerated expressionism. This taste for ritual and romance lies at the heart of Kit's violence; Malick's visuals show us that we are also susceptible to their charm" (9). Much of the stunning cinematography recalls John Ford, for its vast, formally composed landscapes, which contribute greatly to the sense of liberation for this outlaw couple on the road. The minimal(ist) dialogue (linking it with *Two-Lane Blacktop* and *Vanishing Point*) mirrors the sublimely vacuous, almost abstract compositions; these latter seem self-referential and ironic more than romanticized. The visuals, like the characters, are beautifully distant.[23]

Yet such majestic imagery serves an illusionism more self-conscious than Ford's. Throughout *Badlands*, the visual compositions tell the story (Malick's ensuing *Days of Heaven* (1978) goes further in this direction). Moreover, the often breathtaking cinematography integrates reference to its own contrivance. One telling example would be during the "tree house" sequence, where Holly looks into a viewfinder at old photographs. First the camera looks "through" her point of view at the photos in the viewfinder, with the interior of the viewfinder included in the frame. Soon the camera cuts in closer, absorbing the photographic image into the filmic image, becoming a poetic montage—of what she is looking at, but also of the film we are watching. Balancing nostalgia with irony, this self-conscious tone is further elaborated by Holly's voice-over, which muses innocently and philosophically about her origins and destiny, detached from the fictional moment.

It is precisely through such subtle tonal and aesthetic emphasis that Malick renders such a compelling portrait of the American psyche. Through its quirky journey of violence and escape, *Badlands* probes the paradoxical tensions of a modernized frontier, affectionately deconstructing America's Rebel-with-a-Cause mythology. Near the end, the film actually raises disturbing political questions, but in a refreshingly indirect way. Rather than making half-baked, fleeting attempts at cultural critique (along the lines of *Five Easy Pieces, Two-Lane Blacktop,* and *Vanishing Point*), Malick dredges up the specter of an ideological contradiction at the heart of America's Heartland.

As the film draws toward its conclusion, Kit and Holly need to get gas from a big rig parked at an isolated construction site. When the truck driver declines to cooperate, Kit pulls out his gun with boyish bravado, only to have such bravado immediately mocked by an arriving police helicopter (which Holly points out to him). Kit goads her to hop in the car and make yet another dash for it; but she does not move, shaking her head, claiming she does not feel like it. He gets livid, but she refuses to play outlaw anymore, confirming what the audience has suspected all along: that she has never

3.13. Kit stages his own capture at the end of a thrilling car chase with the cops.

been an "outlaw," she has just been tagging along by default (though initially she is drawn to his good looks). After making an absurd pact with her (to meet her on New Year's Eve years later), he runs for the car, on his way shooting it out with one cop. As Kit makes his final desperate getaway, Holly approaches the other cop, hands raised.

Then begins the film's culmination, a climactic car chase between Kit and two highway patrolmen. With distinct echoes of *Vanishing Point*, this police chase achieves a furious energy with remarkable traveling shots and a dynamic crosscutting montage of both cars speeding down the highway and over off-road terrain. From a low angle in the passenger seat (suggestive of Holly's absence, now filled by the camera), we observe Kit checking his appearance in the mirror, making sure his hair is just right. After running out of ammunition, he pulls over and builds a little rock monument to himself, waiting for the cops to arrive, anticipating the "dramatic" significance of his capture, mocking both the cops' hot pursuit and the film's own focus on "following" him. The film's end of the road seems distinctly 70s in its cynical emphasis on futility, where the journey/chase simply ends by running out of fuel. But a more important inflection here is Kit's hyperself-consciousness as a celebrity, suggesting that the visionary rebellion of *Easy Rider* has been overtaken by a media-savvy posturing (or: a media-saturated sense of self-as-image). Even *Bonnie and Clyde*'s emphasis on fame set the outlaw couple fundamentally in opposition to the mass media. As noted earlier, Bonnie and Clyde self-consciously exploit the newspapers, an offensive gesture against the distorting empire of public images.[24]

In the backseat of the patrol car, Kit's jittery twitching, slightly distracted stare and smug nonchalance bear little trace of such visionary rebellion. Kit seems like a godfather to the twenty-something slacker—another way the film is truly prophetic, possessing a lasting relevance. Along these lines, and resituating the film in relation to the road movies previously discussed, we should note how the film renders visionary rebellion not as a "presence" (of deliberate, sometimes righteous confidence in utopian social changes) but as an "absence" (a lack of vision and motivation, a haphazard and aleatory momentum).[25] As the three drive back to town, after the "capture," one cop finally notes how much Kit looks like James Dean, to which Kit responds with bashful aplomb. A rapport develops between them as they exchange chit-chat about firearms, despite the cop's superior disbelief regarding Kit's murder spree. Kit even expresses an interest in joining the force, pathologically naive about the fate awaiting him. The perturbing affinity suggested here between lawman and outlaw comes to a subtle but startling fruition, when we cut to Kit standing at a small airport, bound and chained, waiting to be shipped out to prison, surrounded by police and a military squadron. Their curiosity about him betrays empathy, even admiration: his "freakishness" becomes a mirror, within which they see themselves, if slightly distorted.

This scene articulates the road movie's spectacle-ization of the driver, familiar from previous road movies discussed, where a stable, passive audience in the film admires the mobile rebel. The genre's driver is an antisocial antihero, but society is interested in "following" him. More importantly, the scene seems to question the very notion of criminality. Who is the criminal here? The line between law and disorder has become blurred. Kit is glorified within the film by the police-audience, and by the film itself, showing him to be charming, endearing, responsive, and unpretentious—not at all the image of the evil, deranged serial killer. The disturbing power of Kit's characterization is that he is as likable as James Dean; but also, he is so much like any one of us (or your local police officer or marine). Rather than demonize the cops, the film pulls off a compelling antiauthoritarian critique by ironically linking the cops with the killer. Thus, the film's glorification of Kit gives pause to righteous condemnation of him, but one that also causes us to question the definition of heroism, and the social, conventional (thus in many ways arbitrary) distinction between good and evil, law and disorder.

The very end of *Badlands* follows through on this questioning of moral and legal boundaries—not, however, in a heavy-handed, overt way (as in the endings of *Bonnie and Clyde* and *Easy Rider*), but in a poetically ambiguous way that resembles the endings of both *Five Easy Pieces* and *Two-Lane Blacktop*. Riding in the plane together (flying across the landscape they had been driving across), Kit and Holly exchange smiles. Then Holly peers out the window, and we cut to a point of view shot of sky and clouds and sunshine. But this last shot is much more than Holly's point of view; it is actually an aerial shot outside the plane, suspended, floating, angelic, but also ironic, as we listen to Holly's voice-over describe Kit's trial and execution, then how she goes on to marry the son of her lawyer. Though its outlaw couple gets captured and its lead male gets executed, this road movie's sense of violent doom finally becomes an ambiguous exaltation and exhalation. Holly will return to normal society (she never had really left), while Kit is punished with death offscreen, postnarrative. Our last image of him as smiling innocence and cocky confidence (so "American"), taken together with the last aerial shot of heavenly clouds gliding across the screen, challenges the audience to both sympathize with and analyze a "killer on the road" (à la the Doors' song "Riders on the Storm"). In any case, we may clearly contrast this disturbingly ironic and ambiguous tone with *Easy Rider*'s final aerial shot.

As I have suggested throughout this chapter, the irony that permeates the early-1970s road movie bears within it a more politically conservative angle, one that dilutes (without eliminating) the genre's driving core of cultural critique and rebellion. *Badlands,* for all its artistic prowess, testifies to this tendency. As Kinder puts it, "The final irony is that both of these 'outlaws' really belong *within* society" (7), and that "even their rebellion is culturally determined; like the police, the outlaws merely reflect the society and its limitations" (10). Malick himself observes this conservatism when he remarks that Kit "thinks of himself as a successor to James Dean—a Rebel without a Cause—when in reality he's more like an Eisenhower conservative." More revealing with respect to the film's conservative streak is how Malick tried to minimize references to specific time periods (1950s or 1970s), going instead for a fairy-tale feel "outside time, like *Treasure Island*" (Walker, 82).

This choice, given that Kit and Holly live in a kind of fairy tale, makes brilliant artistic sense. But let us acknowledge in following the road movie's generic unfolding how such a timeless, universal, and childlike context renders rebellion more innocuous and less politically articulate.

The Road Taken: The Film School Generation

In drawing this chapter to a close, let us acknowledge the peculiar importance of the road movie for the early years of the "film school generation." Bred on countercultural values, European New Waves, and classical Hollywood, most of these directors began their careers just after the *Bonnie and Clyde* and *Easy Rider* phenomenon. Before they "saved Hollywood" (Biskind) with the blockbuster/"high concept" film of the late 70s, these "post-baby boom movie brats . . . test-drove the genre's highways at least once" (Atkinson, 14). The generation of filmmakers Biskind labels "sex-drugs-and-rock-'n'-roll" includes Dennis Hopper, Arthur Penn, Robert Altman, Bob Rafelson, Monte Hellman, and Hal Ashby, who all made at least one road movie between 1967 and 1973. But the more specific "film school generation" or "movie brats" made the following road movies: *The Rain People* (Coppola; discussed above), *Paper Moon* (Bogdanovich), *Duel* and *The Sugarland Express* (Spielberg), *Boxcar Bertha,* and the less road movie–esque *Alice Doesn't Live Here Anymore* (Scorsese). George Lucas can be included peripherally (as producer of *The Rain People,* but also notably for *American Graffiti*'s focus on cars and driving).[26]

Before turning to the road movies of the ultimate movie brat, let us take note of the one "film school generation" director who contributed *the least* to the New Hollywood blockbuster. Based on Bertha Thompson's *Sister of the Road, Boxcar Bertha* was produced by Roger Corman's American International Pictures, and thus possesses a trashy, low-budget, Hollywood-schlock look and feel, as well as plenty of explicit sex and violence. Set during the Depression like *Bonnie and Clyde* (and like Altman's more ironic, less politicized *Thieves like Us*), *Boxcar Bertha* is not really an "outlaw couple" film, though Bertha Thompson (Barbara Hershey) and Bill Shelley (David Carradine) form a loosely romantic union, one inflected by a posthippie free love. While at times on the run, these lovers roam the country more on a quest: in Bertha's case, for a sensually fulfilling life; in Bill's case, to fight capitalist greed and galvanize the unions. Bertha's father is killed in a plane crash (due to the money-grubbing negligence of the plane's owner) when she is a mere teenager, so she is forced to hit the road. She hooks up with radi-

3.14. *The Sugarland Express* merges the outlaw couple with the cop-hero.

cal leftist union organizer Shelley (they first have sex in a traveling boxcar), roaming the country with him and his small gang (including one black man). While Shelley often has specific destinations related to his political activities, Bertha suggests a more liberated and open wanderlust. Somewhat like the Girl and Holly, she goes along for the (male-driven) ride, yet displays a more detached, inspired, and truly free mobility. Unlike the Girl and Holly, Bertha is the main character of the film.[27] Together she and Bill live a life of crime on the run while trying to forge a socially meaningful alternative.

Steven Spielberg's early road movies achieve a different but related de-politicized effect. His career was truly born with the road movie, his first two features being the made-for-television *Duel* (1971) and *The Sugarland Express* (1974). *Duel* is a significant contribution to the road movie horror film (*Detour, Delusion, Speed, Breakdown*), where a traveling businessman becomes terrorized inexplicably by a mysterious, murderous truck driver. *Duel* fits well into our discussion of early-70s road movies, for its infamous minimal dialogue, as well as its "incoherence" regarding the purpose or meaning of the killer truck driver. *The Sugarland Express*, however, is more interesting for the cultural conservatism it anticipates, in its desperate attempt to restore the family, and in the alliance it creates with the police.

Despite Kinder's grouping, *The Sugarland Express* is a much more conventional "outlaw couple" road movie than either *Badlands* or *Thieves like Us*—no surprise considering the director, who more so than Coppola would go on to "save" Hollywood with *Jaws* (1975). In *The Sugarland Express*, Lou Jean Poplin (Goldie Hawn) helps break her husband Clovis (William Atherton) out of prison so they can drive to see their son, presently in a foster home. As the police pursue them, it becomes increasingly clear that their hope is a futile one, a desperate, doomed flight from the law in the name of true love on the run. And yet, unlike the films discussed above, *The Sugarland Express* is hardly pessimistic or cynical: their determination, their vision of a family restored, their clear purpose and goal all render the film's journey much more classical than modernist.

3.15. Conformist tendencies: a police escort for the outlaw couple's family reunion.

Moreover, the film displays considerable sympathy for police authority. Once on the road, our outlaw couple befriends a policeman, Officer Slide (Michael Sacks). Initially they were forced by circumstance to abduct him. But gradually, by virtue of being in their car, on "their side" of the law, he "joins" them. This bond between outlaw and lawman results in a situation more sentimental than ironic (as in *Badlands*): a police caravan escorts them to the home of their son (strangely anticipating the O.J. Simpson police caravan back from the Mexican border). So in a sense, the police (society's law enforcement) are facilitating their journey; more than that, they make the journey *with* the outlaw couple, rendering the latter not really outside the law. Rather than questioning their authority, as *Badlands* does with its disturbing blurring of boundaries, *The Sugarland Express* rehabilitates the authority of the police as sensitive to the desire of the outlaw couple—a desire that in essence is rather conservative and conventional to begin with.[28] Put differently, *The Sugarland Express* portrays its cops as desperate victims— quite a contrast from *Bonnie and Clyde* and *Easy Rider* (and looking forward to *Thelma and Louise*'s Inspector Slokum). Though Clovis is killed in a melodramatic shoot-out, we should take note of the film's final shot: a shimmering, high-contrast long shot of Slide alone on a beach, perhaps poised to become the good husband and father.

As one of the "last" road movies before the lull until the mid-1980s, *The Sugarland Express* distinguishes itself from most other early-70s road movies in ways that signify a transition to the genre's next phase. First of all, the film does *not* use irony or minimalism in its tone and presentation. Conversely, its narrative structure is much more reflective of the classical Hollywood model, rather than the European modernist narrative of existential wandering. Despite having Vilmos Zsigmond behind the camera, the film also possesses a distinct made-for-television quality (carried over from *Duel*) that is not only transparently illusionistic (as opposed to self-conscious) in style, but looks rather flat, rather unfilmic. Most important is the film's cartoonish quality (a quality Spielberg will expand and refine into the 1980s), which combines a slapstick/screwball type comedy with heavy-handed sentimentalism (again, no irony here). This cartoonism comes through in the film's portrayal of violence, at once sanitized and sensationalistic.[29]

Such unself-conscious utilization of cartoon conventions ultimately renders *The Sugarland Express* quite the conservative, depoliticized road romp, where cops and outlaws travel together. This road movie softens cultural critique by fusing rebellion and conformity in an ambiguous, socially detached tonal context (the "fairy-tale" quality of *Badlands* is relevant here). Finally, the conservatism and conformity that dominates *The Sugarland Express* seem an extreme expression of the overall trend I have described throughout this chapter, where the genre's rebellious core gets psychologized and depoliticized. In many ways, the road movie road trip that began with Bonnie and Clyde's first robbery ends in the congested, uniform parade of police cars that *is* the sugar-coated Sugarland Express.

The Road Warrior
Repo Man
Paris, Texas
Stranger than Paradise

Drugstore Cowboy
Raising Arizona
Wild at Heart

Chapter 4 ....

BLURRING THE BOUNDARIES
The 1980s Postmodern Road Movie

The road movie fizzles out in the mid-1970s, perhaps the inevitable destination of its existential meandering, but also probably a result of being driven off the road by the conservative convoy of New Hollywood blockbusters during the latter part of the decade. Several Hollywood road comedies appear, among them *Smokey and the Bandit* (1977), *Convoy* (1978), *Bronco Billy* (1980), *Cannonball Run* (1981), *Honky Tonk Man* (1982), and *National Lampoon's Vacation* (1983). In my view, most road movie comedies, especially of the Hollywood variety, do not incorporate any visionary rebellion, and in fact do not really emphasize road travel. Not coincidentally, this wave of road movie comedies occurs during the New Hollywood's revival of the patriarchal action-hero, heralding the Reagan-Bush era (*Rocky, Star Wars, Rambo*, etc.). These late-1970s versions are "played for broad farcical laughs and car-crash pyrotechnics" (Hark, 207).[1]

The road movie returns during the mid-1980s, its rebirth driven by the postmodern quirkiness of a thriving American independent cinema. As a label for this new version of the road movie, "postmodernist" is to be conceptually hyphenated. Just as romanticism both precedes and informs modernism, so too modernism both precedes and informs the postmodern. At least in terms of the road movie's history, the postmodern should not be understood as distinct from (after) modernism, but rather as a commercialized, or depoliticized, repackaging of modernist aesthetics: something like modernism gone mass media. The postmodern road movie thus modifies *but continues* the genre's modernist impulse. Still restless, rebellious, and independent, the postmodern road movie exaggerates irony and cynicism through stylized spectacles of sex, violence, or simple tongue-in-cheek cool. Generic elements become driven by style (think fashion), transformed into images of and for mass popular culture.

This period of the postmodern road movie seems exemplary of Thomas Schatz's notion that a genre's typical evolution ends in a revisionist, self-reflexive phase (36–41). While it is true that the postmodern road movie is characterized by revisionism, self-consciousness, and irony, this phase is no end point. On the contrary, here the genre thrives more than it ever has previously. The road movie therefore is in no sense a classical genre but an independent, postmodernist one: its "classical" phase, its soul, is rooted in late-1960s countercultural modernism, while its generic flowering reflects the advent of postmodern culture at large.

Indeed, Hollywood appropriations continue to crowd the genre's highway at this time, car-jacking the genre as a vehicle of farce and/or romantic comedy (Cohan and Hark, 10). Partaking little of the genre's modernist narrative structure elaborated between 1967 and 1975, they likewise dilute visionary and existential themes with heavy doses of trite and sentimentalized values (e.g., "friendship is more important than greed"). In many ways, these Hollywood road movies seem to be generic skeletons gutted by an "entertainment" mentality. Examples would include the *Cannonball Run* films (1981, 1984), *Lost in America* (1985), *The Sure Thing* (1985), *The Journey of Natty Gann* (1985), *Midnight Run* (1988), *Planes, Trains, and Automobiles* (1988), *Rain Man* (1988), and *Homer and Eddie* (1989). Continuing into the 1990s, these more "fun" and accessible road trips provide a pop culture mirror for the equally numerous but far more compelling films following the independent road movie trend.

Utilizing a postmodern tone and look (which does often incorporate comic elements of farce and satire), these road movies stick more closely and self-consciously to the genre's original terrain of rebellion and cultural critique.[2] Postmodern road movies like *Paris, Texas* (1984), *True Stories* (1986), *Something Wild* (1986), *Near Dark* (1987), *Down by Law* (1986), *Leningrad Cowboys Go America* (1989), *Drugstore Cowboy* (1989), and *Wild at Heart* (1990) are more self-conscious of, and usually mock, their own generic status and modernist roots.[3] To poke fun at a genre does not automatically preclude a social/political critique. On the contrary, as I have suggested above, rebellion and cultural critique still furnish the fundamental drive of these films. But their subversive edge is typically softened by a cleverly ironic tone. Albert Brooks's *Lost in America* is instructive here. Bearing traces of both the Hollywood comedy and independent postmodern road movie, the film parodies *Easy Rider* from a yuppie perspective: "Born to Be Wild" blasts as David Howard cruises away from his advertising job in a Winnebago. But the film's parodic attitude is insidiously driven by a reactionary political agenda. Howard is earnest in his frustration and search, but the film makes fun of his earnestness, inviting the audience to laugh at him. His journey becomes a pretext for comic gags that "criticize" him for criticizing American culture. Not surprisingly, he returns to the fast-paced materialism of corporate America—a happy conformist ending.[4]

From this angle, many postmodern road movies that appear subversive can just as easily be read through their ironic mockery of subversion. In contrast to the dark, moody and meandering irony of the early-1970s road movie, the irony of the postmodern road movie is more heavy-handed, often cartoonish. More importantly, this postmodern irony embraces posturing: the artificiality of performance and the performance of artificiality. Generally speaking, the postmodern road movie prefers to tease and dazzle, rather than critically engage, the audience. This sense of postmodern road movie dazzle—stunning mobile camera work, excessive violence, over-the-top performance, deadpan irony—can be understood in terms of Corrigan's notion of the "hysterical": "representations overdetermined by their materiality and no longer even interested in accommodating history and cultural change" (151). The overall effect tends to depoliticize the genre. On these postmodern highways, visual thrills and reflexive in-jokes supplant a lack of historical, social, or political grounding.

Baudrillard's Hyperreal America

To further bring into focus the sensibility of the postmodern road movie, let us turn to Jean Baudrillard's description of road travel in his book *America*. While he does not use the term "postmodern," his characterization of contemporary American cultural identity in terms of speed on the highway resonates for the road movie generally, and for our present discussion.[5] The concept of hyperreality he develops goes far in characterizing the postmodern road movie because mobility through open space becomes crucial to his description of contemporary, hyperreal America. Moreover, the archetypal deserts and highways that figure prominently in his version of hyperreal American cultural identity are crucially linked with movies and images. "[I]t is Disneyland that is authentic here! the cinema and TV are America's reality! The freeways, the Safeways, the skylines, speed, and deserts—these are America, not the galleries, churches, and culture" (104). As in the postmodern road movie, this sense of space and mobility is intractably bound up with America's "cinematic" essence, its hyperreality where images *are* reality:

> The cinema has absorbed everything—Indians, *mesas*, canyons, skies. And yet it is the most striking spectacle in the world. Should we prefer "authentic" deserts and deep oases? For us moderns, and ultramoderns, as for Baudelaire, who knew that the secret of true modernity was to be found in artifice, the only natural spectacle that is really gripping is the one which offers both the most moving profundity *and at the same time the total simulacrum of that profundity.* As here, where the depth of time is revealed through the (cinematic) depth of field. Monument Valley is the geology of the earth, the mausoleum of the Indians, and the camera of John Ford. It is erosion and it is extermination, but it is also the tracking shot, the movies. All three are mingled in the vision we have of it. (69–70)

As in the postmodern road movie, representation playfully subsumes reality, imagery ironically consumes politics.

Such rendering of reality and politics as nothing but image invariably yields a depoliticized, ultimately conservative context if not content. This becomes one of the most consistent underlying characteristics of the postmodern road movie, which basks in its own image construction, not so much to provoke critical reception, but in celebration of the hyperreal culture of consumption. While the reflexivity of the early-1970s modernist road movies confronts the spectator with the creative film process, linking this process with the fictional theme of the journey, the postmodern reflexivity here emphasizes genre conventions, film history allusions, and self-conscious special effects. In the postmodern road movie, visionary rebellion and existential roaming become saturated with a ludic irony and tongue-in-cheek posturing. Rather than conveying an existential loss of direction, the postmodern journey going nowhere and/or anywhere signifies a derealized, depoliticized embrace of a synthetic cultural space. By blurring all borders under the banner of Artifice, the postmodern road movie tends to nullify transgression, rebellion, and cultural critique.

Heading toward the Postmodern Wasteland: *The Road Warrior* and *Repo Man*

Let us begin our journey through the postmodern road movie with two films that may not be the most compelling examples, but that embody many of its most important features: *The Road Warrior* (George Miller, 1982) and *Repo Man* (Alex Cox, 1983). Part of their significance is chronological, since they engage the genre at a time (the early 1980s) when it was still sleeping. In a sense, they foretell the (postmodern) return of the genre in the mid-1980s. We should proceed somewhat tentatively with *The Road Warrior,* since it is an Australian film that in many ways reflects uniquely Australian themes regarding national identity and landscape.[6] On the other hand, the film enjoyed a substantially popular reception in the United States, and therefore speaks in some ways to American culture.

As conveyed by its title, *The Road Warrior* is more of a road movie than either of the other two films in the Mad Max trilogy, the preceding *Mad Max* (1979) and subsequent *Mad Max: Beyond Thunderdome* (1985). Very much about mobility through a postapocalyptic wasteland, the film is replete with driving sequences, traveling shots, open landscapes, and car culture fetishism—often at the expense of plot and character. In many ways, it is a kind of futuristic *Two-Lane Blacktop*. But unlike that film's lackadaisical journey of drift, *The Road Warrior*'s "journey" is more narrowly conceived as a somewhat tiresome series of speeding car and motorcycle chases. But the film proves a good starting point for considering the postmodern road movie. Set in the desolate desert(ed) aftermath of a world war over oil, *The Road Warrior* stars Mel Gibson as Max, a ravaged wanderer who stumbles upon a "commune" of survivors. As the film begins, the latter are being attacked by a roving biker gang, "scoot jockeys." A pastiche of postpunk, heavy-metal Hell's Angels, this motley crew scavenge the land and terrorize the commune like wild Indians from an old Hollywood Western (Falconer, 259). What the scoot jockeys want from the commune is the "petrol" the latter are refining, so as to make a trek to "the Gold Coast" and start a new life. Having rescued one of their members, Max is allowed to enter the commune. Initially he just wants some gas, but eventually agrees to drive the oil rig for them through the ominous desert outback and the impending onslaught of the scoot jockeys. The body of the film focuses on preparations for the drive, and the drive itself. In an ironic twist that invokes the futility of the existential road movie journey, Max learns at the end that the big rig was full of sand, and that he was a decoy so the commune could make its *real* escape to freedom. Like Ethan from *The Searchers,* he returns to his solitary wandering as the film closes.

The Road Warrior extends several features of the modernist-existentialist road movie. The film has minimal dialogue and plot development, focusing instead on driving for action and suspense; characters too are sketched in thin strokes. The main character, Max, walks and drives in a stoic aura:

he speaks in Eastwood-esque grunts, never revealing much about himself or where he comes from. Though we may know from the first film that he has suffered the horrible personal trauma of losing his family, this character information is barely referred to in *The Road Warrior,* which instead portrays Max mostly as a cipher of postapocalyptic isolation, despair, and survivalism. Such tight-lipped, jaw-clenching mutism recalls not only *Vanishing Point* and *Two-Lane Blacktop* but also *Easy Rider*'s Captain America. As in those films, this road movie driver channels all his passion into being on the road.

But this road movie driver is a road *warrior.* Attending to this notion reveals how *The Road Warrior* anticipates some important generic shifts. Riding the early-1980s wave of popular science fiction/action films, *The Road Warrior* turns the notch up on road movie violence, and helps rehabilitate the loner as hero, in contrast to the modernist road movie's *anti*hero (Broderick, 256–61). The film participates in the trend exemplified by the *Star Wars, Indiana Jones,* and *Star Trek* film serials, as well as the reactionary, vigilante films of Eastwood, Stallone, and Schwarzenegger. Regarding costume, physical attributes, and performance style, Max resembles Stallone's Rambo and Schwarzenegger's Terminator. Thus, Max seems a good example of a Reagan-era "hard body," the "normative body that enveloped strength, labor, determination, loyalty, and courage" (Jeffords, 24). Max likewise mobilizes on a symbolic plane the return of the patriarchal hero, with the future of the human race as his "family."

This is not to say that the film transparently transmits conservative Reagan-era values. On the contrary, the film also illustrates Constance Penley's "critical dystopia," where a horrific vision of the future comments critically upon the present. From this angle, the film's emphasis on gasoline and cars as the precious remnants of an industrial society that destroyed itself is not only a clever pretext for reinventing the road movie's car fetishism; it also achieves disturbing political resonance by alluding to the oil crisis of the late 1970s. On the one hand, the film bashes fetishized car culture by showing the doomed aftermath of society's obsession with it; on the other hand, the film resurrects car culture by building the entire story around driving, car chases, road violence, and of course, acquiring fuel.

Moreover, the film rearticulates the genre's early-1970s existential pessimism and irony as postmodern, postpunk nihilism. Though the commune possesses a clear destination, the body of the film uses their desperate drive as a narrative pretext for elaborate car stunts, explosions, crashes, traveling shots, and sundry blood-curdling violence. The fact that Max's drive turns out to be a ruse underlines this drive as a relatively pointless or "empty" (yet

4.1. *The Road Warrior*'s spectacular postmodern war on the road.

spectacular) exercise in road violence and pyrotechnics. Max's decoy drive has a narrative "point," allowing the commune to reach their destination. But the film wasn't "about" that: we don't see them arrive; we see Max wander off alone. The film's spectacular and pointless road violence is mirrored, in a way, in the blanched, arid desert landscape, adding to the impression that the journey is furiously going nowhere. It is a never-ending, never-changing landscape, so there is no sense of passing through it (recalling the landscape imagery of *Badlands*). The laborious traveling shots, driving stunts, acrobatics, and pyrotechnics exist in a kind of representational vacuum: a meaningless series of stimulations displace the journey and, to a large extent, the plot itself.

Through its postmodern mode, *The Road Warrior* minimizes visionary rebellion, cultural critique, the existential search, even the detached, ironic ramble. The postmodern road of *The Road Warrior* is illustrated by what I would call the film's "deliberate camp" quality.[7] Its over-the-top, tongue-in-cheek attitude drives the plot to the brink of the ridiculous. While the film employs a fairly realistic (not very reflexive) cinematic approach, it becomes postmodern in its narrative content, specifically its mise en scène. The science fiction plot pretext itself renders the material "unreal." But the film's specific dystopian production design aims for a cartoonish quality: characters, costumes, dialogue, and story all reek of comic-book fantasy. This is not to suggest that every science fiction film is postmodern. The postmodernism engaged in by *The Road Warrior* is its brazen, exaggerated mockery of its own status as fantasy. That is, the film does not take its production of fantasy too seriously; rather, *The Road Warrior* flaunts its garish artificiality (again, in the plot, not the film style). Its "cartoonism" is thus less insidious, more overt than that of the classical-modernist *The Sugarland Express*.

Repo Man, we should clarify at the outset, is not really a road movie. It belongs to the non- or semi–road movie tradition of *American Graffiti, Taxi Driver,* and *Speed*—movies about driving and cars, but within the city limits. Like *Five Easy Pieces* in relation to the existential road movie, *Repo Man* is relatively "weak." But it articulates much better than *The Road Warrior* the features of the postmodern road movie. Like *The Road Warrior,* it focuses crucially on cars, driving, and car culture; also like *The Road Warrior,* it is a science fiction film. But *Repo Man* engages postmodern reflexivity and pastiche stylistically as well as thematically. Whereas *The Road Warrior* mitigates its ridiculous, cartoonish production design and characters with a critical dystopian narrative, *Repo Man* is blatant mock science fiction, a boisterous, no-budget pastiche. Basking in its own phoniness, subverting classical realist genre aesthetics, the film takes itself much less seriously than *The Road Warrior.* Yet *Repo Man* too operates through deliberate camp and self-conscious farce. Cynically and humorously removed from its own pretenses to narrative coherence, *Repo Man* makes fun of everything—including and especially itself.

More than *Taxi Driver* or *American Graffiti, Repo Man* focuses on car culture, and possesses a road movie sensibility even though its topography is primarily urban. Director Cox inflects the film's opening classic road movie imagery—the maps, the open highway, the speeding car, and the police pursuit—with a distinctive punk/postmodern tone. A kind of Brechtian self-consciousness operates here, playfully foreshadowing the contrivance of the film's absurd plot. Exemplifying postmodern pastiche, the mysterious contents of the car's trunk invoke through low-budget shorthand B-grade 1950s science fiction and horror films.[8] Yet the film's punk sensibility (itself a symptom of the broader postmodern condition) mobilizes a cultural critique fundamentally different from its modernist predecessors. This critique can best be understood in terms of a "disappearance" of critical distance, where the film text embraces the object of commentary. Parody becomes pastiche, satire becomes ludic imitation.[9]

Certain elements of the plot further elaborate the postmodern road movie sensibility. The story focuses on Otto (Emilio Estevez)—that is, "auto"—a young L.A. punker whom we first meet working as a stock clerk in a super-market. Developing the tone of the opening scene, the market is coded as comically hyperreal, since every item in the store is generic: it is not a *real* market, but a "fake" market; rather, it is both real *and* fake. After being fired, aimlessly marching down dilapidated streets, Otto is "picked up" by Bud (Harry Dean Stanton), a repo man who tricks him into repossessing a car. As Otto gets lured into the repo man world, driving around with Bud, he and Bud become "buddies."[10]

Though confined to the sprawling suburban wastelands of the Los Ange-les area, *Repo Man* integrates driving into its plot in the tradition of the road movie. Otto and Bud or Lite (Sy Richardson) have their most impor-tant conversations while driving. Otto is first introduced to the "intensity" of repo man life during the senseless "off-road" car chase with the Rodriguez brothers. When he first meets Leila (Olivia Barash), Otto is driving while she walks; then, after he drives her to work, they first have sex in his car (shot in fast motion, another example of the film's comically artificial quality). Per-haps most significantly, *Repo Man* cleverly weaves automobility into its nar-rative through the unhinged and alien-possessed Chevy Malibu first driven into Los Angeles by the lobotomized nuclear scientist (Fox Harris) in the be-ginning. The repo men, the Rodriguez brothers, Otto's former punk friends, the FBI, and other aliens in the film end up pursuing the car, which keeps changing hands yet somehow keeps moving, even and especially at the end where it turns into a spaceship and takes off into the skies over Los Angeles.

Within this narrative focus on the "life in the fast lane" of stealing or "repossessing" cars in Los Angeles, one tangential theme is especially signifi-cant for appreciating the postmodern road movie: the film's attitude toward the counterculture. As I've suggested throughout, the counterculture in many ways signifies the "birth" and the essence of the genre. *Repo Man*'s overall at-titude can be characterized as derogatory, deriving from its punk sensibility, and the more general postmodern culture to which punk (perhaps uneasily) belongs. Here, the counterculture is either explicitly mocked, or is decon-textualized and appropriated as fodder for commercialized imagery. Such mockery becomes viciously sardonic in the portrayal of Otto's parents as burned-out hippies who sit stoned in front of the TV, mesmerized by tele-vangelist Reverend Larry. This portrayal recalls *Vanishing Point*'s born-again hippies in the desert. Yet a significant distinction is that in *Repo Man*'s post-modern world, the television mediates the couch potato hippies, whereas in *Vanishing Point*'s desert, actual hippies are actually present, unmediated. In other words, the distinction suggests that the counterculture's previous "outsider" relationship with dominant conservative culture has been reinscribed "inside," thus neutralized through the recuperative power of television.

The film's other cipher of the counterculture is Miller (Tracey Walter), the "junkyard mystic/fool" of the repo men. Miller is treated with considerably more sympathy than Otto's parents. In his ritualized burning of the "possessions" of the repossessed cars, he seems a remnant of the sixties' visionary, alternative lifestyle. Coded as an "outsider" within the repo man tribe, he "is precisely the type of character which the normative hegemony of the neoconservative eighties relished in excoriating—not only as a nonproductive, worthless fool, but in their most damning judgment and for quite transparent ideological reasons, as a '60s burn-out.'" While Miller does not escape the film's irrepressible mockery, he emerges as a "quietly adversarial and totally unrecuperated" hero who literally "transcends" the film's postmodern wasteland in the Malibu-turned-UFO (Goshorn, 68–69).[11]

Yet I wonder if Miller isn't finally "recuperated" through the final "transcendent" gesture he makes, by lifting off. Recuperated, not by neoconservative culture, but by the film's own depoliticized tongue-in-cheek tone and (anti)aesthetic strategy of pastiche. When Otto chooses to leave Leila behind and follow Miller's silent beckoning, climbing into the Malibu (especially alluring now that it has become a spaceship), the film is making a choice too: an absurd resolution to an absurd film about an absurd world.[12] Not coincidentally, the car is the vehicle of this fantastic, absurd escapism (such escapism posturing here as subversion). Miller, the one who can not and will not drive ("The more you drive, the less intelligent you are," he says earlier in the film), is ironically the only one able to approach the radioactively fastidious spaceship and "drive" it away. (When Reverend Larry approaches the car, his Bible gets zapped into flames.) The male buddy road pair takes flight from their troubles, the urban dilapidation, the greed and betrayal and postmodern inauthenticity, as if on an amusement park ride.

More heavy-handed satire and irony emerge in the film's final science fiction pastiche. With the lights of Los Angeles superimposed across Otto's stargazing face, the finale alludes ironically to that modernist classic of the counterculture era: *2001: A Space Odyssey*—a hugely expensive, hugely serious film, diametrically opposed to *Repo Man*. Then, the film's final shot seems a reference to *Star Trek,* when the car surges into "warp speed," the stars blurring past in a stream of hyperlight. Yet *Repo Man*'s ending also, perhaps unwittingly, anticipates the flying spaceship-car that ends *Back to the Future* (1986). Both films reflect the cartoonism prevalent in 1980s Hollywood. But while the latter film takes itself seriously as big-budget comic book–style fantasy/entertainment, *Repo Man*'s independent, no-budget quirkiness conveys a savagely ironic mockery, one that imitates and incorporates what it despises.

Coming Home and Going Nowhere:
Paris, Texas and *Stranger than Paradise*

Repo Man's cinematographer Robby Muller and co-star Harry Dean Stanton would team up again the following year, in 1984, on an important road movie: Wim Wenders's *Paris, Texas*. During the late 1970s, ironically enough as the American road movie went into a lull, Wenders relit and carried forth the torch of the genre, establishing himself in Germany as the premier road movie director (eventually naming his production company "Road Movies"). Films such as *The Goalie's Anxiety at the Penalty Kick* (1972), *Alice in the Cities* (1974), *Wrong Move* (1975), and *Kings of the Road* (1976) clearly take their inspiration from *Easy Rider* and *Two-Lane Blacktop,* but push the genre in a distinctly European modernist-auteur direction. Eschewing outlaw rebellion in favor of the existential quest, these films display both suspicion and admiration toward American cinema (Kolker and Beicken, 28–42). *Paris, Texas,* Wenders's first American production, proves a useful if anomalous bridge from *Repo Man* and *The Road Warrior* to *Stranger than Paradise.*

Part of this anomalous quality derives from the director's European perspective on American mobility and landscape. Written by celebrated American playwright Sam Shepard and set in Texas and California, *Paris, Texas* inflects the American genre of rebellion and alienation with a foreign accent. Another facet of its anomalous status as postmodern road movie is how the film "belongs" with the early-70s road movies, displaying a "nostalgia" for the "Road Man" featured in those films (Hark, 212). Beyond Hark's "Road Man" connection, *Paris, Texas* may also be linked with films like *The Rain People* and *The Sugarland Express* for their shared focus on the family, its dissolution and restoration. Though *Paris, Texas* deals with the social outcast, this figure appears in the context of a family melodrama, emphasizing emotional and psychological turmoil more than overt political/cultural critique.[13] With its digressive, languorous narrative and aura of angst, the film seems a road movie out of time, a delayed contribution (a decade late) to the existential road movie. Yet several elements of the film articulate and anticipate features of the postmodern road movie, features quite different from (but complementary to) those of *The Road Warrior* and *Repo Man.*

To begin with, *Paris, Texas* deemphasizes road travel, employing a journey structure that literally stops and starts, with substantial pauses. Exagger-

4.2. *Paris, Texas*: two alienated brothers (Dean Stockwell and Harry Dean Stanton) reunite in the desert.

ating the genre's lack of motivation and direction in the early 1970s, many postmodern road movies break up the journey. *Paris, Texas* likewise treats the literal journey as a metaphor for an internal, psychological journey. In the film's opening sequence of aerial shots, Travis Henderson (Harry Dean Stanton) emerges alone, wandering through the Texas desert. Invoking a staple of the genre, the film explains later that he is returning from a four-year odyssey of delirium throughout Mexico, an odyssey that served as refuge from his past life and previous identity crisis in America. In a near catatonic state, he finally comes to temporary rest at a clinic in Terlingua, while his brother Walter (Dean Stockwell) is notified. After flying out from Los Angeles, Walt has to drive around the Texas desert in his rental car, searching for his brother, who would not stay put. Once Walt finds him, Travis begins to come out of his state, but insists that he cannot fly, which leads to their road trip home.

Their drive home is largely noncommunicative, due mainly to Travis's reticence about responding to Walt's queries. Gradually, however, Walt and Travis reacquaint themselves; but Travis clearly cannot talk about what has happened to him. As is typical of Wenders's road movies, the drive serves as therapeutic interlude, bringing Travis back to culture, back to himself, back from the hellish past he cannot yet confront or express. Such communication breakdown and breakthrough on the road evoke the early-70s road movie. But *Paris, Texas* moves toward family reconciliation and stability more quickly and directly than does *The Rain People, Five Easy Pieces,* or *The Sugarland Express.* The destination of the film's first road trip furnishes Travis with the first part of his cultural and emotional restoration. Once back at Walt's house in Los Angeles, Travis convalesces, gradually reconstructing himself. He learns to confront his past—largely through watching the Hendersons' home movies, but mostly through encountering his own son Hunter, whom the Hendersons have "adopted" while Travis was "away." Being reunited with his son most forcefully reintegrates Travis with his former identity, and with society. Significantly, this partial family reunion inspires him to hit the road.

Yet the road trip he takes with Hunter, the film's second road trip, is not back out into the wilderness, but further into the realm of convention and stability: the urban metropolis of Houston, to seek out his estranged wife Jane (Natassja Kinski).[14] This second drive from Los Angeles to Houston functions as the second part of Travis's process of cultural reconciliation. Previously Travis came out of his deranged state, back into culture and into his former identity as father; here on the road he further reestablishes his bond with his son, aiming toward reunion with the wife/mother. Mobility in *Paris, Texas* is thus a journey *back to*—not away from—home, family, and society. Once father and son find Jane working at a peep show/porno house, the film's "movement" comes to a dramatic and telling standstill. More precisely, it becomes transformed into a purely metaphoric journey into the past. The literal journey back home and the metaphoric journey into the past constitute parallel lanes of the postmodern road movie's more conservative highway.

After reuniting Jane with Hunter, Travis drives off into the night, alone. The last shot echoes a film like *Five Easy Pieces* or *Two-Lane Blacktop,* a classic road movie ending where the journey continues with no clear destination. But the difference here betrays the conservative turn of *Paris, Texas.* While we do not know where Travis is going, and he probably does not himself know, he has achieved a certain "destination"—the restoration of his family—even though he is not part of it.

Jim Jarmusch's first feature film, *Stranger than Paradise* (also 1984) works well as a companion piece to Wenders's film. Clearly descending from the 1970s existential road movie, it too brings a European perspective to the American landscape. Like Wenders, Jarmusch has established himself as a provocative and unique independent film voice largely through road movie revisions: *Down by Law* (1986), *Mystery Train* (1989), *Night on Earth* (1991), and *Dead Man* (1995) all possess vital generic traces. At the same time, like *Paris, Texas* and more reflective of the postmodern mode, *Stranger than Paradise* stops and starts at a listless and jaded pace, as though world-weary of roads (and road movies).

Stranger than Paradise is historically significant as a watershed film of the mid-1980s American independent generation that includes Spike Lee, John Sayles, Jonathan Demme, David Lynch, and the Coen brothers.[15] Moreover, it links well with road movies previously discussed, curiously revising the search for fulfillment structuring the narrative of *Easy Rider* and the minimalist character sketches, plot, and overall aimless journey of *Two-Lane Blacktop*. But Jarmusch's film takes the idea of "nothing happening" to a new extreme, one laced with a postmodern tongue-in-cheek hipness and deadpan irony. Lumbering with ironic urbanite "attitude" and ennui, the aimless purpose of the film's journey is revealed in the stationary scenes as well as the driving scenes. Stability in the film is so exaggerated it becomes an excessive caricature, the extreme opposite of movement and motivation, an "emptiness" in the mise en scène, a void that only mobility can fill. Yet mobility too will be "empty," unfulfilling, a rearticulation of nonmovement. Beyond such a paradoxical elaboration of mobility, *Stranger than Paradise* seems most exemplary as a postmodern road movie for its distinctive humor: restrained irony that affectionately mocks the pathetic characters and their journey.

Comprised of three distinctly titled sections, *Stranger than Paradise* focuses on two "beautiful losers" in New York City, Willie (John Lurie) and Eddie (Richard Edson). Their vacant, mundane existence is interrupted by the arrival of Willie's cousin from Hungary, Eva (Eszter Balint). On her way to their Aunt Lotte in Cleveland, she is forced by circumstance to stay with Willie longer than expected. Part 1, "The New World," focuses on Eva's stay with Willie, where she is mostly bored, with nothing to do, since he does nothing. She finally departs for Cleveland. Titled "One Year Later," Part 2 focuses on Willie and Eddie making a visit to Eva. As if Willie and Eddie's very presence breeds banality, the three of them quickly become bored, disillusioned also by the cold weather. So they decide to go to Florida. The last section, "Paradise," portrays them traveling there, as well as their brief stay.

Before turning to some of the details of the film, we should note that *Stranger than Paradise* possesses little of the driving fetishism of most road movies previously discussed. Yet its detached, blasé, nonchalant interest in driving is characteristic of the emergent postmodern road movie, where driving is treated as a kind of joke. A distinctive "been there, done that" attitude prevails among the characters, who often literally or figuratively smirk at the road trip. Like everything else in the film, and like most postmodern road movies, *Stranger than Paradise* makes fun of the drive it nevertheless embarks upon. This jaded road movie attitude is conveyed through a film language that is subtly self-conscious and self-reflexive. Notable for being composed entirely of one-take sequence shots, the cinematography graphically exaggerates compositional dynamics. At the same time, the camera movement, and movement within the frame, remains conspicuously, sometimes uncomfortably static: in some shots, the only movement is the shifting of someone's eyes. Drawing attention to itself as artificial cinematic construction, the film presents an interesting example of hyperrealism. This metacinematic aura— achieved largely through its distinctive black-and-white, low-key cinematography—becomes quite a contrast to the reflexivity of *Two-Lane Blacktop*'s burning filmstrip or *Vanishing Point*'s freeze-framing play with narrative realism. Such formalistic film distortion, in fact, will be more prevalent in *Drugstore Cowboy* and *Wild at Heart*. *Stranger than Paradise* uses cinematic restraint to achieve a sublime artificiality.

While the film minimizes driving per se, the theme of travel and migration is built into its fundamental framework. The first shot shows Eva watching a plane land; then she turns with her bags and walks out of the frame, while another plane on the ground lumbers forward. Overall suggestive of travel, departures, arrivals, and The Journey, this shot sketches the traveler and the vehicle of travel—a plane rather than a car. After "The New World" title appears (connoting, of course, colonial and immigrant discovery journeys from Europe to the Americas), the second shot is a traveling shot of Eva walking down the street. Significantly, the first thing she "does," and the only thing that "happens" in this shot, is to put on her tape deck: "I Put a Spell on You," sung furiously by Screamin' Jay Hawkins. Recurring throughout the film as a synchronous musical motif, the song accompanies her as she moves down the street, and as the camera travels with her, a humorous send-up of the road movie's enthusiastic driving rock soundtrack. In one of the few moving camera shots in the film, we might also note the graffiti she passes: "US out of everywhere—Yankee go home." Such "found" details obliquely refer to the road movie sensibility.

One of the film's trademarks, unique and bizarre for a road movie, is the way "nothing happens," the way the characters are often engaged in doing nothing. The static long take and lack of movement seem a deliberate, ironic subversion of all the necessary staples of Hollywood film: movement, action, emotion "moving" the characters and audience. Many scenes in this first section have extended shots of Willie playing solitaire or watching television. However, the "nothing" that happens here seems by choice, not due to lack, loss, past repressed emotional trauma, or existential confusion. This road movie becomes postmodern by superimposing pathetic banality with casually jaded cool.

Such jaded cool, we come to realize, is to an extent a put-on, a posture. When Eva is getting ready to leave, Willie seems sad to see her go. Eva brought some "life" to Willie's chosen nonlife. "You're all right," he says to her, after she comes home with some shoplifted food. More broadly, she sheds a critical light on the routine of American culture. This is illustrated most comically in the scene where Willie explains TV dinners to her. Through her non-American outsider perspective, she emanates the cultural critique typically associated with mobility in the genre. After she's gone, Willie and Eddie sit drinking a beer in an unbearable silence that again underlines lack of communication, nothing to do, the extreme opposite of the mobility they will eventually engage in one year later as some kind of antidote to their meaningless boredom and empty routine. Both Eva's presence and her absence critically expose their sedentary lives going nowhere. We can therefore credit her with inspiring Willie and Eddie with an urge to travel. At the end too, she seems to have left Willie with GTO's "taste for the foreign," as he spontaneously leaves the New World for the Old.

The catalyst for Willie and Eddie's small-time journey to Cleveland "one year later" is set up rather appropriately in terms of small-time crime: they are caught cheating at a card game. They take off with their booty, pausing in an alley, where Willie suggests Eddie borrow his friend's car so they can "go somewhere." When Eddie suspects Willie of wanting to "skip town" out of fear, Willie denies it (though we may doubt him), explaining instead that they should "see something different." As if the idea is preposterous, Eddie asks where they will go, to which Willie responds, "I don't know." In typical road movie fashion, they just want to go, fleeing a "crime," in need of a new perspective.

The film's first driving sequences are visualized self-consciously in the language of the genre. The camera is positioned in the backseat mostly, though sometimes on the front hood, showing them in the car as they drive, using the windshield as a screen through which we see them, and through which they see the world go by (like images in a movie). We look at them as they look out onto world: they are traveling spectators. Nothing seems to happen in these driving shots, as nothing happens in the world going by. Articulating the film's postmodern contours, these driving scenes beautifully fuse mobility, banality, and reflexivity. The point is that there is no point other than the driving itself. Accordingly, there is nothing restless or desperate about going to see Eva for a flimsy, half-baked "family reunion." Unlike the disassociated, dehumanized cool of *Two-Lane Blacktop,* or the pregnant silences of the brothers driving home in *Paris, Texas,* there is no therapy here, no emotional search, not much being repressed. Yet their silent togetherness while driving is lightly peppered with conversation fragments where, most often, Willie teases Eddie with affectionate sarcasm. If this journey is empty, the film savors such vacuity, redeeming it with a Zen-like quietude. In these driving scenes, subtle humor finds ironic pathos in the tiniest of gestures.

When Willie and Eddie arrive in Cleveland, they find that Eva too has had to embrace "TV-dinner" America by working in a hot dog stand. Later Eddie observes—significantly, at some train tracks—that "when you come to some place new, everything looks the same." Willie pokes fun at this pseudo-revelation. But like Miller of *Repo Man* and GTO of *Two-Lane Blacktop,* Eddie has expressed a key theme of this road movie, and the road movie generally: wherever you go, you have really gone nowhere (again, obliquely suggestive of Zen philosophy, perhaps Jarmusch's importation of Ozu). At the same time, Eddie's observation betrays a longing for the visionary inspiration promised by the mythical mobility of *On the Road.* An ironic climax (that is, an anticlimax) to their Cleveland foray occurs when the trio silently observes a frozen Lake Eerie: all around them, all they can see is a white nothingness. They decide that "Cleveland is a drag." Eddie and Willie then decide they want to go to Florida. After starting out, they go back for Eva, who leaves despite the protests of Aunt Lotte. Though Aunt Lotte possesses a certain "old-world" charm and generosity, her home comes to signify a prison house of boredom for the trio, from which they flee. As she walks back into the house cursing, the car pulls away into the distance, toward the horizon.

On their way to "paradise," a series of frontal driving shots frame them through the windshield. They appear (not surprisingly) lackadaisical and bored. Echoing the opening traveling shot of Eva's arrival in New York, the main thing that "happens" (aside from switching drivers) is that she plays her song on her tape deck. In an ironic and excessively casual send-up of the genre's driving rock music enthusiasm, Eddie comments, "It's good driving music." After they enter the state of Florida, and sneak Eva into a motel, the film continues in this vein, treating with wry humor the road movie's visionary theme. Willie and Eddie envision excitement in gambling at the races. Eddie insists he has a "good feeling" about the dog races; Willie doesn't like the idea, but they follow Eddie's crackpot "visionary" impulse. Willie and Eddie see themselves as "high rollers," whereas the film maintains a sardonic but affectionate distance from their comically pathetic "vision."

Meanwhile, Eva wakes up the next morning to find she has been left be-

4.3. On the road to "paradise" in Florida: *Stranger than Paradise*'s Willie (John Lurie) and Eva (Eszther Balint).

hind, with no note of explanation. Her rage is conveyed in a compelling shot typical of the film's graphic irony: the camera pans with a car off in the distance, behind a long hedge, all the way to the ocean's edge, where she sits staring at the sea, her tape deck silent next to her. This scene in fact reveals her as the film's true visionary, a road sister to Bonnie and the Girl: her excitement about exploring some unfamiliar terrain reflects the spirit of Kerouac and *Easy Rider*. But it has been squashed (by Willie and Eddie, and by the postmodern version of the genre), poignantly conveyed in her motionless gaze, as well as the camera's arrested movement on her, becoming a static (frozen, paralyzed) long take.

As expected, Eddie was wrong about his "vision." When they come back, having lost most of their money, Eddie sincerely offers up more platitudes: "That's the name of the game, you can't win 'em all." Such futility in the context of a "game of chance" recalls *Easy Rider*'s money in the gas tank, and the wagers propelling the journeys of *Two-Lane Blacktop* and *Vanishing Point*. Whereas Eddie readily throws his hands up in the face of such futility, Willie has a harder time accepting such senseless loss. A slight caricature of the earnest modernist road movie driver, he paces toward and away from the camera (one of the film's most dynamic movements within the frame), striking matches and flicking them. Invoking classic road movie restlessness (Bonnie comes to mind), he is trapped in a motel room, and by the static camera frame, yet ready to "make a move." But he comes up with nothing original or daring, despite all his intense concentration (compared to Eddie and Eva, Willie is not much of a visionary). He and Eddie make another desperate attempt at gambling—this time at the horse races.

While they are gone, a marvelous scene of mistaken identity occurs, re-igniting the stalled engine of the narrative. As she is out walking near the ocean, Eva is mistaken for a drug dealer, and is handed a bag stuffed with money. She leaves Willie and Eddie a note, some money, then goes to the airport. In the spirit of the film's postmodern articulation of mobility, here an ironic and absurdly comical coincidence—the mistaken identity—fuels the film's drive, propelling her to "make a move" and move on. In a further ironic twist, Eddie and Willie have won back their money. Thus, for them too the "game of chance" procures the money necessary to get the journey going again. When they discover what Eva has done, they go to the airport to try to stop her from returning to Hungary. At the airline counter, Willie tells Eddie he has to buy a ticket so he can get on the plane, to reach her before takeoff. He arranges to meet Eddie at the car. When we cut to Eddie leaning against the car, watching as a plane takes off, we realize as Eddie does that Willie is on the plane. Then Eddie drives away, wondering aloud what Willie will do in Budapest.

In the film's final ironic surprise, the last shot reveals Eva returning to the motel. She takes her hat up off the bed (the hat that caused the mistaken identity earlier), leans back against the bed, then looks into camera. Evoking the endings of *Five Easy Pieces, Two-Lane Blacktop*, and *Paris, Texas, Stranger than Paradise* concludes with each of the three characters isolated, in transit, with no clear sense of destination or direction. But there seems to be much less at stake in the postmodern film, where the pointless journey becomes a pretext for comically ironic reversals, and where a listless "whatever" attitude smirks in the face of wanderlust.

From "Crossroading" to a "Regular Guy":
Drugstore Cowboy

Released in 1989, Gus Van Sant's first feature film, *Drugstore Cowboy*, further extends many of the postmodern road movie characteristics described above. In its insidiously conservative values and playfully self-conscious visual effects, the film anticipates *Wild at Heart*. Like *Paris, Texas* and *Stranger than*

Paradise, Drugstore Cowboy conveys an overall feeling of transience, a sense that the characters are dislodged, adrift, wandering aimlessly. But also like those films, road travel as narrative drive is minimized, occurring as a turning point rather than as a continuous fluctuating state. As we have seen, and as exemplified by *Drugstore Cowboy,* the postmodern road movie allots substantial attention to scenes of stability within a general context of mobility. Whether through hyperreal artifice or listless narrative entropy, or both, the postmodern road movie journey continues its aversion to high-minded enthusiasm. Cynically distracted from mobility, the postmodern road movie willfully delays itself. In fact, *Drugstore Cowboy* upon close generic examination reveals itself to be a road movie and an anti–road movie combined; more precisely, a road movie that retreats from its own generic status. The first half of the film follows the characters on the road, in their rambling drug-addict lifestyle; but the second half focuses on the main character's journey back home, and what happens to him once he gets there.

Like *Repo Man, Drugstore Cowboy* reinjects the genre with a sense of youthful rebellion, focusing on a gang of wandering drug addicts. The main character of *Drugstore Cowboy* is Bob Hughes, played by Matt Dillon. In addition to the actor's star appeal as young dashing rebel (coded as a contemporary James Dean), Bob's periodic voice-over establishes his point of view: in many ways, this road is his journey. As I have suggested above, the postmodern road movie usually mobilizes many generically familiar elements of the modernist road movie, but puts a new contextual spin on them. *Drugstore Cowboy* is no exception, illustrated by its opening sequence, an interesting variation on the road movie's narrative departure. The first shot is a close-up head shot from above, of Bob's face. In a semiconscious (or altered) state, he stares into the camera; as his voice-over begins, he starts "telling his story," introducing us to his gang of druggies. We realize he is riding in an ambulance, and that this is "the end" of the story. By framing itself with Bob's ambulance ride, the film inaugurates mobility as an overarching theme of the plot. Likewise, the ambulance ride emphasizes a dark fate for the road movie protagonist. Yet unlike the doomed modernist fate of *Bonnie and Clyde, Easy Rider, Vanishing Point,* or *Two-Lane Blacktop,* and foreshadowing the film's postmodern take on mobility, Bob rides as the pampered passenger—driven, not driving.

Before flashing back to show what happened, the film presents a "home movie" sequence (handheld, Super-8) to illustrate Bob's description of his gang: his wife Diane (Kelly Lynch), his good friend Rick (James Le Gros), and Rick's girlfriend Nadine (Heather Graham). While the sequence intends to convey the irreverent freedom of young people on the road, a reading slightly against the grain reveals that this "gang" is really much more of a "family" than a "gang." As Bob's voice-over suggests, Bob and Diane are the "parents," while Rick and Nadine are the "kids." Bob's gang to some degree reincarnates the conventional and conservative family they supposedly rebel against. Aiming for an independent, no-budget, hip film style, such home-movie tactics are obviously derived from MTV. They therefore reflect the postmodern style of recycling images (film footage), but also the distinctly postmodern oxymoron of commercialized experimentation. Beyond the MTV influence, the home-movie effect enhances the "family" theme, since they are being coy, innocent, and silly for the camera. Indeed, we might contrast Bob's gang with the Barrow gang, the latter being composed more of blood and legal ties (two marriages, blood brothers) than Bob's gang, but possessing on the road more socially subversive bite.

This sequence ends with Bob's voice-over invoking a road movie theme already discussed: life on the road conceived as a game of chance, a gamble, a risk. Somewhat suggestive of the racing wagers of *Two-Lane Blacktop* and *Vanishing Point*, he explains that they were playing a game they knew they could not win—but they played anyway. The story then "begins" with a title announcing "Portland, 1971"—the time period, not coincidentally, of the early-70s road movie flourish. Not coincidentally because, as the "game" reference implies, the film attempts nostalgically to invoke the vintage road movies of that time. But this nostalgic glance backward distinguishes *Drugstore Cowboy* from those films in ways that illuminate the postmodern road movie's difference.

Right away the narrative drops in on a classic road movie scene already in progress, where Bob's gang are just starting to rob a pharmacy. After they pull off the heist, they hop into their car, a beat-up Cadillac, and drive away. This generically typical scene (the desperate departure from the scene of a crime) distinguishes itself, first of all, through the unique seating arrangement. Diane is driving, with Nadine and Rick in the front passenger seat. Bob, the leader, is alone in the backseat. On the one hand, this unusual seating arrangement conveys Bob's leadership role, alone on his throne, "above" having to drive (a curious parallel with his being driven in the ambulance). But in tracing the road movie's evolution from modernist to postmodern, from rebellious to conservative, Bob's passivity seems significant. He is a road movie driver who is not driving: as the central catalyst of the film's narrative journey, his aloof distance from the act of driving betrays the postmodern road movie's cynical and ironic withdrawal from taking the road seriously.

Van Sant makes compelling use of this passivity, however, by developing the road movie's visionary motif through Bob's drug-induced hallucination. Bob is in the backseat, we realize, to enjoy a privilege his leadership apparently entitles him to: he can immediately shoot up. This narrative alibi for his being in the backseat, however, does not render his role as road movie protagonist any less passive. On the contrary, in the scene's fusion of the drug trip and the road trip, Bob is clearly more interested in the former, with driving and mobility coded as a necessary side effect of the drug-addict lifestyle. This further elucidates the road movie's withdrawal from active (and activist) search and discovery. Another revealing contextual detail of this first hallucination is that on the car radio, a newscaster is saying something about the "Pentagon Papers." But the news report is barely audible, functioning as innocuous background and backdrop to the drug trip. The film includes a token reference to the politics of the time, yet simultaneously conveys the characters' lack of interest in politics. This is effective characterization; but it also reflects a postmodern depoliticization of the genre, a convenient shorthand reference to political crisis, one that says more about the 1989 Reagan-Bush-MTV era than it does about 1971.

Significantly, this getaway scene culminates in the hallucination itself, the first of several (and they are always Bob's inner visions). It is presented in an overinvested, over-the-top style: superimposed over a close-up of Bob's face are floating spoons, figures, planes, and houses. Additionally, we should note that Diane (the driver) is cursing and almost crashes, uptight and frenetic: driving functions in the scene as an intrusion upon Bob's passive drug-trip haze. The highly formalistic and self-conscious special effects expressing Bob's altered state supersede driving and mobility, favoring the crossing of borders within the mind rather than across state lines. The brevity and relative triviality of the scene likewise suggests that the visionary theme of the road movie has become ever more personalized and gimmicky.

Set in the house they rent, the film's next scene focuses on the drug-taking ritual for the rest of the gang. Conveyed through a montage of close-ups of drug paraphernalia, the scene also brings out the family subtext and hierarchy: Bob and Diane are the parents, Nadine and Rick the kids. When their neighbor David (Max Perlich) comes by to try and trade some speed for heroin, the film further develops this family dynamic by foreshadowing him as the "TV baby" who will later put Bob in the ambulance. David acts like a hyped-up child who Bob and Diane have to control and calm down; then he and Rick discuss recent television episodes (which, again, seems more reflective of 1980s MTV youth than 1971's hippies). In the narrative logic of the film, David's presence seems an omen, not only of the thug he becomes at the end, but also of the cops who barge in upon the heels of his visit, to search the place.

Initially, Gentry (John Kelly), the officer in charge, seems a formidable roughneck antagonist to Bob, forging Bob's road movie outlaw status as a rebel fugitive. Or is he? An interesting and telling detail emerges during the search: their mutual admiration for Bob's golf clubs. It is, of course, ironic that Bob plays golf—ultimate symbol of America's conservative recreation. But that is precisely the point. Bob's (and, by extension, the genre's) subversive, rebellious edge has been softened by an ironic embrace of dominant conservative culture. Put differently, such postmodern irony (i.e., Bob's golf clubs) slips readily from satire to imitation, from parody to pastiche. Indeed, Gentry bonds fleetingly with Bob as he inquires about the golf clubs, which foreshadows their friendship at the end.[16] In any case, Bob's gang is forced onto the road again—but only to get a new apartment across town. One senses that if the cops had not come, they would have been content to stay put in the house. Some road movie.

Drugstore Cowboy trivializes being on the road. There is very little that is serious about the film, which might be better described as "road movie lite." The overall immaturity of the characters comes into further focus when Bob and Diane visit Bob's mother, while Rich and Nadine get the new apartment. Though the film treats Bob and Diane as parents, Bob's mother scolds them with "You can't run and play like children forever." Standing in the doorway to the house, waiting for Bob to collect his things, Diane has nothing to say in response. Parental and childlike, Bob and Diane form a pretty lukewarm outlaw couple. Peter Biskind has noted how such "infantilization" of characters is a prominent feature of the Lucas-Spielberg blockbusters of the 1980s ("The Last Crusade," 121–27). *Drugstore Cowboy*, an offbeat, independent road movie, nevertheless reflects such postmodern Hollywood film culture. Compared to Bob's gang, Bobby's tantrums in *Five Easy Pieces* or the Driver's jealousy in *Two-Lane Blacktop* seem sophisticated.

As suggested earlier, this juvenile and trivializing quality is revealed in the way the film revises the genre's visionary motif. At the new apartment, Bob the wise parent explains his theories of superstition to the gawking, attentive Rick and Nadine, telling stories of how dogs and hats came to signify bad luck. Such a version of the genre's visionary theme ironically elevates a belief in ridiculous hoaxes to a level of mock seriousness. Being able to "read the signs" is presented here as rather juvenile and misguided, perhaps a lasting effect of their drug use. Similar to *Stranger than Paradise*'s cool distance from Willie and Eddie's "big score" aspirations, the film subtly mocks Bob's superstitions with diagonal compositions of each character during this conversation, effective in conveying their off-kilter, altered state of mind (another trace of MTV aesthetics). The fact that Bob's superstitions prove accurate does not redeem him as a true visionary, but rather underlines the film's contrived, tongue-in-cheek tone.

As we have seen in previous road movies, the contrast or flip side to the visionary motif appears often through references to the commercialized "visions" of mass media. *Drugstore Cowboy* bashes television throughout as an oppressive force, one at odds with Bob's "visionary" superstitions. For example, after Bob explains the dog story, dogs keep appearing to him on the television, goading and haunting him. Yet a little later Bob's aversion to television is inverted; that is, Bob's aversion is ironically mocked. Bob sets up Gentry's partner in a practical joke across the street, and presents it to his gang like a television comedy show, sitting his "family" down in front of the window (screen) to "watch." Anticipating similar sequences in *Natural Born Killers,* the film's heavy-handed formalism enhances the scene's televisual mode: synthetic applause and laughter on the nonsynchronous soundtrack, as well as superimposed hallucinatory bubbles. Here, the film suggests that the television format and visionary hallucination overlap as much as contrast. The scene goes far in characterizing the postmodern road movie, which merges the genre's familiar themes of mass media/popular culture and visionary exploration. *Drugstore Cowboy* criticizes television and "TV babies," but it also reflects and extends television culture.

The next morning Gentry repays Bob for the practical joke by beating him up and chasing him out of town. Echoing Willie's denial in *Stranger than Paradise* that he is skipping town because of the gamblers, Bob tells his gang with forced bravado that it is not Gentry causing their departure, but that they "need a change of scenery." His voice-over then comes in to explain "crossroading," one of the film's more compelling elaborations of the genre, where they drive across country, with no particular destination, sending the drugs on ahead in a bus so they will not get caught with them. This crossroading sequence suggests a subversive passion for mobility. Here the film engages a classic road movie montage of driving shots: one where a cop pulls them over and they dump the drugs through a hole in the floor (not very convincing since the cop is behind them and would see the drugs come tumbling out the back); lyrical rotating aerial shots of them driving; low-angle shots of bridges they cross and pass by; close-ups of their eyes while riding in the car; rainy windshield shots of their faces; and one fleeting allusion to *Easy Rider,* a quick shot of a straight redneck type watching them go by. As part of the driving montage, such a shot illustrates how the postmodern road movie makes trivialized, tokenistic references to the genre's past portrayal of rebellion. Rebellion *is present* in the film; it has not been completely left behind. But it is conveyed through a playfully artificial tone and an ironically superficial journey.

In fact, the one "serious" event that occurs in the film, Nadine's death by overdose, is treated seriously only insofar as it causes Bob to give up the road and go back home. (Even then, her corpse becomes the pretext of a comic scene where Bob has to sneak her body past a group of policemen.) In one small town during their "crossroading" jaunt, Nadine botches a robbery, so they leave her behind in the motel for the next job. Indicative of the film's confined and diluted mobility, Rick and Diane drive around in circles in the parking lot of a hospital, crashing into parked cars; when everyone comes out, Bob slips in and steals some drugs. As it turns out, he has to hide out there all night; Rick and Diane are shown waiting impatiently for him in their parked car (more immobilized mobility). When they all end up back at the motel the next morning, they discover that Nadine is dead from overdose. While Rick and Diane gaze at Nadine's corpse, Bob comes through the front door spouting the ironic line "Honey, I'm home!" But the irony Bob intends is also nonironic; for when he discovers the body, he has to become Father Knows Best and figure out what to do. In his confusion and anger, he refers to Nadine as a "TV baby." Then the film initiates its crucial antiroad movie turn, where he proclaims to Diane that he is tired of life on the road.

Thus, Bob abandons his "family" so he can return home. Other circumstances at this narrative juncture combine to heighten this conformist shift in gears. First of all, let us note that the narrative trivializes Nadine's death by "using" it to motivate Bob's return home. This becomes underlined in the ensuing comic scenes where first Bob tries to hide her body, then has to furtively transport it out of the motel, which happens to be hosting a sheriffs' convention. Surrounded by the law, Bob makes a "deal with God" that if he can get out of this situation, he will go straight. Then, further driving Bob homeward bound, the police become another sign for him to read. Though he is not high on any drugs, he has visions of handcuffs, a courtroom, the bars of a prison cell, all exaggerated with a sound montage of gavels pounding and prison sentences being declared. After they do manage to sneak the body out, they drive in two cars out to an isolated spot in the forest, where Bob buries Nadine. After completing the deed, he has another reactionary hallucination—again, he is not high on drugs, thus presumably truly "seeing." Staring into his hand, he then looks around him, and sees floating hats in the sky. In a powerful scene that culminates the film's turning point, he emerges from the forest, silently walks past Diane, gets into the other car, and drives away—all shot in one long-take long shot. Here, the visionary serves not rebellion against but reinscription into society. Halfway through the film, renouncing his outlaw couple wife and his "drugstore cowboy" life-style on the road, Bob heads home.

Bob's newfound resignation from the road is first suggested by the bus rides he takes back to Portland. The film's second journey montage implies that Bob has become like the drugs of the "crossroading" sequences: an object (not subject) of transport. As a series of aerial shots and point of view shots out the rainy windshield portray his arrival in Portland, "For All We Know" plays on the soundtrack. While poignantly conveying the uncertainty of life's journey, this song is a pop standard that connotes mainstream sentimentalized romance (the antithesis of "Born to Be Wild"). Thus, it seems an appropriate commentary on his renunciation of rebellious mobility in favor of settling down. The road montage of busses on highways transforms into a city montage of streetlights and sidewalks, as Bob checks into the St. Francis Hotel.

A rather conspicuous sound bridge introduces us to Bob's new world of stability. As we observe the final shots of the city montage, we hear Bob answering tiresome questions at his interview for acceptance into a detox clinic. When we cut to the scene, the mise en scène prepares us for the fact that the receptionist/counselor is black. This seems a peculiar (but revealing) coding of stability, conflating oppressive bureaucracy with racial difference. The camera slowly dollies down from a picture of Martin Luther King Jr. on the wall to the woman, establishing a connotation for this bureaucratic hassle in terms of black political protest. Literally separating Bob from her, the editing then shifts into more typical shot/reverse shot as they continue conversing. In this way, the film groups black activism, social programs, and institutional bureaucracy together, with Bob (for the moment) on the "other side" of such "regularity." The point of the scene seems to emphasize (and empathize with) Bob getting buried by red tape. Yet it also touches upon Bob's self-centered immaturity about answering those very questions. This contradiction is resolved dramatically with Bob lecturing her about "his kind of people" and how she does not see them or know them. Though exposing his juvenile, uncooperative attitude, overall the scene exalts his rebellious posture, critical of the bureaucracy that she is made to represent. In yet another way the film betrays its conservative makeup by associating African American political struggle with stagnating, oppressive bureaucracy. As we have seen, road movies such as *Vanishing Point, Easy Rider,* and *Bonnie and Clyde* often use blacks as parallel but tokenized social outcasts. Like *Drug-*

4.4. Bob (Matt Dillon) comes home from a life of drugs on the road to rehabilitate himself, hanging out with Father Tom (Beat guru William S. Burroughs).

store Cowboy's "social program" woman, they understand, want to help, have "suffered." But the genre rarely permits them to drive.

Beyond this problematic portrayal of racial difference, and further elucidating this road movie's postmodern turn toward stability and conformity is the character—or, rather, the actor who plays the character—of Father Tom Murphy, portrayed by William S. Burroughs. The legendary beatnik/punk author brazenly plays himself, revealed not only in the unlikely persona of a priest as lifelong drug addict, but also in his acting style, with eyes glancing distractedly around (perhaps at the film crew, or dialogue cues). Additionally, his dialogue lines are made up primarily of contrived, aphoristic comments on drugs and culture—lifted most likely from his books. More self-conscious and playful than *Two Lane Blacktop*'s rock stars, this cameo brings a tongue-in-cheek tone to an already ironic film. Perhaps most significant in terms of the postmodern road movie—and most ironic—is the allusion embodied by Burroughs to the Beat culture so formative to the emergence of the genre. As mobility has been arrested by a conservative, domestic urge, one of the Kings of the Beat Road appears as a caricature of himself, an aging resident of the hotel, who takes Bob on walks. His very presence, combined with his ironic role as priest, winks at the camera.

Despite the bohemian drug-guru "star" presence of Burroughs, and in conjunction with its heavy-handed irony and stylistic self-consciousness, this road movie has become an anti–road movie. Bob gets a job working in a factory, starts drinking tea, goes to "rap" sessions with other addicts, reads books in his new place of residence. He has become a "regular guy," as he puts it. Then Gentry comes to visit him. Though the cop waits intrusively inside Bob's apartment, unexpected and uninvited, Bob warms up to him quickly, revealed through the camera blocking. At first they are on opposite sides of the room, their past antagonism defining their space; but midway through the conversation, Bob moves closer to him and sits next to him. Their conversation too starts as contesting jabs, but quickly becomes a sincere exchange, with Gentry querying "what happened out there" to make Bob change. As Gentry leaves, they are more or less buddies. Significantly, Gentry will reappear once more in the film, as concerned pal, while Bob is carted away in the ambulance.

Diane, however, does not fare so well as Gentry in the film's perspective, suggesting perhaps that *Drugstore Cowboy* is more of a buddy than an outlaw couple road movie. In fact, she comes to visit Bob soon after Gentry leaves, which implicitly links the two visitors as rivals for Bob's affection. The film's less favorable attitude toward her becomes clear as she gets out of the car: the director uses a rather clichéd close-up of her leather boots landing on the pavement, accompanied by the sounds of alley cats screeching. This shot is then crosscut with a close-up of water boiling in Bob's apartment, emphasizing both that Bob does not know she is coming, and that she represents "hot water" for him, capable of scalding. When she arrives, he informs her that the boredom and routine of the straight life is not so bad. She, on the other hand, reveals that she has betrayed him: she is Rick's "old lady" now. Before departing, she leaves him some drugs—which further demonizes her. As with *Two-Lane Blacktop*'s Girl, Diane proves more road movie–esque than her male counterpart. But more like Holly and Palm, she has to pay for it by being stereotyped: not as passive or hysterical, but as a femme fatale. Let us admit that, in fact, Diane's role in the film is rather minimal: this is *his* story, even though as she leaves his room she embodies the sensual and restless road movie lifestyle. Stuck in a depoliticized, postmodern road movie framework, she is a stepdaughter of Bonnie and Bertha, with much less narrative significance than either.

As it moves toward its conclusion, *Drugstore Cowboy* further articulates an inverted or "immobilized" road movie, since Bob is literally stationary in his new settled and stable life, while people "pass through" to visit him. *They* are mobile, on the road, while Bob stays put (even Gentry the cop patrols the streets). His last visitor, in fact, will prove to be his nemesis. Bob walks down the hall to give the drugs Diane left behind to Father Tom, who gratefully receives them. Meanwhile, David and his buddy, sporting ski masks, have hidden in Bob's room, and mug him when he returns. Like the ironic reversals closing *Stranger than Paradise,* Bob used to bully David, but now the latter has grown into a formidable street punk/gangster. Bob's new conformist lifestyle proves pathetically vulnerable here. Also like the irony of *Stranger than Paradise*'s mistaken identity around a drug deal, they think Bob has drugs—which he did just have and could have given them. But the Game of Life, which appears throughout the genre, here has dealt Bob yet more ironic tough luck. As they beat him to the ground, his voice-over comes in, explaining the "dark forces" he is surrendering to, conceding that you can never really "buck the system." Then David shoots Bob. A caricatured, rather cartoonish old lady in the next room hears the trouble (significantly, while watching television), and calls the police. Aloof and somber in his aged wisdom, Father Tom peers from his apartment window as Bob is brought into the ambulance. Gentry arrives at Bob's mobile bedside, asking Bob who did this to him. Bob mumbles about telling Diane to watch out for "the hat," and that it was the "TV baby" who shot him. Gentry does not comprehend, so Bob says, "Never mind, I'll tell her myself." The lack of communication between cop and outlaw is belied by their union together as the film ends: Gentry has been redeemed from being a rough cop; Bob has been redeemed from being a rambling drug-addict rebel. The mise en scène here figuratively suggests that both have been brought closer together.

As he is carried off to the hospital (the first shot of the film), Bob's voice-over returns, offering some final road movie philosophy that reiterates the genre's themes of rebellion and cultural critique. He explains that life for most people is unpredictable, but that the drug addict's life is ordered by the predictable need for drugs. He reasserts the importance of being able to "read the signs," and the irony of the "chickenshit cops" escorting him to the "fattest pharmacy in town." He hopes they will keep him alive. These thoughts suggest that he may go back to drugs, that perhaps he has rediscovered his (and the genre's) antiestablishment, visionary impulses. There is also a sense that he will subversively use The System against itself. Moreover, this ending invokes the early-70s road movies, and the genre generally, with a scene of ambiguous mobility, traveling into the unknown. It remains unclear whether Bob will go back to drugs or not, and whether he will live or die.

But these intimations of rebellion come too little, too late. The very end of the film, the coda during the credits, returns to hopeful affirmation and lukewarm irony with more home-movie sequences, where the family is resurrected as MTV-esque celebration. This renders unconvincing Bob's ambulance-ride invocation of the rebel road movie, especially given the numerous conservative turns throughout the film. The song playing during these closing home movies, "The Israelites," contains the line "I don't want to end up like Bonnie and Clyde." No, this road movie certainly does not end up like *Bonnie and Clyde*. As the credits appear, we again are treated to the family of four "acting" as "stars," bopping and posing for the camera. Thus, in a sense, the "family" of the film's first part, broken up midway, is resurrected as nostalgic memory for narrative closure. In sum, this home-movie ending reiterates the film's themes of home, family, and celebration in terms of image and ironic posing. It therefore serves to neutralize the narrative's previous open-ended ending, providing a reassuring destination for the journey of the narrative. This in turn reasserts *Drugstore Cowboy*'s conservative route, coded as postmodern independent, where mobility, rebellion, and cultural critique take a backseat.

More Family Values:
Raising Arizona and *Wild at Heart*

Before turning to David Lynch's *Wild at Heart,* the road movie that culminates the postmodern trends of the 1980s and spearheads them into the 1990s, let us consider briefly a film by the Coen brothers from a few years earlier, *Raising Arizona* (1987). This semi–road movie serves especially well as preface to the Lynch film, largely because the films share so many qualities. Taken together, they vibrantly sum up the postmodern road movie. Often mentioned in the same film history textbook breath, the Coen brothers and David Lynch best represent the more general (i.e., non–road movie specific) postmodern independent film sensibility of the 1980s. Characterized by a quirky, offbeat tone and self-conscious, often dazzling stylistics, their films tend to revise Hollywood genres with plenty of hip irony. Much as it helped define the New American cinema of the late 60s, the road movie participates crucially in creating 1980s independent film. Along with Jonathan Demme, Jarmusch, and Van Sant, Lynch and the Coens turn to the genre.[17]

Raising Arizona is of interest because it illustrates certain tonal qualities that vividly describe the postmodern version of the genre. The film features an outlaw couple, H. I. (i.e., HI; Nicholas Cage) and Edwina (Holly Hunter); it also has quite a bit of driving in it. But this "outlaw" couple want to start a family rather than hit the road and rob banks; likewise, the driving in the film, conveyed through some amazing moving camera shots, mostly takes place within a suburban neighborhood near Tempe, Arizona. These two general aspects of *Raising Arizona* crystallize the way the road movie has become circumscribed, literally and figuratively, by its conservative subtext. The latter, in fact, is no longer subtextual but overtly textual (thus, to my mind, more ideologically forceful).

Accompanying this more blatantly conservative framework is a sarcastic tone and ironic presentation. As *Raising Arizona* no doubt illustrates, such irony has plenty of subversive edge toward, for example, the family. But this ironic, subversive edge always runs the risk of being (mis)read as literal rather than ironic. The postmodern irony of *Raising Arizona* relegates road movie rebellion to the subtextual realm, while textually foregrounding conformity. Such ironic humor, let us note, links the postmodern indie road movie with the Hollywood road movie comedies. Both forms restage the genre's rebellion and cultural critique as a posture to be smirked at.

And *Raising Arizona*'s irony is quite heavy-handed. It seems to be ridiculing the small-town, hick, "white trash" personas of its two stars (though all other characters are equally ridiculed, exemplifying the film's across-the-board mockery). Like *Drugstore Cowboy*'s Bob, HI is the compulsive small-time thief who narrates the film. As the film begins, he is being photographed for a mug shot in the police station; Ed (short for Edwina) is the cop taking his picture. HI seduces her on his second visit, where she is crying because her fiancé has left her. Vulnerable and hysterical, she absurdly falls for his absurd proposal of marriage. Perhaps ironic, it is nevertheless revealing of the film's conformist twist that this outlaw couple meet in a police station, and that one of them is a cop. This seems a bizarre, postmodern revision of the cop-outlaw camaraderie begun in *The Sugarland Express*.

In fact, Speilberg's family focus in that film is also the main attraction in *Raising Arizona*. After they get married, they acquire a "starter home" (a mobile home out in the desert) and want to start a family, but Ed cannot have children. Unlike their outlaw couple predecessors (save, significantly, Lou Jean and Clovis of *The Sugarland Express*), HI and Ed are driven to crime because they *want* a family and a stable home environment. *Drugstore Cowboy*'s Bob chose the life of a "regular guy" halfway through the film's journey; HI and Ed choose it at the outset. No doubt, the film mocks such stability; HI comments in his voice-over that his job was "just like prison." Yet the film equally betrays a tongue-in-cheek affection for such stability. Desperate — for their family stability—HI and Ed decide to steal a baby from local furniture retailer Nathan Arizona, whose wife just had quintuplets. "Raising Arizona" turns out to refer, not to the desert landscape, but to the stolen baby.

FOR OFFICIAL USE ONLY

4.5. *Raising Arizona*'s ironic revision of the road movie: half the outlaw couple is a cop (Holly Hunter).

That night, HI has a dream that further distills this road movie's post-modern generic revision. He has a "vision" of the "Lone Rider of the Apocalypse," a demonic biker who seems an over-the-top pastiche of the Road Warrior by way of the Hell's Angels. The Lone Rider, the film's most road movie–esque figure, is also the film's Other: a macabre mercenary, a hilarious and hysterical caricature. Additionally, this vision becomes an omen of the future, for the Lone Rider does truly exist in the film's narrative, as Leonard Smalls (Randall "Tex" Cobbs), who is tracking down the stolen baby for the reward.

Raising Arizona's dazzling, manic driving sequences begin when HI decides impulsively one night to hold up a convenience store for some Huggies, while Ed and baby wait in the car. As the sirens come, and Ed realizes what HI has done in the store, she peels away in a rage, abandoning him. A crazy car chase ensues, full of cartoonish coincidences, where excessive acts of violence are answered with outlandish rebound, where people get smashed and shot and appear out of nowhere (e.g., the convenience store clerk suddenly in the middle of the street aiming a rifle at the oncoming car). In a send-up of the Keystone Cops, the police chase HI through the neighborhood and a supermarket, a satirical slapstick romp replete with grotesque housewives in curlers and wild killer guard dogs. Eventually, miraculously, Ed's speeding car finds HI: she picks him up, and he scoops the Huggies up off the street as she peels away from the camera. The ironic coincidence of *Stranger than Paradise* becomes ludic fantasy in *Raising Arizona*: slapstick histrionics prevail, hilariously safe because they are so obviously unreal, trivializing any subversive bite the film's irony may possess.

Ensuing driving sequences continue in this direction. Uncertain about whether he is cut out for family life, HI leaves a good-bye letter for Ed, planning to accompany Gale (John Goodman) and Evelle (Will Forsyth) on a bank heist. Meanwhile, Gale and Evelle learn the details of the reward for the baby, and kidnap the kid, taking him instead of HI on the bank heist. At one point in the car, Gale utters a road movie maxim, "I love driving." But he is admiring the baby, not the road. The road movie gets further infantilized when they have to stop for diapers, and accidentally leave the baby behind. In another example of the film's cartoonish mode, the baby supposedly fell off the hood as they drove away, but landed upright on the pavement, just fine. Then the film's juvenile cartoonism kicks into higher gear, when Gale and Evelle realize as they drive down the open highway what has happened: in a frontal two-shot through the windshield, they scream like cartoon characters. They screech to a halt, make an about-face on the open road, and go back for baby, who is revealed in low-angle close-up waiting placidly alone on the highway. This image—of baby on blacktop—occurs several times in this part of the film, and seems an apt visual metaphor for the road movie's infantilized and comic-book treatment in the late 1980s.

While they make their bumbling getaway, Ed (donning her police uniform) and HI are also ripping down the highway, trying to get "their" baby back. An explosion causes Gale and Evelle to crash just as HI and Ed approach. But the Lone Rider too is approaching fast, inaugurating the film's open-highway climax. He scoops up the baby (who again has landed upright and pristine on the pavement), destroys HI and Ed's car, then does extensive battle with HI, beating him almost to death. But HI has managed to pull out the rings of the grenades attached to Smalls's jacket. His exploding body graphically symbolizes the film's cartoonism: a sick joke.

Raising Arizona then initiates what may be the happiest of road movie endings thus far in the genre's history. HI and Ed return baby to the Arizona family. Nathan Arizona catches them in the act, and they confess their crime. He does not turn them in, however, but instead encourages them to work out their marital problems. After this scene where both families, in a sense, restore each other, the film ends on another dream "vision" of HI's. Consider this montage of things to come: Gale and Evelle return of their

4.6. The road movie gets cute: baby on blacktop in the cartoonish *Raising Arizona*.

own accord to prison; Nathan Jr. gets a mysterious present at the Arizonas' Christmas; Nathan Jr. becomes a high school football star (HI's wish-come-true). Finally, the dream converges with the film itself, with HI and Ed as grandparents of a large family, presiding at the head of a long dinner table, in a land not too far away, "maybe Utah." HI does not know who the family is, nor how he and Ed could have a family. This codes the family as generic, a fantasy family. That is, his "vision" is a sublimated version of his (utterly conventional) desire, a "wish fulfillment" that here reflexively invokes the cultural institution of the Hollywood "dream factory" itself.

With aloof and condescending irony the film mocks conservative America—but makes fun of its own mockery. Not unlike *Drugstore Cowboy*'s road movie that quits halfway and returns home, *Raising Arizona* illustrates a kind of rebellion against rebellion. Early in the film, HI in voice-over expresses suspicion about what a "good guy" President Reagan is supposed to be. But Reagan's America is celebrated more than critiqued by *Raising Arizona*. All crimes are redeemed; the baby is returned to its real family; the film's conclusion renounces the outlaw lifestyle through an embrace of the American Dream—as a literal dream of the American family.

David Lynch's *Wild at Heart* (1990) travels much more furiously than *Raising Arizona* in its postmodern irony. Given its huge commercial and critical success, the film seems a road movie watershed, cutting loose the popular 1990s road movie trend of ever more graphic high-tech spectacles of violence (e.g., *Natural Born Killers* and *Kalifornia* discussed below, as well as *The Doom Generation, True Romance, Freeway,* and *Crash*). More significantly, *Wild at Heart*'s darkly comic tone and surrealistic histrionics displace any social or political grounding; its outlaw couple has not the slightest interest in rebellion, preferring to settle down and start a family. Likewise, they *pose* as rebels throughout, with the acting and cinematography baldly exaggerating such posing.[18] By not being interested in rebellion, and by pretending to be rebels, the film's outlaw couple carry out a viciously sardonic mockery of the genre (a mockery, let us note, that dovetails with the conservative values prevalent in 1980s America).

The style of *Wild at Heart* seems the epitome of cinematic postmodernism: flashy, bizarre camera techniques; a recycling and blending of genres; extreme self-consciousness and posturing; an ironic condescension toward the suburban culture of Middle America (or, in this case, the South). Yet just beneath the surface of the film's hip veneer, one discovers a depoliticized, neoconservative view of the road, and of the world. Aside from the film's notorious racism and sexism,[19] any trace of modernist rebellion has been collapsed and flattened out into an oddly sensationalized celebration of the traditional white patriarchal family. This is in fact what Sailor (Nicholas Cage) and Lulu (Laura Dern) aspire to. Compared to many road movies of the mid-1980s, *Wild at Heart* reignites the genre with wild energy and enthusiasm. But it also exaggerates violent road movie rebellion to an almost ridiculous degree—unabashedly recontextualizing it through excessive special effects and sadistic humor. More to the point, such "special effects" offer the spectator "an uneasily and unevenly infantile point of view" that, according to Sharon Willis, invites us "to protect ourselves from history and politics by imagining that everything comes down to a private psychosexual adventure" ("Special Effects," 279). *Wild at Heart* therefore culminates the juvenile irony and depoliticized cartoonism that began with *The Sugarland Express* and that continued to swell through *Lost in America, Drugstore Cowboy,* and *Raising Arizona.*

Before turning to some of the specifics of the film, let us first establish its narrative framework by noting its similarities to *Raising Arizona.* Regarding plot and character, Nicholas Cage's persona and performance are strikingly similar: the rebellious, dashing criminal who lives on the edge, acted by Cage over-the-top. With deadpan delivery of highly artificial lines, Cage is ironically distanced from his character, throughout striking poses that cite Presley and Dean. In both films, the male lead is in and out of prison, while the female lead waits dutifully. Moreover, in both cases the outlaw couple's desire to start a family is playfully mocked yet fulfilled. With respect to tone, both films poke fun at southern culture: HI and Ed have conspicuously extreme southern accents; Sailor and Lulu are southern, *Wild at Heart* taking place mostly in New Orleans and Texas, reinventing gothic southern stereotypes throughout. While *Raising Arizona* features a parody of *The Road Warrior,* *Wild at Heart* cleverly creates a running patchwork of parodic allusions to *The Wizard of Oz.*[20] Both films use cartoonish, over-the-top screaming. *Wild at Heart* answers *Raising Arizona*'s allusions to *Bonnie and Clyde* with its own—Lulu's father's name is Clyde. Both films use the image of fire in close-up as symbolic motif.

This image, in fact, becomes *Wild at Heart*'s notorious signature. A micro-close-up of a match striking into flame opens the film, a compelling visual suggestion of the rebellion of the outlaw couple. The first title too invokes the road movie: "Somewhere between the border of North and South Carolina." The introductory narrative sequence shows Sailor "defending himself" at a dance: actually, the threat of knife-bearing Bobby Ray Lemon (Gregg Dandridge) is obviously a pretext for the horrific scene of Sailor beating him to death.[21] He goes to prison for this, but the story skips to the end of his term, where Lulu picks up Sailor in her car as he is waiting nonchalantly outside the prison. They want to start a family together, but Lulu's mother Marietta (Diane Ladd) despises Sailor because he had rejected her sexual advances (at the dance in the opening sequence, we learn later). Additionally, she suspects that Sailor witnessed the murder of her husband Clyde, which she orchestrated. Thus, she is desperately intent on keeping Sailor and Lulu apart, setting gangsters after them to murder Sailor. But our outlaw couple is just as desperately determined to be together, so they hit the road.

Their first motel scene initiates the film's ridiculing revisions of the genre's visionary theme. Recalling *Drugstore Cowboy* and *Raising Arizona,* Lulu reveals her "vision" as mock apocalyptic (the sun will burn a hole through the earth), while Sailor's is pseudoprofound (Buicks will drive to the moon): surely we are meant to laugh at both of them here. Sailor suggests they drive out to California, even though he will be violating his parole. Though this renders him a kind of lukewarm outlaw, their primary desire and impetus is to start a family, a "normal" life away from their pasts and her family. This brings us to one terribly significant aspect of *Wild at Heart*'s conservative revision of the road movie: namely, that Sailor and Lulu are running *from* the gangsters (though he is initially coded as a criminal). To achieve their dream of happiness (stability and conformity), they must escape the hit men Marietta has set on them. Like other postmodern road movies, the driver is trying to *get back to* mainstream society, not away from or beyond it. Exaggerating the classical underpinnings and conservative ideological subtext of the road movie discussed previously, this shift in emphasis severely sanitizes any politically rebellious point of view.

But before following our outlaw couple on their journey out West, we should note another aspect of *Wild at Heart* inaugurated in this first motel scene: what I would label their mock pop-therapy confessions. Employing a complex, haunting flashback structure organized around the match-striking visual motif, both their childhoods become confessed/represented as sexually abusive and traumatic, especially Lulu's. These Remembrances of Crimes Past recur throughout the film, and instructively distinguish it as a truly revisionist, conservative road movie. First of all, such confessed memories—coded always as spectacularly traumatic and lurid—function to "ground" or delay their journey forward and away from Marietta's mobsters. Through the narrative setup of their intimate and ritualized postsex conversations, the film delves lasciviously into their memories during extended scenes of nonmovement, which "weighs down" their mobility. This links *Wild at Heart* with other road movies previously discussed in this chapter, where because of various strategies the genre's journey narrative gets diluted, restricted, circumscribed, and minimized.

In other words, though ostensibly Sailor and Lulu are on the road running from Marietta's mobsters, the film makes it clear that they equally are running from their pasts. Unlike *Detour,* where the past constitutes the body of the narrative in typical noir fashion; and unlike the existential psychological emphasis of the 1970s road movies, *Wild at Heart* seems distinctly 1980s in its lavish ridicule *and* celebration of our culture's apparent obsession with televised public confession (that is, psychotherapy gone mass media). In the postmodern context, to ridicule and to celebrate are reversible and interchangeable, as illustrated by both *Wild at Heart* and numerous popular tabloid TV talk shows. *Wild at Heart*'s fascination with their lurid psychosexual anecdotes displaces the genre's core of cultural critique: no radical Freudianism connecting the personal and the political here. It also trivializes these anecdotes into a surreal freak-show spectacle, a pretext for Lynch's trademark excessive, sometimes sadistic formalism. Such sensationalizing of traumatic and dysfunctional childhood, interwoven with playful allusions to Elvis Presley and *The Wizard of Oz,* renders this road movie a lateral offshoot of the early-1980s Lucas-Spielberg blockbusters—that is, an amusement park ride road movie that infantilizes the audience and that both mocks and exploits sexual abuse.

As they drive, first into New Orleans, then through Texas, the film's style of presentation continues in its highly contrived and excessive mockery. Not really taking itself seriously, the film teasingly (under)mines its own representational mode. The windshield wipers cut the rain while the car top is down. As they cross a state line, he corrects her: he is not a "murderer" but a "manslaughterer." Mimicking countless starlets, Lulu says, "You ain't let me down yet," to which he responds, "You please me too, peanut." Bred on the all-pervasive postwar consumer culture of images, they pose and sing while listening to music on the car radio, as if onstage (recalling *Drugstore Cowboy*'s home-movie sequences). The film's abrasive foregrounding of performance forms a crucial component of its excessive artificiality: Sailor's "performances" are as baldly phony, forced, and unconvincing as Cage's. Such Brechtian tactics, however, serve no political critique. Not surprisingly—for the road movie generally, but for this neoconservative one especially—Lulu's "performance" is simply to display her body: she stands in her seat as they head into New Orleans.[22]

Meanwhile, this driving sequence is crosscut with Marietta at home mobilizing her devilish scheme. First, she assigns her boyfriend Johnny Farragut (Harry Dean Stanton) to get Lulu away from Sailor in New Orleans (we see

Johnny driving at night). Then she asks her other boyfriend/gangster Marcello Santos (J. E. Freeman) also to help; we learn he has put into motion a hit on both Johnny (his rival for Marietta) and Sailor. This crosscutting can be contrasted with that of *Vanishing Point,* which through radio commentary invokes black political struggle as parallel to Kowalski's manic journey. In *Wild at Heart,* the crosscutting is more bound to the conventions of suspense typical of a crime/thriller film. Additionally, Marietta's obsession with stopping the outlaw couple and killing Sailor is conveyed through the trope of "home," since in these initial scenes of planning (and throughout most of the film), she is coded through costume and acting as an extension of her decadent, grotesquely ornate domestic environment. The latter proves a compelling and ironic contrast with Sailor and Lulu's road trip, since they are trying to get to their own home, yet are haunted by memories of their past home lives.

Part of the exciting tension around *Wild at Heart's* portrayal of Sailor and Lulu is that they connote very little of the conventional homeyness they nevertheless aspire to (and travel toward). Indeed, one feature of the road movie *Wild at Heart* dynamically develops from *Bonnie and Clyde* (more than most road movies since then) is the theme of sensuality and sexuality. Their hot, kinky sex scenes, explicitly presented, seem a direct effect of being on the road and on the run. After Sailor comments that she is "hotter than Georgia asphalt," one scene begins with a close-up, high-speed shot of asphalt whizzing by, then dissolves into a close-up of their bodies in rocking motion. After they leave New Orleans, another scene suggests Lulu's feverish sensuality as fuel for their flight. At a gas station, while Sailor fills the tank, the old black attendant rocks in his chair, smiling at her, admiring her.[23] Their sensual fury is then vividly expressed in a scene where she is behind the wheel on the highway. On the radio, all she can get are news reports of violence. She pulls over and screams hysterically and histrionically that she wants some music, and that the world is going to shit. Manly Man that he is, Sailor finds some music, which not surprisingly is heavy metal. As the music blasts from the car, they jump out and thrash-dance violently, kung fu style, on the desert shoulder. The camera cuts to a high-angle extreme long shot, then tilts up to frame the sun setting in a golden fury on the horizon above them. To my mind, the scene exemplifies the film's irreverent immersion in contradiction (à la *Repo Man*). The scene portrays uncritically how they partake of what she just previously could not take (violence). Celebrating their hypocrisy as appropriate antidote to social decay, the film embraces their mindless, eroticized embrace of what she despises.

Their drive continues into the night, where one of the film's more compelling takes on the genre occurs. Sailor finally "confesses" his past connection with her father Clyde's death: that he was there outside the house as it burned, working as a driver for Santos. A flashback presents the fiery memory. The image of the burning house with Father Clyde inside recalls the gothic domestic inferno of *Badlands*. But here, Sailor is passive witness; not even that, since he did not see what everyone thinks he saw. His "vision" is empty, or ignorant; he is innocent of the "crime" Marietta accuses him of. In any case, distraught over this revelation, Lulu glances up into the passing night sky, and has her own "vision": the Wicked Witch of the East flying alongside them. We should note that this vision is an "already received," or recycled, image from an old Hollywood movie. Likewise, the film's discourse does not clarify whether it is an internal or external vision, since it is shot as "really there" (indicative of Lynch as a contemporary surrealist). Both qualities—pastiche, and the blurring of boundaries between real and imaginary—are symptomatic of postmodern style, deployed here to poke fun at a more typically modernist moment of visionary inspiration. Upset by the bad news that led to her bad vision, she concedes, "We're out in the middle of it." This in turn leads them to a bad accident. They come upon a car wreck (one staged in a way reminiscent of the car crashes of Godard's *Contempt* and *Weekend*), where bloody bodies and overturned cars are spread on the highway shoulder in a conspicuously contrived arrangement, under artificial, glowing lights. Similarly, the girl they discover stumbling and mumbling wears fake blood. She dies an over-the-top mock-Hollywood death in front of them. Very much like Bob in *Drugstore Cowboy*, Lulu "sees" this stagy roadside attraction as an omen.[24]

And very much like the signs Bob reads, Lulu's omen does prove accurate, prefiguring a yet more surrealistic nightmare. The next day they pull into Big Tuna, Texas. She claims to be carsick, but we soon learn she is nauseous due to being pregnant. (The specter of *Raising Arizona*'s infant on the road rears itself.) Actually, Sailor has an ulterior motive in stopping in Big Tuna: to check with a former "acquaintance" from the Santos gang, Perdita (Isabella Rossellini), on whether there is a contract out on him. Yet while there, Sailor and Lulu meet up with a bizarre array of losers and weirdos: obese women making a porn film; a rocket scientist (perhaps alluding to *Repo Man*) with his own "dog story" (perhaps alluding to *Drugstore Cowboy*); a Vietnam vet sporting a Confederate flag; and most importantly, Bobby Peru (Willem Dafoe), another vet who is "from all over." He becomes a most ominous threat, seducing Lulu (without Sailor knowing), then luring Sailor into robbing a bank. Again recalling *Raising Arizona*, Peru's lure preys on Sailor's need to be able to provide for his pregnant wife and start a family.

In fact, Peru turns out to be the hit man hired by Santos, and the robbery is a setup for Sailor's death. The next morning, with Perdita suspiciously behind the wheel, the three drive together to do the job. A cop unexpectedly pulls up as she is waiting outside; when she flees the scene, the cop ends up killing Peru. Sailor gets captured, headed back to prison.

As the title informs us, the story skips ahead "Five years, ten months and 221 days later" to Sailor's second release from prison (a repetition of the opening "in and out of prison" sequence, and a framing device for the narrative as a whole). Despite Marietta's continued insistence that she stay away from him, Lulu drives with their son, now six years old, to meet him. On the way, she almost crashes twice, expressing her reckless, passionate abandon through driving, but also suggestive of the genre's sputtering engine. Another connotation here is her awkwardness as a (female) driver, which links with her tantrum earlier about the car radio. Sailor waits nonchalantly and unfazed near some railroad tracks. As in most previous road movies, such an ending scene suggests narrative closure as a new road with unknown destination.

But *Wild at Heart* undermines this suggestion with the arrival of wife and son; together the three drive on, all in the front seat. The film's final destination of family reunion encounters one last obstacle, as Sailor feels something is not right. Despite Lulu's screeching protest, he gets out of the car and walks down a conspicuously empty street, shot from an extreme long, high angle. Then the film's campy, hysterically artificial histrionics converge. On the one hand, a contrived group of nonwhite male thugs surround him; on the other hand, *The Wizard of Oz*'s Good Witch "appears" to Sailor (and to us the audience) after he has been punched in the nose and knocked to the ground. She advises him: "Fight for your dreams" and "Don't turn away from love," sending him back to Lulu. Of course, this ending recollects (restages) the dream-happy ending of *Raising Arizona*. Both endings import the surrealist strategy of not distinguishing between the dreamworld and the real world (or, put differently, the strategy of making dreams real). As *Raising Arizona* closes while still inside the dream (thus implicating it as "real" on some level), so too does *Wild at Heart* legitimize Sailor's dream-vision of the Good Witch by presenting it as something that really happens. Both films trivialize and ridicule the road movie's visionary impulse by "realizing" it in a context of cartoonish (sur)realism.

But the subversive surrealist would be appalled at the "message" such surrealistic tactics serve. *Wild at Heart*'s mock fantasy of happiness lacks any critical or subversive edge. As Sailor runs back to her, stomping over the deadlocked cars in a sudden traffic jam, the road movie too takes a beat-

4.7. Sailor (Nicholas Cage) stomps across cars to get back to his family, at the end of the road in *Wild at Heart*.

ing, at least in terms of its modernist rebellious origins: this is all postmodern pastiche, tongue-in-cheek sarcasm, a live-action cartoon. Significantly, in the film's final shot, the car (and all it means for the road movie: mobility, rebellion, exploration) is immobilized. Then it "disappears" as the camera shifts to low angle, transforming the car into a "stage," as the outlaw couple stand on the hood for his "performance" (lip-synching) of the song he said he would sing to his wife, "Love Me Tender." [25]

One may argue that *Wild at Heart* does not take its ending seriously. Perhaps its excessive sentimentality is mocking an already melodramatically contrived Hollywood cliché (the happy ending, the union of the romantic couple). [26] Yet I feel the film embraces the very silliness of the fantasy it makes fun of, thus on some level asserting its validity. Put differently, *Wild at Heart* may treat traditional family life with some irony, but this is offset by the fact that Lulu and Sailor *do succeed* in their aspiration. Though *Wild at Heart* is a grotesque road spectacle, it does not end with punishment, apocalypse, tragedy or even an open-road open-ending. It therefore sidesteps the cynical ambivalence with which most previous road movies since the sixties close. Rather, it ends with joyful if trivialized reconciliation: the triumph of the family. *Wild at Heart* effectively dilutes road movie rebellion by decontextualizing and glorifying its signifiers (young rebel lovers on the run) while betraying its signified (rebellion against the dominant cultural values of home and family).

THE LEARNING CENTRE
TOWER HAMLETS COLLEGE
POPLAR CENTRE
POPLAR HIGH STREET
LONDON E14 0AF

Delusion
Thelma and Louise
Natural Born Killers
My Own Private Idaho

The Living End
Get on the Bus
Smoke Signals
The Straight Story

Chapter 5 . . . .

REBUILDING THE ENGINE
The 1990s Multicultural Road Movie

The Road Movie and the Information Highway

Into the 1990s, the road movie gathers considerable momentum, putting more miles on the cinematic highway than ever before—in a plethora of directions, through a diverse array of landscapes, with a multiplicity of multicultural drivers. It is perhaps no accident that this road movie boom coincides with the economic boom of the Clinton era, especially considering the administration's enthusiastic discourse about "crossing into" the next millennium, "bridging" the twenty-first century. According to Clintonian rhetoric, and most economic analysts, the primary "engine" for the economic prosperity of the 1990s was computer technology.

Popular cultural discourse in turn describes the booming computer economy through traveling and highway imagery, to convey its utopian potentialities. The most prominent example, of course, is the Internet, popularly known as the "information highway." Beyond the road connotations of Web browsers named "Explorer" and "Netscape," ads for websites clearly exploit the tension between the virtual road and real roads. A Microsoft television ad campaign beckons with the question "Where do you want to go today?" One website encourages you to "take a trip to the drugstore, without taking the trip." Cameraworld.com ironically proclaims, "Worth the Drive." Travelocity.com more brazenly offers the following: "Road Trip." Monstrous billboards for Apple computers show the standard iMacs "driving," with the message "Internet Expressway."

Other new electronic technologies play on road imagery. An ad for GTE cell phones reads, "No Roaming: No More Long Distance Charges." The ad's glorious "wide-screen" color photograph looks down an open highway through the desert, the horizon off in the distance: an image of deliciously empty space, a staple road movie image. Such an image inscribes our desire to "hit the road." The ad calls forth an idealized image of the road—only to supersede such an image with its own more utopian message: "no roaming, no more long distance . . ." The peculiar and telling irony here is that the advent of electronic technologies like cell phones and the Internet renders roaming and long distances less desirable, less necessary—thus more obsolete. An imaginary, mythical evolution is established between the real road and the virtual road—as though the road disappearing into the horizon line has always been leading to a certain "disappearance" of the highway itself.

In this respect, let us take note of Netscape's home page of July 20, 2001, which celebrates the 75th birthday of Route 66 with the following link: "Kitsch Superhighway: Take a ride along Route 66, the classic American 'Mother Road.'" While this link sells itself as "the ultimate road trip planner," it also invites viewers to browse the "photo gallery"; other links include "quirky landmarks," "more road trips," "lost in America" (an article on drive-ins still in operation), and "The National Historic Route 66 Federation." Perhaps some visitors to this website plan and actually take a Route 66 road trip. But most no doubt just "cruise" the website itself. In any case, we can appreciate the rather un-Kerouacean implications of how the Internet further extends the tourist industry's packaging of road travel, in many ways absorbing and recycling road travel as a virtual activity.

Droves of Drivers: The Road Movie Boom

Perhaps an alibi for gradually displacing real road travel, American commercial culture clings to the highway by resurrecting it as image and metaphor. The 1990s road movie fever can be partially understood as a response to the encroaching phenomenon of the virtual highway.[1] The genre continues to drive primarily down the two main narrative highways of the late 1980s: the postmodern independent road movie (the focus of the previous chapter), and the Hollywood comedy road movie. Yet in the 1990s we also witness a refreshing reinvention of the visionary, politically rebellious spirit of *Bonnie and Clyde* and *Easy Rider*. Mostly within the postmodern independent context, though at times through the Hollywood mode, the genre's repoliticized, reinvigorated cultural critique in the 1990s usually derives from new drivers—notably gays, people of color, and women. The 1990s road movie therefore comes back to itself, in a sense, to embrace its original, countercultural purpose. Many 1990s road movies seem fueled by a mission to return to society's fringes and borders, to travel transgressively, challenging conservative mainstream culture. While these repoliticized road movies shall form the central focus of this chapter, we should first acknowledge how more conventional road movies prevail at this time as well.

Certainly the postmodern independent road movie discussed in the preceding chapter continues to broaden its approach and appeal. Recalling that "independent" usually designates a type of *Hollywood* film in the 1980s and 1990s,[2] most of these road movies rely on postmodern stylistics and sensibility, informed by varying degrees of irony and reflexivity. Ranging in tone and style from garish, tongue-in-cheek cartoonism to a more grim, irreverent realism, these road movies offer various versions of outlaw ultraviolence. Taking *Wild at Heart* as a prototype, such 1990s outlaw road movies include *Guncrazy* (1992), *Kalifornia* (1993), *Natural Born Killers* (1994), *Love and a .45* (1994), *Freeway* (1995), *From Dusk to Dawn* (1995), *The Doom Generation* (1995), *Lewis and Clark and George* (1996), *Niagara, Niagara* (1998), *Outside Ozona* (1998), and *Another Day in Paradise* (1999). Oliver Stone's *Natural Born Killers*, a watershed of this road movie strain, will be discussed in more detail below.[3]

For the moment, let us note *Kalifornia*, which sanitizes the outlaw couple, not through family values or excessive cartoonism, but through shallow postmodern reflexivity (Atkinson, 17). Specifically, *Kalifornia* "doubles" its outlaw couple, pitting white trash serial killers against middle-class yuppies. Brian (David Duchovny) and Carrie (Michelle Forbes) are hip New Yorkers doing a book on serial killers. At the end of their artistic journey, they reflect upon the road nightmare they have survived while driving with Early (Brad Pitt) and Adele (Juliette Lewis). Like the 1980s postmodern road movies, *Kalifornia* pays much attention to sleek traveling shots, glistening surfaces, formalistic lighting, and the graphic spectacle of excessive violent outbursts. Moreover, the film's nasty use of lower-class serial killers to slap intellectuals in the face becomes a cheap thrill and a cheap shot—revealing a rather Reagan-esque attitude toward both the poor and the artist-intellectual.

The widespread cultural currency of such ultraviolent outlaw couple road movies is further evidenced by the success and popularity of foreign English-language road movies in this vein, such as the Canadian *Highway 61* (1992), the British *Butterfly Kiss* (1994), and the Australian *Kiss or Kill* (1997). Cleverly directed by Bill Bennett, *Kiss or Kill* is exemplary of the 1990s attraction to the violent outlaw couple. Edited almost entirely with jump cuts, the film features grifters Nic (Frances O'Connor) and Al (Matt Day), who come to suspect each other of murdering their roadside hosts. Nic is haunted by childhood traumas; their criminal files are dynamically crosscut with blistering traveling shots on the highway; an Aboriginal seer helps the sleazy, inept police track them down. But the film's real demon is a retired futbol celebrity. At the end, Nic and Al get off and come clean. Like *Kalifornia*'s road couple, they settle down to domestic placidity—he working for a winery, she "hanging out" and painting. Their lingering mutual distrust is hinted at, but mainly as a disturbing joke: she pulls a knife on him in the kitchen, "just kidding."

In addition to the popularity of such hip, trendy, and ultraviolent outlaw couple road movies, the 1990s saw a flock of independent postmodern and Hollywood road movies in the quest vein, deriving more from the existentialist/psychological emphasis of the genre's early-1970s phase. As in *Five Easy Pieces* and *Two-Lane Blacktop,* these films tend to portray the singular male or male buddy pair or group in a wandering, searching narrative framework, with less emphasis on desperate flight from the law. Hollywood furnished several versions of the buddy/quest road movie, including *Breaking the Rules* (1992), *Calendar Girl* (1993), *Dumb and Dumber* (1994), *Good Luck* (1996), *My Fellow Americans* (1996), Terry Gilliam's hallucinogenic version of *Fear and Loathing in Las Vegas* (1998), and *Road Trip* (2000). *Flirting with Disaster* (1995) is another telling example, a screwball road movie with more flirting than disaster. Appearing to be an "outlaw threesome" film, it actually focuses on one man's search for his real parents, so he can name his son and have sex with his wife. As suggested by *Flirting with Disaster,* most of these films code the quest road movie through sentimentalized, heavy-handed melodrama and/or comedy, focusing on the male journey as a means of self-confrontation and revelation. A significant variation on the male buddy road quest in the 1990s features young boys. These films represent a more accessible form of the postmodern cartoonism and juvenile humor discussed in the previous chapter, as in *Beavis and Butthead Do America* (1996) or *Larger than Life* (1996); or a conservative, "family values" emphasis on the regeneration of patriarchy, as in *Josh and S.A.M.* (1993), *A Perfect World* (1993), and *Wild America* (1997).[4]

Despite these conservative tendencies, some powerfully challenging single male quest road movies appear in the 1990s, from distinctly independent directors. *Roadside Prophets* (1992) is a good example, an interesting companion piece to *Lost in America* as a 90s (rather than 80s) revision of *Easy Rider.* Perhaps the first road movie written and directed by a woman (Abbe Wool, assistant director to Alex Cox on *Repo Man* and scriptwriter to his later *Sid and Nancy*), the film also employs *Two-Lane Blacktop*'s road movie–rock star liaison, by featuring Los Angeles punk band X's John Doe as one of the two buddies who embark on a motorcycle road trip to transport the ashes of a fellow biker to Nevada. Along the way they encounter an array of bizarre characters; overall the tone is ironic and aloof, coding revelation on the road as cool ethnographic amusement. Like *Drugstore Cowboy*'s cameo of William Burroughs, *Roadside Prophets* nostalgically references the counterculture with an appearance by Timothy Leary. Other provocative male quest road movies would be Jim Jarmusch's *Dead Man* (1995), Robert Duvall's *The Apostle* (1997), Finn Taylor's *Dream with the Fishes* (1997), and John Sayles's *Men with Guns* (1998).

In the midst of all this road movie traffic, a distinctly revitalized and re-politicized version emerges, where the genre gets driven by drivers previously consigned to the sidelines: women, people of color, gays. As we shall see, when such new/"Other" drivers take alternate routes, the genre's core of rebellion and cultural critique becomes greatly enhanced and expanded. As Katie Mills notes, genre revisionism is key to this phenomenon: "The once-masculinist road story of the lone anarchist on the run is reborn when genre becomes a vehicle for the representation of 'otherness' along the lines of marginalized class, race, sexuality, or gender" (323). While I shall focus primarily on multicultural road movies in the postmodern-independent vein, we should note that the incorporation of the racial and sexual Other into the genre pervades the Hollywood road movie too. Perhaps the most significant example is *Thelma and Louise,* a Hollywood road movie with screwball comedy elements, but one that in many ways attacks both patriarchal oppression in society and the patriarchal underpinnings of the genre. The film's politically subversive bite may be partially due to director Ridley Scott, a British "outsider" with a fresh generic take. But probably more so it is due to the script by Callie Khouri, which infuses the narrative with the independent spirit of a woman's perspective. In the wake of its success, other multicultural/feminist Hollywood road movies appear, such as *Leaving Normal* (1992), *Boys on the Side* (1994), *To Wong Foo, Thanks for Everything, Julie Newmar* (1995)—the latter a Hollywood appropriation of the more compelling Australian *Adventures of Priscilla, Queen of the Desert* (1994), and *Tumbleweeds* (1998). These Hollywood ventures raise issues of race and gender, but often in a sappy, derivative, or superficial manner.[5] More fruitful to explore are those films in the 1990s that reclaim and revitalize the genre's independent spirit of cultural critique by traveling on the edges of Hollywood formula and appropriation, generating an edgier, more socially subversive multicultural perspective.

A Postmodern Detour: *Delusion*

Before turning to those multicultural road movies, and as a transition from the previous chapter, let us briefly consider Carl Colpaert's *Delusion* (1991). A little-known independent film, *Delusion* is an engaging road movie that neatly combines the outlaw and male quest narratives, while simultaneously possessing a feminist sensibility. Moreover, the film elaborates a compelling hyperrealism, where the vast, empty desert landscapes of California and Nevada seem to engender a disorienting series of reversals for the film's protagonist driver. In *Delusion,* as its title makes blatant, the real is forever derealized—an uncertain image, a lure. Along these lines, the film also self-consciously constructs a pastiche of film noir and the Western. Thus, *Delusion* functions well as a bridge between the postmodern road movies of the 1980s and the multicultural, repoliticized road movies of the 1990s.

The plot premise of the film revisits a road movie noir like *Detour,* but also anticipates a horror road movie like *Breakdown* (1996).[6] As the film opens, George O'Brien (Jim Metzler) is the head of a start-up computer team being bought by "the Gladstone Group." Having just completed a new computer program called "Mirage," he is angry and frustrated about the merger, and decides to embezzle about $500,000 so he can start his own "alternative" company and keep the team together. After securing the cash, he drives out to his warehouse in Reno, where he plans to start the company. To be sure, he never arrives at his destination.

The film possesses notable cultural resonance for how it dresses up road movie rebellion in corporate attire. In this respect, *Delusion* is more compelling and disturbing than the Hollywood screwball/romantic comedy road movies like *Lost in America* and *Something Wild,* which also feature yuppies "rebelling" on the road. In a subtle sting to capitalism's goal-oriented celebration of clear destinations (the most direct, cost-effective route being the most profitable), *Delusion* articulates the journey as a nightmarishly ironic series of accidents. Such accidents that happen are both literal (in the stranded couple who have had an accident on the desert highway) and figurative (in the unexpected plot turns that perpetually detour into a series of delusions). At the same time, the journey is motivated by both rebellion (the envisioned, authentic company) and a crime (the embezzled money). Thus, George embodies both the searcher and the outlaw, driving as a fugitive yet driven by his "vision," one ostensibly anticorporate, pro-creative.

Delusion clearly harnesses the look and feel of the genre soon after George starts his journey: from a heat-glazed eye-level extreme long shot of the highway, with the car heading into the camera; to a close-up of George driving; to a point of view shot of the highway racing toward the car; to a rearview mirror shot that reveals, a moment later, a tiny speck behind him racing toward him. Gradually this speck becomes a wildly skidding car that flies past him. Around the next bend, he sees that the car has crashed, and pulls over to help. Ironically foreshadowing ensuing plot twists, a certain lack of vision on George's part figures strongly here: he does not see the car crash. More importantly, he seems blind to how this other car is coded in terms of excess: its headlights on in the bright, midday glare; its speed and lack of control. Most symbolic, portending George's fate, their car is turned upside down. As the camera cranes up and away from George's car pulling off the road toward the overturned one, the film suggests George's loss of perspective and judgment, as well as the fate (or trap) he has just driven into.

In distinctly postmodern fashion, the film toys with absurd coincidence and mistaken identity in a self-conscious context. *Delusion*'s fateful road terror comes from an outlaw couple, Chevy (Kyle Secor) and Patti (Jennifer Rubin), the survivors of the overturned car who will soon turn George's world upside down. Colpaert builds subtle tension as initially the three of them ride together, effectively using the enclosed traveling space within the car to express George's entrapment. The film further creates ironic road movie tension by destabilizing George more specifically in terms of mobility. Chevy and Patti clamber for their map—which turns out to be of Oklahoma. Then, George insists he knows where they are going. But of course he does not know where he is going; he is in "territory" as unfamiliar and distant as Oklahoma. When they pull into a gas station, George scolds himself for being an "idiot" as he looks at himself in the bathroom mirror (a scene faintly reminiscent of Bobby's confrontation with his reflection at the end of *Five Easy Pieces*). The desert, the highway, and his unexpected road fare are turning him, as we shall see, into someone else.

Suddenly Chevy and Patti are "driving" the journey; they are taking him for a ride. In an absurdist play on appearances, Chevy now seems to be an assassin sent to kill George for his crime. At gunpoint, he takes George on a "detour." Chevy offers some road movie philosophy in the tradition of Palm, GTO, and Miller when he responds to George's demand to "get to the point" by suggesting George look out into the desert, where there is no point. George has been deluded by his own paranoia. It turns out that Chevy has car-jacked George to carry out an assassination of someone else.

After Chevy leaves George for dead in the desert, absurd fate arrives again, in the form of a female version of *Raising Arizona*'s Lone Rider of the Apocalypse. Clearly invoking the Hell's Angels and *Easy Rider*, a tough leather-clad woman biker spots George's body through her binoculars. As he rides on the back of her motorcycle, she explains how she thought he might be "Bono," her lover lost in "the revolution." "What revolution?" George asks; "The sexual revolution," she replies. A kind of granddaughter to Palm, a postmodern, cartoonish caricature of the 1960s counterculture (not unlike Burroughs's and Leary's cameos mentioned previously), she reflects an ironic attitude toward the road movie's countercultural origin. On the other hand, she is the antithesis of George's corporate yuppie world, and therefore seems symbolic of a new stage in George's rebellion. As the vehicle, in a sense, of his resurrection, she embodies the notion that the mysteries of the road (and the road movie) can work in George's favor. George gets a gun, and wants his money back (it is in the trunk of his car, which Chevy and Patti now drive). Gambling with destiny, he tracks Chevy and Patti to their motel for a final showdown.

During the latter part of the film, Patti develops into a potent third player, deconstructing the face-off between Chevy and George. *Delusion* moves toward an affirmation of the female as truly heroic, by allowing Patti to transcend the male obsession with power. She discovers George's money hidden in the trunk, and hides it from Chevy in her bag. While Chevy is in Las Vegas (first getting paid for his deed, then gambling it away), Patti plans her escape, buying a bus ticket from the motel bartender (played by *Repo Man*'s Tracey Walter). When George appears unexpectedly, she tries to seduce him, but George refuses; she is a femme fatale in his eyes, despite her coy innocence and claim of never having been sexually satisfied. Besides, George is set on confronting Chevy to get his money back (not knowing that Patti has it). When Chevy finally does return, there is a drawn-out shoot-out in the deserted plaza of the motel, one that self-consciously remakes the spaghetti Western's baroque showdown.

As the film concludes, the interwoven themes of greed and gambling become more pronounced, suggesting that George and Chevy are two sides of the same coin. The futile isolation concluding the journey is most clearly embodied by Patti, who finally drives away, leaving them to their "male hysteria."[7] The film's final shot frames George towering over a dying Chevy from a low angle, then the camera glides past them, out of the motel lot and onto the highway, traveling down the road—in a sense, following Patti. *Delusion* seems to be making a political, feminist statement. On the other hand, it also seems to be fashionably reflecting feminism's cultural currency. Like Bonnie, Patti is often portrayed through the "male gaze" as a sex toy who likes "to-be-looked-at" (Mulvey, 11). And yet like the Girl, she stays one step ahead of both George and Chevy, making small but significant gestures of subversion, asserting her own agenda.

5.1. *Delusion*'s ambivalent feminism on the road: Jennifer Rubin as Patti.

Delusion's "feminism" is ambivalent and contradictory, conveyed during the closing credit sequence, where Patti performs "These Boots Are Made for Walkin'" for the camera. As a nonnarrative coda, this performance codes her as a sex object spectacle (she slithers and struts as a sex kitten onstage). The subversive, feminist potential of the song lyrics is located beyond narrative agency or impact. Moreover, the song does have a narrative origin in the film that is rather significant. Patti had been singing this song earlier in the motel, in front of the bathroom mirror, blow drying her hair, bare breasts bobbing—that is, blatantly playing to traditional sexual spectacle. Then George sneaks in on her, throws her on the bed, forcing her to answer his questions—in a sense, punishing her for her "loose," "open" behavior. We can applaud the progressive connotations of Patti's appropriation of the (male) thrill of driving, as well as her independent transcendence of male competition. But we should also note the film's confluence of reflexive hipness and traditional Hollywood gender roles, which results in a lukewarm, problematic feminist cultural critique.

Remapping Road Movie Rebellion:
Thelma and Louise and *Natural Born Killers*

A more successful example of a road movie repoliticized by feminism is Ridley Scott's *Thelma and Louise* (1991). Whereas *Delusion*'s outlaws were passengers, here the outlaws are back in the driver's seat—this time, for the first time, two women. *Thelma and Louise* forcefully fuses classic road movie narrative structure with feminist social critique, jump-starting the genre into the 1990s, reestablishing "the frontier of modern nomadism as the domain of conflicting social forces" (Atkinson, 14). In the introduction to their anthology *The Road Movie Book,* Cohan and Hark likewise single out *Thelma and Louise* as marking "an important turning point in the popular and academic reception of the road film" (10). Linking the film's timing and its controversial feminist politics with the simultaneous appearance of Corrigan's chapter on the genre in *A Cinema without Walls,* they rightly claim that the film "galvanized critical attention on the road movie as an identifiable Hollywood product," and that it "revived the genre" by challenging its previous patriarchal ideology (12). Manohla Dargis puts it more vehemently: "In the absence of men, on the road Thelma and Louise create a paradigm of female friendship, produced out of their willful refusal of the male world and its laws. No matter where their trip finally ends, Thelma and Louise have reinvented sisterhood for the American screen" (18).[8]

Before considering where their trip finally does end—which matters quite a lot—let us first note how the film employs a panoply of classic road movie conventions to crucially link rebellion with driving, mobility and the highway. The plot comprises a balanced synthesis of the genre's quest and outlaw narratives. Thelma (Geena Davis) is a stifled and abused housewife; her friend Louise (Susan Sarandon), a waitress. They are taking a small vacation to a cabin, but on the way Thelma is nearly raped at a bar. Louise ends up shooting the rapist. Afterward, as Louise puts it, a "snowball effect" kicks in where they flee the police, committing crime after crime. They come to embrace their outlaw status: they come alive and come together on the run and on the road. Yet they never become true criminals. As much as they drive *against* circumstance, they often *are driven by* a criminal patriarchal society. Thus, the film uses various strategies to justify their actions. Eventually the police corner them at the Grand Canyon; rather than face prison and the patriarchal oppression they originally fled, they drive over the cliff in an affirmative suicide that, according to some readings, signifies a great triumph.

In terms of mise en scène and tone, *Thelma and Louise* ends, in many ways, where it began: the wide open spaces of the American Southwest. The narrative significance of them being entirely off-road as they face the Canyon's cliff is crucial in characterizing just how far their rebellion has taken them. The film's opening is more conventional, a prediegetic establishing shot that does not really set the scene of the story but symbolically expresses the mood and texture of the film. More important, it lucidly announces the film generically: a highway through the landscape of the American West. Perhaps anticipating the ambivalent death at the end of the film's journey, the sky darkens, then the image fades completely to black as the last opening credits roll.

When we first "meet" Louise's car, a 1966 convertible T-Bird (nostalgically evoking the countercultural era of the road movie's birth), an energetic nonsynchronous rock and roll song plays, initiating the first of many enthusiastic driving sequences (sometimes the music is synchronous, coming from the radio, with them singing along). Here the music also serves to figuratively bring Thelma and Louise together, as it plays during a crosscutting montage between the two of them getting ready to depart. In the first intimate two-shot scene of them driving, Thelma, the passenger for most of the film, checks herself in the mirror. She then does a mock but affectionate imitation of Louise. Yet the gesture is more significant for inaugurating a theme prominent throughout: their special bond that results from their fugitive mobility, itself an expression of the visionary reflections and revelations yielded by highway travel.

Another aspect of the film's initial generic articulation, one more related to gender politics, is how Thelma's marriage and Louise's job are coded as static and enslaving. Both women see their trip as an escape from the "prison" of domestic servitude and economic dependence. The film places more emphasis on Thelma's home life—significant since she will be sexually assaulted, suggesting a spectrum of patriarchal oppression that both her husband and the rapist occupy. Daryl (Christopher McDonald), Thelma's husband, treats her atrociously. We know he is on the other side of the road movie when he trips and falls all over himself as he approaches his ostentatiously red Corvette (Daryl's car is utterly un–road movie, a glaring contrast to Louise's Thunderbird). Later, in the bar, just before getting tangled up with Harlan (Timothy Carhart), the man who will try to rape her, Thelma exclaims to Louise that she has "had it with being sedate." Just after the shooting, in another exemplary reinvention of the genre's iconography, Thelma and Louise find themselves surrounded by trucks on the boulevards near the bar. This not only foreshadows the obnoxious truck driver later but also achieves a powerful visual metaphor (aided by the nighttime setting) for their entrapment within patriarchy: the (male, phallic) trucks towering over them, clogging and blocking their way. To drive the point home further, Louise explains to Thelma that no one is going to believe they acted in self-defense, that they "don't live in that kind of world." After committing her act of visionary rebellion, Louise no longer knows where they are going, but she has to pull over so she can vomit—a vivid point of departure for their real journey. Taking to the road has radically twisted their fate; they no longer have a destination, or a vacation. Louise knows where and how the genre goes, and aims for a motel, symbol of the perpetual fugitive transience awaiting them.

After this point, the film instigates the crosscutting format typical of many road movies. As in *Vanishing Point* and *Wild at Heart,* this strategy juxtaposes the stable, grounded, and oppressive society they are leaving behind with their mobility away from it—with the effect of enhancing the thrill of such mobility. *Thelma and Louise* keeps cutting back home primarily to the plight of police investigator Hal Slokum (Harvey Keitel) and his effort to track them down. An overinvested figure of law and order, he suggests that because they might be crossing state lines, the FBI should be brought in (thus "nationalizing" the case). As the stable male authority figure counterpoint to Thelma and Louise, obsessed with capturing them, his dramatic function often involves exaggerating the threat they pose. (At the end, when Louise sees the army of federal militia lined up against them facing the Grand Canyon, she says, "All this for us?") One "home" scene among many that conveys the link between the stasis of domestic life and the mission of law enforcement is a shot of a convoy of cars rolling in precise uniformity toward the camera, then turning like clockwork one after another into Daryl's driveway. In fact, the cars do not appear to be moving at all: they are static in the frame, a homogeneous, nondescript mass—quite a contrast to the speeding T-Bird.

Meanwhile, in another classic instance of the genre, Louise has decided to get her savings and go to Mexico, to flee legal prosecution, since she did pull the trigger. She explains to Thelma that "everything has changed" (Thelma will later return the observation, in a moment of more visionary insight), and invites Thelma to come with her. Thelma does not know what to do, but Louise insists she has to choose. This insistence on making a choice in the context of sociopolitical criticism (American society is against them, unfairly so) is quite a long way from all the ambiguity, uncertainty, irony, and listless wandering of many previous road movies. Rarely has the road movie drive been so politicized. *Thelma and Louise* makes taking to the road a matter of life and death, freedom or bondage. Moreover, the conventional highway itself proves too conventional for their rebellious flight. Waiting for a train to pass, they decide to take "secondary roads" to Mexico, to avoid being seen.[9] Louise insists on getting from Arkansas to Mexico without going through Texas, because of her own painful memories associated with that state and landscape (a variation on the 1970s road movie's psychological emphasis, but one politicized by the theme of gender oppression). They must take the longer, indirect route, implying the narrative and political significance of the journey rather than the destination.

Despite the desperation of their situation, Thelma and Louise taste liberation and embrace affirmation on the road. Their outlaw rambling generates visionary revelations in the spirit of Kerouac's *On the Road*. One of the film's most compelling moments occurs while Thelma is robbing a liquor store. As Louise waits in the car, the camera arcs around her: she contemplates putting on lipstick, then feels herself being watched, not by the camera, but by two old made-up women gazing at her through a glass window. When she looks at them, the camera cuts not to a literal point of view shot, but to a close-up of them. Instead of chucking her watch, as Captain America does, Louise chucks her lipstick (later she does trade her watch for a cowboy hat). Disturbed by an image of her own mortality, she is more disturbed by the beauty industry's manipulation and definition of female appearance. While Griggers sees Louise's gesture as a sign of "despondency and despair" (139) after having all their money stolen, I see it more as a moment of visionary insight related to the act of looking ("seeing") engendered by road travel. Throughout the film, Louise is seen gazing out of windows or looking at herself in the mirror. She is the contemplative, more stoic Captain America/Clyde type, in contrast to Thelma's incarnation of Bonnie/Billy, more sensual, a little naive, and impulsive.

Toward the end, however, Thelma—like Bonnie especially—develops visionary insight, and articulates the film's most important themes. Just after the heist, she is exhilarated, screaming and howling as they drive away, that she has found her "calling," which is the "call of the wild."[10] Parodying patriarchal attitudes toward female behavior, Louise comments, "You are disturbed"—connoting both mental imbalance but also anger. Significantly,

Scott gives a seductive close-up of the car here, the camera gliding along-side it as they hurl down the highway, a nonnarrative shot symbolic of the inspiration they discover while driving. This inspiration is further expressed more poetically in a night sequence as they ride through majestic desert buttes, light and color designed to convey a serene, ghostly atmosphere. At one point, while cruising through such glorious scenery, the camera dissolves alternating shots of their faces, one to the other, formalistically suggesting a heightened, spiritual bonding while driving. Solemn but finally smiling with secret precious knowledge, they look almost directly into the camera, con-fronting the audience with their transformation, their fusion, their cross-ing from one identity to another. Again, it is Thelma who explains what is going on. First, she is watching the landscape in the side mirror, repre-senting perhaps the past, where they have been and come from. "Some-thing has crossed over in me." She can't "go back, can't live"—implying the link between movement forward and authentic living. Then she looks to the actual landscape before her, commenting that she feels "awake, wide awake," that "everything looks different," and that she has "something to look forward to."

The theme of visionary rebellion so crucial to *Thelma and Louise* is in-vigorated further by the film's patriarchal cultural critique. Yet as we shall see, the film's feminism, like that of *Delusion,* is not unproblematic. We may begin with Thelma's husband, Daryl, a tyrannical brute. He "appears" be-fore we even see him: handheld camera and tight framing on Thelma prepar-ing his breakfast conveys his oppression of her (Daryl then walks in and be-gins bullying her). Not coincidentally, the next male character we encounter is an extension of Daryl: Harlan, the stud in the bar who attempts to rape Thelma. Before doing so, he physically takes possession of her while danc-ing, his muscular arm around her neck, clutching a beer, finally spinning her around into a stupor.[11]

Aside from these two male characters, and before turning to the more ambivalent Slokum and J. D., two encounters with patriarchy on the road are worth noting, coded as they are through classic road movie tropes. First, there is the scene where a state trooper (Jason Beghe) pulls them over. Small gestures speak volumes in this scene. The cop puts on his hat (his identity, his power) before approaching their car; when he brings Louise into his car, he asks her to "remove her eyewear," so he can see her eyes. The mise en scène of the police car interior is likewise effective here: she has been taken from *her* car (her freedom and rebellion) into the car of the law, foretelling imprisonment and enclosure. But Thelma comes over with her gun (which, in a way, is *his* gun—she is aping male phallic power) and takes them both

5.2. Louise (Susan Sarandon) and Thelma (Geena Davis) teach sexist truck drivers a feminist lesson on the road.

out of his car (again, highly symbolic). At this point, his tough outer shell of masculine power and control shatters: he starts shaking and crying, pleading that he has a wife and family. Having rediscovered reality by being on the road, Thelma delivers one of the film's most funny and politically potent lines, advising him to treat his wife nicely or she may end up like them. And yet, Thelma and Louise clearly have *not* become the masculine brutes they ape: they apologize profusely as they gently lock him in the trunk of his own car—ending the scene, again, with a poignant generic reversal (no longer a mobile driver, he has been rendered static, trapped cargo by the outlaws).

A second encounter with patriarchy on the road, one that propels the film to its climax, is the scene with the truck driver (Marco St. John). He has been taunting them while driving—signifying that patriarchal oppression is not so easily left behind. (In fact, as we have seen throughout this study, the road beyond stable society is as much a male domain as society itself.) Finally the two women entice him to pull over, then assault him with questions that expose his "disgusting" (Thelma's term), juvenile, yet abusive attitudes toward women. Let us appreciate the road movie iconography at service here: they sit on top of their car, bolstered by their appropriation of (typically masculinist) mobility; in contrast, he stands away from his truck, nervous, twitching, and awkward. Like Harlan, he will not yield to their words; like Harlan, he only understands violence. In a beautifully ironic twist on the road movie's Western/action film influence, the two women next pull out their guns, first to flatten the tires of his truck (a road movie castration), then fully explode his phallic vehicle.

As the film basks in the pyrotechnic spectacle (police helicopter point of view shots), and as Thelma and Louise hoot and laugh while circling the blubbering fool (Thelma swipes his cap up and wears it to the end), let us further glean a potential meaning for this celebration. His truck transports *gasoline*—the fuel for other masculinist road travel predicated on demeaning and abusing women. Rarely in any Hollywood movie—let alone a road movie—has feminist criticism been so successfully and persuasively integrated into dramatic narrative. The trucker is a buffoon, a cartoonish caricature—and perhaps the scene would have been stronger otherwise. But the power and fury of their words and gestures rings cathartically true.

At the same time, *Thelma and Louise* seems to undercut, or perhaps complicate, much of its feminist critique. Such complication arises regarding two important male characters: J. D. (Brad Pitt), a drifter they pick up who has a fling with Thelma; and Slokum. Initially, J. D. asks Thelma if he can have a ride; later, after eyeing him a few times, Thelma persuades Louise to pick up the sexy drifter. Once he is in the backseat, Thelma seems "behind the wheel" of her own desire and sexuality; her encounter with J. D. will in fact lead to her first fulfilling sexual experience. A closer look at their romantic lovemaking scene in a motel, however, reveals that Thelma's "control" over the situation is highly mitigated—if not a delusion. Despite starting off as her boy-toy, he actually ends up seducing her. With his shirt off, he "performs" for her the process of holding up a store; he is the "sex object," yet he instructs her, standing above her, in the how-to of being an outlaw. This educational performance becomes a preface to the sexual performance, where he again edifies her, liberating her passion and pleasure. Later, when she performs her own interpretation of "being an outlaw," actually robbing a convenience store, we are enthralled by her gutsy bravado. Yet the narrative has "taught" her through the authority of the male. Has she appropriated his knowledge, or is she subservient to it? [12]

In considering this question, we should note that the Thelma-J. D. rendezvous is crosscut with Louise and her boyfriend Jimmy (Michael Madsen) in another room. Jimmy was supposed to wire her savings, but instead tricks her by showing up. Offering a rose, he asks her to marry him, mainly out of desperate jealousy (jealousy over an imagined rival lover, but also over her independence through fugitive mobility). Louise calls him on his male power trip, deconstructing his self-serving "concern." Though they end up kissing, he agrees to trust her and to follow her instructions. The crosscutting format seems to render Louise's bedroom scene a critical commentary on Thelma's simultaneous romantic fantasy. And on some level it is a fantasy: J. D. steals all their money.

But Investigator Slokum is the most disturbing character in the film, from the perspective of gender politics. While his narrative function is to lead the effort to capture Thelma and Louise, his thematic function is to protect and "save" them. Slokum, that is, is the exception to the Male Rule. Genuinely concerned for their welfare, he berates J. D. for taking their money and forcing them to steal. On the phone, he asks Louise, "Are you OK?" Later he tells her, "I feel like I know you," to which Louise responds, "No you don't." Yet it comes out that, in a way, she is wrong: he *does* know about "Texas" (he knows more than she thinks he knows). The film's narrative organization further conspires in redeeming Slokum: the fact that Louise keeps calling him lacks any plausible motivation, functioning as an artificial pretext to allow Slokum's "sensitivity" to emerge. Somewhat ironically, the most developed male character comes off finally as the most unrealistic. At the Grand Canyon standoff, he is the only one worried that they will get shot by the police. The film's formalistic aesthetics drive the point home further. Just before they drive over the edge, he is framed with them in a highly significant deep-focus shot, with him in the foreground, them in the distance. They are miles, worlds apart, and yet they occupy the frame together. Additionally, nothing happens in this shot, so its framing is the main point. Let us also note that he is closer to the audience, they farther away, forging a perhaps subtextual audience identification with him as they go over the edge. Slokum is shown in slow motion chasing after them when they start the car, as though he "knows" what they are about to do—the slow motion and insight combining to convey *him*, the male investigator, as the last visionary of the film. Moreover, the slow motion links his gesture formally and morally with theirs: he shares in their glory and dignity, he sympathizes with them, the film sympathizes with his sympathy.

This ambivalence around J. D. and Slokum reflect the larger debate about the film's feminist politics. *Thelma and Louise,* that is, mobilizes an ideological tension similar to that surrounding the more politicized 1960s road movie. This tension, which informed much of its popular, controversial reception, might be generalized as the following question: Is *Thelma and Louise* an effective feminist critique, or does it betray feminism to patriarchal Hollywood narrative? For example, the film seems to substitute a female buddy pair for the traditional male one, a depoliticizing gesture of assimilation. On a certain level, Thelma and Louise seem to be acting like men. Yet the film complicates this assimilation to a male genre by its very articulation of resistance to patriarchal oppression. At the very least, their flight on the road is doubly motivated by rebellion against patriarchy: to get away from a male-dominated home (Thelma) and workplace (Louise); and more emphatically, to evade a patriarchal legal system that legitimizes rape. Though *Thelma and Louise*'s articulation of rebellion is sometimes humorous, it is never ironic or even self-conscious. The film positions itself as rebellious and thus repoliticizes the genre.

Nowhere does the film's ideological tension become more pronounced than in the film's cathartic ending. They choose to "keep goin'," the ultimate road movie solution to rebellion, the ultimate testimony to society's inability to contain them: death, the ultimate leap. In one sense, the film refuses rather conventionally to follow through with its feminist mobility and rebellion, by eliminating them in the guise of a sentimentalized martyr-dom (which from this perspective becomes all the more disturbing since the film has them choose self-destruction). In another, contrary sense the film exalts their resistance by taking it to a dignified extreme. From this angle, the fact that they *choose* their own death distinguishes it from most other rebel road movies. Their embrace of their fatal destiny signifies a potent form of trenchant subversion: a slap in the face of patriarchy. And then again, the bloodless, happy white light washing out their slow-motion leap signifies patriarchy's (and Hollywood's) insidious capacity to absorb and sanitize subversion.[13]

While not postmodern stylistically, *Thelma and Louise*'s references to mass media and the culture of images link it with the postmodern road movie. Images constitute a subtle but significant motif of the mise en scène, and of the overall narrative. At the outset, just before departing, Thelma and Louise take a Polaroid photo of themselves, bonding in the process of producing the image, taking control of the photographic apparatus and reflexively turning it upon themselves. Their image shall not be taken by others. More importantly, this photo "frames" their journey. After they take it, this first photo is freeze-framed by the film, in anticipation of the final freeze-frame of their leap to death, which has the effect of immortalizing them. Not coincidentally, the Polaroid photo flies out of the car as they leap, articulating within the narrative what the discursive formalism (slow motion, freeze-frame, fade to white) also expresses: the transcendence (continuity) of Thelma and Louise as images, as mythical icons. After the fade to white, a montage of selected sequences, or narrative "snapshots," resurrects them from the dystopian (imagined, not seen) car and body mutilation. The (postmodern) point here is that the film flaunts its own cinematic, artificial construction of their immortality. While classical Hollywood stars became "immortal" by virtue of the staying power of their fictional presence on celluloid, *Thelma and Louise* impatiently inscribes its own mythmaking as fictional coda.

Related to *Thelma and Louise*'s emphasis on images is its emphasis on performance, also a trait of the postmodern independent road movie. In one of their first conversations while driving, Thelma imitates, or "performs" Louise (something of Mansfield's send-up of Marilyn in *Gentlemen Prefer Blondes*). Later, when Thelma performs J. D.'s performance of an outlaw, it is captured on the store's surveillance video. Quite poignantly, all the men back home view Thelma's outlaw performance on a video monitor, in stunned disbelief—exaggerating the "star" aura emanating from the two women outlaws.[14] As noted above, the shooting and exploding of the truck driver's big rig likewise plays like a performance, with him the stunned one-man audience (Louise explains to Thelma that she learned to shoot like that "off the TV").

In concluding our discussion of the film, we should take note of *Thelma and Louise*'s sticky and tricky manner of portraying racial otherness, and people of color. As we have seen throughout this study, the representation of people of color forms a peculiar conservative backdrop to an independent genre of rebellion. That is, the portrayal of race in the road movie points up its whiteness. In *Thelma and Louise,* with its feminist rebellion so clearly articulated, this portrayal becomes all the more striking for its glaring contrast with the film's liberal, angry feminism. Let us begin with the road movie staple of the specter of Mexico. Narratively speaking, their fantasizing about Mexico is understandable: it is in their character, and it makes geographic sense as a haven destination. But such fantasizing nevertheless rearticulates the exoticizing tendency that permeates the genre, where freedom beckons across the national border, down south, in the "primitive" underdeveloped country. A more ambiguous iconic "message" regarding race and gender occurs during the ending car chase, where the first two policemen we see in close-up chasing them are a black man and a white woman together in the car. The quick shot perhaps suggests an affinity between the black man and white woman as minorities within white patriarchy; it also may suggest a "conflict of interest" for them in their pursuit. But the shot's fleeting, nonnarrative quality renders it a superficial token.

Surely the most compelling and problematic image of race in *Thelma and Louise* is the Rasta mountain-bike rider (Noel Walcott) who finds the police car with the state trooper in the trunk. As an overdetermined stereotype, it is no surprise that he does not have a speaking part. Instead, sporting dread-locks and an athletic uniform, he listens to music and gets stoned. Associated with drugs, sports, and music, he embodies tired movie clichés about blacks. Equally significant, he appears in the film as comic relief, when he blows pot smoke into the trunk. This is the point of his scene. The comedy thus sanitizes and depoliticizes his presence. The film seems to want to "use" him as an ally of the two women: he is a kind of outlaw too, alone in the desert on the high-way, stoned. His dreadlocks invoke the rebellious, politicized spirit of Bob Marley (he is listening to reggae music); and yet such "politics," such "rebel-lion," is only faintly implied through appearance/costume. Perhaps the scene makes a powerful statement of resistance through humor; but it also plays into traditional conservative stereotypes. Moreover, it treats him purely as a symbol, static despite his riding on the highway.

Natural Born Killers is another road movie from the early nineties that had a popular and controversial reception. In ways distinct from *Thelma and Louise, Natural Born Killers* likewise reignites the genre's rebellious core at-titude. While *Thelma and Louise* dynamically challenges the genre's patriar-chal underpinnings, fusing mobility with feminist cultural critique, *Natural Born Killers* routes itself through the more traditional hetero outlaw couple. But from within that convention, it uniquely deploys a "massive attack" hyper-MTV film language, a frenetic compendium of experimental film techniques. Through its visual barrage, the film assaults the viewer with a superstylized, unrelenting reflection of screen violence. A self-conscious de-scendant of *Gun Crazy, Bonnie and Clyde, Badlands,* and *Wild at Heart, Natu-ral Born Killers* repoliticizes the genre by addressing the connection between violence and mass media in American society. In Stone's typically brazen, heavy-handed manner, the film confronts this issue rather squarely, in a vehe-ment antiestablishment attitude (the latter missing from the genre for quite some time).

Yet this frontal political attack on violence and mass media by no means reveals an unproblematic or coherent cultural critique. In fact, by virtue of the film's bold political attitude, the contradictions that haunt the trailblaz-ing road movies *Bonnie and Clyde* and *Easy Rider* reemerge. Like *Thelma and Louise, Natural Born Killers* possesses its own subtextual conservative politi-cal baggage. With *Thelma and Louise,* the central political contradiction is between its critique of patriarchy and its reiteration of patriarchy (not only in the typically patriarchal Hollywood codes it employs, but also in "substi-tuting" women for typically male characters). Something similar occurs with regard to the politicized rebellion of *Natural Born Killers.* The film critiques the mass media's obsession with violence, yet the film exploits and sensationalizes such violence; that is, the film embraces exactly what it opposes. Essentially, the film wants to have its cake and eat it too. Its postmodern packaging of modernist social critique is in fact the vehicle of its political contradictions.

The first hour of *Natural Born Killers* is of more interest to us, since this is the section where Mickey (Woody Harrelson) and Mallory (Juliette Lewis) are on the road. The second hour takes place mostly while they are in prison, and focuses on Wayne Gale (Robert Downey Jr.)—host of television's *American Maniacs*—and his interview with Mickey. But the first hour is packed with an entire film's worth of road movie conventions and imagery—all radically reinvented. Mickey and Mallory are "killers on the road" (cf. the Doors' "Riders on the Storm," and the credit sequence of Stone's *The Doors*) who have also become the superstars of popular culture. Harnessing the early-1970s road movie emphasis on psychological motivation, *Natural Born Killers* shows through flashback how both Mickey and Mallory had abusive childhoods. But more in line with *Wild at Heart*'s postmodern excesses, their childhoods are presented as garish and sensationalized, especially Mallory's "television sitcom" childhood. A brilliantly disturbing stroke and a variation on the postmodern cartoonism discussed earlier, the sitcom mode suggests the film's explanation of why Mickey and Mallory became "this way": they watched too much television. These two social factors—family abuse and media abuse—combine to propel them onto the road and into their killing spree. Throughout, Stone uses a dynamic montage editing approach, derived from (and reflecting upon) MTV but also from the likes of Eisenstein and Brakhage. The film's rapid-fire assault on the audience seems both an appeal and a challenge to the savvy but often superficial visual literacy of the youth market.

The opening segment of *Natural Born Killers* is worth looking at closely. Set to Leonard Cohen's eerie, mystical ballad "Waiting for the Miracle," the opening shots invoke the road movie landscape, shifting freely from black and white to color, with close-ups in the desert (a snake, a hawk, a rotting carcass) eventually cutting to the genre's classic roadside diner, out in the middle of nowhere. Before moving inside the diner, let us note the significance of the Cohen song. As a celebrated visionary troubadour of the 1960s era, poet and novelist Cohen is a kind of counterpart to Bob Dylan, a recluse who lives on a Greek island. Starting the film off with him singing of "the miracle" evokes a mystical and romanticized mood, further emphasized through the song's gently pulsating rhythm, and Cohen's raspy, whispering vocal style. Since the film ends with another visionary/apocalyptic Cohen song ("The Future"), Stone frames the film musically in terms of the voice of the poet as visionary, revealing Stone's glorification of his two antiheroes, despite his criticism of them throughout.

Such ambivalent glorification is played out dramatically inside the diner. Like the opening nonsynchronous music, the film's hyperformalism cues us to the scene's "perspective" and attitude. Rather than the Cohen song, here the spectacular camera work seems to "express" Mickey and Mallory, thus privileging them in relation to the setting and the other characters. Through fragmented close-ups, oblique diagonal compositions, and "floating" camera movements (a trademark of the Stone/Richardson collaboration: cf. *The Doors, JFK,* and *U Turn*), we see Mickey ordering key lime pie at the counter, while Mallory peruses the song list of the jukebox. Mallory puts on a song and starts dancing, embodying the visceral, sensual charge of the road movie rock music soundtrack (though not driving, they are obviously on the road, stopping for a bite). Mallory's attire is clearly coded as retro hippie, a twentysomething go-go girl dancing in psychedelic free-form. This counterculture reference foreshadows the ensuing violent clash with the rednecks who pull up in their pickup truck. In a way, *Natural Born Killers* begins where *Easy Rider* ended, striking back at redneck America with brutal vengeance. In the postmodern vein of *Raising Arizona, Wild at Heart,* and *Kalifornia,* the southern color of the film's "good ol' boys"—the film's first victims—is done in cartoonish caricature. The southern rednecks enter the diner after their car has overheated (foretelling Mickey and Mallory violently overheating). Along with the waitress, they possess no redeeming qualities: they are ugly gothic caricatures of southern dumbness. On the one hand, they seem to get what they deserve (the scene literally bashes conservative intolerance). But the film has "framed" them into deserving it. Like the truck driver in *Thelma and Louise,* as targets of political critique they are too easy.

Whereas *Wild at Heart* opens with an ultraviolent scene related to an Oedipal drama (mother tries to fuck/kill daughter's boyfriend), here the ultraviolence is situated in a more political framework (redneck versus rebel). But the cartoonish excesses of the film style make it difficult to take this political framework seriously. Just before Mallory unleashes her assault on the cowboy who obscenely flirts with her, the jukebox changes discs to a violent heavy-metal song (again, the music is "with" them; she is "in tune"). Kicking the shit out of the macho sexist pig, Mallory briefly seems a stepdaughter to Thelma and Louise. But any feminism is strictly pseudo and superficial: Mallory is tough but sexy throughout—both hypermasculinized femme fatale who "wants new clothes" and gullible, dependent sweetheart. The cartoonish nightmare format trivializing her feminism reaches a crescendo when the camera follows in slow motion the spinning knife Mickey has flung at a fleeing redneck. Her "eenie meanie" song, determining which of the remaining two shall be killed, further celebrates their juvenile attitude, itself a facet of the film's cartoonish, tongue-in-cheek mode.

As Mickey and Mallory kick ass, their coolness becomes the film's reluctant preoccupation. The film sides with them and against the forces of mass media culture—even though they are a direct product of mass media culture. This is revealed in certain "media" details of the opening scene. Before the burst of violence, we see "Mickey and Mallory" in the headlines of the newspaper Mickey reads, clarifying at the outset that they are "stars" in the narrative (as well as stars of the film). A more intriguing aspect of the mise en scène is that the television is on behind the dining counter, where we glimpse a rapid succession of images: a "Leave It to Beaver"–type sitcom, Nixon, and a screaming demon face. Throughout the film, whenever Stone shows television images, they themselves are constructed as a symbolic montage. In this first instance, for example, we see the "lie" of 1950s America, first in the sitcom, then personified in Nixon (Stone's own demon of deceit and political corruption, cause of the Vietnam War). The third image, the screaming demon face, represents perhaps the fury beneath the surface of conservative repression and media distortion, unleashed here and recurring throughout as a distilled cipher of Mickey and Mallory.

At the end of the scene, they leave one witness to "tell the tale"—and they make sure he gets their names right. The outlaw couple here want more than a mere 15 minutes of fame. They strut and pose like stars, and this, along with their serial killing, makes them stars. Significantly, the scene ends with a surrealistic rear projection on the wall of the diner behind them as they embrace in a kiss. When they say "I love you" to each other, it sounds like a cliché they learned from television and the movies: pure artifice, mock sincerity, *media*ted, as the rear projection too implies.

In the spirit of this mass media and film reflexivity, the ensuing credit sequence offers further compelling revision of road movie imagery. Basically a driving montage set to rock music excerpts, the sequence is contextualized as media-saturated and therefore artificial, through more elaborate use of rear projection. Rather emphatically, Mickey and Mallory are not going anywhere: the car is obviously phony, the "landscapes" they pass through are images projected behind them. An irreverently effusive display of the postmodern disappearance of the road, the sequence flaunts its own pretentiousness. Discontinuous images full of potential symbolism abound: an eye close-up, them kissing, a 1950s movie monster, horses galloping, headlines of their killings, skyscrapers. This visual collage of collisions is matched by an

5.3. Killers on the road, stars of the culture: Mickey (Woody Harrelson) . . .

aural montage: a film noir voice-over speaks, Patti Smith's "Rock and Roll Nigger" fades in and out ("outside of society, that's where I wanna be"). Finally, their car stalls in the desert, as the director's name appears on screen.

Despite the stalling of their car, the first narrative scene codes their frenetic, nihilistic mobility in terms of a recycled visionary freedom and rebellion, a pastiche comprising both romance and mockery. In this way, and throughout, *Natural Born Killers* evokes a peculiar ambivalence, an identification with and analysis of its outlaw couple. Probably alluding to the scene in *Badlands* when Kit and Holly dance to Nat King Cole, Mickey is seen urinating beneath the moonlight as Mallory dances on the hood of the car (both shot in extreme canted angles). His urinating undercuts the pretentious earnestness of his clichéd vision of the apocalypse, as he muses aloud, "The whole world's coming to an end, Mal . . ." This moment is similar to Lulu's impersonation of a visionary for Sailor, in the motel in *Wild at Heart*. Both scenes mock poetic vision through a 90s "whatever" attitude. Meanwhile, Mallory talks of "seeing angels"—and we see an angel in the sky descend, at once legitimizing her vision, yet making fun of it, since it is such a blatantly retro special effect (like the "Good Witch" at the end of *Wild at*

5.4. . . . and Mallory (Juliette Lewis), the ultimate outlaw couple.

Heart). Claiming to be able to see "the future" (which links with the final Cohen song), she "sees" Mickey "riding on a horse." Mickey describes her thoughts as "poetry"—but his over-the-top delivery of the term puts quote marks around it. The film's discourse is likewise over-the-top: the lighting enshrines her in a halo, making fun of her visionary impulses, yet glorifying them. The excess of the cinematic cliché forms just one facet of the film's other excesses: their murders, their stardom, the often hysterical formalism of the camera work. Such excess, applied on so many levels, constitutes the root of its thematic and political contradictions.

More postmodern revision of classic road movie elements occurs in the portrayal of the past home lives of the outlaw couple. The genre's typical rendering of home and stability as oppressive and confining is given an excessive, cartoonish twist in *Natural Born Killers*. Through the use of the "I Love Mallory" television sitcom, the film is able to ridicule the family, the home, and mass media as interlocking structures of control and abuse. As we watch Mallory's grotesque home life, we also watch ourselves watching. Moreover, such reflexive foregrounding of the sitcom insists that celebrity culture and the privacy of domestic living, formerly opposites, now inextricably influence each other. Mallory's father (played against type by Rodney Danger-field) is a patriarchal pariah in the mold of Marietta from *Wild at Heart*, a demonic parent "responsible" for turning Mallory into a killer. Whereas *Badlands* faintly suggests a repressed Electra complex between Holly and her father, *Natural Born Killers* becomes furiously explicit about molestation—perhaps too explicit to be taken seriously.

It is significant that during part of the "I Love Mallory" sequence, Mickey is in prison (for auto theft). This implies a parallel between her home as prison, and his prison as home: both must be broken out of. As he and some other prisoners are on work duty with some horses in a corral, a twister emerges in the distance. Everyone but Mickey is blown away; he sees the twister as an emissary of opportunity, an ally. He steals a horse and rides directly into the twister, howling ecstatically. Cleverly citing the Western genre, this visually captivating scene suggests that the fits of Nature reflect Mickey's wild fury, "naturalizing" him as a "natural born killer." Aiding his escape, the twister poses no threat to him, but rather expresses his *amour fou* and his visionary rebellion. Like Mallory's halo a few scenes earlier, this scene establishes his mystique, but in a comically baroque manner that is sledge-hammer ironic, begging not to be taken seriously. Not coincidentally, this is where Mickey's literal cartoon character counterpart is interwoven into the live action. This animated action-hero appears sporadically throughout, exploiting and critiquing the cartoonism of postmodern culture.

More road movie elements are hurtled over the edge of the genre, extending its boundaries. Mickey goes back to rescue Mallory from her domestic sitcom hell, murdering the father and "burning down the house" (Talking Heads)—all reminiscent of *Badlands*. While Holly is rather indifferent about being "rescued," Mallory jumps for joy like a cheerleader. Then, Mickey and Mallory "get married," the scene ritualized, not so much through their rather banal and adolescent blood-letting bond, but as a union on and with the highway. Parked on a bridge towering over a deep vast ravine, they throw over all their previous belongings, Mickey declaring that "the road to hell is in front of us." He then proposes to her, the bridge their "church." As the road is the determining setting for the consummation of their love, so too it figures prominently in their conflicts with each other. For example, when Mallory becomes jealous of the female hostage Mickey has taken, she vents her anger by driving. Eventually she seduces a gas station attendant on the hood of a Corvette, then kills him. When police investigator Scagnetti (Tom Sizemore) arrives on the scene, he notes her bodily imprint on the hood, then "sees" her reflection there, smiling back at him. Automobility functions here as the site of her jealousy, but also Scagnetti's psychosexual obsession, reflecting in the very surface of the car the skewed pathologies on both sides of the law. We should note that though she has just committed murder, Scagnetti's depraved "vision" reframes *her* as victim (not of mass media here, but of hypocritical, corrupt law enforcement), revealing again the film's uneasy but compulsive fetishism of its outlaw couple.

The existential road movie's search for meaning is referenced in a later scene when driving through the desert they argue about not knowing where they are going. High on mushrooms, they turn off the road, where Mickey vomits, his face contorting in a hallucinatory revelation of the monster/cartoon character inside him. Mallory screams at him for calling her "a stupid bitch," like her father used to. Coming apart at the seams, the thrill seems to be gone. Insert shots of animals and plants are intercut with their arguing, again recalling *Badlands* (and *Days of Heaven*), "naturalizing" their rage at each other. (Later, in the Wayne Gale interview, Mickey articulates this montage, explaining his behavior in terms of the "laws" of nature.) At this point, they are out of gas, literally and figuratively lost. This lull, however, leads them to a special encounter with America's own history of serial killing as genocide. Looking for gas, they stumble upon a run-down shack that by nightfall turns into a makeshift sweat lodge. The Native American who dwells there welcomes them inside. The sequence immediately sets up the Old Indian (Russell Means) as a visionary, with Mickey and Mallory the "objects" of his insight: "demon" and "too much television" are projected onto their chests. Instead of images being projected behind them, with them as the "stars," now they have become the screen onto which images (text, in this case) are projected. Here the film's over-the-top formalism collaborates with the Old Indian's visionary insight: these words are what he sees. (Dying from Mickey's gunshots, he claims he saw them in a dream twenty years earlier, and has been waiting for them.) From another angle, though Mickey and Mallory are the objects of this visionary commentary, they also become aligned with the Indian's vision, since all along they too are coded as seers who act out their "natural-born," primeval instincts. Seeing as the Old Indian does, Mallory informs Mickey that "we are the demons" he senses.

The Old Indian proceeds to tell a snake story, exemplifying the storytelling motif of the genre that often accompanies the visionary theme: seeing clearly and telling stories on the road go hand in hand. (Later, Mickey will tell a story to the guards that distracts them so he can escape—again linking him with the Native American.) Though spoken in a Native American language, the fable along with the campfire seems to lull Mickey and Mallory to sleep. As with Bonnie and Clyde and other outlaw couples, respite from the road does not bode well. Mickey has a nightmare about his own abusive childhood; he wakes up and shoots the Old Indian. One possible meaning of this overloaded gesture is that the repressed violence and neurosis of the white nuclear family is unfairly vented on innocent people of color. At the same time, Mickey's natural-born killer instinct *embodies* the bloody American imperialist history that is in fact anything but "natural." Such an interpretation of his act of murder undercuts his pretenses as an "outsider" to American culture. Along these lines, Mallory vehemently scolds him for doing such a "bad" thing—peculiar since she feels no remorse for their other innocent victims. In narrative terms, she singles out the Native American and justifies her sympathy because he took them into his home. But more likely the film's ideological reason behind her sympathy is that, as a Native American, he is a "victim" of American society like they are (the Old Indian's son was killed in Vietnam). As the film mystifies Mickey and Mallory, so too it exoticizes the Native American. Both Mickey and the Old Indian are victims of his unconscious (his dream), itself created by America's history of imperialist racism.

Ideologically loaded, this scene proves to be penultimate to the capture of the outlaw couple. At the same time, the film continues to code them in visionary terms. Mickey says the shooting was an accident, but Mallory counters that "there are no accidents"; that is, they are fulfilling some fate or destiny, they are driven by some force or plan beyond them. As they try to leave the Old Indian's abode, Mallory and Mickey get trapped by an army of snakes; Mallory gets bitten. When the police finally capture them outside the drugstore where Mickey has stopped for some snake-bite medicine, it seems that their karma is catching up with them. They get caught, not only when they stop moving, but also when they try to heal the wound inflicted by the snake. In a sense, the Old Indian has led them to their capture, a just comeuppance. And yet this capture turns out to be an extended detour on their ferocious journey.

Let us concede that the Old Indian is the film's most intriguing embodiment of the exoticized, nonwhite figure, slightly more elaborate than *Thelma and Louise*'s Rasta bicyclist. The film's general manner of representing people of color is entirely in keeping with the road movie (and Hollywood cinema generally). That is, race in *Natural Born Killers* is cast as Other —either as secondary, background color, or as overinvested, exoticized symbol, as in the case of this Native American, who carries "positive" values. Most other nonwhites in the film do not fare so well. We might note the Japanese television crew at Mickey and Mallory's capture, ridiculed for packaging the (tragic) event as titillating export; the Asian drugstore clerk, who is presented as buffoonishly obese; the truckload of Mexicans who ride by on the bridge during their "marriage" (Mallory curses them for interrupting); lastly, the cop following them at one point, who appears to be a person of color, but who oddly does not pull them over. His role in the film—like that of people of color in so many other road movies—is a brief symbolic flash.

The prison sequence, one year after their capture, focuses mainly on Mickey's interview with Wayne Gale, and its apocalyptic aftermath. Throughout, Mickey seems caught in a trance; Mallory too in her cell appears possessed. This contrasts sharply with the demonized caricatures of the representatives of the law, such as Gale, Scagnetti, and the prison warden (Tommy Lee Jones). Whatever the film may be saying about its outlaw couple—and perhaps it does not know what it is saying—one thing is clear: the film cannot help glorifying them. Mickey's shaved head and serial killer philosophy mesmerize Gale and the others present. To be sure, Gale admires Mickey for the ratings he will bring, but does not take his visionary ranting seriously. From the film's perspective, this is a crime much worse than anything Mickey and Mallory have done. In fact, Gale is punished for his "crime," while the outlaw couple go free. Mickey himself distinguishes between his murders, which are "pure," and the media's impure interest in sensationalizing them. When he utters the film's title, "natural born killer," describing his calling, the words seem to possess magical power, instigating an anarchic, rebellious riot throughout the rest of prison. The irony, and the contradiction, is that his words and image are transmitted on television to the rest of the prisoners. Television takes a beating throughout the film as a heartless vehicle of evil—yet it aids Mickey and Mallory to freedom, facilitating a furious subversion of authority.

In crosscut, Stone shows the riot gathering momentum while the interview proceeds. Additionally, Mickey seems "aware" of the riot. As the interview pauses for some guards to check on the disturbance, Mickey tells a tale to lure the remaining guards into a mesmerized stupor, so he can stage his glorious escape. Suddenly overpowering everyone, he insists Gale and a cameraman come along and record the spectacle. Mickey seems to be playing Gale's game so as to push Gale's face in the evil hype he manufactures, making him stew in his own mess. Gale, however, believes he and Mickey are now "buddies," and actually becomes Mickey's accomplice. But Gale—and all he represents—has been duped; he can never be "one of them." *Natural Born Killers* suggests that Gale's mass media machine is the inauthentic mass murderer who must be destroyed, Mickey and Mallory the "natural born" authentic killers who keep driving at the end.

The film concludes with a powerful synthesis of road movie mobility and mass media imagery. We watch through Gale's video camera as Mickey and Mallory execute him. This televised image then blips into a channel surfing montage, revealing O. J. Simpson, Rodney King, the Waco siege, then a series of screaming demons. At the end, while Leonard Cohen's "The Future" plays, Mickey and Mallory are on the road again, driving a mobile home, not just free, but with a family of kids. The irony of Mickey and Mallory's continuing mobility disturbs, not only because they have moved into a middle-class family vehicle, but also because such irony is easily rendered impotent as a coda to a film that cannot help romanticizing them. As the closing credits roll, we see a montage of previous scenes from the film. Though not resurrected from death as in *Thelma and Louise*, the outlaw couple is revived by this montage, as star outlaws. Such reflexivity does not engender critical analysis or distance, but rather celebrates (their) celebrity status—not unlike the endings of *Drugstore Cowboy*, *Delusion*, and *Thelma and Louise*. With conveniently ambiguous irony, the ending montage basks in the very celebrity culture that much of the film energetically bashes.

The Gay Highway: *My Own Private Idaho* and *The Living End*

The road movie of the early 1990s further reignites the fire of the outlaw couple by incorporating significant gay and lesbian characters and themes. While Hollywood churns out sentimental and derivative fare such as *Boys on the Side* and *To Wong Foo*, more compelling gay road movies appear from the independent sphere. Two notable examples from 1992 are Gus Van Sant's *My Own Private Idaho* and Gregg Araki's *The Living End*. Both films distinguish themselves from *Thelma and Louise* by operating through a more postmodern, expressionistic style and possess a more edgy, independent sensibility than the Hollywood feminist film. Like the latter film, however, they dynamically combine both the quest and outlaw road narratives, refueling the genre by exploring rebellion and cultural critique from a gay perspective.

My Own Private Idaho focuses on two gay male hustlers who ramble through the Pacific Northwest, Mike (River Phoenix) and Scott (Keanu Reeves). As Thelma and Louise replaced and revised the male buddy and hetero outlaw road movie couple with two women, *My Own Private Idaho*'s two "buddies" likewise challenge the genre's traditional buddy format, but "from within," embodying it through a different form of masculinity. But we should note at the outset that the film pairs an authentic gay outsider (Mike) with a poseur (Scott) who eventually returns to his conservative, upper-class home and family—and to his straight sexual orientation. While their mutual affection constitutes the emotional core of the film, this tension between the two buddies allows the film to combine romantic-modernist and postmodern sensibilities. More significantly, it allows the film to explore the genre's rebellion/conformity dualism in terms of economic class and sexual identity.

The film's iconography and narrative invoke classic scenes from the road movie's past, but also offer dramatically new configurations, mostly related to the gay politics driving the film. The laser disc cover of the wide-screen version features the most popular publicity photo from the film, which shows the two main characters, Mike and Scott, in two separate fragmented photos, sliced up vertically, laid over another photograph of the classic road movie icon: an empty highway through sprawling open landscape. This publicity image clearly situates the film generically within the road movie, specifically suggesting its early-1970s sense of fragmented identity on the road. Likewise, the "message" on the cover claims, "It's not where you go, it's how you get there," further framing the film's packaging as a self-conscious generic revision. The narrative proper begins with a title, "Idaho," designating the setting but also suggesting the state lines that will be crossed later. Throughout the film, different sections begin with titles reading "Portland" or "Seattle" or "Roma," underlining the narrative as structured by travel from one place to another. *My Own Private Idaho* is not the most mobile road movie; much of the film takes place in one place. But overall the film deals explicitly with being homeless and on the road. This theme gets articulated on various levels—for example, in these "state" titles, suggestive of the crossing of borders and a peripatetic narrative.

The first image of the narrative is likewise imbued with vintage road movie imagery: Mike standing on the open highway. More precisely, an extreme long shot frames the open highway through a deserted landscape. Then, Mike walks into the frame, his head now in close-up, transforming the shot into a jarring deep-focus shot (the radical distance between his head and the horizon). Such composition suggests Mike's identity as bound up with the road, the latter supplying the visual context he enters. His opening monologue proves a confessional discourse on the meaning of the road. He explains: "I always knows where I am by the way the road looks"; he knows he has "been here before." Then he describes the road meeting the horizon and mountain range as a "face, a fucked-up face." Put differently, the road is where he lives, what he keeps returning to. Let us also note that this same scene ends the film, framing the story within the visual and thematic motif of being on the road.

My Own Private Idaho continues its reinvention of road movie imagery by intercutting into this scene dreamlike shots of the sky, with clouds rolling in

5.5. Distance and intimacy: Mike (River Phoenix) framed with the road he knows so well.

fast motion. Instead of movement on the road, the clouds in the sky rapidly cruise, suggesting motion in overtly expressionistic terms. Cars are conspicuously absent. Mike is stationary; soon he will collapse from his narcoleptic condition. But this image of the still road with the "moving" sky seems obliquely to foreshadow his oncoming seizure. It also inverts road movie mobility without abandoning it altogether, projecting it (in both the literal and Freudian sense here) into the environment. Such paralyzed wandering in turn seems bound up with Mike's memories (and sense of loss) regarding his mother. After Mike collapses, the director initiates a series of flashbacks of Mike with his mother (often presented as home movies, a visual strategy familiar from *Drugstore Cowboy*). In his deep sleep, he seems to be "returning" to her. Here, she actually "appears" on the road, holding his head in her lap, coaxing him not to worry. Mike's quest for his lost mother, in fact, proves to be the crucial driving force of the film's mobility—but also of its gay outsider point of view.[15] In any case, these recurring visual motifs—the fast-motion clouds, the return to Mother—form part of the film's postmodern style: self-conscious and self-reflexive, ironic and playful. At the same time, through this postmodern aesthetic, the film displays a commitment to cultural critique, by virtue of the gay perspective it develops, repoliticizing the road movie outsider. Similarly, with its emphasis on Mike's psychological and emotional malaise in the context of an open-ended narrative, *My Own Private Idaho* harks back to the early-1970s road movie.

Other aspects of the film link rebellion with mobility in ways that revitalize the genre's culturally critical core. Through its ongoing montage approach, *My Own Private Idaho* inserts symbolic nonnarrative images: salmon leaping upstream against the flow, houses falling and crashing on the open road. While bearing a postmodern veneer (exaggerated, slow motion), such elliptical inserts work to pepper the story with provocative visual messages that convey rebellious mobility. Such rebel mobility occurs in the narrative too. One scene early in the film has Scott put Mike down to sleep, hidden at night on a street in a rich neighborhood. With a domestic argument occurring in a window above, Scott rails theatrically against his father (the town mayor), mocking this "comfy" neighborhood. Additionally, a non-synch organ-grinder version of "The Star-Spangled Banner" plays in the background, politically ironic commentary that recurs throughout the film. Later, with stolen money they buy a motorcycle, energizing their indigent drifting with speed and potential direction. The film aesthetically invests this turning point, isolating them from their environment through an aerial shot, then a low-angle close-up from the handlebars. Finally they pull up in front of the camera, commenting that they are "still alive," and that they are "on a crusade." With little narrative context for the conversation, both comments may be read as allegorically (if elusively) political: surviving AIDS, forced by a homophobic society to battle for their freedom. Such freedom is alluded to, of course, through the preferred road movie metaphor of the journey. While getting out of town is the main attraction, they decide to go visit Mike's brother, in Idaho.

But the road is not necessarily a place of freedom or a way to freedom for two gay men (recall the fate of the two gay men in *Vanishing Point*). Rather than bask in a "freedom" montage of traveling shots, the film cuts directly to them stranded on the highway (the bike won't start). Taking advantage of their arrested mobility, the film explores homosexual intimacy rather poignantly in the deserted "outback" of society. *My Own Private Idaho*'s campfire scene seems a deliberate allusion to *Easy Rider*, suggesting some affinity between Wyatt/Billy and Mike/Scott, as Rebel Buddies with a Cause. But Mike and Scott are "doubly" cast out by mainstream America: young, restless drifters, they are also *gay* young, restless drifters.[16]

As in *Easy Rider*'s campfire scenes, society's conservative attitudes insidiously haunt Mike and Scott's moment of intimacy. First of all, it is Mike who opens up to Scott, expressing his desire to be close to Scott, to be more than friends. The camera blocking is quite effective: Mike is curled up in a tight ball, while Scott is stretched out. Scott, who we know is only "playing" at being a lower-class rough gay hustler, at first resists Mike's suggestion. But he does feel a special camaraderie, and so they hug. However, Scott seems to yield to the embrace as a favor, not sincerely; perhaps this is why he bears the family name "Favor." The embrace is shot in extreme low-key light, so we do not see much. This lack of visibility foreshadows their eventual split, and Scott's insincerity. But it also may reflect a lack of vision on the director's part, an "internalized" homophobic attempt to make the film more palatable to mainstream audiences. On the other hand, the low-key light works nicely as a poetic reflection of homophobic society's refusal to "see" them. (Of course, the dim lighting is naturally motivated by the nighttime setting; but is anything ever "natural" in a film, especially such an expressionistic

5.6. Posing as a road rebel, Scott (Keanu Reeves) does not fear the oncoming highway patrolman, as Mike does.

fiction film as this one?) In any case, the scene is shrouded in a figurative darkness that is suggestive of the taboo, or the crossing of the line, that their embrace involves (and that was initiated, let us recall, by the film's *real* gay rebel, Mike).

In a peculiar aftermath to this special scene, the morning brings the unlikely figure of a Native American highway patrolman. His mere presence sends Mike into a terrified narcoleptic seizure; but he cordially helps Scott start the bike. Again, Scott has less to fear, less at stake, than Mike, because Scott is a poseur, and belongs to a politically powerful family. Like *Thelma and Louise*'s Rasta-rider and the Old Indian of *Natural Born Killers,* the Native American is iconically overinvested: one mobile minority helping another minority to be mobile. Beyond the predictable one-dimensional treatment of this person of color, we might also wonder why the film gives him a curiously conservative tint, as a policeman. In yet another disturbing twist regarding the Indian cop, the film has us observe him a few sequences later giving a citation to Hans (Udo Kier, of Paul Morrissey/Andy Warhol fame), now in possession of Mike and Scott's motorcycle. After visiting Mike's brother Richard (James Russo) in his trailer home, they sold the bike to Hans so they could fly to Italy to continue searching for Mike's mother. It is true that Hans has no straight buddy, no "Scott" on hand, to handle the cop. But the scene does not seem to be "about" Hans as a victim of homophobic authority. Rather, in contrast to Mike's and Scott's (Phoenix's and Reeves's) boyishly handsome "straight" appearance, Hans is overdone as a fag, a stereotypical portrayal of the Gay Eccentric, physically embodying a cross between Peter Lorre and Truman Capote. When we see Hans pulled over by the cop, he is lasciviously fondling the bike. The film perhaps inadvertently implies here that one type of gay man is an acceptable target of the police—and of ridicule. The scene's comic framework is not irrelevant in this respect: the genre's postmodern theme of absurd, ironic coincidence (same cop, same bike, same landscape—different rider) combines with caricatured, cartoonish acting to have a laugh. Yet such a laugh transparently veils archly conformist and homophobic perceptions.

By flying its gay buddy couple to Italy, *My Own Private Idaho* introduces an international (or crossnational) facet to the American genre that nicely complements the expanded boundaries represented by its gay point of view. Rather effectively, it is when they are furthest outside of American society that their quest is revealed as most futile and most ironic. After arriving by taxi at the home in the Italian countryside where they believe Mike's mother to be, they discover that again she is already gone, one step ahead of them, on the move, as they are. In a sense, her perpetually elusive mobility functions as a kind of mirror for their own: she will never be there for them, and they will never catch up with her. The fact that she only appears in the film as a memory, subjective (Mike's memory) but highly mediated (home movies), further conveys the destination of their quest as a ghostly absence, a delusion born from irretrievable loss. This futility is driven further home by an inadvertent but bitterly ironic consequence of their quest: Scott falls in love with Carmela (Chiara Caselli), the beautiful daughter of the family. So the search leads not to its destination, but in an unexpected, tragic, and ironic direction. That is, it leads *Scott* (it was never his quest, but now we see that it really was) to his betrayal of Mike—to his future wife, and to his return to conventional upper-class heterosexual comfort.

More refreshing road movie imagery expresses the plot's turnaround. The moving clouds motif reappears to Mike through the airplane window as he flies back to Portland, alone. Though literally moving, he observes movement in the surrounding environment; he is passive, paralyzed by his new loss, by his return to home(lessness), by his failed, futile journey. Back in the States, a smooth dolly shot from within a car reveals Mike back on the streets, back on drugs. But the true revelation of the shot is its point of view: Scott in a limousine, his new identity expressed through the socioeconomic connotations of the car. At the very end, another road montage— slow-motion leaping salmon, the clouds moving through the sky, the "Idaho" title, and a languorous extended pan of the highway—brings us to Mike on the road again. The synchronous monologue of the opening scene has given way to a nonsynchronous voice-over, suggesting his current disembodied state: he explains that he is a connoisseur of roads, that he has been tasting roads his whole life, that this road will never end. He passes out, and an aerial shot recedes upward—an intriguing revision of the one ending *Easy Rider*.

While that shot withdrew in horror from Wyatt and Billy being murdered by redneck America, this aerial shot conveys Mike's isolation in a more ironic and comic way, indicative of the film's overall postmodern mood. Opting away from *Easy Rider*'s politically ferocious catastrophe, here a truck pulls up, then two rednecks with cowboy hats take his money and his shoes. They violate the gay man's unconscious body, exploiting it but leaving it to continue living/moving. With "The Star-Spangled Banner" playing again, a second car pulls up. We watch from a dizzying height as the driver gets out, pulls Mike into the car, then drives off toward the horizon. Reworking *Easy Rider*'s political commentary, this extreme high long shot exaggerates what occurs in the plot (on the ground): individual identity consumed by the landscape and the highway. More significantly, the extreme distance creates a critical distance for the audience, facilitating the closing image as, again, politically allegorical. The sleeping gay male body, just previously ripped off, next becomes appropriated as cargo for some unknown purpose, with no home, no destination, at the mercy of the twists and turns of the road. The continuing journey of wanderlust that "closes" many early-1970s road movies is invoked here, repoliticized by a gay perspective, yet depoliticized with postmodern humor and artifice. The last shot of the film features a dilapidated house, with the fast-motion clouds rolling above it, then cuts to the message "Have a nice day." This seems a trendy, tongue-in-cheek 1970s reference; but also, perhaps, an ironic comment on the failure of 1970s "liberation" counterculture, suggesting that homosexuals in America cannot "have a nice day."

Beyond the film's linking of rebellion with mobility, the theme of the mobile visionary is developed on several levels in *My Own Private Idaho*. The road movie's visionary perspective, we have seen, is typically bound up with its emphasis on cultural critique, mobility beyond society provoking inspired insight. *My Own Private Idaho* uniquely dramatizes the visionary by contrasting Scott and Mike. Whereas Bonnie and Clyde, and even Wyatt and Billy, share in the visionary experience, albeit in distinct ways, Scott is presented as an imposter, while Mike is the real thing. Beyond the fact that the story is told primarily through Mike's point of view, the film further embellishes this point of view with narcolepsy, yielding a druggie, disorienting, often hallucinatory visual mode connoting the privileged insight of Blake. Let us take more specific note of Mike's particular visionary status. *My Own Private Idaho* alienates Mike from the road itself; the endless, aimless road expresses his state of loss and confusion, but his narcoleptic reactions serve to alienate him from his own lifestyle, paralyzing him on the road, interrupting his mobility, creating a curious dependence and vulnerability where he often needs to be carried away. Moreover, Mike is a distinctly unhip visionary; at a diner, when one of the other hustlers mentions a Sinead O'Connor concert, Mike comments awkwardly that he has never been to a concert. As the first trick for the rich woman near the beginning, he waits for her in her luxurious room, exploring the decorations of the mise en scène. He picks up a large seashell and listens to it. When she approaches him to kiss him, he realizes that she resembles his mother, and passes out.

In contrast to such authentic visionary experience, Scott is presented as the faux visionary, more histrionically embodying postmodern irony through the trope of performance (thus, a 90s version of Kit, a younger brother to Sailor). Because Scott's rebellious posture is a luxury he can afford, his visionary pretensions are—just that, pretensions. They are also rather trite, petty, and juvenile—directed often against his own friends. Early in the film, Scott comes up with the idea of "rebelling" against father-figure Bob Pigeon's (William Richter) scheme to ambush and rob a rock band returning through the park at night. Fueled by an aloof sense of irony, he and Mike ambush and rob *them*. After the joke, Scott confronts Bob and his gang, luring Bob into his predictable cover-up, comprised of baroque fabulation. Bob "tells his story" of what happened, a tall tale indeed, absurdly exaggerating details in the pathological spirit of *Two-Lane Blacktop*'s GTO. In fact, Scott has set Bob up to spin his tale, which dramatically links the road movie's storytelling theme (Bob's fiction) with postmodern posturing (Scott's false rebellion and "vision"). The replaying of Shakespeare's *Henry IV* through loosely intertextual allusion further underlines the artificial context of Scott's visionary posture. Reeves's performance of Scott's performance seems to be forcing the Shakespearean allusions. Even Bob's ludicrous pretensions to heroism and authority are coded as more sincere than Scott's hypocritical performance as an underclass visionary outcast.

When the police bust into the tenement warehouse where they all squat, the fracas blatantly invokes a comic version of the Hollywood staple scene from gangster films, going back to the Keystone Cops. More importantly, the scene stages a postmodern pastiche of Welles's *Chimes at Midnight* (1966) — itself a pastiche of several Shakespeare plays. The cops know Scott through his father's powerful political influence, and let him off, joking with him even as he is in bed with Mike.[17] Significantly, their "bedding" scene is yet another performance, a lie, a ruse (perhaps misleading Mike). Later, Scott's confrontation with his father is, like that with Bob, full of Shakespearean intertextuality and stagy irony, rendering the moment not really a confrontation but a playful father-against-son caricature (again, citing Shakespeare and Welles). Near the end of the film, after Scott has chosen his true, conservative, upper-class, and straight identity, the double funeral scene crystallizes the contrasting codings of visionary rebellion. Bob's funeral, which Mike attends, is full of pagan singing, dancing, and drinking, a carnivalesque celebration, with swinging cameras, swish pans, and garishly colorful costumes; Scott's father's funeral, where Scott sits suited and stately, is utterly conventional and conventionally religious.

No doubt, Scott's posturing as a visionary rebel represents one facet of a larger theme prevalent, as we have seen, throughout the genre's history: performance, fame, and celebrity culture. Beyond but related to Scott's characterization, this theme comes up throughout *My Own Private Idaho*. For example, when we first meet Hans in his apartment, he and Mike are "acting out" — Mike as a French maid, Hans dancing and singing a show tune. Here the trope of performance permeates the sexual-economic hustling relationship: Mike performs for the money, Hans pays to perform for his own sexual stimulation. This performance is then repeated and revised later, when Mike and Scott meet up with Hans before leaving for Italy. Hans again puts on a show for them, here a German Expressionist send-up of a cabaret song. In fact, aside from Scott, the film most cartoonishly invests Bob and Hans with an over-the-top theatrical flair. Both characters are pseudo father figures for Scott and Mike. Scott ridicules and betrays Bob just as the film itself ridicules and betrays Hans as a cipher of a "flaming fag."

At one point, Hans takes out a photo of his mother, which of course disturbs Mike. Mike's own photo of his mother represents a profound loss, whereas Hans's photo signifies a fully realized relationship. Indeed, photographs and movies form another layer of the film's postmodern emphasis on mass media. We should turn first to the bold "magazine cover" scene, which begins with a slow-motion dolly following from behind a cowboy entering a porn shop. Once inside, the camera frames the magazines lining the walls, featuring photos of the main characters. Then, seamlessly, the photos become live action poses, and the boy-toys start talking. It is no coincidence that the sequence foregrounds Scott, since he is the film's most avid performer: he speaks directly into the camera, explaining his plan to "play" at being a hustler so as to infuriate his father, until he is old enough to get his inheritance. This scene effectively combines a campy postmodern stylistic approach with the equally postmodern theme of mass media and performance. Despite being socially marginalized as gay, their bodies are commodities, transformed into images. The reflexivity of direct address and obvious special effects further conveys the notion that their identities are constituted in and through mass media.

Another rather different emphasis on the power of images in *My Own Private Idaho* occurs during their visit with Mike's brother Richard (James

Russo). Mike becomes mesmerized by a photo of himself and his mother. Perhaps projected on the mindscreen of Mike's consciousness, his "home-movie" memories of his childhood with his mother recur at this tense and tender moment (further linking images with memory and desire). At the same time, the film crosscuts to Scott in the bathroom, admiring himself in the mirror. Each image—the photo and the mirror—serve as a symbolic site of reflection and projection for each of the two buddies, distinguishing the two journeys. Scott's journey is more egotistical; he is the comfortable, more aloof passenger; he "comes home" to himself (and to socially "proper" sexuality and class) at the end. Mike's journey, in contrast, is more deeply driven by the quest—to heal his wound, his social isolation, and his emotional pain. Moreover, during this same scene, Richard tells a crucial, reverse-Oedipal story to Mike, where their mother supposedly murdered Mike's father in a movie theater during a screening of *Rio Bravo*. While this tale sends Mike into hysterical denial, it is worth noting that Richard seems obsessed with the fact that John Wayne was up on the screen during the shooting in the audience. We might compare *Repo Man*'s irreverent, postmodern mockery of John Wayne with the more disturbing, modernist insinuation here, that images and reality influence and determine each other with sometimes devastating effect.

Another important road movie of the early 1990s that "revitalizes the road genre" (Mills, 307) is *The Living End* (1992) by Gregg Araki. Released around the same time as both *Thelma and Louise* and *My Own Private Idaho*, *The Living End* likewise politicizes and revises the genre by reimagining its gender roles. But the film too anticipates *Natural Born Killers* for its furiously rebellious outlaw couple, much more irreverent and violent than Thelma and Louise or Scott and Mike. Testifying to the exciting and diverse road movie explosion in the early 1990s, the film races on the fringes of the mainstream: a self-consciously independent, no-budget film bristling with allusions to Godard and Jarman. In *The Living End*, a young gay couple is on the run from the law, but they are also searching, despite and because of their nihilism, for some more intense and fulfilling meaning to life under American patriarchy. Here, the context is more politically volatile than *My Own Private Idaho*'s gay hustlers: the two leading men are HIV-positive. As "infected" and branded rebel drivers of the genre, they travel further outside social norms than *My Own Private Idaho*'s male bodies, the latter jettisoned by commodity fetishism and class hierarchy. As Katie Mills puts it, "These are rebels with a cause, simply by virtue of being gay in a road film" (308). What *The Living End* shares with *My Own Private Idaho* and *Natu-*

ral Born Killers is a postmodern style of presentation that ultimately mitigates its political bite. Yet because *The Living End* rails with more political vigor against homophobic patriarchy, it persuasively reconfigures romantic-modernist cultural critique as radically postmodern.

The first part of the film crosscuts between the two gay buddies/lovers before they meet. Jon (Craig Gilmore), a hip film student and writer living in Los Angeles, has just discovered he is HIV-positive. As a character, following the road movie couple tradition, he is more the homebody, more conventional and cerebral. But he soon gets seduced by Luke (Mike Dytri) and his sensually thrilling life on the edge of legality and morality: he too has recently been informed of his positive blood test. It is significant that the film begins with Luke's rambling adventures on the road, establishing him as the angry fugitive. The film seems in many ways to privilege his perspective and attitude, which is more extreme, less easy to identify with, than Jon's. If Jon negotiates the audience's access to *The Living End*'s world of AIDS, then Luke functions more abrasively, as an instrument of (political) assault on such access. The film's first shot is of some graffiti Luke has just spray-painted ("fuck the world"). Then we cut to him standing alone on what appears to be a mountain highway turnout, chucking a bottle of whiskey out into the sprawling urban metropolis below him.

The crosscutting goes on to link thematically Luke's nihilistic drifting with Jon's grounded nightmare, as the latter learns of his death sentence. In contrast to Luke (who in a way is one step ahead of Jon), Jon tries to cope rationally and conventionally. The suggestion here is not only that their paths will cross (by virtue of the crosscutting, and their shared HIV-positive status), but also that Jon will eventually end up on Luke's road. In one of the film's early sequences, Jon drives past Luke hitchhiking, but is too distracted to notice, as he solipsistically speaks diary entries into his tape recorder. Such a scene instigates the genre's visionary emphasis, since Jon engages in a creative artistic activity while driving. More importantly, the scene also invokes the road movie's ironic sense of absurd coincidence or fate, as their paths literally cross on the road, before they literally meet and hit the road together.

Another early scene before Luke and Jon meet is notable for the generic self-consciousness and postmodern cartoonism that runs throughout the film. Luke gets picked up by two nasty lesbians, who taunt him and plan to kill him. In mocking earnest, they ask him where he is going; he says, "Wherever." His response politically reinvents road movie wanderlust, where "just going" is the only antidote to AIDS and homophobia. From this angle, Bobby (*Five Easy Pieces*), the Driver (*Two-Lane Blacktop*), and Sal (*On the Road*) all seem comfortable middle-class wanderers compared to being a gay man on the run in the 90s with AIDS. On the other hand, his "Wherever" is delivered with a distinctly slacker cool, which the two women call him on. They mock him as a "nomadic drifter," a "lonesome cowboy," like "Jack Kerouac hitching across the country," adding with their own venomous cynicism, "Isn't that romantic!" Further revealing the film's postmodern, punkish theatricality, the scene ends with a quirky take on the road movie's "absurd coincidence" theme. Luke warns the driver about snakes when she goes to pee; then, offscreen she screams, her partner jumping out to the rescue—conveniently leaving the keys and their gun. So he drives off.[18]

But Luke's control over his own mobility and direction is short-lived. In fact, he prefers to be aimlessly driven, a politicized (if irreverent) embrace of his socially cast-out status. He gets a flat tire, then we see him painting "I blame society" in an underground parking lot. This image of the road movie rebel underground in a parking garage connotes an ironic generic lack: a driver without a car, stuck in a place designed to arrest mobility. Again with postmodern wit, the political message he scrawls is trite, perhaps deliberately so: as a form of ironic, ludic subversion, he is "acting out" the cliché mainstream straight society will accuse him of becoming—a "victim" who "blames society." Hitching again that night, he gets picked up by a gay man, who is then murdered by his wife the next morning when she discovers the two men in bed together. As with the roving lesbians, this murder is done as farce, bombastically artificial, distancing us from the action. But one wonders, to what end? Once again, such comic reflexive excess functions at the expense of the female.

The initial portrayal of Luke suggests him as passive road movie cargo, carried along somewhat like Mike in *My Own Private Idaho*. Interestingly, both characters' passivity is due to their biochemical "condition": Mike's narcolepsy and Luke's HIV infection. While Mike suffers from past emotional trauma regarding the loss of his mother, Luke suffers from the more blunt and politically controversial fact of a fatal disease commonly associated with gay sex. Luke's despondency therefore is less psychologically grounded or emotionally justified, more vicious and ominous. The gay men of *My Own Private Idaho*, for example, never directly confront homophobic discrimination. Luke, however, is violently accosted by three gay-bashers (bearing T-shirts reading "Drugstore Cowboy," "sex, lies, & videotape," and "Avenue Pictures," perhaps reflecting Araki's own need to distance himself from so-called independent filmmakers like Van Sant). Somewhat reminiscent of the scene where Louise kills the rapist, Luke shoots all three in a dramatic catharsis—but one that is surely less palatable to audiences than Louise's "killing." The despondency of living with AIDS drove Luke to reckless wanderlust; now the murder of three men who would murder him for being gay drives him to outlaw desperation. In accordance with the genre, he needs a buddy/lover; Luke and Jon thus find each other—of course, on the road. From within Jon's car, we see Luke coming toward us in slow motion, stopping the car and forcing his way in. They come together, not only as a direct result of a political hate crime, but also while driving through a tunnel, visually suggestive of their entrapment by society and their refuge in the moving car.

Once Jon and Luke hit the road, *The Living End* further focalizes its acerbic suggestion that aimless, irreverent mobility—the journey *sans* destination—is the only appropriate political response to living with AIDS in a society that seemingly won't help or even have them. After their San Francisco destination does not work out (ironic, since the town is supposed to be a gay haven in America), Jon wants to know where they shall go, but Luke replies with the question, "What difference does it make?"[19] Later, Luke explains the meaning of the road movie they are driving: because they are "infected" outcasts, they are totally free, they have nothing to lose, they can "fuck the system." As they continue driving, the film presents a series of night shots—unique for a road movie, which typically prefers glaring daylight on blacktop and desert surface. Araki uses abstract patterns of dotted distant lights to achieve a striking poetic effect. Such night driving also underlines their fugitive mobility, perhaps invoking a romantic outlaw couple road noir like *They Live by Night*.[20] Another unique cinematic touch is the somewhat brazen use of tight close-ups during their drive. More typically, the road movie uses extreme long shots to visually emphasize the characters passing through landscape. *The Living End*'s extra-tight framing conveys their claustrophobic enclosure in the car, symbolic of their oppression by society. Yet it also creates a space for their intimacy, an outlaw intimacy that is cramped but nevertheless protected and nurtured by the traveling car. In this way, *The Living End* develops an antiromantic but politicized image of the desert landscape and open highway. Most of the landscapes we do see in *The Living End* during the day recall those near the end of *Easy Rider,* just before they are gunned down by redneck America: "Their trip never takes them through the stock Western topography that symbolizes awesome eternity, like Monument Valley, but reveals only a postmodern wasteland of fast-food joints and ominous highway overpasses" (Mills, 311).

Like most road movies, *The Living End* enhances the narrative spectacle of being on the road by juxtaposing crosscut scenes from "home," here conveyed primarily through Jon's repeated phone calls to his friend Darcy back in Los Angeles. Aside from revealing Jon's clinging conformity, these calls serve as narrative pretext to cut back to her and her unhappy plight as a straight woman trapped by her domestic relationship. However rough it is for Jon on the road as an outlaw, the film insists, going back seems even more depressing. In fact, during one call, not knowing where he is, Jon nearly quotes Thelma by musing that "nothing is the same, everything has changed." As Jon gropes for serious road movie reflection, Luke parades his naked bottom in the background. Whereas earlier the two lesbians poked fun at Luke the Road Man, here Luke mocks Jon's pretensions at making sense of the journey. Jon takes himself perhaps too seriously, a mistake the film punishes him for. As in many postmodern road movies, juvenile humor intervenes to dissolve critical distance—between character and society, but also between audience and film. A similar scene uneasily mixing reflexive humor with cultural critique is an extreme long shot of Luke up on a mountain, pissing, with Jon at the bottom of the frame, leaning on the car. Luke tells an elaborate, moving story of a bag lady who jumps to her death. But given the mise en scène, it is difficult to take the story seriously. At the conclusion of the tragic story, somewhat reminiscent of *Repo Man*'s tone, they decide to go for hamburgers. Swollen with cocky postmodern attitude, the film clearly intends to raise sociopolitical issues, brazenly confronting its audience. At the same time, the film seems compelled to trivialize both the issues themselves and the film's own engagement with them, through irreverent and juvenile humor.

Luke's reckless embrace of violence (which Jon mocks as a "Clint routine") eventually drives Jon to attempt a return home (which Luke mocks as "Toto going back to Kansas"). Both the Toto impulse and the Clint impulse prove dead ends at the end of *The Living End*'s road. However, their final gestures of mutual self-destruction equally reveal mutual affection. Stranded "on the road," off the highway near land's end in the blistering sunlight, they reject the "hackneyed romantic fantasy" of their own road narrative. Yet the film's quintessential desolate, open-ended ending seems an apt vehicle for affirming the journey of Living, of Living with the End, even when there is no place left to go.[21]

Drivers of Color: *Get on the Bus* and *Smoke Signals*

We shall now turn our attention to road movies of the 1990s featuring ethnic minorities—specifically African Americans and Native Americans. As women and gays take the 1990s road movie for a socially critical drive, so too do various nonwhite ethnic drivers give the genre a refreshing, repoliticized spin. However, out of respect for the discussion just preceding, let us clarify as a preface that most of these "people of color" road movies focus on *men* of color. To a degree, they therefore reenact the genre's typical masculinist perspective—the perspective disrupted and revised by the films previously discussed. Thus, from *within* the road movie's traditional male paradigm, we will address how these films use race and ethnicity to challenge the genre's traditional white framework.

As we have seen throughout this study, many road movies feature black characters, but they typically wave, observe from the roadside, or supply the white driver with drugs, perhaps inspiration. In any case, they are usually weighed down with a one-dimensional "meaning" to their racial otherness.[22] Historically speaking, the first black road movie may be *Sweet Sweetback's Baad Asssss Song,* starring and directed by Melvin Van Peebles, released in 1971. The film is more politically charged than its white existentialist counterparts from the early 1970s, largely due to its black perspective, which does not possess the luxury of alienated wandering. Born of the African American civil rights movement, *Sweet Sweetback* feels more like *Easy Rider,* though the film actually has little driving. This "lack" seems a political reflection of economic hardship and racial discrimination: blacks having minimal access to white middle-class America's car (whether for commuting, tourism, or lighting out from the suburbs). The narrative follows the desperate flight of its protagonist, Sweetback (Van Peebles), for stopping police brutality against another black; he ends up killing one of the officers. For much of the film Sweetback hides out and moves about in the city. Yet toward the end he crosses the threshold from city to wilderness, roaming the desert, finally heading into Mexico with an exclamatory avowal of insurrection. *Sweet Sweetback* is significant as a black road movie, not so much for its narrative emphasis on mobility, but for the way it links mobility with rebellion against racism. Invoking the "Underground Railroad" of the era of slavery, the film infuses its "man on the run" journey with revolutionary anger and incisive political critique.[23]

Not surprisingly, it was Spike Lee who created a landmark road movie in 1996 with *Get on the Bus,* perhaps the first example of the genre that explicitly focuses on blacks on the road. This road narrative, driven by blacks, is mobilized so as to address American social tensions around racism and the historical specter of slavery (as opposed to just putting blacks behind the wheel for a politically innocuous joyride, as in 1998's *Ride*).[24] *Get on the Bus* is a self-conscious example of the genre, infused with a pointed, if sometimes didactic, commitment to visionary rebellion and cultural critique. At the same time, like most road movies, the film is rife with political contradiction, where conformist values harass the journey's progressive forward motion.

Get on the Bus focuses on a group of black men, most strangers to each other, traveling across country on a chartered bus ("The Spotted Owl") to attend the Million Man March in Washington, D.C. Unlike the dramatic focus in typical road movies (whether quest or outlaw) on individual rebellion, this film dynamically reinvents the genre's less common convention of a traveling community. While some road movies use the train, caravan, or bus as a mobile "meeting place" for a cross section of society (*It Happened One Night, The Grapes of Wrath,* Bunuel's *Mexican Bus Ride*), few actually break from the standard one or two main characters typical of the road movie.[25] On this bus, there is no one main character or couple; the *group* is the main character. Additionally, the black male group is the majority, *not* the minority. Most importantly, this group contains a wide range of diversity. Rather than presenting a palatable homogeneous whole, Lee resists idealizing this diversity, instead delving into the nuanced, often tense differences among the black males. From our perspective, it is refreshing to see a road movie with such a multiplicity of traveling characters.

Another significant feature of *Get on the Bus* is that its journey possesses a specific destination (the March in D.C.), one overinvested with meaning for each passenger, and for the narrative as a whole. The bus ride exists by virtue of the all-important destination, an event with pretensions to being historically and politically momentous. From a slightly different angle, the meaning of the destination directly bears on the social and political issues the film explores among the various passengers during the journey. And yet, like most road movies, *Get on the Bus* also emphasizes the journey. While the March hovers on the horizon, generating the political issues in the film, the ride itself receives most of the narrative focus. In many ways, the destination is dramatically minimized: when they finally arrive, they are unable to attend the March. Politically and narratively, Lee emphasizes *going to* the March, rather than the event itself. The March, being literally stationary, seems less significant for the film than the process of moving toward the (idealized) goal of the March. Moreover, the closing speeches by the bus driver George (Charles S. Dutton) and by Pop (Ossie Davis) valorize the "journey" continuing beyond the event: "what is to be done" after the March. Thus, despite the characters' own motivations for going, the March is *not* the end-point destination, but the point of departure. The *real* March, in a way, was occurring on the bus, on the road, as the various characters entered into dialogue about life in America for black males.

The film's powerful credit sequence establishes the political context for the ensuing narrative journey. Visually reminiscent of the credit sequence of his previous *Clockers* (1994), the "floating" titles are intercut with roving close-ups of black men and women, shot in soft, low-key blue lighting. The first shot is of a black man's eye looking directly into the camera; ensuing shots show arms, legs, and necks, sometimes in shackles. As the credits progress, the eyes start to avert from the camera, evocative less of confrontation than of denial, refusal to engage, and frustration. As Michael Jackson sings "Put Your Heart on the Line," these sultry close-ups sketch the fragmented black body as both erotic and imprisoned (by Western representation, and by racism). The film abruptly transitions from this darkly symbolic montage to the narrative proper via a bright, color low-angle shot of a cross atop a church.

The next few sequences introduce us to the main characters before and just after the road trip begins. Though not presented through montage formalism, the characters seem to represent various "types." This is one annoying aspect of the film: the "characters" seem more like symbols of various positions, rather than real people, which in the context of a realistic and topical premise renders some sections didactic and artificial. On the other hand, such exaggerated character symbolism may be an appropriate and necessary strategy for articulating marginalized ethnic perspectives. To break the mold of oppressive stereotype requires a heavy hand indeed. In any case, this road movie's drive is uniquely inhibited by the very topicality that repoliticizes it. No long stationary pauses of existential exploration or ironic paralysis here. *Get on the Bus* is a film that moves a lot (across the span of the United States, for the entire narrative), but that gets bogged down with its soapbox polemics.

We are first introduced to Evan and Evan Jr. (Thomas Jefferson Byrd and DeAndre Bonds, respectively), handcuffed to each other by court order: the son must remain in his father's custody for the next 72 hours. The young teen prefers his "homey" nickname "Shmoove," and calls his father "dog." Throughout the film's journey they embody the "father-son" problem in the black community (see *Boyz N the Hood,* mentioned in *Get on the Bus*), where young black fathers irresponsibly abandon their sons, perpetuating the cycle of alienation, violence, and poverty. This social phenomenon, to be sure, was a primary issue on the agenda of the Million Man March. In fact, Evan and his son are arguing about going when we first see them approaching the bus, the son not wanting to go. Regarding this issue specifically (the need for fathers and sons to bond), the bus they board and the journey they undertake become a more hopeful version of the handcuffs: bringing father and son together, providing a space for them, a space that is intimate and *going somewhere.* At one point later in the film, Evan agrees to take the cuffs off his son. When everyone piles off the bus to watch a fistfight (between a gay black man and a macho movie star wanna-be), Evan Jr. exploits the distraction and dashes off into the woods. An obvious suggestion here is that violence within the black male community is a form of neglect, fostering family disintegration. From a genre perspective, the scene is significant because it occurs when the bus *stops*, and everyone gets *off* the bus (a direct violation of the film's mandate title). Junior's disappearance becomes the new crisis to be dealt with. Consequently, all come together in their search for him. Eventually the father finds him and coaxes him back to the bus, in a long confessional scene, the major turning point in their relationship.

Returning to the departure scene, the second main character we meet is Gary (Roger Guenveur Smith), first seen arguing with his wife in their car near the bus. She feels the whole underlying premise of the March is sexist, exclusionary, and ultimately regressive. But he calmly insists that he wants to go. Gary's character is a compounded cipher of volatile issues. On the road, we learn with the other passengers that (1) his mother is white; (2) his father was a cop who was killed by another black; and (3) he himself has become a cop. As a mixed-race black who also represents the law, Gary provokes much tension and hostility—primarily through contact with Jamaal (Gabriel Casseus). As a member of the Nation of Islam, Jamaal questions Gary's "authenticity," since Gary is half-white. More emphatically, Jamaal reveals that he used to be a "gang-banger," like the one who killed Gary's father. Reformed by his embrace of the Muslim religion, presently a counselor with at-risk youth, he honestly "confesses" that he had "smoked" someone during his gang days. At the end of the ride, Gary vows that he has an ethical responsibility to bring him to trial.

Another important main character is Jeremiah Washington (Ossie Davis), who goes by Pop, first shown escaping from a rest home, pulling off his "shackle" (the name tag on his wrist), then mounting the bus. It is interesting that most of the bus passengers are shown leaving behind some form of institutional stability, whether it be domestic, legal, religious, academic, or medical. Representing the 1960s "civil rights" generation previous to that of the March, radiating quiet dignity and wisdom, Pop serves as a kind of father figure on the ride. At the same time, he reveals that he was a man who worked hard and never "made trouble," but was exploited and eventually disposed of by the "downsizing" system. He explains in ambiguous terms to another passenger that this led to the loss of his wife and family. Later the passengers learn that Pop embarked on the journey to the March knowing that he could easily die from his heart disease (he does die at the end). Before the bus departs, he blesses the journey; the night of the bus's arrival in D.C., after the March and after his death, Pop's voice-over recites another prayer. His character thus forms a "frame" for the journey. It also provides this road movie with much of its visionary element. While the general narrative pretext is driven by the visionary idea of social change for the black male community, Pop embodies the elder, shamanistic visionary. Through his wise words and unassuming insights, he often effects a mystical healing. Pop's centrality in *Get on the Bus* therefore invokes other rare but intriguing road movies that feature elder travelers (discussed below).

Rather significantly, Pop's opening blessing is interrupted by one of the more testy characters, Flip (Audre Braugher), as he gets on the bus late. He is an aspiring actor who is self-centered, but also rabidly sexist and homophobic. The film brings out his homophobia almost immediately, when Flip encounters the journey's gay couple, Randall (Harry Lennix) and Kyle (Isaiah Washington). They too are arguing just as the bus departs: Kyle "needs space" and wants to end their relationship as lovers, but not as friends. Yet another main character is Xavier (Hill Harper), who goes by X and who seems the film's surrogate for Lee himself (at one point he is referred to as a "Spike Lee Jr."). A film student at UCLA, Xavier is shooting a video documentary of the bus ride and the March; throughout he interviews the passengers. Yet he has no pretense of merely observing, and becomes a "son" for Pop, who at one point shows Xavier how to play the African djembe drum. As the journey's young artist, he (along with Evan Jr.) represents the future of black males: the film's penultimate shot, after Pop's death, shows Xavier pounding feverishly on the drum in the back of the bus. Not coincidentally, it is George the bus driver who decides that Pop's drum should be given to Xavier (that the "torch" of ancestral dignity be passed from old to new). George is also one of the crucial characters, especially in terms of the film as a road movie. Lee highlights George's role as the driver of the journey: he becomes the leader, the ringmaster. A younger, more enlightened version of Pop, George makes the film's final speech about the need to continue "the journey" beyond the March. Moreover, throughout the film he negotiates conflict with reasoned insight. While most of the other characters are "extreme" in some way, George seems the most balanced and the most positive character—the journey's "center."

Get on the Bus further teases out the social and political issues expressed through each of the traveling riders, by redeploying road movie conventions. The genre's core of cultural critique uniquely addresses the contemporary plight of black males in American society. George sets the tone in this respect by exclaiming upon departure that they will "ride into history." Then, *Get on the Bus* quickly mobilizes the road movie technique of music-as-movement. Before they leave, someone puts on James Brown, as though the music is crucial to the start of the drive. They all enthusiastically sing along as they start their trip, an invigorating use of road movie music, expressing the thrill of mobility, but also invoking an icon of black pride in the entertainment field. (On the other hand, reading against the grain, Brown is problematic as role model or hero, given his history of drug abuse and domestic violence). The film then goes into a driving montage in rhythm with the music. After the Brown song, the passengers create their own driving music through a "roll call" rap where each character introduces themselves. Throughout the film, music and sing-along invest the journey with political significance.

In a bold gesture, Lee derails the trip almost as soon as it starts, out in the desert (notably, the classic road movie landscape), using the genre's "car accident" plot twist to further contextualize the political meaning of this journey. Significantly, the crash occurs as a result of George wondering aloud to fellow driver Craig (Albert Hall) about Farrakhan, and whether he is good or bad for blacks. The crash thus symbolizes the ambivalent conflicting attitudes toward Farrakhan that are in fact articulated later by the characters on the journey. Here the mere mention of his name causes a crash, suggesting that whatever one's opinion, he is a volatile and controversial black leader. Questioning his leadership can "stall the movement"; or, Farrakhan himself shall "stall the movement" by being so controversial. Another provocative connotation of the crash is that it occurs just after the bus enters the familiar terrain of the genre, the desert landscape. That is, this also "causes" the crash, since blacks have never traveled this generic landscape before, creating a kind of shock to the genre's system. After they "get off the bus," George explains the link between their immediate task—getting the bus out of a ditch—and the plight of their African Zulu warrior ancestors. Initially they cannot budge the bus, but he inspires them with legends of their ancestral history; on second try, they are successful. This is another way the crash becomes politically symbolic. Not unlike the scene later in the film where Junior flees during a fight, here the black male community comes together, despite their differences, to push forward for social progress. But also, it is crucial that they harness their common racial heritage, for strength. In a sense, the bus accident was "necessary" (thus no accident) for the journey to continue.

Yet merely harnessing ancestral energy, the film suggests, is not enough to overcome all obstacles. Once out of the ditch, the bus still will not start, so they have to wait for a new bus. With the arrival of the new bus, yet another "problem" is introduced, as the flip side to a solution. The new driver is

5.7. Jump-starting a stalled vehicle . . .   5.8. . . . means harnessing ancestral energy, in *Get on the Bus*.

white and Jewish, which does not thrill most of the passengers, adding more tension to an already tensely disparate group. Like most of the other characters, Rick (Richard Belzer) represents a "type" in a disconcertingly one-dimensional manner: the naive liberal Jew who tries to bond with blacks. Eventually Rick decides that he cannot continue the journey, that he does not "belong" (perhaps internalizing the film's own attitude: Rick chooses to do what the film thinks he should do). This notion of "belonging" on the bus is developed later, in equally convenient and stereotyping strokes, with Wendell Perry, a Lexus car salesman who the passengers meet at a roadside diner. He asks if he can go along with them. It is against bus policy, but they all convince George that a higher policy is to include all "brothers." Once Perry is on the bus, the film wastes no time in demonstrating that brotherhood has little to do with race. Perry turns out to be a Republican who blames blacks for their own problems; he brags that he is attending the March to try to sell some cars. He gets literally thrown off the bus, a collective action sublimated with slow-motion cinematography, implying a certain alignment between him and Rick as not acceptable in this community of passengers.

Later, in another classic road movie scene, yet another intrusion into their mobile community occurs, in the form of two cops who pull them over. Typically for the genre, as we have seen, the highway patrolman represents an ominous threat to visionary rebellion, society's roving arm of the law, extending its regulations to the fringes. In *Get on the Bus*, the "pull-over" scene is potently infused with the historical resonance of racism and slavery—a resonance white outlaw drivers do not have to contend with. Two Tennessee troopers stop the bus at night. The nighttime southern setting of the mise en scène works poetically and politically here, suggestive of the dark chapter of America's past that is in fact still present. They come onto the bus with their German shepherd "Bruno," claiming to be searching for drug-runners; the scene is coded as a racially motivated invasion. No drugs are found, but it is a tense scene, ending with a series of compelling, confrontational close-ups

5.9. The mise en scène of confrontation: the audience sees through the point of view of racist cops who get on the bus.

of each passenger's face. Shot in a glowing blue light, visually reminiscent of the credit sequence, each face stares blankly, suggesting that despite their differences they are all connected by this all too familiar experience of white oppression. Even Gary, who presumes a professional rapport with his law-enforcement peers, discovers that ultimately he is on the other side of the law, as a black man. This sequence also implies once again that when their mobility gets arrested, antagonistic trouble invades their vehicle (a special vehicle in this case, since it defines their mobile collective identity: the bus).

While *Get on the Bus* clearly repoliticizes the road movie from a black perspective, it also integrates postmodern aesthetics. Quite distinct from the restrained visual style of the early-1970s road movie, *Get on the Bus* seems more under the stylistic spell of postmodern road movies like *Natural Born Killers* and *My Own Private Idaho*. Like most of Lee's films, *Get on the Bus* is highly formalistic. As we have seen, postmodern formalism can dilute the road movie's critical perspective toward dominant culture. At times, the film tries to create a stylized spectacle out of its pressing "realistic" issues. Many canted angles, handheld and sweeping dolly camera movements seem un-motivated. When they are stranded in the desert after their crash, Lee uses a grainy yellow filter, giving an unreal cast to the harsh sunlight, exaggerating the desert setting, yet also emphasizing the construction of the image. In one scene, the camera travels down the bus aisle, with each character looking into the camera as the film switches back and forth between video and film stock. Another fast dolly down the bus aisle at the end of the film shows Pop unconscious in the back. Such visual flair aspires to postmodern flashiness.

Often these postmodern stylistics derive from Xavier's video lens. Such reflexivity seems distinctly post-Godard. But Godard rarely portrays a fic-tional filmmaker character; instead, he draws attention to the making of the film being watched. More typical of Hollywood and American indepen-dent reflexivity, *Get on the Bus* fictionalizes its filmmaking references. As in many postmodern road movies, the reflexivity of *Get on the Bus* partakes of the home-movie/camcorder look that currently saturates commercial main-stream images (such as television commercials) and the indie film scene (e.g.,

The Blair Witch Project). As a twentysomething college student wielding a video camera, Xavier seems designed to appeal to the MTV generation. His hip, off-the-cuff documentary injects the sometimes heavy-handed, didactic, and classically linear narrative with a certain look and feel that aims for postmodern cool (e.g., the blending of black and white with color, the blending of different film stocks).

On the other hand, the film's attention to its own look is not merely style for style's sake; nor does it convey a juvenile, cartoonish attitude of jaded irony. As with *Natural Born Killers* and *My Own Private Idaho*, the film attempts to relate its reflexivity to its political agenda. The shifting from story mode to discourse mode engendered by Xavier's metacinematic interventions adds yet another dimension to the film's critical modernist perspective. In many scenes, Xavier questions the other passengers about why they are going to the March. The film cuts back and forth from his video-image point of view, to the "real" film-image point of view. This brings attention to the narrative's construction, which effectively heightens the questioning going on between the characters. One important interaction occurs when Xavier asks Randall about his "role as a gay man" attending the March. Through Xavier's viewfinder, we see Randall taking photos of Xavier shooting the video, returning and challenging Xavier's inquisitive, documenting gaze. Likewise, he "returns" Xavier's question—a narrow-minded one that forces Randall into a sexual category—by asking "what's your role as a filmmaker?" Such reflexivity—unlike the hyperreal, depoliticized variety—situates the fiction, and the filmic production of the fiction, in a political context.

For all its progressive reflexivity, and for all its politicized revisionism of the genre in terms of race, *Get on the Bus* is haunted, as most road movies are, by its conservative sexist male perspective. Indeed, precisely because the film challenges sexism on many fronts, it becomes all the more frustrating when it repeatedly lapses all too readily into reactionary male attitudes. For the majority of the entourage of diverse male characters, women represent— big surprise—either sex or mothering. Gary seems to embody the Positive Alternative, often articulating sensitivity toward women and hostility toward the misogyny and homophobia prevalent among his "brothers" on the bus. He boasts fidelity and respect for his wife. Yet the film insists on relating his "new man" sensitivity to the fact that he is half-white. This is a disturbingly naive (if not racist) implication: that "softness" and femininity come from being white. It is therefore no surprise that Gary often comes off as contrived and didactic, not authentic or "natural"—that is, in the film's view, not really black.

More to the point, this link (sensitive male = white) actually serves to avoid the gender issue by transforming it into a racial issue. During the card game near the end between Jamaal, Gary, and Flip, they banter about their first "whipping" by their mothers. Gary reveals that he was only "lectured" by his mother, never beaten; Jamaal and Gary insist this is due to her being white. An argument heats up around "white" behavior versus "black" behavior. Yet this conflict overshadows the exaggerated (male) perception shared by all the men (including Gary) of mothers as punishing matriarchs. In the crucial scene with Pop and Xavier drumming, Pop instructs Xavier to "make love" to the drum, not just play it. This is supposed to be a tender moment of bonding in terms of racial and ethnic heritage, of transference between "father" and "son" around preserving black authenticity and history. But the notion of women as sex objects is just beneath the surface of Pop's metaphor. *Get on the Bus* attempts to shed a critical light on the sexism of its male entourage. Unfortunately, it is not too successful in this attempt. The film seems more concerned with celebrating the dynamic racial complexity of its Men's Group. Derogatory remarks and attitudes toward women, according to the film, are necessary ingredients to its portrayal of black male authenticity. One wonders how necessary such ingredients are, not only to the film, but to its Million Man March politics of "taking responsibility."

Smoke Signals (1998) is a more recent entry in the multicultural road movie vein, one worth discussing in comparison with *Get on the Bus*. *Smoke Signals* reworks the genre in the direction of Native American identity and history. Like Lee's film, it falters at times with moments of heavy-handed sentimentalism. Again, this is perhaps due to a marginalized culture trying to effectively appropriate a Hollywood-independent genre—"effectively" so as to be popular, and "effectively" so as to convey ethnic authenticity. Directed by Chris Eyre, scripted by Sherman Alexie (from his story collection *The Lone Ranger and Tonto Fistfight in Heaven*), *Smoke Signals* is notable for being the first feature film with a major release about *and authored by* Native Americans. An independent venture full of Hollywood clichés, the film is curiously marked by classical, visionary, existential, and postmodern road movie characteristics. More importantly, as in *Get on the Bus,* the ethnic minority perspective driving the narrative reclaims the culturally critical potential of the road movie journey.

In fact, the film has a clear precedent in 1989's *Powwow Highway,* which deals with many of the same issues. Influenced by William Least Heat Moon's novel *Blue Highways, Powwow Highway* features two tensely complementary Native American buddies on the road in a beat-up Chevy. On their way to New Mexico, one is a "fool" who believes in the old traditions and rituals, while the other is a modern, more cynical political activist. As they travel, they rediscover their "roots" through encounter with the land-scape, simultaneously confronting contemporary social injustice. Like *Smoke Signals, Powwow Highway* unevenly flip-flops between independent modernism and heavy-handed Hollywood sentimentalism and slapstick humor. Less direct precursors to *Smoke Signals* are the revisionist Westerns of the New American cinema, such as *Tell Them Willie Boy Is Here* (1969), *Little Big Man* (1971), and *Billy Jack* (1971), where the Indian is revised as hero, romanticized as the sympathetic outlaw. *Smoke Signals* is not a Western; rather, it is a contemporary Native American road movie that derives much of its culturally critical resonance from the specter of the Western genre. The latter, we know, influenced the road movie; but more significantly it manufactured skewed images of Native Americans, images that *Smoke Signals* rebelliously revises.

Very much a male buddy quest road movie, *Smoke Signals* offers a refreshing alternative to the Old Indian of *Natural Born Killers*. The film focuses on Victor Joseph (Adam Beach) and Thomas Builds-the-Fire (Evan Adams), childhood friends on a Coeur d'Alene reservation in Idaho who make a bus journey to Phoenix, to retrieve the body of Victor's recently deceased father, Arnold Joseph (Gary Farmer). Along the way, they relive Native American oppression as well as confront the current contradictory state of Native American identity. As a preface to this journey, *Smoke Signals* opens with an intriguing allusion to *Vanishing Point*. The voice of the radio announcer at KREZ recalls Supersoul, setting the tone of the film during its opening establishing shot. As a voice-over, we hear the "traffic report," where "a truck just went by." Classically road movie, a high-angle long shot reveals an old beat-up trailer parked at a vacant highway crossroads. The self-conscious, slightly self-deprecating humor of the DJ's voice-over conveys a certain bitter embrace of the socially isolated landscape of the reservation. Even at the very start of the film, we can distinguish such irony from the postmodern irony of, for example, *Stranger than Paradise*. As in the latter film, here on the reservation there is not much happening; the inhabitants are socially disenfranchised and geographically isolated. Yet the community (represented by the radio announcer) embraces this status, through an irony grounded in social commentary, one full of political, satirical bite. The irony of *Stranger than Paradise*, let us recall, is grounded in aloof urban cool: an affordable, hip alienation.

The film's initial portrayal of Victor's father generally invokes the early-1970s road movie emphasis on psychological trauma. First, Thomas's voice-over recounts the aftermath of the crucial house-burning incident of their childhood, where Victor's father, an alcoholic, accidentally started the fire that killed Thomas's parents. Yet the infant Thomas was saved by the father. Then we observe how Victor's father "practiced vanishing" (his term for repeatedly abandoning his family) as a way to (not) deal with the memory of the tragedy. As he drives away in a pickup truck, the idea of "vanishing" characterizes both driving, and running away from emotional trauma and family responsibility. Significantly, vanishing here is conceived not as some mystical, nihilistic convergence of speed, but as a direct reaction to the difficulty of working through family dynamics in the shadow of genocide. This gets further developed a bit later in another flashback with Victor as a child, riding with his dad in the pickup, the latter talking about making everything—the white people, the reservations, the history of oppression—disappear. The image of the burning house—the destruction of "home"—as narrative point of departure also recalls *Badlands* and *Wild at Heart,* expressing a traumatic inferno that consumes stability and comfort. But in contrast to the modernist ambiguity and postmodern gothic stylistics of those two films, *Smoke Signals* concretely situates its destruction-of-home in the context of the social disease of alcoholism within the Native American community, a disease in turn symptomatic of a broader subcultural plague.

While the film possesses many classic driving montage sequences, especially during the bus ride, one entirely unique driving sequence occurs before the bus ride begins. Two young women, friends of Victor and Thomas, are driving *in reverse* down the highway, this for no apparent reason, a spectacle of sheer road movie absurdity. And yet, "driving backward" garners political resonance as commentary on the socioeconomic status of Native Americans, going "backward" as the "society" that conquered them "progresses." Such driving backward becomes subversive driving "against the grain" of the genre and of the highway. The gesture becomes not so much illegally or immorally subversive (no outlaws here), but rather an inventive deconstruction of the road itself—a corrosion of its pretense to (metaphoric) forward motion. We might read the scene as suggesting that such a metaphor (that is, the road movie) has not worked for Native Americans. Delving more specifically into the scene, we should appreciate the gender dynamic at play: the two men are *walking* down the highway, while the car is being driven by two women. When the car stops for them, they all joke around together, until finally Thomas "barters" with them for a lift to the bus station, offering them "a story." While iconically the two women buck the trend of road movie driving, narratively they function to aid the two buddies on their journey, by driving them. In this way they repeat the conservative subtextual conventions of the genre. On another level, this scene instigates both the storytelling motif and the visionary theme of the genre. Here, storytelling on the road possesses a specific political meaning, as the dying oral tradition of an oppressed people. By having Thomas "trade" his story for the ride, the film suggests an equivalence between fiction and journeys (e.g., *Two-Lane Blacktop*'s GTO). The story buys them a ride to their bus ride; conversely, their bus ride is full of stories (memories, visions, traditional parables, etc.).

Smoke Signals clearly articulates their bus journey to Phoenix in terms of their outsider, marginalized status as Native Americans. But it also emphasizes the poverty integral to such status. Unlike *Drugstore Cowboy*'s bus rides, which simply gloss over lack of money, the bus ride here explicitly denotes economic hardship: Victor has no car for the trip (his mother needs it for work); he does not even have enough money for the bus fare. He is only able to go after Thomas offers to help pay for the trip—on the condition that he is allowed to come along. As we have just seen above, *Get on the Bus* too uses the bus ride to portray a socially marginalized collective group, but it does not address the issue of economic hardship. No fault of the film, most of its characters seem to be taking the ride rather comfortably. And yet Lee's bus ride does convey the social status and history of black America, evoking the segregated buses of the South, but also more generally the primary transportation mode of the underclass (within cities and from state to state). In this sense, the centrality of bus transportation in both films seems crucially bound up with their focus on marginalized people of color. From this angle, the staple element of the genre—owning a car and driving it for leisure or exploration, or even escape—takes on an aura of middle-class privilege.

Once Victor and Thomas embark on their bus ride, *Smoke Signals* further politicizes this mode of transport by dramatizing their Other status within the mobile space of the bus itself. As they "get on the bus" (Victor says this line to Thomas), they are observed by the other passengers as ethnic freaks, conveyed effectively through a first-person moving camera. The passengers look directly into the camera, at them, but also at us; thus the audience is made to feel the subtle but arrogant "gaze" of the dominant culture. In contrast to that of *Get on the Bus*, the tension on this bus is between the dominant culture and a marginal community (significantly, a "community" of only two). The impact of the sequence is additionally heightened by the fact that the bus driver is the first to give them (us) "the look." As they make their way through the bus, subjected to more suspicious glances, the film crosscuts to close-up inserts of the driver starting the bus. Such a montage suggests a parallel between the looks thrown at these cultural Others, and the mode of the journey. The movement of the bus and the bus itself become yet another "colonized" space. Victor and Thomas are not just passengers

5.10. On the road, no money for a car, waiting for the bus: Victor (Adam Beach) and Thomas (Evan Adams) in *Smoke Signals*.

on the bus, but second-class passengers. Unlike those going to the Million Man March, Victor and Thomas can find no solace in their driving space.

Almost immediately, their interactions with the other passengers become tense. A young white girl from Texas sitting across from them says, "You're Indians, right?" She is congenial, but betrays an insidious liberal racism, which Victor reacts to. Eventually Victor catches her in a lie, and insults her by calling her on it. I think we can take this "little" lie to represent the "larger" lie of the imperialist history informing her patronizing, if innocuous arrogance. After she moves to another seat, Victor tells Thomas that "you can't trust anyone"—something he has learned from the White Man. Thomas refuses to adhere to such an attitude; he sees Victor's acceptance of it as yet another victory for the White Man. Thomas prefers to preserve traditional Native American ways. Yet moments later, two redneck cowboys steal their seats; a confrontation ensues, with Victor and Thomas having to move to the back of the bus. Grumbling brash bigoted comments, these rednecks are more overtly racist than the young woman. Yet both the passenger moving away from them and the passengers forcing them to move away signify complementary forms of isolating Native Americans.

As Victor and Thomas grudgingly move to the back of the bus, Thomas observes with trenchant humor that the "cowboys always win." Once in their new seats ("moved off" their original seats/homeland), Victor and Thomas begin chanting a song they seem to spontaneously invent, about not ever seeing John Wayne's teeth. Unlike the songs on Capra's bus in *It Happened One Night* or on Lee's bus, here no one joins in the singing; in fact, their raucous rendition becomes a bizarre spectacle that further disturbs the other passengers. In this sense, the chant becomes an expression of resistance to dominant (white) social etiquette. The song achieves a deconstruction of the "cowboy" myth, and the racist/imperialist history packed into it, by mocking John Wayne. This instance of cultural critique is further enhanced by being slightly reflexive, focusing on *the* movie star icon who embodies the frontier expansionism that oppressed and annihilated Native American culture. (There is also a suggestion here of *Repo Man*'s critical and comedic references to John Wayne.)

The road movie's visionary theme becomes especially important to *Smoke Signals,* since it dovetails with the film's Native American perspective. Put differently, *Smoke Signals* reinvents the visionary politics of *Easy Rider* by reviving the visionary tradition of Native American culture, yoking together, in a sense, this tradition with the genre. Thomas is the film's primary vehicle of the Native American visionary tradition. As in *Powwow Highway* (and most road movies), the two travelers driving *Smoke Signals* form two parts of a whole. Thomas embraces the "old ways"; he is a talker, funny and foolish at times. Victor is more modern: jaded, cynical, and repressed. In the lineage of the road movie visionary "fool" (Bonnie, Miller, and GTO), Thomas is a spinner of tales, challenging the border between fact and fiction. His awkward clothes signify his social ineptness. More importantly, his overwrought glasses draw attention to his "vision": the clumsy, outdated spectacles help him see, give him perspective, insight. An idealist, he articulates the meaning of their journey in terms of magic, revelation, and existential healing. Thomas has dreams and visions that we actually see; he still believes in his people's traditions, in contrast to Victor's bitter pragmatism. When Thomas returns from the journey at the end, his mother asks him not only what happened, but what *will happen*. Then Thomas closes his eyes and goes into a dream-trance: gliding aerial shots over a river finally find Victor on a bridge, wailing in agony for his father. The film closes with Thomas's voice-over (the disembodied, visionary voice) asking a series of compelling, contradictory questions about "forgiving our fathers" (a poem by Dick Lourie).

At times, such modernist, visionary articulation of rebellion and cultural critique achieves a humorous, postmodern feel. Not unlike *The Living End* and *My Own Private Idaho*, *Smoke Signals* periodically invokes a tongue-in-cheek tone, making fun of itself. Ironically, such self-conscious reflexivity occurs mainly through Thomas. This is ironic because, as suggested above, Thomas is the preserver of "the traditions," the seer; yet he constantly makes fun of these traditions. Perhaps more precisely, he makes fun of contemporary Western culture's fetishism of them.[26] He characterizes his story to the two girls as a "fine example of the oral tradition," mocking both his own pretensions and the Western tendency to exoticize such tradition. Earlier, Thomas claims to Victor that he heard of Arnold's death "on the wind"; but it turns out he also heard it from Victor's mother. Such humor occurs again, with more mysterious connotation, when Thomas and his mother seem to know that Victor is coming to ask Thomas to accompany him on the journey. The film also employs the postmodern strategy of eclectic citation of popular culture, with constant references to the likes of *Dances with Wolves*, John Wayne, Houdini, Charles Bronson, Superman, and Kafka (the unlikely name of Arnold's dog).[27]

As a palimpsest of the road movie's historical phases, *Smoke Signals* also bears a significant relation to the existentialist/psychological early-1970s version. This emphasis comes primarily from Victor's point of view, especially his flashbacks. Complementing Thomas's visions, these flashbacks also structure the film. Moreover, both the flashbacks and the visions call upon the past to improve the future. For Victor, remembering the past is a painful side effect of hitting the road, having suffered growing up in a "dysfunctional" family (which in turn reflects the "dysfunctional" social situation of his people). Many of his flashbacks return to the fateful night of July 4, 1976, when Thomas's house was accidentally burned down by Victor's father. This reference to the founding of America, its "independence," is politically ironic in the context of Native Americans, for it marks an official starting point in their extermination and forced dependence. For mainstream American culture, the date commemorates breaking away from colonial Britain; but this breaking away, we are reminded by *Smoke Signals,* was predicated on the gradual elimination of the "Other," indigenous Americans.

As such, Victor is forced—by American culture, and by his own unconscious—to commemorate (and replay) the origins of his own troubled childhood. Upon arriving at his father's trailer home in Arizona, these flashbacks more insistently come to the surface of Victor's mind, dredging up his need (a need he is reluctant to embrace) to reconcile himself with his dead father. As is characteristic of the early-1970s road movie, Victor's journey is conceived primarily in emotional and psychological terms, focusing on "internal" exploration and personal redemption. But, by virtue of its politicized ethnic minority perspective, *Smoke Signals* crucially contextualizes this existential emphasis. Victor's inner emotional terrain of pain is also historical and cultural. *Smoke Signals* renders the personal political, not in an abstract or universalizing way, but in the specific context of the Native American identity crisis.

In many ways, this identity crisis reaches a crescendo during their drive home from Phoenix, in Arnold's pickup truck. Victor and Thomas have a heated argument about Victor's repressed anger. The scene is overinvested aesthetically and generically: they are no longer passengers on an antagonistic bus, but driving their own car. This sense of control over their mobility and their direction is conveyed through some classic generic aerial shots of the car driving. While screaming at each other, they have an accident, crashing into an oncoming car. Unlike *Wild at Heart*'s accident, coded as a "weird" but trivial spectacle, more like *Get on the Bus*'s accident, this crash becomes a major turning point in their relationship, and in the narrative journey as a whole. The cause of the accident is the oncoming car, a white drunk driver with his family. Of course, he accuses Victor and Thomas of causing the accident. Reading the scene symbolically, as I think we are intended to, their mobility, their forward motion, is violently interrupted by both their own interpersonal conflicts, and by the irresponsible head-on collision of dominant white culture (which proceeds to "blame the victim"). The film suggests that both causes of the accident are interdependent: the white man smashes into them because they are arguing; they are arguing because the White Man has been smashing into them for hundreds of years.

Their journey is thus forced into a detour through the nearest town, where they must deal with the police. Initially, the encounter looks like a scene from *Easy Rider,* where the minority outsider is about to be "railroaded" by white middle-class conservative America. The police chief (Tom

Skerritt) starts off extending the racist attitude of the white driver, and of small-town America: they are to blame because they are Indians. But in a conspicuously abrupt reversal—a cheap Hollywood twist, it seems—the chief suddenly changes his mind, takes their side, congenially allowing them to go free. Such a reversal lacks the political bite and historical resonance of, for example, the police confrontation in *Get on the Bus*. Instead, it reflects an idealized exchange, one that echoes the police-bonding of *The Sugarland Express* and, more recently, *My Own Private Idaho* (recall that the cop there was Native American!). Though not impossible, the scene seems almost irresponsible in instantly forgetting the historical or political relationship of "cowboys and Indians." Though the film is not obligated to reflect this relationship, the scene reeks of Hollywood deus ex machina.

After they elude this potential trouble, their car refuses to start. As in *Get on the Bus*, overcoming the one obstacle to mobility (the auto accident) leads to another obstacle (no ignition from the car). Whereas in *Get on the Bus* George is able to muster the physical strength of the men through an invocation of their spiritual and cultural African roots, in *Smoke Signals* a more literal and contrived repair gets the car started. Conveyed through suspenseful crosscutting, Suzy Song (Irene Bedard), the woman who was living with Arnold, prepares to set Arnold's trailer ablaze. Simultaneously, Victor keeps trying the ignition, which finally turns over once her fire starts. Invoking a vast repertoire of road movie imagery, the pyrotechnic destruction of the mobile home "causes" the car to start; mobility is rediscovered as the fire consumes the family and the past. Put differently—and, again, more in terms of the existential road movie—Victor must let go of the pain associated with his father, so as to find himself in and through forward motion.

And yet, this forward motion is also a return home. Likewise, Victor's severance from his past is also a return to his past, the past of his people. This in fact is the crucial lesson of Victor's journey: he can embrace his authenticity only by embracing his ethnic heritage. Because of its unique ethnic framework, in other words, this road movie emphasizes *returning home* as a politically subversive direction to take. The film's return home occurs on many levels: Victor's journey to his father; their return back to the reservation; and a more general return to their vanished ancestral "home," the traditions of their people. Such returning home is not a conservative turn away from rebellion. In the context of ethnic minorities who have had their home taken from them, the real return home becomes a politically potent form of rebellion, a mobility beyond typical road movie mobility.

Returning and Leaving Home:
The Straight Story

Another road movie that revitalizes the genre by reinventing the notion of home is David Lynch's *The Straight Story,* released in October 1999. It seems a fitting but also provocative conclusion to the American road movie of the 1990s. The director who gave us *Wild at Heart* and *Lost Highway*—the latter a "road movie" of the psyche, a confusing experimental feature that pushes road noir to psychotic extremes—now invites us to follow a story that is "straight." Not wild, not lost, but straight—in both a narrative and a topographical sense. Instead of moving all over the map in a fugitive frenzy, or through a demented, alienated mental landscape, *The Straight Story* travels in a fairly straight line. Closing out the genre's multifarious saturation of 1990s film culture, this road movie brings the genre full circle, back to road movie basics, with an enigmatic simplicity that recalls *The Grapes of Wrath.* Harping on the combination "G" rating and Disney distribution, most movie reviewers went out of their way to "warn" audiences that this is *not* your typical David Lynch movie, because it is so conventional. For Kenneth Turan of the *Los Angeles Times* (October 15, 1999), the "heartwarming" film is "the equivalent of David Lynch doing 'Little House on the Prairie,'" therefore "a suspect enterprise." *The San Francisco Bay Guardian* review by Cheryl Eddy (October 20, 1999) suggests that *The Straight Story* "treads close to Hallmark Hall of Fame territory."

The *Straight Story* does possess some politically straight, conservative dimensions—not surprising given our previous reading of *Wild at Heart.*[28] And yet our consideration of the film as a road movie will reveal nothing so straightforward. In fact, by reading the film through the lens of our historical survey, its peculiar and striking qualities become more tangible. *The Straight Story* marks an appropriate coda to the genre's 1990s formulation, as it intelligently synthesizes conformist trends with revitalized rebellion. Not only does Lynch suddenly move in a straight line; as we shall see, this "straight" road movie harbors within it subtle curves. Whereas the bombastic fury of *Wild at Heart* betrayed a conservative "family values" heart, here the conservative veil of *The Straight Story* modestly reveals a more radical route.

Based on a true story, *The Straight Story* offers a significant rearticulation of the road movie, first of all, because it extends the growing body of unique contemporary road movies that feature elder citizens on the road. As I have mentioned earlier, such elder road movies find literary precedent in Steinbeck's *Travels with Charley;* important cinematic versions include Bergman's *Wild Strawberries* (discussed in the next chapter), *Harry and Tonto*

5.11. Challenging the genre itself: elder farmer Alvin Straight (Richard Farnsworth) drives his John Deere lawnmower hundreds of miles across country.

(1974), and *Over the Hill* (1993).²⁹ *The Straight Story* focuses on one Alvin Straight (Richard Farnsworth), an elder farmer who drives hundreds of miles from Iowa to Wisconsin on a lawnmower, to visit his estranged brother Lyle (Harry Dean Stanton) who has just had a stroke. As with most other elder road movies, the distinguishing feature of *The Straight Story* is how the genre's themes of cultural critique and visionary rebellion are expressed through the travels of a senior citizen. As we have seen throughout, the genre is born in and through the counterculture, and is driven essentially by *youthful* rebellion against stability, conformity, and tradition. More typically in the road movie, senior citizens signify such stability and tradition, epitomizing the law and home, both in terms of character (harking back to the "old days") and their physical limitations. Driving the genre with an elder senior, therefore, automatically inclines toward sanitizing its culturally critical core. As with road movies featuring children, such a perspective renders the genre more palatable, more family-oriented, more conventional—and less culturally critical.

On the other hand, driving the road movie with a senior can become a challenge to the genre itself. Indeed, in Lynch's hands the focus on a senior driver becomes the starting point for a surprising twist. Like that of women, gays, and people of color, this elder perspective becomes an outsider perspective within an outsider genre, a fresh revitalization of the typical young white male point of view of most classic road movies. Lynch digs beneath the surface of the film's sentimental sympathy for an old man. The fact that this is a true story, and such a strange one, further enhances its power to challenge (no "wild" fiction from Barry Gifford here). Driven by the likes of

Straight and Lynch together—the archsurrealist to the true, straight story—the genre gets fresh fuel from the new/"old" perspective behind the wheel.

The Straight Story offers yet another illustration of the tension within the genre itself, discussed throughout this book, between rebellion and conformity. While extending the bounds and contours of the road movie's culturally critical core, the film also celebrates the concepts of family and home, concepts usually at odds with the genre's visionary rebellion and modernist wanderlust. Whereas most road movies proffer rebellious attitude haunted by the specter of conformity, this road movie, in a way, articulates conformity haunted by rebellion. This is what makes the film such a peculiar and provocative version of the genre: reflecting a certain conservative takeover of the genre, the film also demonstrates how rebellion and cultural critique can be subtly reconfigured. Aping the *Bonnie and Clyde* approach, *Wild at Heart* pretends to be rebellious, resolving itself with home and family; conversely, *The Straight Story* pretends to be conservative, deconstructing its own mainstream, sentimental veneer with subversive ironic twists. Here, irony serves rebellion, not conformity. Somewhat akin to the politicized notion of "home" as articulated in *Smoke Signals* and other road movies by marginalized drivers, *The Straight Story* reinvents the meaning of home and family without sacrificing the road movie's drive to get outside of society and look critically at both. If the road of *The Straight Story* brings one back to home and family, it is with a renewed, defamiliarized understanding of those terms, one more critical of traditional connotations. Demonstrating Wolfe's (very road movie) adage that "you can't go home again," Straight comes back home figuratively (arriving at his destination, his brother's home), but not to the same home he left behind. As suggested by the archetypal journeys of Odysseus and the Prodigal Son, and as intimated by *The Straight Story*, being on the road *changes the meaning* of home and family.

And though family and home are prominent themes developed by the narrative, forming its beginning and end points, most of the film takes place on the road, filtering these themes critically through the tropes of mobility and the highway. Straight's journey constitutes the film's main substance, in both a qualitative and a quantitative sense. The opening sequence furnishes a compelling portrait of the tension between stability and mobility, privileging the latter. A "cosmic" shot of stars in deep space is followed by a series of sweeping aerial shots of midwestern farming landscapes, which in turn dissolve to high-angle shots of a small-town Main Street, then a suburban home. This introduction establishes the town and house (stability) within the framework of—literally framed by—images of outer space, then movement across the landscape outside the borders of home and commerce. These aerial long shots are establishing shots typical of most types of narrative film. But here they possess an aesthetic beauty related, I think, to the film's generic status as road movie: through the canted, conspicuous high-angle moving camera shots, we seem to be looking down on the town and house from the perspective of motion itself.

As the film focuses on Straight's home situation, stability is treated to subtle negative connotations. The scene of a woman sunbathing and eating on the lawn of the house is laced with familiar Lynchian irony and ridicule. She is absurd in her normalcy; more importantly, she is absurd and disturbing largely by virtue of being sedentary, stationary. Perhaps an extension of this "ill" state, Straight himself, we discover, is collapsed on the kitchen floor: to be immobilized and unhealthy are interdependent. When we next see Straight, he is revving up a car; then, he is on his lawnmower, which will not start. Thus, the narrative's character introductions are coded through images of stifled or repressed mobility. Soon we do see Straight driving the mower on his front lawn, but in the context of later plot developments, this too becomes an image of confined mobility. He will drive the mower hundreds of miles, far beyond the limits of his plot of land.

Conversely, *The Straight Story* begins to elaborate the lure and utopian promise of mobility by articulating the motivation for the journey. After hearing of the stroke suffered by his brother Lyle (to whom he has not spoken in years), Alvin informs his daughter Rose (Sissy Spacek) that he must go "back on the road," implying that in his youth he was a highway traveler. This suggestion is significant in that it sets him up as *returning* to the impulses of his youth (returning also to the genre itself and its "youth" attitude). Likewise notable here is that his impulse is quite irrational: he cannot explain it or justify it, but he *must* go. Though the goal of seeing his brother is the ostensible motivation for hitting the road, he is driven by a kind of wanderlust. This irrational quality is further underlined by the fact that he plans to drive a lawnmower. It is an absurd notion, one that fits nicely into Lynch's surrealistic vision of suburban America. But it also emphasizes the desire to go as more powerful than practical considerations or social convention. In fact, as we see in later sequences of him driving, he moves so incredibly slowly, and is such a visual anomaly on the road (he doesn't belong there) that he flies in the face of road movie conventions themselves. The genre's fetishism of speed, and of the car itself, is thrown out the window by this absurd driver and vehicle. The snail's pace of the lawnmower towing a small trailer perfectly embodies the senior citizen driver. Neither car nor driver fit the genre's mold—thus breaking that mold. Unlike a postmodern road movie like *Wild at Heart*, but similar to one like *The Living End*, this road movie casts a critical eye on both social and generic conventions.

Other details and strategies continue to renew road movie conventions. When Straight first hits the road on his lawnmower, nonsynchronous fiddle music begins to play, conveying the leisurely, elderly yet fully committed pace of this journey. In contrast to the genre's typical driving rock music score, this musical piece is a relaxed yet upbeat, country-tinged motif that becomes the musical theme of the film. Harking back to its opening sequences, *The Straight Story*'s gorgeous and precise aesthetics further celebrate his departure, with some serendipitous traveling long shots of the mower-trailer passing through the landscape. For example, a high angle of the road that cranes slowly down to a low angle of the sky, then tilts back down to the road again. The cinematography emphasizes wide-open spaces surrounding Straight; close-up tracking shots peruse the highway pavement rolling beneath him. Gliding by, he waves to a mother and son on their front lawn. Especially with the shot's slow motion, there seems to be a touch of *Blue Velvet*'s ironic affection for suburbia here. But where *Blue Velvet*'s suburbia bears beneath its surface a dark perversity, here Straight's passing, mobile perspective offers a more subtle critique of stable domesticity. Though Straight belongs to this domestic culture (he waves to the suburbanites, sharing more affinity with them than Wyatt and Billy do with the poor southern blacks they wave to), in his mobility he moves past and outside it, further enhancing the already disturbing, dreamlike quality of the image of the mother and son. Like *Blue Velvet*'s Jeffrey, Straight is implicated in a bizarre mainstream Middle America; but unlike the sensationalistic nightmare *Blue Velvet* explodes from within American stability, *The Straight Story* maintains a quiet but critical distance.

The film further develops the theme of repressed mobility first suggested in the opening sequences, by articulating Straight's departure in terms of overcoming obstacles. His vehicle breaks down not long after he starts off, so he has to be brought back to town by a pickup truck. The mower's breakdown symbolizes Straight's worn, elderly physical condition; but it also serves to reveal his determination to make the trek. The obstacles to his desire to drive seem intent on keeping him home "where he belongs." Undaunted, he shoots his old tractor, blowing it up—evocative of shooting a horse with a broken leg, but also reconfiguring the pyrotechnics of *Easy Rider*, *The Road Warrior*, and *Thelma and Louise*. After buying a spanking new John Deere lawnmower, he starts out again. The film sharply distinguishes the dignity of his "visionary rebellion" (his determination to go)

5.12. Straight as a senior rebel with a cause, leaving behind small-town conformity.

from the slightly buffoonish group of old-timers who make fun of him in the local hardware store. A similar, more tender and tense connotation occurs in a dramatic pullback traveling shot as he drives away from Rose on the front lawn, exaggerating his mobile separation from home. Also underlined here is the daughter, the younger family member, staying put, while the elder father moves away.

Back on the road, this time until he reaches his destination, Straight has a series of encounters that, from a variety of angles, dramatize his traveling in terms of visionary revelation and cultural critique. These encounters also situate the film in relation to the early-1970s road movie driven by psychological pain and emotional scars. Kreider and Content suggest this connection by rightly seeing Straight's journey as an oblique confrontation with "his own crimes and failures," with "his own denial." In true existentialist road movie form, these unarticulated failures revolve around his "sundered" family (28–29). His first encounter is with a runaway teenage girl who turns out to be pregnant. An unnerving sight, she is first seen hitchhiking; though he does not pick her up, she shows up at his campfire on the side of the road that evening. Recalling *Easy Rider* and *My Own Private Idaho* among other road movies, many of *The Straight Story*'s "encounter" scenes occur as nighttime, off-road campfire conversations. In classic road movie fashion, such scenes serve to punctuate Straight's journey with reflective pauses—a time and space for processing the rambling daylight adventures. Like most other conversations in the film, their exchange is moving but unsentimental; they speak little, with long silences as they stare into the fire, cooking their dinner. She is reticent to answer his few queries; he in turn shows little interest in pressing her, or in helping her.

Gradually, however, they become magnetically drawn into the road movie ritual of exchanging stories. He explains to her about Rose being mentally "slow," about how her kids were taken from her by the State, about her great ability to memorize. In more evasive terms, the teenager tells of why she is running away. Humble and scarred by his own past family pain, all Straight can offer her is an anecdote about the strength and importance of the family bond. In the morning she is gone—no good-byes, no thank you—but she has left a sign that she has learned from his anecdote. Though she may be heading back home, one senses that she is empowered, more independent, or at least clear-minded, by virtue of her road encounter with Straight.

Other defamiliarized road movie sequences emphasize Straight as generically unstraight, an anomaly. A huge group of bicyclists pass him by, dynamically conveyed through a series of swish pans and jump-cut point of view shots. He stops to observe this spectacle of youthful pumping bodies and high-speed travel. Then a bird's-eye aerial shot of all the bikes swarming past the mower-trailer concludes the scene. Later in the evening he arrives at their camp, conversing with the young riders, responding to one query that "the worst thing about being old is remembering when you were young." These trim and fit young bike riders, mechanically pumping their pedals, decked out in designer bikewear, signify uniformity on the road. They constitute a traveling social entity, conventionalized (thus, to a degree, conventional) in terms of sport training and fitness trends. As suggested above, visually *Straight* is the outsider, a challenge to their social body. At their camp, they question him as if he were an alien. In his aged, slightly cantankerous and aloof wisdom, Straight ironically seems far more "countercultural" than this traveling mass of preppies.

Another day, not surprisingly, the requisite car accident scene occurs, but with some peculiar Lynchian twists. A car speeds past him, then offscreen we hear screeching brakes and a collision. A hysterical woman rants about hitting *another* deer—she has hit thirteen in seven weeks—and she loves the animals. Recalling the accident scene in *Wild at Heart* (with its own deranged female), as well as sequences from *Weekend* (discussed in the next chapter), this scene may be the most Lynchian in the film—its quirky surrealism thinly veiling an antiliberal, sexist stereotype. Straight silently (and somewhat aloofly) absorbs her unhinged diatribe. In a cut that further judges her as absurd, we next observe Straight cooking and eating the deer at his

5.13. Straight becomes a road visionary, a mysterious stranger who leaves his mark on Dan Riordan (James Cada) during one of Straight's highway breakdowns.

campfire, the horns now attached to the front of his mower-trailer. A group of fake deer seem to be watching him, one of the few overtly surrealistic, postmodern scenes in the film.[30]

More covertly postmodern is the penultimate crescendo of the film, beginning with Straight's near-fatal descent down a huge hill into a small town. As he loses control and speeds downward, another spectacle is occurring for members of the suburban community below: a house is burning, but we learn this is simulated, a practice drill for the local fire department. The image of the burning house is of course a highly charged road movie motif — and certainly here Lynch's trademark postmodern irony is unmistakable, undermining the scene's modernist rebellious coding (destruction of home) with the smirking lure of hyperreal artifice.[31] On the other hand, the fake emergency is interrupted by a *real* emergency — Straight's lawnmower caravan speeding out of control. The suburban comfort of controlled spectacles becomes rattled by the figure of Straight's bizarre mobility. Since his vehicle needs some serious repair, he stays for a few nights with one family, the

Riordans, out in their garage. As an elder wanderer derailed from his strange journey, as an "alien" presence in their home, Straight clearly has a subtle disturbing impact on the couple—especially the husband.[32]

The tentative affection between Dan Riordan (James Cada) and Straight signals the film's subordinate buddy motif, which is further developed when Straight drives into town with Riordan's father. In a bar, the two trade World War II stories. Straight confesses that he probably accidentally killed one of his own men in a "friendly fire" incident (an anecdote that invokes Vietnam more than World War II). For his part, Grandpa Riordan reveals how his entire unit was killed in an attack that he alone survived. Given the mystically mute reunion between the two Straight brothers at the end (discussed below), this scene appears to be the film's emotional catharsis. The notion of "trading war stories" illustrates another reflective pause in Straight's journey. But here it also further demonstrates the film's somewhat insidious buddy theme. Despite Straight's tender relationship with his daughter Rose, and despite the scene with the runaway, *The Straight Story* is driven by male bonding. Though Straight travels alone, he experiences a deep connection with both father and son Riordan, later a priest, and finally his brother Lyle. Another peculiar instance of the film's buddy theme is when two twins fix Straight's vehicle. As they bicker, while trying to overcharge him, Straight straight-talks them down on the price. More importantly, he straight-talks them about the importance of being brothers. "A brother's a brother," he says, guiding them, like the runaway earlier, back to what they have obviously strayed from: an appreciation of family. Straight becomes a traveling messenger, a reluctant prophet, waking people from the suburban stupor of their straight lives. In the early morning, from the confining frame of his front window, shrouded in a lingering melancholy, Riordan watches Straight pull away on his lumbering caravan as if watching his own brother depart for war.

As Straight gets closer to his destination, a few sequences intensify the meaning of his trek, with its "unusual mode of transport," as the priest shall put it. First he crosses the Mississippi River, photographed in a series of compelling point of view shots that render this crossing symbolic as much as literal. Lynch builds suspense into the sequence, but nothing happens other than the crossing itself, monumental and glorious. The next night he is camped in a graveyard where a priest comes out to chat with him around the fire. Straight confesses the gist of his estrangement from his brother Lyle, a "story as old as the Bible." "Anger, vanity, liquor": vague terms that sequester the real story, which does not seem to matter as much as his present crossing toward reconciliation does. As he gazes at the stars—a visual motif

5.14. Resolute, despite the perils of highway driving, Straight follows his vision . . .

recurring throughout the film, coloring his journey with a cosmic dimension and a greater spirituality — he talks of making peace.

After having his first beer in years, Straight follows the dirt road toward Lyle's shack — "if he is still there," the bartender says, invoking the generic specter of the futile journey or absent destination. This connotation is further dramatized when Straight's mower mysteriously stalls on the cusp of arrival. A series of dissolves suggests not only the passing of time, but also a penultimate fusion between Straight, his lawnmower, and the road. A dreamlike moment of frustration and anguish on the road he has traveled so long, this delay will be the last pause for reflection before the journey's end. Its significance seems to revolve around the metaphoric value of the vehicle. Another larger tractor (a big brother?) passes him by, and the passing presence seems to revive his tractor, which starts up just as mysteriously as it first expired.

After following the big tractor down the road, Straight pulls off at his brother's shack. Lyle comes out and asks, "Did you ride that thing all the way out here to see me?" He responds, "I did." Lyle and Alvin sit silently together on the front porch a long time before the camera cranes up to the sky, then dissolves into the stars, the camera moving now through the cosmos, ending the journey and the film with an image of mobility through outer space. Such an ending deliberately sidesteps narrative closure. The meaning of the journey, the details of their estrangement, and the future of their relationship are all left to the wind. "The point here is not to supply an answer to the open-ended question posed by this image, but to explicitly acknowledge that it remains open-ended" (Kreider and Content, 32). Straight's arrival, utterly distilled, refers the audience by default back to the journey itself, where mobility yields cultural critique, enriching self-reflection, and an enhanced perspective on that other journey: life. In this way, *The Straight Story* rearticulates but also quietly expands the genre's visionary potential. In its elusive, enticing simplicity, *The Straight Story* reclaims for the road movie what most road movies in fact speed past: the ineffable mystery of perpetual change.

La Strada	Kings of the Road
La Strada	*Kings of the Road*
Wild Strawberries	*Vagabond*
Weekend	*Bandits*

La Strada
Wild Strawberries
Weekend

Kings of the Road
Vagabond
Bandits

Chapter 6 . . . .

TRAVELING OTHER HIGHWAYS
The European Road Movie

Let us conclude our journey through the history of the American road movie as many of these films themselves close: by embarking on a new journey. To be sure, this is no conclusion at all, but rather a provocation to follow a new road through a new landscape. In the spirit of the genre, then, our critical survey ends with an open-ended continuation of our exploration in Europe.

Such exploration helps to "define" the genre by way of contrast with the formative American version. In venturing to Europe, we can more lucidly appreciate the cultural specificity of the genre's American development and influence. Indeed, many contemporary European road movies seem a reaction to, or reformulation of, the American genre. At the same time, this reaction is driven by uniquely Continental journey narratives that explore issues of national identity, politics and philosophy. Moreover, since the postmodernist genre was originally influenced by the European New Waves, it proves appropriate and fruitful to return to Europe. Our reading of the European road movie aims to glean distinctive elements, but also to further appreciate the ideological contours of the American road movie map. Along these lines, we might speculate that the American road movie is the perfect vehicle for the post-1960s (postmodern) global exportation of American culture. In *Kings of the Road*, Wenders refers to such a notion as the American colonization of the European cultural unconscious. On various levels, the European road movie reflects the European-American dialogue so crucial to the genre.[1]

Generally speaking, European road movies seem less interested than their American counterparts in following the desperately rambling criminal exploits of an outlaw couple; or, in romanticizing the freedom of the road as a political alternative expressing youth rebellion. Rather, the exploration of psychological, emotional, and spiritual states becomes more important to the Continental drive. Overall the European road movie associates road travel with introspection rather than violence and danger. Put differently, traveling *outside* of society becomes less important (and perhaps less possible) than traveling *into* the national culture, tracing the meaning of citizenship as a journey. With smaller countries sharing more national borders, the European road movie explores different national identities in intimate topographical proximity. Therefore, these non-American road movies tend toward the quest more than the flight, and imbue the quest with navigations of national identity and community—navigations that often take on sophisticated philosophical and political dimensions.

Many European road movies express this more cerebral mobility through the trope of the caravan, or the carnival: traveling troupes and troubadours prevail over serial killers and rebels.[2] The genre's core drive of cultural critique thus becomes more explicitly linked to spiritual and artistic reflections upon the collective soul of the national landscape. While obviously sharing some traits with the American existentialist 1970s road movie, the European journey on film distinguishes itself with important features: characters on the road out of necessity rather than choice, seeking work, family, or a home; less valorization of the individual Road Man or the outlaw couple, more emphasis on the traveling group; less fetishism of the automobile; less emphasis on driving as high-speed action-spectacle. The European road movie foregrounds the *meaning* of the quest journey more than the *mode* of transport; revelation and realization receive more focus than the act of driving.

To illustrate such European trademarks, let us begin with Federico Fellini's *La Strada* (1954) and Ingmar Bergman's *Wild Strawberries* (1957). Both films are early masterpieces by two prominent visionary auteurs of the postwar art film generation. More relevant to the road movie, Bergman and Fellini helped forge the modernist cinematic language and landscape that paves the way for the French New Wave, which, in turn, influences the road movie's New American cinema. While neither *Wild Strawberries* nor *La Strada* even remotely resembles the first American road movies of the late 60s and early 70s, both films rely on a journey narrative where mobility yields visionary experiences. Instead of emphasizing the high-speed, thrill-seeking driving typical of American road movies, these films emphasize introspection and reflection; passage through the landscape becomes an allegory of a lost soul seeking the meaning of life.

La Strada is notable as a European road movie for several reasons. Translating literally as "the road," the film features a female protagonist—quite an accomplishment for a road movie from any country (as we shall see, European road movies are, like their American counterparts, typically male-driven). Anticipating in some curious ways the female protagonist of Agnes Varda's *Vagabond* (discussed below), the pathetic waif of *La Strada*, Gelsomina (Guilietta Massina), is the passive but sympathetic eldest daughter of a poor Italian woman. The mother "sells" her daughter to Zampano (Anthony Quinn), the traveling "strong man" entertainer. Interweaving ominous references to home and death, the opening segments establish the context for the ensuing journey in terms of economic dependence and patriarchal hierarchy. Rosa, Gelsomina's older sister, had previously gone off with Zampano; he has presently returned to tell the family she is dead. Despite his suspiciously evasive visage as he grumbles this information, the mother needs money so desperately she gives her next daughter to him. Gelsomina does not want to go, yet is attracted to the prospect of getting out and "seeing the world"; she also is drawn to the idea of performing. Clearly the mother does not want Gelsomina to leave home; Gelsomina too breaks down crying, reluctant to venture out into the world.

Gelsomina's departure in the shadow of death, and her ambivalent attachment to home, distinguish the start of this road movie journey. *La Strada*'s focus on poverty as catalyst for mobility recalls Depression-era classical American road movies. "With such a beginning, the film could become an essay on the devastations of poverty which condemns its victims to cycles of bondage and death and prevents their ever escaping the margins of society" (Marcus, 88). Yet *La Strada* puts a European modernist twist on such socioeconomic thematics. Its narrative structure meanders, more concerned with character than plot; this character focus in turn emphasizes the pursuit of creativity in the context of emotional and spiritual alienation.[3]

The distinctly European features of *La Strada*'s mobility come into focus through a gypsyesque paradigm: poor outcasts who live on the road as a form of survival; like Jews of the Diaspora, gypsies are archetypal people of exile and Continental wandering—homeless, of mixed race, characteristically migrating from country to country, from ghetto to ghetto. The characters of *La Strada* are not gypsies ethnically speaking, but they are clearly underclass southern Italians, and have suffered economic and ethnic prejudice. Zampano's motorbike is a shoddy hodgepodge, a pastiche of paucity: a truck mounted onto a motorcycle. He wears a ragged leather jacket, carrying his "home" around on his bike like a sack of potatoes on his back. In contrast to the American road movie representation, home here is not a place

6.1. Zampano (Anthony Quinn) ponders his unglamorous life as a traveling entertainer, in *La Strada*.

to reject or leave behind; home is not an option. More literally than in many American road movies, the road *is* home.

The barren landscapes they travel through further emphasize the paucity and emptiness haunting them within and without. In concert with such striking location mise en scène, the film uses effective road montages, as well as traveling shots looking backward out the back of the truck, from Gelsomina's perspective; or forward down the usually desolate road that seems to go nowhere. Beyond these driving montages, *La Strada* integrates a mobile sensibility into many scenes, by using elaborate moving camera shots. For example, in Gelsomina's first public performance with Zampano, a circular panning shot follows her as she moves before the crowd. This reflexive (or at least cinematically conspicuous) camera movement unifies her transient physical state with her talent, and social impact, as a performer. Later there is a conversation with a nun at a convent, where Gelsomina explains that they travel because of their work, not for pleasure; the sister responds that the nuns travel too, so as to honor God by never forming material attachments. Again, a lyrical tracking shot conveys their movement, relating two types of transience. Even though they are not driving, the camera is "driving" alongside them. Such elaborate moving camera shots will become part of Fellini's auteurist signature (in *8 1/2*, for example, the lyrical moving camera links dreams, flashbacks, and reality). Here in *La Strada* they aesthetically convey the film's road sensibility.

Despite the sometimes brutal abuse Zampano deals out to Gelsomina, the film follows a fanciful trajectory as they roam the countryside together, earning their keep by performing for small village audiences. Inextricable from Fellini's auteurist vision of Life as Carnival, mobility in the film—even forced, sometimes miserable mobility—inspires the characters. A sense of celebration, a gleeful tone, emanates from their wandering. *La Strada*'s mobility achieves a poetic resonance rare in American road movies: on Fellini's road, the journey going nowhere becomes an affirmative metaphor for the Journey of Life. Fellini's signature traveling circus motif redeems the drifting characters, yet forces them to confront the meaning of existence. On the road, Gelsomina discovers her own creative talents as a performer. More importantly, she realizes her mobile "place" in the beautiful and dangerous world beyond her home.

La Strada is not desperate to get outside or beyond the culture; rather, it ventures into and through the culture. However, Gelsomina does develop a critical attitude toward Zampano, and the world around her, that links the film with most any road movie. This notion of her expanding critical perspective is further developed through her encounter with the Fool (Richard Basehart), first at a religious procession. Prior to meeting him, she is being pushed along by the crowd, adrift in the flow of life, embracing and enjoying such propulsion. Significantly, she first sees the Fool as a "star," during his performance on the tightrope. Let us appreciate how this spectacle is modernist, not postmodern: he balances on a high wire *above* the masses, a quintessential modernist icon. At the same time, this modernist performance is highly mediated for the masses by the amplified announcer he works with. As the star of the spectacle, the Fool will lead Gelsomina to visionary revelations; he becomes her shaman, evoking Shakespeare's wise fools. Their union is framed by the mise en scène of mobility: they first make eye contact after he gets into his car, through the window of the car as he drives away.

The Fool, to be sure, is the most road movie–esque character in the film, the most articulate, the one who self-consciously embraces life on the road (anticipating road "clowns" like *Easy Rider*'s George Hanson, *Two-Lane Blacktop*'s GTO, and *Repo Man*'s Miller). He states almost enthusiastically that he has no home, and that, as a vagabond, he will die soon (which comes true). *La Strada*'s visionary, he sees the future; he sees that Zampano *does* love Gelsomina, even though Zampano does not know it (and will realize it too late at the end). In a way, Gelsomina learns this from the Fool, deciding tragically but with transcendental devotion to stick with Zampano.

Like life, *La Strada*'s journey seems to move from beginning to end, but actually has come full circle. An existentialist, archetypal circus tour from innocence to experience, from ecstasy to agony, *La Strada* is a distinctly European road movie in its bittersweet embrace of life on the road.[4]

Though quite different from *La Strada*, Bergman's *Wild Strawberries* possesses many similar European road movie elements. The existentialist search for meaning of *La Strada* becomes more verbally articulated and symbolically visualized in *Wild Strawberries*. The voice-over of Dr. Isak Borg (Victor Sjostrom) that opens the film introduces us to another unique road movie protagonist, not in gender (as Gelsomina is) but in age: an old man facing retirement but also death. Having explained that he has withdrawn from social life because "people tend to criticize each other," the estimable professor of medicine makes a road trip through the Swedish countryside to accept a jubilee promotion from the University of Lund, on the fiftieth anniversary of his graduation. Opting spontaneously not to take the train, he drives with his daughter-in-law, Marianne (Ingrid Thulin), presently separated from her husband (his son). The meaning of his life, and the specter of his death, both hover conspicuously throughout his journey. On this general thematic level, *Wild Strawberries* proves an important if unlikely pre–New Wave precursor to the American existentialist road movie of the 1970s. Moreover, the film explores the dialectic between passion and reason through a strikingly reflexive film language, employing complex dream, memory and fantasy sequences.

As *La Strada* is unmistakably marked by Fellini's worldview, *Wild Strawberries* is full of Bergman's signature tone and philosophical preoccupation.[5] Like *La Strada*, the film transforms the literal road trip into an allegorical contemplation of the Journey of Life. We should note first that Borg decides to drive rather than take the train after having a disturbing dream. In this dream, visualized for the audience with surrealistic cinematography, Borg has lost his way on empty streets; then he confronts his own corpse in a coffin that has fallen off a passing carriage. The dream's content itself relates to the road movie: he is unsure of where he is going, unsure of how to go. Then, as the horse-drawn carriage goes past, its wheel gets stuck on a lamppost. The wheel careens *toward him* (the rolling wheel accosting him, beckoning him). The carriage continues on without the wheel, but the coffin falls out onto the street—again, beckoning Borg. Though he may not consciously note it upon waking, signifiers of mobility figure in the dream, inspiring him

6.2. Shifting perspectives on uncomfortable intimacy . . .

6.3. . . . inside the front seat of Bergman's *Wild Strawberries.*

to drive. Moreover, like the specter of the death of Gelsomina's sister in *La Strada*'s opening, here Borg's vision of his own death hastens a departure on a journey.[6]

Quite similar to *La Strada*, the film intersperses brief driving montages (close-ups of the highway, low-angle shots of passing trees, etc.) with ensuing interpersonal confrontations. Once on the highway, Borg and Marianne immediately engage in a tense and frank conversation about how each feels about the other. It seems that the forced intimacy of the car interior, traveling across the landscape, has in some sense provoked the dialogue, furnishing a kind of liberating distance from their traditional (repressed) familial roles, at home. This first conversation is conveyed through dynamically composed shot/reverse shots and frontal two-shots through the windshield, as well as moving cameras within the front seat, all bringing the driving setting to bear on their dialogue. We should note that *Wild Strawberries* does not take the "campfire" approach of so many road movies, where soul-searching discussion occurs in mobility's pauses. Rather, by linking passage through space with the passing of time, the film portrays the moving car as a metasocial space, a space outside of society yet with its own social functions.

Bergman explicitly uses Borg's literal journey as catalyst for his spiritual and emotional journey back in time, back to his origin. Borg's death-dream may have inspired him to drive, we realize, so he can visit the summer house of his youth, as well as, further on, his mother in a retirement home. Borg comments that the memory is "more clear" than reality. This notion becomes the essence of the journey's visionary motif: the imagination is more real than reality. In the modernist reflexive framework of *Wild Strawberries*, being on the road provokes the language of memory, which in turn infuses the language of the film itself.

Soon Borg's drive begins to resemble a caravan, perhaps even a traveling circus, as the car gets more crowded with different symbolic characters: the elder, lonely scientist; the betrayed wife; the young beautiful but naive woman; Anders and Viktor, the two men vying for her love, representing poetry and science, respectively. Indeed, one of the film's central themes is this tension, between science as cold isolation, and art/religion as passionate connection. Such thematic tension is further embodied in Alman and Berit, a couple they give a ride to whose car has crashed. Like *La Strada*, *Wild Strawberries* distinguishes itself from the American road movie's frontier spirit and Whitmanesque pastoralism, with an allegorical exploration of ethical and philosophical issues derived from the likes of Descartes, Kant, Kierkegaard, and Nietzsche.

The film continues to develop uniquely European road movie imagery. After a high-angle extreme long shot of the car on the highway, we enter the region where Borg first began his practice; they pull into a gas station where the attendant's family recognizes and welcomes him. Throughout, there is something of the celebrity about Borg; he is not a flashy outlaw, but he is a renowned intellectual. For the entertainers of *La Strada*, for Borg the accomplished doctor, and for most other European road movie travelers, recognition becomes an ambivalent encounter with one's reflection, rather than a vehicle of fame. Equally distant from the American road movie, road notoriety in Europe is rather coded as tepidly criminal. Borg's "crime," it seems, is lack of feeling, and lack of self-awareness.

Marianne, on the other hand, enjoys a privileged critical perspective in the film, revealed in the fact that she drives most of the time. Conversely, Borg's passivity as passenger renders him especially susceptible to the impact of the journey. In a sense, Marianne (along with the car and highway) is the instrument of his journey. Driving onward, rain pounding the windshield, Anders strumming a guitar in the backseat, Borg is lulled into another dream, where he is "tried" for his "crimes." (*Wild Strawberries* seems a remarkable precursor to *The Straight Story*.) And yet Marianne too is making her own journey. She narrates for Borg her last encounter with her estranged husband, Borg's son, Evald (Gunnar Bjornstrand). Significantly, she is not asleep but wide awake as the film visualizes the scene—which takes place during a drive, on the highway. As throughout the film, the car and the road figure prominently here as context for the confrontation, itself a flashback from the present car and road. Taking a drive means getting distance from repressive domestic routine, so as to engage (often uncomfortable) communication and reflection.

The journey of *Wild Strawberries*, to be sure, is more important than the destination. As a "lifetime achievement" award ceremony, this destination renders Borg's journey all the more allegorical of a quest for the meaning of his life. During the procession of the ceremony, he explains in confessional, interior voice-over that he sees a "logic" in all the strange events of the day's drive. That night, he attempts to be more compassionate with his servant Miss Agda, his son Evald, and Marianne. The journey has changed him, has brought about a revelation. As he dozes off to sleep, he recalls yet another scene from his childhood—making one last journey. More than that of *La Strada*, the journey(s) of *Wild Strawberries* delve into memory and the psyche through surrealistic visions and dreams, all provoked by being on the road.

Released the same year as *Bonnie and Clyde*, Jean-Luc Godard's *Weekend* (1967) furnishes yet another distinctly European contrast with the American genre. Like most road movies, *Weekend* is driven by a cultural critique of Western middle-class society, articulating this critique in and through a mobility narrative. Yet *Weekend* engages a radically politicized cultural critique that leaves American road movies in the dust. In this respect, *Weekend* essentially turns the road movie on its head. The most important contrast is that Godard uses cars and travel as an indictment of the very conformity *Bonnie and Clyde* critiques. Unlike Penn, and most American road film directors, Godard displays little sympathy for his couple: they are unfaithful, greedy, ultimately barbaric, as they drive around the French countryside. He likewise has no sympathy for road travel, refusing to valorize it as a means of flight from or rebellion against society. Rather, it becomes the ultimate symbol of society's materialism and decadence. From this angle (and in contrast with *Bonnie and Clyde* and *Easy Rider*), we can appreciate the disturbing, elaborately staged apocalyptic imagery that the film associates with the road.

As a distinctly European road film, *Weekend* helps define the American road film's cultural significance, by its very difference. Yet *Weekend* also is a singular European road movie. In contrast to the earnest existentialist modernism of *Wild Strawberries* and *La Strada*, *Weekend* develops a macabre histrionic strategy that gleefully dismantles cinematic realism and illusionism. Anticipating the postmodern antics of David Lynch, this road movie's modernism invokes the theater of the absurd derived from Jarry and Brecht.[7]

Weekend loosely interweaves the narrative of a bourgeois couple's "weekend" drive to visit the wife's mother (to try to get an advance on their inheritance) with many digressive, documentary-like sequences and surreal apparitions. *Weekend*'s French countryside sardonically deconstructs the tourist myth of idyllic wine tasting and charming chateaux; here, it is laden with noisy, unending traffic jams and gory car accidents. The couple's drive is constantly being rerouted by various mishaps and crimes. Due not to existential confusion, but rather to their nasty greed, they end up perpetually detouring (going nowhere) for most of the film. Unlike the digressive wandering narratives of most early-1970s road movies, *Weekend*'s aimless driving is frenetic and manic, driven by consumerism gone insane.

In the film's opening narrative conversation between Corinne (Mireille Darc) and Roland (Jean Yanne), they wish a fatal car accident upon her father. She then becomes coolly fascinated with a news story where seven people were killed in a car accident. Meanwhile, offscreen we hear angry, frantic back-and-forth honking between two cars in the parking lot below their apartment balcony (this is where the "Weekend" title appears). A long, high-angle shot exaggerates the cars as "characters" more than the people (since the latter are so tiny in the frame), as two cars back into each other. The occupants then get out and fistfight. As demonstrated here, Corinne and Roland's relationship—full of hate, distrust, and selfishness—is contextualized by cars as vehicles of violence, extensions of human domination and abuse.

Beyond its disturbing vision of middle-class values skewered through the lens of grotesque driving mayhem, what further distinguishes *Weekend* as a road movie is its self-reflexive style. The film elaborates the affinity between the camera and the car, conspicuously interrelating the traveling shot with the traveling car, using the car windshield or rearview mirror as a striking allusion to cinematic reflection. The notoriously long tracking shot of the nearly endless traffic jam early in the film conveys a mechanical and ontological kinship between cinema and cars—focalized around the moving camera, the traveling shot. Let us recall Timothy Corrigan's explanation: "In this genre, the perspective of the camera comes closest of any genre to the mechanical unrolling of images that defines the movie camera. As with the movie experience, time on the road becomes figurative space" (146).

Against a yellow field periodically lined with trees along the highway, the endless series of stopped cars features people playing cards, throwing a ball back and forth, overturned cars, kids playing, various farm animals— a surrealistic caravan of middle-class "weekenders." Though the cars are paralyzed on the highway—a generically subversive road movie image—the camera moves fluidly, panning forward and backward as it rolls by. Finally the cause is revealed: bloody dead bodies on the road, a gruesome car accident. Yet the scene reeks of theatrical artifice—as does the entire tracking shot, too conspicuously and elaborately staged to be even remotely realistic. This suggests that "good" middle-class people out on their weekend are false, prone despite the veneer of civility to cruelty and barbarism. Moreover, the traffic jam suggests a *social* phenomenon, which Roland and Corinne embody.

The next sequence articulates the sociopolitical dimensions of mobility in yet another way, more characteristic of the film's numerous nonnarrative digressions. With the camera focused tightly on Roland and Corinne in their car, we see a sports car and a farm tractor drive in and out of the frame, then hear them crash offscreen. In a cutaway to the aftermath of the crash, we see that the male driver of the sports car is dead. The young woman covered in blood argues with the driver of the tractor over who had right of way. Stylistically, this represents a constrast to the ensuing American approach, which prefers to exaggerate action, collision, and driving pyrotechnics as visual spectacle. Additionally, their argument quickly transforms into a screaming debate between working-class and leisure-class perspectives. Again, Godard configures political conflict in terms of driving. In his trademark reflexive setup, drivers stare into the camera, one after the other, confronting the audience with their respective political positions, but also with the artifice of cinema, the *fact* of cinema.

More reflexive devices create a disturbing, surrealistic image of driving. The road becomes a treacherous path laden with violent materialism that erupts into bloodshed and crime. As Roland and Corinne drive on, hands reach in from other passing cars (physically impossible), grabbing at her; here the camera position unites the frame of the film with the car interior, underlined by the startling use of offscreen space. Recalling *Detour* and anticipating *Delusion,* they are waved down by a girl seemingly in distress; but her two male comrades appear from behind a wrecked car, and car-jack Roland and Corinne. These three armed hippies turn them around, back the way they came, foreshadowing their attempt to "turn them around" politically. Corinne and Roland call out for help to passing cars (an inversion of the hands previously reaching into their car). To be sure, none of their fellow weekenders stops to help—just as they themselves would not stop to help them.

The leader of the hippie trio is the film's first visionary road character. Speaking in surrealistic anomalies, he lectures them about their lazy, crass ways, and produces miracles (pulling a rabbit out of the glove compartment). As these gimmicky cinematic "magic tricks" are performed, he discourses about how "flamboyance in cinema is lacking." As a spokesperson of the counterculture, viciously deconstructing the weekend couple, he may embody the attitude of the film itself. Yet as the film playfully foregrounds its own artifice, so too this hippie—and the counterculture in general—is not treated with complete reverence. In contrast with the tongue-in-cheek trivializing of the American postmodern road movie, the motivation here for such satire is to probe cinematic illusionism and political ideology.

The mise en scène of *Weekend* likewise deconstructs the road movie pastoralism informing a film like *Easy Rider*. After escaping from the hippies, Roland and Corinne scour the countryside for a car to drive, continuing their descent into a Bosch-like inferno. Walking on the road, through flaming wrecked cars, they ask dead bodies for directions. Often Godard uses formalistic windshield shots as they speed, the blurred reflection of the landscape passing over them, distorting them, connoting their alienation and cruelty through the visual trope of fast driving. Upon arriving at the home of Corinne's mother, they waste no time in gruesomely murdering her, for her money. Interestingly, they "hide" her body in a staged car accident, similar to how Zampano hides the Fool after murdering him.

Weekend dramatically anticipates the postmodern sensibility, in both its reflexive, formalistic film techniques, and in its satirical, cool distance from its characters. Yet I see the film as essentially modernist. Despite its irreverent, vitriolic satire of weekend driving, *Weekend* does use mobility to sincerely question "the meaning of life," as *Wild Strawberries* and *La Strada* do. Beyond the hippie car-jacker's commentary, or the revolutionary diatribes spoken directly into the camera, the film imports Brecht, Jarry, and Eisenstein in a generalized revision of the French Revolution as Situationist subversion. One notable encounter in this regard is when Roland and Corinne run into Lewis Carroll and Emily Brontë wandering in the woods, reciting poetry and philosophy. Though they speak in Borges-like non sequiturs, they verbally explore the nature of reality. Here Roland and Corinne meet literal "characters" who offer wisdom and revelation. This in turn reflects Roland and Corinne's own status in the film *Weekend* as characters. But Roland and Corinne can not and will not appreciate such poetic inquiry; they goad the two romantic authors about directions to Oinville, site of her mother and the money. Finally, they set fire to Miss Brontë. Roland says she is just imaginary, but Corinne asks why she is crying as she dies.

In the vein of both *Wild Strawberries* and *La Strada*, the film here suggests that the imaginary is more real than reality. Like the car crash in the small town, her burning body is done offscreen—reflexively drawing attention to the frame, and to the looks of Roland and Corinne. Again, this offscreen action can be distinguished from the American road movie's preference for visual spectacle. The artificiality renders a distance to it all, yet not so as to deride or trivialize the scene. In fact, it becomes one of the film's truly tender and sad moments, as Roland and Corinne miss (and destroy) an opportunity to become visionary outlaws, opting instead to cling to their ruthless opportunism.

In the early 1970s, Wim Wenders established his career as a compelling director of the New German Cinema with a series of road movies. Perhaps his masterpiece of this series, *Kings of the Road* (1976) provides yet another European variation on the genre. Apparently a paean to American existentialist road movies of the early 1970s, *Kings of the Road* gives the genre's sense of lost wandering and identity crisis its most lavish treatment, yielding a near plotless glorification of being on the road. The film brazenly harnesses the American spirit of *On the Road,* invoking Ford and Ray as cinematic forefathers (Kolker and Beicken, 34–41). Unlike *Weekend*'s antipathy toward American capitalism and its automobile culture, this European road movie displays ambivalent affection toward the specter of the American highway. The German-American dialogue mobilized by *Kings of the Road* synthesizes the Western's yearning for the frontier with the gothic, dreamy introspection of Werther, Heine, and Caspar David Friedrich.

Kings of the Road is an epic road saga that begins with Robert (Hanns Zischler) driving his car into a lake, where Bruno's (Rudiger Vogler) truck is parked. During the next three slow hours Robert accompanies Bruno on his job—repairing broken film projectors. With lengthy and gorgeously shot traveling sequences, languid pauses along the way, and a bluesy Pink Floyd–style music soundtrack, *Kings of the Road* pushes the aimless, nomadic road narrative to new extremes. In ways very different from *Easy Rider* and *Weekend,* the film's conspicuous style intimates affinities of mobility between the characters, the car, and the camera. Moreover, mobility becomes a sacred key, a marginalized ritual where motion yields emotion, where motion/pictures produce "emotional intensity" (Kolker and Beicken, 67–68). The film's two disenchanted kings of the road are emotionally scarred and isolated, but find therapy and even redemption in their languorous wanderings.

Kings of the Road reflects upon postwar and post-Nazi German national culture through a reflection upon cinema itself. With more social and historical scope than *Wild Strawberries,* the search through the landscape here becomes a search for reconciliation between personal confusion and the untenable, even inexpressible national past haunting contemporary culture. The opening titles inform us the film was shot along the East German border, invoking the crossing of borders, and exploration of the social and national fringes.[8] In the first scene, Bruno is fixing a film projector, chatting with the theater owner, who turns out to be a former Nazi. This sequence-shot prefaces the film's journey with the horrific shadow of the Nazi past, but also the reflexive theme of "fixing cinema" (a similar scene occurs at the end of the film).

The road narrative proper begins in the next sequence, a vast deserted expanse spotted with weeds. The camera slowly pans right along the horizon line, where gradually a speeding car emerges out of a trail of white smoke. The visual effect of the extreme long shot is that the landscape "produces" the moving car. From a medium shot just outside the window of the speeding car, we observe Robert driving; he rips up a photo (presumably of his home and family), at one point driving with his eyes closed. Here *Kings of the Road* cues us to its primary focus on individual crisis, within the overarching context of the critical state of film art and the nation. A frontal traveling shot shows trees racing across his windshield—an image that recurs throughout the film. Like Godard's use of the same technique in *Weekend,* the reflection distorts the driver with an image of his own speed and mobility, fusing him visually with movement, but also turning movement into a moving image, referencing film itself. These opening driving images seem a dreamy, modernist revision of the genre's existentialist white-line fever.

Robert's furious driving is crosscut with Bruno and his huge repair truck parked at the lake, dramatically contrasting the serenity of Bruno's (temporary) stability. As Bruno gets dressed, it becomes obvious that he lives out of his truck, recalling Zampano and his motorcycle-wagon in *La Strada.* As Bruno hears the racing car coming, he looks back through the passenger seat window (the seat Robert shall soon occupy), then gets out to watch. The camera cranes up, reframing Bruno with the road behind him, where Robert's car is seen off in the distance, coming toward Bruno and the camera. This crane-up recurs throughout the film, visually shifting the mise en scène so as to inscribe the character into the highway landscape.

In one of the most compelling sequences in the genre's history, Robert speeds into the lake, sitting in his car as it starts to sink. Wenders's camera frames Robert again within the car door window, then crosscuts to Bruno watching, also framed by his car door window. Bruno's expression seems amused and remotely empathetic. In fact, the formal shared element of the car window renders the editing more like shot/reverse shot than crosscutting. Indeed, this nonverbal shot/reverse shot "conversation" foreshadows the film's minimal dialogue, preferring instead the silent communion of men on the road, where there seems to be no need to talk (recalling *Two-Lane Blacktop,* and the Western in general). Such verbal minimalism will come to signify their sublime automobility, but more importantly the repressed emotional pain of each man.

6.4. Road therapy: Robert (Hanns Zischler) and Bruno (Rudiger Vogler) find themselves, and each other, on the road.

Wenders carries this notion further, articulating a poignant blend of alienation and serendipity on the road. When Robert emerges from the lake, they do not speak to each other (perhaps embarrassed by Robert's absurd suicide attempt). Instead they walk over and stand in front of Bruno's truck, their new vehicle, the traveling space that will bind them. Once again the mise en scène "speaks" for them, framed together in the same shot (no longer separate and crosscut). Silently following some mystical road movie impulse, they climb into Bruno's front seat and drive away. Several shots here emphasize the long vertical rearview mirrors on each door, suggesting that the road (the life) left behind is an image.

In fact, the film's antidote to the mass culture of images is the aimless journey, which gradually restores the ability to communicate. While fueling up, Robert goes to a phone inside a window across the street, starts to dial, then hangs up. The more time he spends on the road, the more space he covers, the closer he will get to completing this phone call—symbolic, to be sure, of reconciliation with his past, but also of communication itself. The landscape here, as in most of the film, is deserted in a rather contrived way (not very realistic), thus representing the internal emotional isolation of each man. Not quite "outside of society" as a restless (American) rebel, Robert rather is out of touch with society, accompanying Bruno by default, without knowing where or why—at this point, without caring, either.

Kings of the Road turns in a more affirmative direction when nonsynchronous rock music comes in, lending a liberating lilt to their isolation on the road. Robert suddenly leaps over a sand dune; Bruno, in an extraordinarily honest scene, walks over a hill and defecates. These empty, wide-open landscapes and languorous traveling shots connote a sense of freedom and refuge. It is therefore significant that at this point they finally introduce each other: communication begins, after some good driving. At the train station where Robert intends to return to his former life, he vomits after putting his own clean clothes on for the first time since the lake. He then articulates his true mental state (as well as a major theme of the film, and the genre): he does not know where to go. Both men seem amused by Robert's reluctance to "go back," and by his titillation at the prospect of continuing on the road. The ensuing traveling shot first reveals the train Robert *should* be on (trains signifying controlled, regulated, destination-oriented travel). But then Bruno's truck pulls into the frame (with Robert in the passenger seat), leading to a road montage, a series of dissolves of the rolling front tires and the truck's windshield, aesthetically condoning Robert's decision to stay with the open road.

They pull off the road at night—again echoing in look and tone similar scenes in *La Strada*—to sleep in the truck, where Bruno has ample sleeping quarters ready (a true Road Man). Robert wanders off to watch the trains go by, musing perhaps on the road he has chosen. On another night, again camped out off the highway, Robert begins to tell his "story." Thus, these familiar pauses in mobility, usually at night, facilitate reflection, introspection, and here, communication—since previously there was very little between the two travelers. At the same time, this scene dramatizes how mobile communication involves risk and uncertainty. The repression afflicting both men runs deep, and is not shed easily. Thus, just as Robert starts to "open up," the two men get on each other's nerves, resulting in Robert deciding to sleep in another part of the truck. The ensuing extended episode with the man mourning his wife's suicide (Robert discovers him at the top of a nearby rock quarry) elaborates storytelling as a crucial, therapeutic side effect of being on the road.

Possibly inspired by the grieving man, Robert leaves Bruno for a while to make his own individual pilgrimage to his father, from whom he is estranged (echoes of *Five Easy Pieces*). Not unlike Borg in *Wild Strawberries* going to visit his mother, this gesture links road travel with "travel" into one's past and toward one's very origins. Insisting that his father not speak, but listen,

Robert's confrontation is crosscut with Bruno's experiences. The crosscutting between Robert and Bruno invokes the beginning of the film, at the lake: two separate yet parallel identities who mystically crisscross on the road.

While Robert journeys into his past, Bruno delves into the unwholesome landscape of contemporary cinema. He meets a young woman at a bumper car ride in a funfair. Significantly, their meeting revolves around, on the one hand, her not being allowed to ride in one of the cars; and on the other, a prize she has won, a candle in the shape of Hitler's bust. The context for their tryst emphasizes how commercial kitsch trivializes as "amusement" both the freedom of the road and the ultimate twentieth-century nightmare, Germany's fascist dictator. Later that night, he meets her again selling tickets in the booth of a movie theater. The porn film being projected malfunctions, as the projectionist masturbates. Bruno repairs the projector, then makes his own film loop and screens it privately for the woman after the theater closes. The film loop is all sensationalized sex and violence. This seems not only Bruno's (and Wenders's) commentary on contemporary popular film, but also an illustration of how the latter blocks communication, since Bruno and the woman sit gazing, distracted by pure sensation and redundancy. Just as Bruno has prepared this message for her, Robert (we observe in symbolic parallel cutting) has prepared his own message for his father, who has collapsed asleep on the printing press where he was at work. Both instruments of mass media are appropriated by our two Road Men to communicate the fact that the media "speak" for them, displacing authentic communication.

Robert's visit to his father provokes a similar inclination in Bruno. After Bruno arrives at the printing press to pick up Robert, they enthusiastically decide to make a detour from Bruno's repair route, so as to visit the towns where each man grew up. They stop briefly in Robert's hometown (mainly to borrow a motor scooter), then head for the summer home of Bruno's family, nestled on a tiny inlet. With a more vigorous rock music accompaniment, their riding is dynamically conveyed in traveling shots that frame them alongside another moving train. In a sequence evoking *Easy Rider,* their more creative and free motorcycle mobility is fervently distinguished from rail mobility (as well as from their oversized lumbering repair truck). However, the mood soon changes when they arrive at the water's edge, night falling and a storm looming. After taking a boat out to the abandoned summer home, Bruno falls under a spell of mute, morose reminiscing: he throws a brick through a window, recovers childhood objects hidden beneath the front porch stairs, insists to Robert they cannot sleep inside. As throughout the film, the extended pause during the journey borders on paralysis, a dramatic contrast to their inspired mobility on the road.

Kings of the Road initiates its denouement with subtle suggestions that the road for these kings is coming to an end. In one town, they decide to leave during a film screening, but run in the wrong direction. In another town, the camera dwells on an "easy rider" they encounter, who was seriously injured in a motorbike accident. Most significantly, the film engages in a prolonged encounter with the shadow of World War II, and postwar American cultural influence. They arrive at night at an old abandoned American military station. This destination will prove to be the end of the road, on many levels. They drive up against a huge fence, a barrier into East Germany. This intimates a certain poetic irony, in that the American Road (and American cinema) obviously inspires the film; yet here the American political legacy (which includes geopolitical divisions in topography and nationhood) prevents further movement. They peruse the "American graffiti" scrawled on the walls inside. When Robert somewhat absurdly tries the phone, all he can hear is an American operator, who cannot understand or even hear him. Both the Nazi past, and the ensuing, so-called rehabilitating American commercial intervention prove stifling forces that finally provoke violent revelation. Drunk on whiskey, they confess their deepest fears, get into a fistfight, then pass out.

As *La Strada* comes full circle from day to night on the beach, and as *Wild Strawberries* frames its journey with a dream, so too *Kings of the Road* suggests a cyclical journey. Like the one near the start of the film, a long slow pan the next morning traces the distant horizon line, across a vast empty landscape, ending finally on Bruno's truck. While Bruno sleeps, Robert has gone to the train station — symbolic, we know, that he is going "home." But he will return to himself differently, rejuvenated by road travel, suggested in his trade with a young boy at the station, for the latter's notebook. Now he can write; now he can reflect and create. Indeed, when Bruno emerges from drunken sleep, he discovers a note from Robert on his windshield. Throughout the film, this oversized windshield has served as a kind of film screen within the film. It reflects the two Road Kings, but also becomes the frame through which they perceive the passing landscape, transforming mobility into vision (and vision into mobility). Thus, here, it bears the film's closing message: "everything must change." For *Kings of the Road*, the road and the journey represent the process of change itself. When we go on the road, we learn that we *are always* on the road.

Bruno's histrionic reaction to the note is to let out a Munchian scream, suggesting that he too will embrace the vital change road travel elicits. However ambiguous in motive, Bruno's wail seems a liberation of all the pent-up moping and silent lapses that have marked the journey thus far. It is a kind of inversion of silence, an inarticulate, perhaps preverbal release of emotion. In a glorious road movie finale, both men are traveling separately, in separate vehicles, on separate roads (Bruno in his truck, Robert on the train). Yet the crosscutting insists that they are still "together" by virtue of traveling, and by virtue of having traveled together. Recalling the silent "conversation" shot/reverse shot cutting when they first met, here they may not see each other, but they sense each other, even "speak" to each other through the driving vehicles themselves, as their paths cross in a mystical farewell.

Agnes Varda's *Vagabond* of 1985 further distinguishes the European from the American road movie, on a variety of fronts. One of the few road movies directed by a woman, *Vagabond* features a Road Woman—perhaps the genre's first serious Queen of the Road.[9] As we shall see, life on the road for a woman does not offer the same adventure and romance as for a man (at least not until *Thelma and Louise*, whose heroines enjoy their share of adventure and romance, and who die more heroically than *Vagabond*'s antiheroine). Beyond its unique gender focus, *Vagabond* also deconstructs and reinvents the genre in terms of narrative structure, film style, and thematic tone.[10] *Vagabond* bears substantial traces of the French New Wave, and displays notable affinity with Godard's *Weekend*, especially regarding the conspicuous and elaborate use of traveling shots.[11] As in *Weekend*, but perhaps even more meaningfully, *Vagabond*'s moving camera becomes the central expression of the film's theme of mobility.

Vagabond is a compelling and disturbing portrait of a young single woman, Mona Bergeron (Sandrine Bonnaire), living on the road, drifting with no place to call home, nor any desire to claim one. While the action dramatizes Mona's aimless mobility, it is really the moving camera that conveys it with forceful if oblique pathos. In many respects, *Vagabond* is a semi–road movie: there is not much emphasis on driving, as she is a homeless drifter— hitchhiking often, riding as passenger, or simply walking down highways. Yet, as we have seen, the European road movie overall is less preoccupied with driving as primary action. Likewise, Mona does not cross many borders, in terms of state or nation, but circulates *within* a relatively limited geographic area in the south of France. This too has proven another European distinction from the American version of the genre, where the crossing of vast empty spaces and state lines is important. In the European road movie, the space of mobility is more confined, culturally and nationally (Italy, Sweden, Germany—now France). Additionally, we should note that the film starts at the *end* of the journey, also the end of her life (she is dead in a ditch). As in a road noir like *Detour*, there is no "open road" in *Vagabond*.

Instead, the film creates a trapped, closed-off road movie space, one that emphasizes Mona's socially disenfranchised isolation. In a boldly political move (explored more fully below), *Vagabond*'s trajectory looks *backward*, the journey's destination foreclosed as the film departs.

Vagabond becomes a blistering version of the existentialist road movie, full of enough truly severe "pathos of failure" to make *Two-Lane Blacktop* seem like a joyride.[12] Mona is the ultimate hippie/punk waif: she shows little emotion, has no direction, does not care what happens to her, nor where or how she goes. In relation to the road movie canon, she has no ambitions of rebellion, cultural critique, escape, or violence. A living symptom of cultural malaise and hopelessness, her apathy seems at times terrifying, at other times pitiable. Yet we do glimpse beneath the surface of her raw veneer: something soft, scared, full of pain and longing.

Whatever visionary strength Gelsomina possesses is not an option for Mona: hers is a bitter embrace of the dirty, hungry life of drifting. Gelsomina was an ultimately doomed gypsyesque artiste; Mona is "homeless." And yet, surprisingly, the dismal rambling of this apathetic, nihilistic drifter becomes the starting point, in Varda's hands, for a uniquely political criticism of French culture and French national identity. By virtue of its multi-leveled narrational strategy, *Vagabond* engages in an incisive cultural critique. Generally, the film exposes and explores the oppression of the culture at large in terms of its reaction to the "empty space" Mona embodies. She passes through the lives of various characters—that is, through a landscape as much social as it is literal—provoking various reactions.

Though sometimes dramatized in narrative form, these reactions are mostly presented in a mock-interview style, invoking documentary codes of realism. The film shifts back and forth from these "investigation" scenes (the camera often peers over a policeman's shoulder) to the episodic narrative fragments of Mona's aimless wandering. An intriguing variation on the picaresque road novel, this strategy inverts the more typical road movie narrative structure, where the ephemeral encounters of the driver are brief and secondary. Here, Varda equalizes such encounters with the traveler's actual route, underlining the sociopolitical dimensions of the latter. Put differently, Varda's strategy situates Mona's aimless nihilism and lack of direction within a cultural context. Taken together, in both the "documentary" and narrative sequences, the individuals who survive her and comment upon her represent, at least to some degree, the culture at large.

In radical contrast to the "audiences" within *Bonnie and Clyde, Easy Rider, Vanishing Point,* or *Badlands,* the characters who observe Mona's movement do not admire or glorify her; she does not become a "star." In foregrounding the social matrix Mona passes through, Varda implicitly challenges the road movie's tendency—within the narrative, and as a genre—to romanticize the rambling outlaw.[13] Mona's culture, it seems, does not know how to deal with such aimless wandering; most of those interviewed cannot make sense of her. Throughout, the film suggests that the culture that in some way spawned Mona may have inadvertently contributed to her tragically meaningless death.

Perhaps the ultimate road movie outcast, Mona does not cruise the highways on a sleek motorbike, sporting a sexy leather jacket, wreaking subversive havoc. This European road movie refuses to romanticize rebellious driving/traveling, as most American road movies (whether visionary, existentialist, or postmodern) do. In Varda's and Bonnaire's iconoclastic interpretations of the French Female Lead, Mona is ugly and disheveled; she has no car nor any impulse to drive, a truly disturbing homeless drifter. By deconstructing its own generic patterns and perspectives (e.g., romanticized male mobility), *Vagabond* anticipates the repoliticized multicultural American road movies of the 1990s.

The opening sequences of the film establish the unique relation of the moving camera to Mona's homeless mobility.[14] Rather than convey the spectacular action of driving, *Vagabond*'s traveling shot captures a more subdued but more critical sense of motion. The film begins with a slow zoom across a damp, wintry field of crops, which subtly conveys a road movie sensation of movement over landscape (not unlike Lynch's aerial shots opening *The Straight Story*). Then the film cuts to a tracking shot of a man walking until he comes upon a corpse. Thus, the moving camera brings us into the narrative and to her dead body; somewhat disturbingly, the moving camera also introduces us to her final road encounter, as it follows the footsteps of the anonymous farmhand who finds her body. Varda's voice-over narration then speculates that "she must have come from the sea," a visionary fantasy of Mona's origin, which contrasts starkly with her corpse. As the voice-over speaks, the film cuts to a beach scene, where the camera tracks closely over delicate patterns in the sand, linking the moving camera with the director's voice, and her "vision" of Mona's mythical origin. *Vagabond* establishes the journey as a story that comes to life in the telling of it; this telling in turn is driven by the director's visionary imagination.

As sound bridge to the next scene, the film's signature theme music comes in. Disturbing in its minor keys, almost atonal at times, this nonsynchronous modern classical quartet accompanies the camera tracking along the highway, then tilting up to Mona hitchhiking. Such conspicuous tracking shots, accompanied by this theme music, occur throughout the film, often stopping on some obscurely symbolic or graphically suggestive object. Sometimes the camera tracks with Mona, then continues on without her, resting on a patch of branches, a tractor, tires hanging on a racetrack fence, or a phone booth. Heightened by the music, these scenes of the camera moving beyond her poetically suggest how life will continue after she dies (a notion conveyed, from another angle, by the interviews looking back on her life). These recurring, almost nonnarrative traveling sequence shots convey her wandering mobility with more coldness and distance than a more typical road movie driving sequence. Moreover, they link mobility specifically to her body, rather than to the body of a car (as in the American road movie).

Mona's "sans loi" identity as social outcast is developed on many levels, all reflected through her drifting motion. She camps in the winter, off-season, when it is freezing; one perplexed campsite owner interjects, "But no one's here"—to which Mona responds, "I am." One morning finds Mona's tent set up in a graveyard; she is chased out. Mona gives blood to survive on the road. Such hardcore hardship is almost unthinkable in an American road movie (e.g., Kit is out of work, but looks and acts like James Dean). An encounter with a truck driver early in the film invokes the oppressive patriarchal law she refuses to comply with. A forefather to *Thelma and Louise*'s truck driver, he gives her a ride, assuming she will have sex with him. When she does not concede, he asks her to get out. In his "interview," he says nothing about this dimension of their encounter. (Thus, we learn he is lying, a warning not to trust the documentary appearance of these segments—and documentary in general.) This encounter is important, since a similar scene occurs near the end. Again in interview, one of her last "boyfriends," David (Patrick Lepcynski), laments that he could have pimped her for a lot of money.

Varda's critique of such abusive male figures garners further dimension with a teenage girl who sits at a table in the window of her home/prison, enviously praising Mona's "freedom." This girl's perspective seems allegorical of the American road movie, which romanticizes the freedom of the road. But what does freedom on the road really mean? Here, something other than what the American road movie portrays. Something more difficult, less attractive—less free. Read through *Vagabond*'s lens, the freedom symbolized by the American road movie turns out to be idealized ruse, an ideological construction.

Further deconstructing American road movie sensibilities, two subplots of *Vagabond* seem to rework the genre's countercultural perspective: Mona's encounter with a hippie farmer and his family, and with Madame Landier (Macha Méril), a university professor. Both encounters are developed over several sequences, and both begin with a moving camera point of view shot from within the car of each driver approaching Mona on the highway. The goatherd (Stéphane Freiss) gives Mona shelter on his farm, offering her a job and the chance to work the land. But unlike Wyatt in *Easy Rider*, Mona is not so impressed with the idea of working on a farm. On a strictly impulsive (rather than rational) level, she seems averse to any form of stability or domesticity. "Rebellious to the core, she appears to have no sense of what she might be revolting against" (Flitterman-Lewis, 291). More importantly, the hippie-farmer with a Master's in philosophy shows paternalistic condescension toward her negative, lethargic attitude. After she steals from them, he throws her out. In many ways, he represents the late-1960s counterculture, even the film *Easy Rider* itself: he has lived "on the road." In his "interview" segment, he evaluates her road as leading to "destruction" and "loneliness," as "withering" rather than "wandering." Perhaps intimating a link between the truck driver and the hippie goatherd, Mona meets a hooker on the road just after leaving the farm, signifying her refusal to "sell" herself—for sex, but especially for anyone else's values.

One might expect Mona to be drawn to the hippie's lifestyle, but she is not; the subplot involving Madame Landier proves even more surprisingly complicated. When the professor first questions Mona after picking her up, Mona invents a past for herself; then, she freely admits that she is "making things up." Recalling of course a road tale–spinner like GTO from *Two-Lane Blacktop*, the scene suggests that homeless roaming engenders a certain poetic license to re-create one's identity (the more ominous version of this notion portrayed in road noir like *Detour* and *Delusion*). Madame Landier is intended, I think, to represent a potential role model for Mona. Perhaps this is related to the sequence's resemblance to the American road movie. First of all, there are more traveling shots that emphasize driving; secondly, Mona and the professor come to form a kind of "couple" on the road. At one point, Mona puts some rock music on while driving; they eat pizza and drink beer in the car. In one of the few moments in the film where she seems happy, Mona claims that she likes being in the car with her. There is even the sense that Mona *teaches her* some unique road movie joy and wisdom: when the professor asks her why she "dropped out," Mona replies that champagne tastes better on the road.

As with the hippie goatherd, Madame Landier seems to embody a positive, progressive opportunity for Mona. Yet both ultimately alienate Mona, in part through trying to help her. As Mona accompanies the professor in her research on the disappearance of plane-trees, one senses a subtle irony: Landier displays more deep concern for "the environment" than for a desperate human like Mona. In this way, *Vagabond* is truly a punk film (in attitude if

6.5. Mona (Sandrine Bonnaire) stares out the passenger window, as her temporary "buddy" Professor Landier (Macha Méril) looks forward through the front windshield.

not look): Mona thumbs her nose at both the conservative work/home ethic *and* the liberal sixties alternative. It is especially intriguing that Madame Landier has a vision of Mona (in a somewhat contrived scene where she is almost electrocuted), after having finally dropped her off on the road. She "sees" in her vision that Mona is in danger, and regrets having left her. In fact, we learn, Mona was attacked and raped while hiding in the woods near where the professor dropped her off. This parallels the hooker Mona encounters after leaving the hippie's farm; both sequences conclude with images of Mona as a (discarded) body circulating on the fringes of society, subject to (sexual) exploitation.

It seems Mona is destined to never have a home, and to die on the road. Near the end she moves in with the Moroccan farmhand Assoun (Yahiaoui Assouna), where she seems genuinely but briefly content. Significantly, Assoun has no lofty pretensions of "saving" Mona. Labeled "dirty" by other French villagers, Mona probably identifies with him as an ethnic outsider. But the other Moroccan farmhands returning from vacation refuse to let her stay. She gets sick and vomits in a train station, then almost perishes in a fire while squatting. The final blow comes in the form of a peculiar pagan wine ritual she stumbles into in one village. Unaware of the "rules of the game," she gets doused with wine dregs. Terrified and traumatized, she wanders through a nearby wine orchard, finally tripping into a ditch face-first, unable to get up again.

Vagabond articulates an unsentimental social indictment, one without overt political slogans that simplistically point a finger of blame. Here no one is to blame. Mona is no victim. Yet the film insistently contextualizes Mona's fatal mobility with her social interactions. Unlike in most American road movies, this road is no refuge from home, no vehicle of revelation or redemption or critical insight—except, perhaps, for the audience, testimony to the film's unique form of cultural critique, which occurs not so much *within* the film but rather as a result of watching it.

Conclusion: A Postmodern Visionary Road Movie

We will conclude our survey of the European road movie—and our exploration of the genre as a whole—with the striking recent German film, *Bandits* (Katja von Garnier, 1997). In many ways a follow-up to *Vagabond*, *Bandits* more significantly projects a promising future highway for the road movie, one that balances social criticism and postmodern hip. The film focuses on a female rock band on the road, and engages in a dynamic political critique of popular culture. *Bandits* signals a vision of the road movie for the next century, articulating a coherent convergence of most road movie tendencies described throughout this book.

As a "rock 'n' road" movie, *Bandits* reinvents the genre by integrating the visionary, rebellious energy driving both rock music and road tripping. Let us recall that the rock music film genre emerges in and through the same countercultural context as the road movie. Thus, *Jailhouse Rock* (1955) becomes a companion to *The Wild One* (1954); *A Hard Day's Night* (1964), *Magical Mystery Tour* (1966), and *The Harder They Come* (1973) parallel *The Wild Angels* (1966), *Easy Rider* (1969), and *Badlands* (1973). Indeed, both genres seem driven by the same "inner form," to use Buscombe's term: youth culture rebellion, visionary exploration, critique of mass/celebrity culture. Furthermore, the road movie's journey across the landscape in a car and its literal distance from social conventions becomes, in the rock music film, a journey "up" the socioeconomic ladder. Usually the rock antihero "travels" from anonymous authenticity, to fame, cynicism, and corruption, then back "down to earth" as some form of retribution (often death) or revelation— see, for example, *Tommy* (1975), *Quadrophenia* (1979), *Sid and Nancy* (1986), *The Doors* (1991), *Velvet Goldmine* (1998).[15]

Bandits infuses the rock 'n' road movie with a fiery feminist perspective that recalls *Thelma and Louise*, but goes further. Beyond exposing patriarchal oppression in many levels of German society, the film also features an exciting blend of MTV-style visuals. In its unique integration of the rock music film, the outlaw road narrative, and a refreshingly nondidactic feminism, *Bandits* heralds the politicized European postmodern road movie. The starting point of prison is certainly familiar to the road movie, whether figuratively (Thelma's home) or literally (*I Am a Fugitive from a Chain Gang, The Sugarland Express, Natural Born Killers,* etc.). *Bandits* maximizes its gender concerns by making explicit the link between oppression of women and incarceration, reversing *Thelma and Louise*'s use of home as a metaphor for prison: here, prison is a metaphor for home. Further revising *Thelma and*

Louise's trajectory, here the women *begin* their journey as convicted outlaws. Their outlaw status at the outset is exaggerated when they form a rock band, since rock music too possesses certain connotations of rebellion; that is, to be a rocker in prison is to be an outlaw among outlaws who wants to be a star. Opposing their confinement and social isolation with their visionary creativity (and vision of fame), these road protagonists are triply marked as outlaws: prisoners, rockers, women.

As *Bandits* begins, three of the musicians—Luna (Jasmin Tabatabai), Marie (Jutta Hoffmann), and Angel (Nicolette Krebitz)—are holding auditions for a drummer. As the group runs through a rousing rendition of Bob Dylan's "All Along the Watchtower," the film crosscuts to the arrival of Emma (Katja Riemann), a terse and solitary individual who will eventually become the drummer. Before the other three discover her, the stakes of completing the group get raised: the government has offered the group a chance to perform at the Policeman's Ball. Given what occurs at the performance, it is important to note that the film dramatizes this "offer" as politically motivated, since the prime minister (a woman) is up for reelection soon. The performance would be an opportunity to show off her reformist political approach (reintegrating prisoners socially; encouraging creative expression in prison).

The nature of Emma's audition is also worth noting, since it occurs accidentally but in and through the context of confinement and rebellion (thus, especially powerful as road movie point of departure). After Marie attempts suicide, all the women are lined up outside their cells and searched. Emma protests this unfair treatment, and the implied accusation, by beating against the wall. Other inmates join in; but Luna and Angel notice her great sense of rhythm (which emerges in reaction to a specific instance of social oppression). Later, the three overhear her drumming, and officially bring her into the band. Together they arrive at the road movie–esque name "Bandits," and in one rehearsal seem to reincarnate the Who as they flail about, smashing up their gear. In terms of the genre, this opening sets up an extreme form of stability and immobility; it also prepares for a specially exhilarating road romp, since their escape from prison will turn them into rock stars.

Yet the most tangible catalyst for their fugitive mobility is clearly gender oppression. As the foursome waits in the police truck outside the Policeman's Ball, one of the male prison guards begins to taunt them, making lascivious, abusive sexual remarks. Then, he tears up a photo belonging to Marie. When the guard gets the signal to bring them inside to perform, he unlocks Luna's handcuffs. She cannot help unleashing her fury; as she beats him to a pulp, she exclaims, "You just don't get it, do you?" Pounding nonsynchronous rock music accompanies her outburst, linking their creativity, as well as their future fame, with rebellion against institutionalized patriarchal abuse. Luna's violent "rage against the machine" gains further political nuance by being crosscut with the pomp and circumstance occurring onstage inside the ballroom. The prime minister is awarded for the "success" of her prison plan. She introduces "Bandits" as a model experiment in rehabilitation. But when the curtain goes up, there's no one there.

After Luna uncuffs the other three, they make their getaway in the police truck, smashing into parked cars and running down officers chasing them. Having appropriated the official vehicle of their incarceration (and of their own exploitation as "models" of so-called reform), they make the first of many implausible but politically symbolic escapes. Somewhat similar to *Vagabond*'s "documentary" interviews, the initial police investigation sequences serve to give profiles of each woman. Now invoking *A Question of Silence* (Marleen Gorris, 1986), each profile reveals a dubious "crime" that more likely was some form of subversive reaction to criminal male authority. Marie poisoned her husband in reaction, it is implied, to his abuse of her (now she repeatedly tries to kill herself); Angelika was married to two men; Luna stole from a male proprietor; Emma shot a man who exploited her musical talent and beat her. These "investigation" profiles are dynamically crosscut with scenes of their newfound rebellious mobility (handheld windshield shots of them driving, standing around the truck out in the countryside, etc.). Yet this newfound rebellious mobility, or "freedom," is not treated simplistically. Like *Get on the Bus* and especially like *Hard Core Logo*, *Bandits* yields a more multifaceted journey by exploring four (rather than one or two) road characters, each with distinct personal and political "baggage." Luna is frenetic and impulsive, a road warrior; Angel is more timid and conventional, immediately questioning whether they should go back and turn themselves in; Marie seems semicatatonic but enjoys herself on the road; Emma is the most solemn and enigmatic, following her vision of escape to Guyana.

Once on the road and on the run, they really become bandits—and the Bandits. Driven to drive the highways, forced into a fugitive concert tour, the group's musical identity ironically takes off. They arrange to leave the country on a boat, but have to wait a few weeks, driving around in hiding. *Bandits* is full of such contrived, even far-fetched plot points (as it is equally full of postmodern reflexivity and playful artifice). Yet this plot contrivance, which delimits their mobility, pioneers some significant road movie terrain. First of all, the delayed boat ride forces their mobility in circles; under pressure to evade the police, and without destination, the Bandits must drive round

6.6. Escaping prison, stealing cars, going on tour: the outlaw female rock band of *Bandits*.

and round. Secondly, they must remain within German borders as they drive, which permits the film to critically reflect on the political landscape of German national identity and culture. This national/cultural commentary occurs primarily through the advent of the band's popularity, a crucial plot development that depends upon the "trapped" waiting period. Lastly, the boat trip, promising the refuge of the expatriate, rewrites the road movie notion that one journey leads, not to destination, but to another journey. Likewise, the boat trip invokes culturally exotic or Other shores, idealized here as antidote to the national "home" culture that both hunts and celebrates them.

Bandits blends the outlaw and quest road narratives, dramatizing throughout how the fugitive mobility of the women engenders visionary insights. Like *Bonnie and Clyde, Thelma and Louise,* and *Natural Born Killers, Bandits* integrates the fame motif into its visionary ramble, developing its patriarchal critique through the expanding popularity of the group. An early scene of their life on the road seems a feminist stab at male cruelty and gun fetishism. In a deserted, mountainous region, they come upon a small group of men shooting dogs; we observe the Bandits surround them. The sequence then jump-cuts to the women driving away in their car, laughing. Such editing, which occurs throughout the film, is slightly comic and unrealistic (we do not see how they overtake the men). Next we learn on a news broadcast that they had stripped the men naked and covered them with dogshit. Through such playful plot twists and film style, *Bandits* establishes its "bandits" as cartoonish heroines. But the European cartoonism here, unlike that of most American postmodern road movies, is driven by an earnest critique of male cultural authority.

It is also driven by a critique of mass culture, clearly on display in the next sequence. In a diner, they see a "top story" on the television news, about two men who escaped from prison. But there is no news of *their* escape. Luna becomes irate, insisting that they should get the publicity that is their due. Again invoking key scenes in *Bonnie and Clyde* and *Natural Born Killers,* Luna intuitively envisions combating mass media sensationalism "from within," by appropriating it. Yet there is an added political undertow to their desire to be stars, since this desire emerges in reaction to the media's privileging of the male. They contact a television station and agree to meet an interviewer on a rooftop, where they are videotaped, first speaking directly at the camera, then breaking into a song. Especially through its flaunted lip-synch and sudden appearance of instruments (Emma drumming on garbage cans), the song performance evokes the playful artifice of *A Hard Day's Night,* and music videos in general. It is exhilarating to witness the Bandits create their own mythology, controlling the destiny of their public image. As they serve the media by furnishing a story, the media serve them by providing the spin. The film language itself of *Bandits* reflects their rising stardom: narrative realism is gradually left behind in favor of lip-synching artifice, formalist musical numbers, and idealized plot contrivances. The more popular they get, the more the film becomes a road musical, integrating performance seamlessly and implausibly into the narrative.[16] Perhaps revealing a certain political naiveté (or at least political idealism), the popularity they gain creates a literally artificial world for them, where anything is possible because they are *media*ted stars.

This suggestion of popular culture and the mass media being to some extent aligned politically with the Bandits is further developed when the news team that interviewed them is scolded by the police. Throughout, "the people" support the group, while the police are against them. Unlike many road movies we have discussed, *Bandits* dramatizes a certain utopian potential for popular culture and popular rebellion to join hands. Let us bear in mind that mass culture in Germany (and other European countries) differs from that of America by being (generally speaking) less sensationalistic and market driven, more socially conscious and government sponsored or influenced. In this context authentic cultural commentary seems more possible within popular culture, relieved from American-style bottom-line commercialism. The synergy in *Bandits* between the outlaws and the masses seems more central than, for example, in *Bonnie and Clyde* (where the Depression populace is mostly invisible) or in *Natural Born Killers* (where the masses are thinly sketched with a few sound bites, and ridiculed as dupes). Clearly in the film the masses gain access to the group by virtue of the television and pop music recording industries.

On the other hand, a more cynical version of mass culture is illustrated when they first hear one of their songs being played on the radio. This occurs during a remarkably evocative scene out in the forest, where they are digging for a "buried treasure" Angel claims to know of. Instead, they uncover a dead bomb from World War II. It seems no coincidence that at the moment when they encounter an ominous trace of Germany's Nazi past, they hear their "art" being exploited by a record company that had previously rejected them. In a brazen, unrealistic but politically charged scene, they head straight to the record company to confront the smarmy producer, demanding a contract with royalties. Again mobilizing the film's mass media/artiste dialectic, the scene concludes with the producer trying to swindle them. But they end up swindling him, pouring coffee all over his designer rug. Though the building is surrounded by police, they escape with the money they need—disguised with sunglasses. Such comic, postmodern cartoonism again serves a culturally critical point: here the police are coded as an *arm* of the media, both institutional forces intent on exploiting/capturing the group.[17]

The women mostly enjoy being outlaws, and will soon revel in huge popularity; yet the road movie's more introspective, visionary theme is always clearly motivating their journey. While hiding out in a nightclub one night (watching a somewhat drab male band onstage), Marie explains to Emma that she wants "to burn," she does not want to be merely "eaten by worms." Evoking the live fast–die young mythology encompassing James Dean and Jim Morrison (but also *La Strada*'s Gelsomina), she yearns for even a few days of meaningful existence. The rock music film that partially defines *Bandits* will channel such visionary drive into their ensuing fame, while the film's road movie facet channels it into their automobility. This visionary drive is Marie's chance to "seize the day" (she will burn up in a car near the end).

The next chain of events seem to bear out Marie's driving vision. During the male band's break, the Bandits leap up onto the stage, first seducing the audience with a crooning ballad, then (after a mere swish pan) invigorating them with a hard rock song. The crowd goes crazy, freeze-frames of each Bandit foretelling their immediate future as pop idols. When the police arrive (the bartender recognized them, not as stars but as outlaws), they are in the middle of performing a song. Somewhat safe up onstage, with the public "protecting them" from immediate police action, they pull a hostage from the crowd, a guy named West (Werner Schreyer). An American whom Angel had been doting on earlier, West seems a playful allusion to Brad Pitt's character from *Thelma and Louise*—a boy-toy for the girls to have fun with. In another unlikely escapade, they overcome the police, using their hostage as leverage. The hilarious sequence concludes with the Bandits driving onto a freeway off-ramp *the wrong way*, summing up the present extremity of their rebellious, fugitive mobility. Interestingly, such driving onto the off-ramp recalls the two women driving backward in *Smoke Signals*. Both scenes dramatize feminist critique in terms of "wrong" (different) driving.

Other sequences suggest visionary political potential in the context of

6.7. Postmodern fame: the Bandits are exceeded by their public image.

postmodern fame. One night, as Angel seduces West with song and dance in their motel room, Luna and Emma confront each other on a deserted street. Throughout the film these two have been butting heads—the two toughest women. This evening, after exchanging personal stories of past abuses by men, they enjoy a moment of intimacy and affection, where they come to understand each other. Significantly, the scene concludes with them looking up to see a huge billboard image of "The Bandits" towering over them; they express shock at their own success. This moment suggests that their public image exceeds them, yet is driven by their private painful histories.

Their rapidly swelling popularity comes to spectacular postmodern fruition in the next sequence—a ludic, liberatory mass cultural "happening." While stuck in a traffic jam on the freeway, the Bandits are recognized by other drivers; soon teenagers are out of their cars, demanding autographs. The dominant elements of the road movie—the road and cars—become here foundation for the spectacle of rock music. Recalling similar scenes from the film *Fame,* as well as the last song of *Wild at Heart,* the freeway transforms into a stage, the packed, immobilized cars transform into an audience, as the Bandits sing and dance through the traffic. When the police arrive, the crowd (as in the earlier bar scene) helps the band escape by blocking the police. Unlike in *Weekend, Five Easy Pieces,* and other road movies, the traffic jam here is utopian rather than dystopian; it makes possible a cathartic connection between the star outlaws and their adoring public, a popular/populist convergence, over and against the police. In another nod to *A Hard Day's Night,* the film shows in extreme high-angle long shot how they dash in and out of shopping malls, sporting new clothes, further eluding the police, shielded by the costumes of pop culture.

As their postmodern fame reaches a certain apex (dolls appear on the market), they are forced to withdraw from culture into nature, hiding out deep in a forest. In scenes reminiscent of *Badlands,* their tree house and the nearby lake connote an Other zone, "outside" of society. Laughing and swimming in the lake, they seem truly (if temporarily) free. When dark storm clouds appear, we know that this idyllic consummation of their mobile re-

6.8. "Rock 'n' road" movie hysteria:
stuck in traffic, the Bandits perform a
song for their adoring and protective
fans.

bellion and fame will begin to take a downward spiral. West betrays Angel
for Luna; Angel accidentally reveals their whereabouts to the police.

Such signs of foreboding come to bitter fruition when Marie dies (for no
apparent reason) in the backseat as they cross a bridge. This bridge, it turns
out, is also the site of a trap set by the police. As if "seeing" their imminent
capture, Marie's last words are "No more life on the road." They stop the car
on the bridge, shocked by her death, overwrought, yet comprehending that
now she is finally "free." Despite the police ambush they see coming, they
remain devoted to her (and to the group bond), granting her wish "to burn"
by setting fire to the car with her in it, the car then exploding in slow motion. With the police chasing them down, Angel and Luna leap into the water
below, making another over-the-top and unlikely escape (the entire segment
is an affectionate send-up of itself, with slow-motion photography and aerial
shots). Emma hesitates, reaching back to retrieve her precious necklace that
had slipped off, and gets caught.

Before their final destruction, the remaining Bandits enjoy one more
glorious subversion of patriarchal authority. Against all odds and all reason (marking the film with a certain Hollywood idealism, if not postmodern cartoonism), Luna and Angel decide to break Emma out. They trick the
two primary investigators, Schwarz (Hannes Jaenicke) and Ludwig (Andrea
Sawatzk), in an underground parking lot, taking them hostage to enter the
police station. While Angel holds a gun on Schwarz (quoting Janis Joplin),
Luna poses as an officer and frees Emma. As the police scramble to figure
out where they will turn up, the film crosscuts to close-up inserts of them
buying musical gear. Once again refashioning *A Hard Day's Night*, they appear on a rooftop near the boat dock, departing with their last parting shot,
for their fans and the police: a farewell concert. An adoring mob gathers
on the streets below, as the police make their way to the roof. Then, culminating the film's political postmodernist representation of the Bandits as
rock star/superrebels, they dive into the crowd. The crowd, in turn, aids
them one last time, cushioning their fall. All done in self-conscious, over-
the-top, and tongue-in-cheek slow-motion photography, Luna, Angel, and

6.9. Heading for the "undiscovered country": the Bandits' farewell concert on the roof, near the boat docks.

Emma run toward the boat platform. At land's end, at the end of the road, the Bandits are running, not driving. Here *Bandits* goes out of its way to invoke a melodramatic Hollywood ending—only to subvert it with a more bitter modernist political statement in the spirit of *Bonnie and Clyde* and *Easy Rider*. This last border crossing of ultimate escape, away from the land and the nation, also leads to death.

The particular staging of their death reveals a firm commitment to bashing the patriarchal law. First of all, the visionary rebellion that has driven the women all along crystallizes when they "see" (the dead) Marie waiting for them on the boat. While this image of Marie is a hallucination reflecting their desired goal of freedom and togetherness, it also foretells their doom: if they can "see" her, they are already crossing the final threshold. Before crossing onto the boat, they turn for one look back, pull out their guns—and drop them. But Schwarz has misunderstood the gesture, and orders the police to fire. We hear the gunfire, but see a close-up low-angle shot of three hands reaching out to join the one (Marie's). Rather than show bullets ripping their bodies, the film opts for symbolic formalism, emphasizing the visionary bonding of the women in death. Additionally, during the slow-motion crosscutting montage of this finale, a close-up insert reveals Ludwig closing her eyes in empathy, shame, and disgust, realizing helplessly how her male partner has misunderstood the final gesture of the women—as he has misunderstood them all along.

Unlike the outlaw couple of *Thelma and Louise*, the Bandits are gunned down for being misunderstood. In contrasting *Bandits* with *Thelma and Louise*, we should note that the policeman of *Bandits* is the *instrument* of their death, unlike Slokum, who runs after them trying to save them (thus redeeming *himself* and, by extension, the law). No such redemption for the law in *Bandits*, which overtly incriminates the male investigator in their death. Moreover, in choosing to "escape" through suicide, Thelma and Louise let the police off the hook. Though there is a sense in which Thelma and Louise refuse to be victims, dignified by an affirmative abandon, there is another sense in which they do the dirty deed to themselves, for the police. The women of *Bandits* are martyred, victims of patriarchal abuse, especially in the end. Yet this ending seems politically more daring and disturbing, following through on (rather than sanitizing) its critique of patriarchy.

Unabashedly alluding to *A Hard Day's Night* and other rock music films, the grrrl group of *Bandits* seems a politicized antidote to the Spice Girls. Traveling the postmodern cultural landscape with fervor and insight, *Bandits* paves the way of the future road movie. The film boldly combines dynamic reflexive techniques and a collage of film stocks and styles to produce a politically engaged road saga that nevertheless winks at the audience. Intelligently blending rock music, Hollywood, modernist and postmodern cinematic codes, *Bandits* mobilizes a visionary deconstruction of culture and power. Such driving vision is the hallmark of the road movie's power and appeal.

They have been driving for days, hounded by both the police and the masses. They are not two, but four, one of them already dead. They have been abused. They have been to prison. They have scaled the heights of stardom and tasted the sweetness of liberation on the road.

Despite being surrounded by an army of police and fans, they continue their journey. They join hands and throw down their guns. They make their leap, discovering the undiscovered country, shot down by the law.

THE LIBRARY
TOWER HAMLETS COLLEGE
POPLAR HIGH STREET
LONDON E14 0AF
Tel: 0207 510 7763

We shall not cease from exploration.
—T.S. Eliot

I wanna go to a different land.
—P.J. Harvey

NOTES

Chapter 1

1. Anne Friedberg provides a fascinating and complementary prehistory to my focus on the convergence of automobility and film in her *Window Shopping,* in which she discusses the "mobilized virtual gaze" cinema inherits from "other cultural activities that involve walking and travel," such as arcades, shopping, and museums (2–3).

2. Another complementary study that links the present one with Friedberg's is Lynn Kirby's *Parallel Tracks,* in which the author discusses the railroad as "an important *protocinematic* phenomenon, a significant cultural force influencing the emergence and development of the cinema during the silent period." For Kirby, the railroad furnishes not only a "mode of perception" film would draw upon (like Friedberg's "gaze"), but also a "highly charged cultural image"—that is, subject matter (2–3).

3. Consider one of the signature slogans of the period: "The whole world is watching." Paradoxically, it refers to the concrete political impact of, for example, the Vietnam War protests (modernist) while simultaneously conveying the mass media's absorption and dilution of *any* political impact (postmodernist).

4. Neil Nehring offers an incisive discussion of this reactionary side to modernism. He shows how postwar (and, not coincidentally, postmodernist) academia defines modernism primarily as apolitical and highly formalistic, disinterested in "everyday" culture. What became suppressed in this "definition" of modernism, according to Nehring, was the revolutionary and politicized works—what he calls "the avant-garde"—that engaged the everyday and the social in a radically political way by attacking the cultural establishment (38–44). This latter visionary, political modernism is essentially what drives most road movies.

5. This tension between rebellious activism and conservative elitism within modernism is crystallized in two of its more compelling manifestations, both of which (like the road movie) reflect upon the human-machine fusion. Italian futurism and Russian constructivism both fetishized industry and technology with the promise of liberation; yet these movements became shadowed, respectively, by fascism and totalitarianism.

6. Henry Nash Smith's classic study *Virgin Land* situates political philosophies as distinct as Jefferson's and Whitman's within the compulsion (whether economic or poetic) to travel westward, so as to integrate nature as an ideological precept into the nation's cultural identity (3–48).

7. Nash Smith's discussion of this literature as it develops Western heroes like Buffalo Bill remains illuminating (51–120); see also Richard Slotkin's updated discussion in *Gunfighter Nation* of these same Western heroes (63–87), as well as more recent dime novels and pulp Westerns (125–228).

8. Leo Marx emphasizes the novel's "pastoral ideal" in connection with its social criticism and wandering plot structure, in his *The Machine in the Garden* (319–41).

9. Like that of his American counterpart Henry Miller, Lawrence's antipathy for home and his embrace of the road seems distinctly pre-Beat. The British modernism of the Bloomsbury crowd, in contrast, emphasizes a more tame mobility, traveling back and forth between country homes and city houses. See Pamela Todd's *Bloomsbury at Home*.

10. On American highway literature and the transcendentalist tradition of Whitman and Thoreau, see Lackey. See also Patton (12–13).

11. Two other important Depression-era road novels—both turned into road movies in the early 1970s—are Edward Anderson's *Thieves like Us* and Bertha Thomson's *The Autobiography of Boxcar Bertha*.

12. Cynthia Golomb Dettelbach notes that for Kerouac "the car functions as a catalyst" in terms of writing style, and that his style changed after driving with Cassady, writing "fast, wild, and free" (38–39). Though titled *In the Driver's Seat,* her study—a good one—emphasizes the automobile in American literature as icon more than narrative vehicle.

13. Stephen King's novella about a ghost driving the highways, "Riding the Bullet," was a publishing landmark as the first work of fiction to be "published" on the Internet, in March 2000. For more on horror road movies, see Morton, "Road Kill."

14. For an excellent discussion of *Blue Highways,* see Lackey (54–61).

15. Busses and trains provide this, but it is a less intimate and private space, such intimacy and privacy being crucial to the road movie's sense of *individual* adventure and rebellion. Conversely, the riding sequences in *Easy Rider* where the two bikers "communicate" seem rather forced and awkward.

16. We are beginning to describe what Rick Altman calls the "semantic elements" of a genre, its "building blocks" (219). Edward Buscombe suggests that what distinguishes a film genre is "what we actually see on the screen," "the visual conventions" that "provide a framework within which the story can be told" (13–15). Enumerating this "outer form"—setting, costumes, props, and other elements of the mise en scène—helps specify a particular film genre; the level of "inner form" or subject matter, in contrast, may be shared among various film genres. The second half of Buscombe's essay rightly recognizes how the outer and inner forms of a given genre are interdependent; my discussion, like his, addresses first the outer form, then the inner form, for clarity.

17. Some of these city driving films do, however, link discovery with driving. Sargeant and Watson note that cities have some narrative significance for the road movie, sometimes serving as a "microcosm of the larger country" (13).

18. See Creekmur (101–3); see also Sargeant and Watson (17–18).

19. On the narrative and symbolic uses of cars in American films, see Mottram. See also Orr (127–31).

20. For an excellent discussion of Italian futurism's car fanaticism, see Silk (57–71).

21. Corrigan can therefore aptly subtitle his chapter on the genre "The Road Movie in Outer Space," intimating how science fiction and road movies are linked not only by the journey motif ("Space: The Final Frontier") but also by the theme of technology. For more on the road movie–science fiction link, see Phillips.

22. "If it is the Western genre that provides the epic landscapes, the belief in freedom, the search for a better tomorrow, and the outlaw mythology, then the other influence on the road movie is the youth culture and the juvenile delinquency exploitation film" (Sargeant and Watson, 9).

23. Bruce MacDonald's films *Roadkill* (1989), *Highway 61* (1991), and *Hard Core Logo* (1996) are intriguing rock music road movies. Beyond the countless "concert tour" rockumentaries, see also Frank Zappa's *200 Motels* (1971) and REM's *Road Movie* (1996). More recently, the popular 1970s period piece *Almost Famous* (Cameron Crowe, 2000) possesses elements of the rock music road movie. And for something way out on the periphery of the road movie–music connection, let us note the name of the Swiss jazz/classical/rock ensemble led by Michael Wintsch: Road Movie.

24. Stringer makes a similar suggestion regarding the road movie's "two narrative situations": "In the first, one or more goal-oriented protagonists take off as a means to escape, either from pursuers . . . or from a hitherto boring lifestyle. . . . In the second, one or more protagonists seek to 'find themselves' existentially, either through sex . . . violence . . . or by messing with nature" (165).

25. Lackey discusses *On the Road*'s gender hierarchy as "a vestige of the old domestic romance, a twinge that dies hard, even in novels of rebellion against the postwar nesting frenzy" (138–41).

26. Corrigan sees road movies as "markers" of a crisis in genre and in gender, "the breakdown of male subjectivity" (137–43).

27. See also Willis's "Race on the Road" (287–306).

28. See Sargeant and Watson (7–9). See also Roberts, "Western Meets Eastwood," and Watson, "From Riding to Driving."

29. See McBride and Wilmington, *John Ford*, especially Chapter 3; see also Kolker and Beicken's discussion of *The Searchers* (28–36).

30. Ryan and Kellner note that the series of films about the Depression made during the Vietnam era reflects the social and political upheaval that characterizes (and connects) both periods (19). Not coincidentally, many of these Vietnam-era Depression films were road movies: *Bonnie and Clyde*, *Boxcar Bertha* (1972), *Paper Moon* (1973), *Thieves like Us* (1974), *Bound for Glory* (1976).

31. See Roddick (123).

32. For more on the film noir–road movie link, see Bryan.

33. Compare James Allen as well with Fonda's earlier incarnation of Joad as Eddie Taylor in *You Only Live Once* (1937).

34. Cohan has argued that Hollywood, and showbiz in general, forms a disturbing backdrop to *Detour*'s journey, a dark contrast to Hollywood's utopian wartime image of itself (127–28).

35. On the contrast between the wandering theme in *Detour* and *I Am a Fugitive*, see Polan (270–71).

36. Britton discusses this decision, and the film's gender politics, in terms of Al's "unreliable narrator" status (176–82).

37. According to Britton, she "acquiesces in the quotidian brutality of capitalism with exemplary ruthlessness, but, even as she does so, she is struggling against masculine dominance" (180).

38. As Cohan reminds us, this ending was "enforced" by the Production Code, as "the only possible means of bringing such a circuitous road to closure" (128).

39. Cohan discusses some "road movies" of the 1950s, such as the Hope-Crosby *Road to . . .* pictures. But they fall somewhat outside my own scope and definition of the genre, since they are, to my mind, more comedies than road movies, overtly conservative, more about "being at home" than being on the road.

40. On the Autobahn's links with Nazism, see Dimendberg (94–116).

41. The PBS documentary *Divided Highways* (based on Lewis's book) emphasizes the short-sightedness of this highway construction, and the destructive effects mentioned. For a more elaborate discussion of this issue, see Jane Holtz Kay's *Asphalt Nation*.

42. Cohan discusses *The Long, Long Trailer* in terms of "home on the road" and "showbiz culture" (136–39).

Chapter 2

1. The "Easy Rider" essay in the recent anthology *Lost Highways* makes a similar point: "For all their rebellious posturing, their West Coast cool, Wyatt and Billy are not quite the new American heroes they would like to be, and they know it. Their behaviour often has little to do with the utopian principles of hippie culture and more to do with its flip-side of self-serving irresponsibility" (Daniel, 76). But this point about the film is not new. See, for example, James (14–18); Ryan and Kellner (25); and Laderman, "What a Trip" (48).

2. Eyerman and Lofgren agree that if we focus on films "where the road and the journey (most often in an automobile . . .) have a central function," then "the genre was institutionalized during the 1960s and 1970s" (60). Orr likewise states that the "popular genre of the 'road-movie' makes its entry in the 1960s with location shooting and the mobile camera" (130).

3. For more on biker films and the road movie, see Morton, "Rebels of the Road."

4. Two years earlier Fred Zinneman used a similar railroad/horizon shot for narrative tension in *High Noon*, also produced by Stanley Kramer.

5. Kenneth Anger exaggerates this motorcycle fetishism, and the subculture of motorcycle gangs in general, in his experimental film of 1963, *Scorpio Rising* (a film that serves well as a link between *The Wild One* and *The Wild Angels*).

6. During an appearance on the Bravo cable channel's *Actor's Studio*, Penn insisted that the piece of Clyde's head being blown off at the end—scarcely visible—was a direct reference to the Kennedy assassination. See also Cawelti. Cagin and Dray contrast *Bonnie and Clyde*'s politicized rebellion with the other huge counterculture film of 1967, *The Graduate*, which they see as "scarcely threatening" and politically "prudish" (24–25).

7. This moment recalls the famous scene in Capra's *It Happened One Night* where everyone sings together on the bus. For a discussion of how *It Happened One Night* (and the prewar road movie in general) articulates "the people" as a community on the road, see Schaber (17–30).

8. Man describes Bonnie's melancholy moodiness in terms of the modernist influence of the French New Wave and its existential antiheroes (9). See also his excellent extended discussion of her complex shifts in attitude (13–18).

9. Leong, Sell, and Thomas discuss this political contradiction on a different level, where the film's life as stylistic fodder for consumer culture undermines its intended narrative social critique (77–81).

10. "At the end of the film's journey, there is really nothing but the characters' deaths. The lack of destination, which has haunted the narrative throughout, is finally eradicated in the spectacular eruption of blood, as if this were the end of the road of desire and not just the end of the road" (Russell, 180).

11. Kolker sees *Bonnie and Clyde*'s iconography—including its mobility—as an "inversion" of the gangster genre, "paradoxical" when measured against the early gangster classics (43–44). He also contrasts the "intangible adversary" of "Society" in *Bonnie and Clyde* with Muley's more politically expository flashback in *The Grapes of Wrath* (35–36). For a good discussion of *Bonnie and Clyde*'s antiestablishment "transformation" of the gangster genre, see Man (22–31).

12. Two other American films worth mentioning that came out in 1969 are the hugely popular *Butch Cassidy and the Sundance Kid,* a modern Western with vital road movie signs (two outlaw buddies who ramble across the country); and the remarkably prescient *The Honeymoon Killers,* a quirky "true crime" B-movie in the road gangster/noir tradition of *You Only Live Once* and *Gun Crazy.* Here, the male member of the outlaw couple seduces rich old ladies so as to murder them. Driving from victim to victim figures prominently. Additionally, we should take note of Jack Cardiff's *The Girl on a Motorcycle* (1968), an interesting pre-*Easy Rider* British road movie that contains all the hallmarks of the genre. Focusing quite uniquely on a female biker (Marianne Faithfull) who flees her boring role as housewife, the X-rated film goes far in exploring her erotic fusion with her motorbike. Thanks to David Gresalfi for bringing the film to my attention.

13. Hill opens her book on "the ultimate road movie" with the following: "*Easy Rider* was the little road movie that came out of nowhere to change Hollywood forever." Conceding that this description is "one of film culture's most enduring myths," she nevertheless contends that the film "has remained that rare beast: the commercially successful cult film" (8).

14. For an elaborate discussion of the contemporary buddy road movie, see Hark.

15. With perhaps convenient hindsight, Dennis Hopper makes this point on the analog track of the remastered laser disc of the film.

16. Daniel reads these flash-forward montages differently. Their "most potent effect is to prime us for tragedy. There is a heavy sense of determinism in the flash-forward/back structure, a suggestion that the story has already been written which undermines the character's perception of the road as a source of unlimited freedom" (78).

17. Rather unexpectedly, these spectators built into the film's "background" anticipate what Mark Crispin Miller describes in the "merger" endings of 1980s blockbuster movies: "Hollywood's new happy ending: a moment of euphoric melding, as the audience within the frame looks on and cheers" (235–38).

18. Hill points out that the original script had scenes of developed interactions with black characters, but these scenes were dropped for the final cut (42).

19. Ryan and Kellner discuss the narcissism operating beneath the surface of the film's alienation and rebellion (24–26).

20. Though it may be a peculiar gesture in the context of *Easy Rider,* I would invoke Laura Mulvey's classic account of the male gaze in Hollywood cinema, where this gaze either fetishizes the woman as reassuring and erotic spectacle, or sadistically demonizes the woman on a narrative level—to be punished, cured, etc. Wyatt, Billy, and George seem to be trapped

by both gazes here, split between male and female, suggesting that the counterculture out-sider, regardless of sex (or race), shares some affinity with women (and minorities) in rela-tion to the dominant culture. See Mulvey's "Visual Pleasure and Narrative Cinema."

21. Hill puts it mildly when she notes how all the women in the film are "supporting charac-ters" (54); Ryan and Kellner state the critique more emphatically: "Women are noticeably marginalized in the film; they appear as compliant sexual partners, prostitutes, or devoted wives. . . . This narcissistic vision is coupled with paranoia or distrust regarding everything that curtails male desire" (23–24).

22. Hopper and Fonda discuss these aspects of the framing on the remastered laser disc's second audio track.

23. Though perhaps not clear from the film, Fonda offers this interpretation—that Wyatt ini-tially believes the truck drivers are coming back to help—on the new laser disc's second audio track.

24. Daniel discusses this scene in terms of the "ambivalence" of "the counter-culture itself" (74–75).

25. James links the film's ideological and financial need to finally "destroy Captain America and Billy" with Wyatt's "We blew it" line, the latter an inadvertent allegory of "the failure of Hopper and Fonda to make a film adequate to the ideals of the counterculture" (15–16).

Chapter 3

1. Despite being inherently modernist and self-reflexive, the road movie too follows Schatz's schema, becoming increasingly self-conscious, as ensuing chapters will demonstrate.

2. Atkinson suggests that such cynicism about the road movie quest is essential to "real road movies": "Whatever might be found on the road, it won't resemble any universal truth, it will elude those explicitly searching for it, and it won't be easy to tie to the hood and bring home" (17).

3. Leo Charney discusses "drift" in reference to the birth of modernity, modernist aesthetics and early cinema's mode of address. Charney's descriptions resonate with the road movies currently under discussion: "The logic of drift meanders, digresses, floats" (17).

4. Though he does not name the 1970s specifically, Baudrillard sees late-capitalist "transpar-ency of evil" as emerging out of a period he describes as "after the orgy"—a period we can infer, I think, as "after" the 1960s counterculture: "Today, everything has been liberated . . . and we find ourselves collectively before the crucial question: what do we do after the orgy?" (*La Transparence du Mal*, 11–12; translation mine).

5. See Kolker (8); see also Cook (11–12).

6. As Peter Cowie recounts in his biography of Coppola, *The Rain People*, based on an ex-perience from Francis's childhood, was produced in emulation of European directors like Claude Lelouch and their "personal" films: "It was the first of the screenplays that Coppola was able to write and make as he pleased. Today he regards it as an attempt to imitate the Antonioni–Monica Vitti creative symbiosis" (45–46).

7. Coppola takes the theme further in *The Conversation* (1973).

8. Cagin and Dray describe BBS as a "small, independent production company" that "served as a haven for . . . Hollywood 'outsiders.'" Embodying "aspects of Hollywood legitimacy *and* rebelliousness," BBS was a crucial production source for the rise of the road movie; Fonda, Hopper, Nicholson, Hellman, Rafelson et al. were all connected with it (62–64). See also Biskind's *Easy Riders, Raging Bulls*, especially 52–80 and 110–40.

9. In an alternative reading from my own, Cagin and Dray see Palm as "an extreme version" of Bobby, "disaffected to the point of absurdity," serving "as a subtle warning and an implicit criticism of Bobby's own obsessive and hostile frame of mind" (67).

10. As reported by Cagin and Dray, Nicholson suggested changing the ending from Bobby and Rayette going over a cliff in their car, to the one adopted, because "the time was right for something other than a sensational blood-and-guts finale like the one that capped *Easy Rider*. Bobby Dupea would live, despite his inability to conform" (69).

11. As Elsaesser puts it, "[T]here is only the merest shadow of an intrigue, the action provocatively avoids the interpersonal conflicts potentially inherent both in the triangular relationship and in the challenge personified by the Warren Oates character, and finally, the film toys with goals (the race to Washington) in an almost gratuitous way. On this level, Hellman has made, and doubtless intended, an anti-action film" (14).

12. David Seed observes how throughout the film, "rapid movement is contrasted with immobility," an attempt by the filmmaker to undermine a sense of movement with the ironic notion of going nowhere (108–9).

13. The tension between the Driver, the Girl, and GTO seems an interesting example of Stringer's notion of the road movie's "traveling trio," where "the emphasis is usually on how a single female gets to be passed between the hands of two men within the terms of an erotic triangle" (172). *Two-Lane Blacktop* both exemplifies and subverts Stringer's discussion of such road movie "intimacy": the Girl does change hands, but of her own volition, deconstructing the genre. More broadly, the "intimacy" upon which such love triangles are typically based is here, as we have seen, starkly unemotional.

14. In this respect, she anticipates Mona in *Vagabond*, discussed in Chapter 6.

15. Orr illuminates this highly experimental aspect of *Two-Lane Blacktop* (and many early-70s road movies) by describing what he calls the neomodern (60s and 70s) cinema's "challenge to the conventions of perception. For the neomoderns the camera's powers of perception remain frail and partial. . . . In the absence of absolute values lies a vision of the uncertainties of all knowledge. Through its vexing quest narratives [neo]modern cinema reaffirms Merleau-Ponty's assertion of the inherent ambiguity of the visual field of perception" (9).

16. Noting that GTO "gets the best lines in the film," Webb emphasizes Oates's acting and character as saving the film from zero audience identification (84–85).

17. On the reemergence of neo–film noir in the early 1970s, see Ryan and Kellner (81–85).

18. Sargeant discusses Kowalski's utter disinterest in sex in terms of the film's postcounterculture alienation: "by negating sexual contact Kowalski is negating the possibility of the emergence of his own identity, suggesting once more that he has entered an abyss of nihilism" ("*Vanishing Point*," 95).

19. Indeed, "easy riders" seem to make up many of the sideline spectators at the radio station, and at the film's final spectacle of explosion. As we shall see, the 1980s postmodern road movie will undertake outright parody of *Easy Rider*.

20. Kinder comments that "we wonder whether he really loves her . . . , or whether he is more enamored with the romantic idea of having such a passion" (8). Malick himself has said that Kit "doesn't really believe" any of the banal aphorisms he records while holding the rich man hostage in his own house, but that "he envies people who do" (Walker, 82).

21. The first thing Holly explains to viewers in her voice-over is that her mother died when she was a little girl, so they moved to Montana. Thus marking the mother's absence, the film implies that Holly may fill the role of both daughter and wife for her father.

22. Kinder notes this scene's evocation of "romantic myths, which glorify killers," not only

"*Bonnie and Clyde*, but from many genres which embody these fantasies—westerns, jungle films, horror movies, cops and robbers, adventures of Marco Polo, and other wanderers" (9). Malick himself suggests such influences, citing "books like *The Hardy Boys, Swiss Family Robinson, Tom Sawyer, Huck Finn*—all involving an innocent in a drama over his or her head" (Walker, 82).

23. Discussing the couple's "outsider status" in terms of "the disappearance of traditionally ascribed borders," Sargeant notes how the film's "*mise-en-scène* reiterates this narrative trajectory of the borderless state . . . here the great plains are shot as an almost hellish infinity of flat, empty miles, mirrored by the flatness of the sky above them. . . . The geography is filmed to emphasise its collapse, until the horizon seems to vanish into pure flatness; world and sky as one massive blank canvas" ("Killer Couples," 153).

24. On the distinction between Bonnie and Clyde's use of the media and Kit's, see Kinder (8) and Corrigan (148–51).

25. In this respect *Badlands* seems a precursor to the Sex Pistols' song "Pretty Vacant" of 1977, the pretty vacant teenagers of *River's Edge* ten years later (1987), and Mickey's postured, laconic mystique in *Natural Born Killers* (1994).

26. The road movie–film school generation link comes full circle, in a sense, with Coppola's reported project of filming Kerouac's *On the Road*.

27. We should hesitate, however, to buy into the film's "women's liberation" theme: like many so-called feminist films in the early seventies directed by men, this film "liberates" Bertha by allowing her to actively pursue sexual pleasure and sensual thrills. In other words, it's a substantially patriarchal film posing as "feminist."

28. Kinder has remarked that the film's sympathetic treatment of the police suggests that the cops and outlaws have much in common, as individualist outsiders to society (4–5). Kolker situates the film's "befriending" of the police, and its overall sentimentality about restoring the family, in the context of Spielberg's commercial and ideological career in the 1980s, as "the great fantasist of recuperation . . . assuring the family that everything will be fine" (265, 280).

29. Noting this cartoonish quality, Kinder brings our attention to the highly symbolic sequence where the outlaw couple are watching cartoons on the television in a camper, and the husband realizes that "these farcical catastrophes foreshadowed his own doom" (7–8).

Chapter 4

1. "It is notable that, in the few road movies—frequently comedies—that neither depict youth, nor emphasize a move to a youthful state of mind, the protagonists often experience the road trip with a mixture of confusion, befuddlement, and even fear. . . . [T]he middle-aged protagonists are too old, too conservative, and ultimately too scared to undertake the psychic journey that is part of the geographical voyage" (Sargeant and Watson, 9).

2. On the complex relationship between postmodernism and film, see J. Hill (100).

3. Some lesser-known independent road movies from the 1980s that stay closer to the early-70s spirit are *Candy Mountain* (1987, directed by Beat road photographer Robert Frank, written by *Two-Lane Blacktop* scriptwriter Rudy Wurlitzer), *Miles from Home* (1988), *Out* (1988), and *Miracle Mile* (1989).

4. "In ridiculing *Easy Rider* by revealing the comic underside of its overly serious themes and episodes, *Lost in America* not only denies the possibility of a political critique in the past but

also expresses doubts about its possibility at the present time or in the future" (Zavarzadeh, 165–66).

5. Cohan and Hark cite *America* on the first page of their introduction to *The Road Movie Book*. Sargeant and Watson also refer to *America* in their introduction to *Lost Highways*.

6. See Falconer; see also Rayner.

7. I borrow the term from Susan Sontag's "Notes on 'Camp,'" where she distinguishes between "naive and deliberate camp"—the former more "pure" because "unintentional," thus more "satisfying" (282). Other "notes" scattered throughout her essay intimate the aesthetic links between camp and the postmodern, and resonate with the road movies being discussed: "the way of Camp, is not in terms of beauty, but in terms of the degree of artifice, of stylization"; "the camp sensibility is disengaged, depoliticized" (277); "camp sees everything in quotation marks" (280).

8. Specific allusions may include the atomic suitcase of *Kiss Me Deadly*, and the scene in *Psycho* where Marion is approached by the highway patrolman.

9. See Goshorn on the film's dialectic of resistance and recuperation (38–39).

10. Bud seems to embody both Hark's "high flyer" and "neurotic," espousing paranoid and contradictory repo man philosophy—which turns out to be a watered-down, caricatured version of conservative American economic values (Goshorn, 62).

11. We might link Miller's science fiction discourse to an earlier road movie visionary/fool, George Hansen from *Easy Rider*, who half-jokingly speaks of Venusians secretly colonizing Earth.

12. As an aside, the film's homoerotic subtext comes to the fore in this penultimate scene, where Miller and Otto gaze into each other's eyes, in what is no doubt a campy send-up of classical Hollywood romantic scenes.

13. Speculating on Shepard's influence, Kolker and Beicken discuss the "family melodrama" aspect of *Paris, Texas* in terms of "the interlacing of modernist exploration and more traditional narrative development, the sequestering of new positions in old conventions" (122).

14. As Hark points out, Travis will not become a "high flyer" like Walt (211–12). But her linking of Travis with a Road Man like Dean Moriarty seems unconvincing. Travis may be restless, but he is too psychologically self-absorbed to engage visionary, mobile exploration. More a family man than a road man, Travis resembles *Walt* in his "drive" to get his family back together.

15. *Stranger than Paradise* is often singled out as the starting point of the contemporary American independent film, as suggested by Geoff Andrew's recent study of the topic, titled *Stranger than Paradise*. For a more sociohistorical (rather than auteur-based) discussion of the American independent film, see Emanuel Levy's *Cinema of Outsiders*.

16. *Drugstore Cowboy*'s cop-outlaw bond recalls *The Sugarland Express*, which in turn suggests the unlikely link between Van Sant and Spielberg: starting as an independent road movie director, Van Sant goes on to make such mainstream Hollywood fare as *To Die For*, *Good Will Hunting*, the unforgivable remake of *Psycho*, and *Finding Forrester*.

17. The Coen brothers' recent *O Brother, Where Art Thou?* (2001) offers a postmodern yet provocative riff on the Depression road movie (notably *I Am a Fugitive from a Chain Gang*, *It Happened One Night*, and *Sullivan's Travels*), as well as Homer's *Odyssey*.

18. Sargeant notes such "conservatism" in the post–*Wild at Heart* "killer couple" films. In contrast with *Badlands*, these films "play with images of alienation and angst, but always resolve the protagonists' dilemmas with a return to the conservatism of 'being' (be it via the

mechanisms of an arrival at the destination, or the destruction of the killer). The potentialities of chaos remain ungrasped. Rebellion is rendered merely as a pastiche of previous
rebellious icons" ("Killer Couples," 167).

19. See Sharon Willis's "Special Effects: Sexual and Social Difference in *Wild at Heart*" for a
thorough—and thoroughly incisive—critique of the archly conservative racist and sexist attitudes of *Wild at Heart*. Parallel to my more genre-focused discussion, she concludes that
"*Wild at Heart* is aiming for an audience that would accept its own strategies for neutralizing
racist and sexist fantasies as ironic" (290).

20. For an interesting discussion of Lynch's road movie–esque *Lost Highway* in terms of *The
Wizard of Oz*, see Celeste. See also S. Mitchell.

21. Willis discusses the scene's "anxious fantasy" regarding race (Lemon is black), but her description of the scene suggests pronounced generic features of the postmodern road movie.
"Such an overt commitment to special effects, staging violence that is orchestrated as driving repetition, helps to figure the murder more as spectacle than event, in a maneuvre of
spectacular aestheticization" ("Special Effects," 276).

22. On "performance" as a significant theme of the outlaw couple road movie, see Creekmur.

23. For Willis, such a scene constitutes one of many "minor special effects" that "implicitly
[structure] the film as a road movie. These effects are almost 'decorative': they present themselves as 'local color,' literally" ("Special Effects," 288).

24. Willis emphasizes the context of the scene, in terms of race and gender: it begins after Marietta's repulsive bathroom-vomiting scene; it is crosscut with Johnny's murder by people
of color; and it precedes the infamous "fuck me" scene in Big Tuna. "The accident scene
is structurally pivotal for it signals an acceleration of the film's progressively intensifying
fetishism directed toward women" (ibid., 286).

25. Willis suggests this last scene is seen from the point of view of their son, Pace. The infantile and ironic connotations of such a point of view corroborate the generic tendencies I
have described: "In some way, this six-year-old's point of view is the symbolic *home* that we
finally reach; it is the *home* of the film's gaze and of our own, and, figuratively, the source
of these fantasies" (ibid., 284).

26. For Kaleta, "the romantic streak of the ending" reflects the film's confrontation of its "disillusioned" 90s audience. But the neoconservative features I emphasize remain: "*Wild at
Heart* echoes the grandeur of the film epic while it approaches the bold, bright colors and
gestures of the animated movie cartoon" (167–69).

Chapter 5

1. Perhaps an altogether different kind of cultural response to the encroaching virtual highway
would be Mark Pinkosh's one-man theater performance, *Road Movie*, written by Geoffrey
Hamilton, which toured the United States in 1998.

2. See Kleinhans (316).

3. An interesting and exceptional example worth mentioning is Jon Jost's *Jon Jost's Frame Up*,
released in 1994. Totally overshadowed by *Natural Born Killers*, the film treats the classic
road movie outlaw couple in a truly disturbing manner, pushing the minimalism of *Stranger
than Paradise* and *Two-Lane Blacktop* to an extreme that verges on nonnarrative.

4. Most recently, Hollywood and popular culture have displayed a penchant for reviving the
action and comedy racing film, with *Driven* (2001), *The Fast and the Furious* (2001), *The
Rat Race* (2001)—a loose remake of *It's a Mad, Mad, Mad, Mad World* (1963)—and USA

cable television network's "reality" series broadcast in August 2001, *Cannonball Run 2001,* a "real" road race inspired by the *Cannonball Run* films.

5. Mills refers to these Hollywood formula road films as succumbing to "banal commodity" (324). See also Willis, "Race on the Road."

6. Donald Lyons's review of *Delusion* situates it in relation to *Detour* (2–3).

7. Corrigan sees the road movie as a hysterical genre because of its "crisis in representation" and "breakdown of male subjectivity," expressed through "obsessive repetition" and "excessive theatricality" (142–43). The overinvested masculine standoff concluding *Delusion* seems an intriguing example of this. Moreover, *Delusion*'s "feminist" response to this impasse dramatizes the "other cultural and other gendered geographies" the road movie can explore in the wake of such crisis and breakdown (160).

8. See also Willis, "Hardware and Hardbodies, What Do Women Want?" and Griggers.

9. Hark notes the "isolated secondary roads favored in road movie iconography" (207).

10. Hark observes that "wild" is "the privileged adjective Hollywood employs to describe the liberatory yet dangerous road ethos" (227).

11. The beer-drinking motif connects Harlan the rapist with Daryl the husband, who later is watching football and drinking beer when Thelma first calls him from the road.

12. Other disturbing ambiguities around gender and sexuality occur in this sequence. Just before meeting J. D., Thelma is shown sunbathing in a bikini at a dingy motel. The camera eroticizes her, perhaps inappropriately soon after she was almost violently raped. Then, she seems a little too eager to get into bed with J. D. so soon after such a traumatic experience. I don't insist that Thelma's character be traumatized. But I do question whether the film may be retroactively trivializing the rape scene, in its rush to get on with the sexy stuff between stars Geena Davis and Brad Pitt. Let us also note that as she eyes J. D. in the rearview mirror (typically the visual domain of the male driver to observe the female passenger, as in *Five Easy Pieces*), we are looking at *her* putting on lip gloss. The scene renders her the erotic object while she gazes at the male.

13. For more on the various political readings of *Thelma and Louise,* see "*Film Quarterly* Roundtable: The Many Faces of *Thelma and Louise.*"

14. This moment in *Thelma and Louise* is noted by Creekmur in support of his argument regarding the importance of fame and performance for the outlaw couple (95).

15. Robert Lang argues that, unlike Scott, who "plays" at being gay, Mike will never find his mother, will never be able (like Scott) to "come home," because he is a gay outsider in a patriarchal society (343).

16. On the other hand, perhaps Wyatt and Billy *are* victims of patriarchal homophobia, when they are attacked ("gay-bashed"?) for being effeminate hippies. See discussion of *Easy Rider* in Chapter 2.

17. I am grateful to Scott Simmon for pointing out the *Chimes at Midnight* connection. Lang discusses *My Own Private Idaho* for its allusions to *The Wizard of Oz* (341–43). *Chimes at Midnight* seems more significant to *My Own Private Idaho*'s postmodern pastiche.

18. It is "unfortunate," as Mills puts it, that *The Living End* "perpetuates a cinematic tradition of hostility toward women" (309). Such easy ridicule of a homosexual in a gay film also recalls *My Own Private Idaho*'s treatment of Hans.

19. Luke's question, which crystallizes this road movie's gay cultural critique, probably is an allusion to a song of the same title by The Smiths, from the mid-1980s. While the film is replete with rock music references, those to The Smiths and Morrissey are especially relevant, since they became pop icons for gay audiences.

20. Mills notes the influence of Lang's *You Only Live Once* (1937) on Araki's film (316).

21. "*The Living End*'s heroes break out of the genre's strictures, and although driven by AIDS, their end is living . . . The road motif symbolizes the movement of gay bodies not only through the landscape, but especially metaphorically forwards into the future when there might be a cure to the disease" (Mills, 325).

22. As Willis notes, even when mobile, blacks usually "need" (according to genre and culture) to be accompanied by a white person ("Race on the Road," 304).

23. Another notable black "road" picture of sorts from the early 1970s is the revisionist Western *Buck and the Preacher* (1972). The first film directed by Sidney Poitier, it also stars him and Harry Belafonte as the two buddies leading a wagon train of former slaves to homestead out West.

24. We should take note of two African American films from the early 1990s that predate *Get on the Bus*, and that feature a journey at their center: Carl Franklin's *One False Move* (1991) and John Singleton's *Poetic Justice* (1993).

25. Mills anticipates our current discussion, arguing that when the road movie is appropriated in the 1990s by "subculture communities," individual drivers represent "a group fantasy which celebrates its difference from the norm. The once-masculinist road story of the lone anarchist on the run is reborn when genre becomes a vehicle for the representation of otherness along the lines of marginalized class, race, sexuality, or gender" (323). In *Get on the Bus*, despite being of "marginalized" race, the community is still "masculinist." A good, provocative example of such a "subculture community" road movie, one complementary to *Get on the Bus* and *Smoke Signals*, is Peter Bratt's *Follow Me Home* (1996).

26. Quart offers a relevant description of irony in the Frears-Kureishi films, which explore "themes built around issues of race, class, and gender with a passion for ambiguity and contradiction" (242).

27. *The Living End* constantly cites movies and rock music. *Get on the Bus* too is full of pop culture references, among them Denzel Washington, the NBA, the O. J. Simpson trial, Rodney King, *The Defiant Ones*, Jesse Jackson, and James Baldwin. Such pop culture pastiche thus seems a prevalent component of the multicultural postmodern road movie, one with politically critical potential.

28. In his somewhat rabid review titled "Golly," John Patterson rightly describes how the film "unfolds gently with an evenness and rural patience that call to mind those allegedly 'better times' that Gingrich, Armey and Robertson would like us all to choke on" (*L.A. Weekly*, October 15, 1999).

29. Complementary to this subcategory are recent documentary films exploring elders on the road, such as *Roam Sweet Home* (1996) and *Grey Nomads* (1998).

30. Kreider and Content see her as a reflection of Straight's own "continuing inability to take responsibility for the terrible (and not unpredictable) consequences of a heedless urgency." Likewise, the "inexplicable herd of statues of deer who seem to be watching him" is "not just a cheap sight gag; these stolidly haunting presences represent the accusing memory of his human victims" (29).

31. Kreider and Content note the fire motif connecting *The Straight Story* with Lynch's previous films (30).

32. In a narrative setup deriving from works as diverse as Pasolini's *Teorema* (1968) and Soderbergh's *sex, lies, & videotape* (1989), Straight is the "mysterious stranger" (Twain), the unexpected and enigmatic visitor who shakes up the family identity and the "Comforts of Home" (to cite a short story by Flannery O'Connor that uses this same narrative paradigm).

Chapter 6

1. With regard to this European-American dialogue, we should note road movies about Europeans coming to America: *Strozek* (1977), *Leningrad Cowboys Go America* (1989), and *Mr. Universe* (1989).

2. This carnival/caravan quality is also present in road movies from Mexico and Latin America, which often portray a quest for national meaning and identity in the shadow of North American economic, political, and cinematic influences. For example, *Mexican Bus Ride* (1955), *Bye Bye Brazil* (Brazil, 1979), *El Norte* (1983), *El Viaje* (1992), *Guantanamera* (1995), *Deep Crimson* (1997), and *Central Station* (Brazil, 1998). See Laderman, "The Road Movie Rediscovers Mexico."

3. Fellini on getting the idea for *La Strada:* "I seem to remember hazily that I was driving my car past the fields around Rome in that lazy relaxed way I have of wandering, which perhaps made me catch a glimpse of the characters, the feeling, the atmosphere of that film for the first time" (Grazzini, 109).

4. Fellini returns to the road movie in *Toby Damit* (1968), a short film compiled in the European Edgar Allan Poe trilogy *Spirits of the Dead.* Here, Terrence Stamp plays a bitter pop idol driven by the paparazzi to take a surrealistic, suicidal drive. Other Italian modernist road movies of note include Rossellini's *Voyage in Italy* (1953) and Dino Risi's *Il sorpasso* (1964), the latter discussed by Restivo (233–48). A recent crossnational Italian road movie, which engages contemporary political issues regarding neighboring Albania, is *Lamerica* (Gianni Amelio, 1995). See also Amelio's previous *Stolen Children* (1992).

5. As with Fellini, many Bergman films incorporate the journey narrative in some way: consider *The Seventh Seal* (1957) and *The Magician* (1958). At one point in *The Magician,* the dying actor Spegel says, "Motion itself is the only truth."

6. Törnqvist links the black hearse with Isak's old black car, and the accident in the dream with the actual accident on the road later (115–33).

7. Another French road movie worth acknowledging, one that dates from the time period of *La Strada* and *Wild Strawberries,* is Henri-Georges Clouzot's masterpiece *Wages of Fear* (1955). See also Godard's *Bande à Part* (1964) and *Pierrot le Fou* (1965) for the director's earlier contributions to the genre. Alain Tanner's *Messidor* (1977) is an interesting precursor to *Thelma and Louise.* Recent multicultural and/or gay French road movies of note include *Western* (Manuel Poirier, 1966), *Those Who Love Me Can Take the Train* (Patrice Chereau, 1998), and *Adventures of Felix* (Olivier Ducastel and Jacques Martineau, 1999).

8. The film's trajectory through small towns along the East German border invokes both the geopolitical "frontier" of "the realpolitik of Germany in the seventies," as well as "the frontier of the American Western" (Kolker and Beicken, 63–64).

9. Jonathan Demme's B-biker flick *Crazy Mama* (1975) offers a campy crime spree by three women. A more significant precursor to *Vagabond* would be *The Girl on a Motorcycle* (1968), cited in Chapter 2. In any case, both films were directed by men, and do not approach the depth of *Vagabond's* exploration of female gender on the road.

10. Hayward notes how *Vagabond* deconstructs the road movie genre, from a feminist perspective: tracking shots going right to left ("going backwards down the road"); the flashback structure; no point of view for the traveling "roadster"; the "roadster" being a woman; no "discovery" or "self-knowledge" (290).

11. Without detracting from Varda's originality, Flitterman-Lewis quite rightly situates *Vaga-*

bond, and Varda's work generally, between Godard's "political and discursive strategies" and Resnais's "temporal dislocations" (298).

12. Varda on *Vagabond* (cited in Flitterman-Lewis): "The film *wanders* between Mona and the others. We *glimpse* their lives, and then move on. I really liked all the characters in this story, *here and there,* like small 'figures' in a winter landscape, where, coming toward us, walking, is a *rebellious* girl" (286; emphasis added).

13. Guy Austin suggests this reading when he notes how Mona and David are "self-effacing," in contrast to the genre's more typical "lovers on the run" who are "self-mythicizing" (86).

14. According to Hayward, "The tracking shot is Mona's sign" (288). Flitterman-Lewis describes the film's moving camera techniques as "investigation, a kind of surveillance . . . that never ceases to imply the *social* inscription of vision" (288).

15. Canadian director Bruce MacDonald has self-consciously developed the road movie subcategory of the "rock 'n' road movie." His films *Roadkill* (1989), *Highway 61* (1991), and *Hard Core Logo* (1996) form a rock 'n' road movie trilogy, where the road movie's rock music accents (driving soundtrack, rock star casting, etc.) become prominent narrative and thematic components. In *Highway 61* the outlaw couple is composed of a shy barber who discovers a corpse and a brassy female roadie who has stolen her band's drug stash. In *Roadkill* a concert promoter searches through the Canadian forest for a lost band, encountering bizarre outcasts along the way. Most compelling is *Hard Core Logo,* which uses the mockumentary style of *This Is Spinal Tap* to focus on an aging punk rock band that gets back together for a concert tour, ostensibly to raise money for an ailing musician friend. The film mobilizes reflexive film techniques on a variety of levels: filmmaker MacDonald is present on the tour, as himself; several driving sequences are portrayed in a playfully artificial style (e.g., using miniatures for the van on the road); the bass player's diary, read at times in voice-over, comments on the interpersonal dynamics of their tour.

16. The roaming outlaw rock stars of *Bandits* thus exemplify and extend Creekmur's argument about the "inverted" kinship between outlaw couple road movies and musicals, a kinship deriving from the trope of fame (91).

17. Regarding the film's antirealistic, Brechtian play with form, Michael Verhoeven's *The Nasty Girl* comes to mind as a fruitful companion piece. Released in 1990, *The Nasty Girl* likewise carries out a potent feminist critique of mass culture (here more specifically relating to Germany's Nazi past), using dynamic reflexive techniques. As in *Bandits,* such presentation looks postmodern, but does not sacrifice a coherent and compelling political critique.

BIBLIOGRAPHY

Altman, Rick. *Film/Genre*. London: British Film Insititute, 1999.

Andrew, Geoff. *Stranger than Paradise: Maverick Film-Makers in Recent American Cinema*. New York: Limelight Editions, 1999.

Atkinson, Michael. "Crossing The Frontiers." *Sight and Sound* 4, no. 1 (January 1994): 14–17.

Austin, Guy. *Contemporary French Cinema: An Introduction*. Manchester: Manchester University Press, 1996.

Bailey, Cameron. "Nigger/Lover: The Thin Sheen of Race in *Something Wild*." *Screen* 4, no. 29 (1988): 28–40.

Baudrillard, Jean. *America*. Translated by Chris Turner. New York: Verso, 1988.

———. *La Transparence du Mal*. Paris: Éditions Galilée, 1990.

Biskind, Peter. *Easy Riders, Raging Bulls: How the Sex-Drugs-and-Rock 'n' Roll Generation Saved Hollywood*. New York: Simon and Schuster, 1998.

———. "The Last Crusade." In *Seeing through Movies*, edited by Mark Crispin Miller, 112–49. New York: Pantheon, 1990.

Britton, Andrew. "*Detour*." In *The Book of Film Noir*, edited by Ian Cameron, 174–83. New York: Continuum Publishing Company, 1993.

Broderick, Mick. "Heroic Apocalypse: *Mad Max*, Mythology, and the Millennium." *Crisis Cinema: The Apocalyptic Idea in Postmodern Narrative Film*, edited by Christopher Sharrett, 251–72. Washington, D.C.: Maisonneuve Press, 1993.

Brougher, Kerry. "The Car as Star." In *Automobile and Culture*, edited by Gerald Silk, 171–74. Los Angeles: Museum of Contemporary Art, 1984.

Bryan, Geraint. "Nowhere to Run: Pulp Noir on the Road." In *Lost Highways: An Illustrated History of Road Movies*. edited by Jack Sargeant and Stephanie Watson, 44–54. London: Creation Books, 1999.

Buscombe, Edward. "The Idea of Genre in American Cinema." In *Film Genre Reader II*, edited by Barry Keith Grant, 11–25. Austin: University of Texas Press, 1995.

Cagin, Seth, and Philip Dray. *Born to Be Wild: Hollywood and the Sixties Generation*. Boca Raton, Fla.: Coyote Press, 1994.

Capote, Truman. *In Cold Blood*. New York: Random House, 1965.

Cawelti, John G., ed. *Focus on Bonnie and Clyde*. Englewood Cliffs, N.J.: Prentice-Hall, Inc., 1973.

Celeste, Reni. "*Lost Highway:* Unveiling Cinema's Yellow Brick Road." *Cineaction* 43 (summer 1997): 36–43.

Charney, Leo. *Empty Moments: Cinema, Modernity, and Drift*. Durham, N.C.: Duke University Press, 1998.

Cohan, Steven. "Almost like Being at Home." In *The Road Movie Book*, edited by Steven Cohan and Ina Rae Hark, 113–42. New York: Routledge, 1997.

Cohan, Steven, and Ina Rae Hark. "Introduction." In *The Road Movie Book*, ed. Cohan and Hark, 1–14.

Cook, David A. "Auteur Cinema and the 'Film Generation' in 1970s Hollywood." In *The New American Cinema*, edited by Jon Lewis, 11–37. Durham, N.C.: Duke University Press, 1998.

Cormack, Mike. *Ideology and Cinematography in Hollywood, 1930–1939*. New York: St. Martin's Press, 1994.

Corrigan, Timothy. *A Cinema without Walls*. New Brunswick, N.J.: Rutgers University Press, 1994.

Cowie, Peter. *Coppola*. New York: Da Capo Press, 1994.

Creekmur, Corey K. "On the Run and on the Road: Fame and the Outlaw Couple in American Cinema." In *The Road Movie Book*, ed. Cohan and Hark, 90–109.

Daniel, Alistair. "Get Your Kicks: *Easy Rider* and the Counter-Culture." In *Lost Highways*, ed. Sargeant and Watson, 68–80.

Dargis, Manhola. "The Roads to Freedom." *Sight and Sound* 1, no. 3 (July 1991): 14–18.

Dettelbach, Cynthia Golomb. *In The Driver's Seat: The Automobile in American Literature and Popular Culture*. Westport, Conn.: Greenwood Press, 1976.

Dimendberg, Edward. "The Will to Motorization: Cinema, Highways, and Modernity." *October* 73 (summer 1995): 91–137.

Elsaesser, Thomas. "The Pathos of Failure: American Films in the 70's." *Monogram* 6 (1975): 13–19.

Eyerman, Ron, and Orvar Löfgren. "Romancing the Road: Road Movies and Images of Mobility." *Theory, Culture, and Society* 12 (1995): 53–79.

Falconer, Delia. "'We Don't Need to Know the Way Home': The Disappearance of the Road in the *Mad Max* Trilogy." In *The Road Movie Book*, ed. Cohan and Hark, 249–70.

Feuer, Jane. "The Self-Reflexive Musical and the Myth of Entertainment." In *Film Genre Reader II*, ed. Grant, 441–55.

"*Film Quarterly* Roundtable: The Many Faces of *Thelma and Louise*." *Film Quarterly* 45, no. 2 (1991–92): 20–31.

Flitterman-Lewis, Sandy. *To Desire Differently: Feminism and the French Cinema*. Urbana: University of Illinois Press, 1990.

Friedberg, Anne. *Window Shopping: Cinema and the Postmodern*. Berkeley: University of California Press, 1993.

Goshorn, A. Keith. "*Repoman* and the Punk Anti-Aesthetic: Postmodernity as a Permanent 'Bad Area.'" *Crisis Cinema*. 37–76.

Grant, Barry Keith, ed. *Film Genre Reader II*. Austin: University of Texas Press, 1995.

Grazzini, Giovanni, ed. *Federico Fellini Comments on Film*. Translated by Joseph Henry. Fresno: The Press at California State University Fresno, 1988.

Griggers, Cathy. "*Thelma and Louise* and the Cultural Generation of the New Butch-Femme." In *Film Theory Goes to the Movies,* edited by Jim Collins, Hilary Radner, and Ava Preacher Collins, 129–41. New York: Routledge, 1993.

Hark, Ina Rae. "Fear of Flying: Yuppie Critique and the Buddy-Road Movie of the 1980s." In *The Road Movie Book,* ed. Cohan and Hark, 204–29.

Hayward, Susan. "Beyond the Gaze and into *Femme-filmécriture*: Agnès Varda's *Sans toit ni loi* (1985)." In *French Film: Texts and Contexts,* edited by Susan Hayward and Ginette Vincendeau, 285–96. London: Routledge, 1990.

Hey, Kenneth. "Cars and Films in American Culture, 1929–1959." In *The Automobile and American Culture,* edited by David L. Lewis and Laurence Goldstein, 193–205. Ann Arbor: University of Michigan Press, 1983.

Hill, John. "Postmodernism and Film." In *Oxford Guide to Film Studies,* edited by John Hill and Pamela Church Gibson, 96–105. New York: Oxford University Press, 1998.

Hill, Lee. *Easy Rider.* London: British Film Institute, 1996.

Interrante, Joseph. "The Road to Autopia: The Automobile and the Spatial Transformation of American Culture." In *The Automobile and American Culture,* ed. Lewis and Goldstein, 89–104.

James, David E. *Allegories of Cinema.* Princeton: Princeton University Press, 1989.

Jeffords, Susan. *Hard Bodies: Hollywood Masculinity in the Reagan Era.* New Brunswick, N.J.: Rutgers University Press, 1994.

Kaleta, Kenneth C. *David Lynch.* New York: Twayne Publishers, 1993.

Kay, Jane Holtz. *Asphalt Nation.* New York: Crown Publishers, 1997.

Kerouac, Jack. *On The Road.* New York: Viking Press, 1955.

Kinder, Marsha. "The Return of the Outlaw Couple." *Film Quarterly* 27, no. 4 (summer 1974): 2–10.

Kirby, Lynn. *Parallel Tracks: The Railroad and Silent Cinema.* Durham, N.C.: Duke University Press, 1997.

Kitses, Jim. *Gun Crazy.* London: British Film Institute, 1996.

Kleinhans, Chuck. "Independent Features: Hopes and Dreams." In *The New American Cinema,* ed. Lewis, 307–27.

Klinger, Barbara. "'Cinema/Ideology/Criticism' Revisited: The Progressive Genre." In *Film Genre Reader II,* ed. Grant, 74–90.

———. "The Road to Dystopia." In *The Road Movie Book,* ed. Cohan and Hark, 179–203.

Kolker, Robert Philip. *A Cinema of Loneliness.* New York: Oxford University Press, 1980.

Kolker, Robert Philip, and Peter Beicken. *The Films of Wim Wenders.* New York: Cambridge University Press, 1993.

Kreider, Tim, and Rob Content. "The Straight Story." *Film Quarterly* 54, no. 1 (fall 2000): 26–33.

Lackey, Kris. *RoadFrames: The American Highway Narrative.* Lincoln: University of Nebraska Press, 1997.

Laderman, David. "The Road Movie Rediscovers Mexico: Alex Cox's *Highway Patrolman.*" *Cinema Journal* 39, no. 2 (winter 2000): 74–99.

———. "What a Trip: The Road Film and American Culture." *Journal of Film and Video* (summer 1996): 41–57.

Laird, David. "Versions of Eden: The Automobile and the American Novel." In *The Automobile and American Culture,* ed. Lewis and Goldstein, 244–56.

Lang, Robert. "*My Own Private Idaho* and the New Queer Road Movies." In *The Road Movie Book*, ed. Cohan and Hark, 330–48.

Lawrence, D. H. *Women in Love*. 1920. Reprint, New York: Penguin Books, 1976.

Lent, Tina Olsin. "As American as Apple Pie: The Road Trip in Postwar Culture." Paper presented at Society for Cinema Studies Conference, Dallas, March 1996.

Leong, Ian, Mike Sell, and Kelly Thomas. "Mad Love, Mobile Homes and Dysfunctional Dicks: On the Road with Bonnie and Clyde." In *The Road Movie Book*, ed. Cohan and Hark, 70–89.

Levy, Emanuel. *Cinema of Outsiders: The Rise of American Independent Film*. New York: New York University Press, 1999.

Lewis, Tom. *Divided Highways*. New York: Random House, 1997.

Lopez, Daniel. *Films by Genre*. Jefferson, N.C.: McFarland & Company, Inc. Publishers, 1993.

Lyons, Donald. "Detours." *Sight and Sound* 27, no. 4 (October 1991): 2–3.

McBride, Joseph, and Michael Wilmington. *John Ford*. New York: Da Capo Press, 1975.

MacMinn, Strother. "American Automobile Design." In *Automobile and Culture*, ed. Silk, 211–52.

Man, Glenn. *Radical Visions*. New York: Greenwood Press, 1994.

Marcus, Millicent. "Fellini's *La Strada*: Transcending Neorealism." *Perspectives on Federico Fellini*, edited by Peter Bondanella and Cristina Degli-Espostim, 87–99. New York: G. K. Hall & Co., 1993.

Marx, Leo. *The Machine in the Garden*. New York: Oxford University Press, 1964.

Miller, Henry. *The Air-Conditioned Nightmare*. 1947. Reprint, London: Panther Books, 1973.

Miller, Mark Crispin. "End of Story." In *Seeing through Movies*, 186–246.

Mills, Katie. "Revitalizing the Road Genre." In *The Road Movie Book*, ed. Cohan and Hark, 307–29.

Mitchell, Edward. "Apes and Essences: Some Sources of Significance in the American Gangster Film." In *Film Genre Reader II*, ed. Grant, 203–12.

Mitchell, Stuart. "How Secrets Travel: David Lynch and the Road." In *Lost Highways*, ed. Sargeant and Watson, 242–56.

Morton, Jim. "Rebels of the Road: The Biker Film." In *Lost Highways*, ed. Sargeant and Watson, 56–66.

———. "Road Kill: Horror on the Highway." In *Lost Highways*, ed. Sargeant and Watson, 120–28.

Mottram, Eric. "Blood on the Nash Ambassador: Cars in American Films." In *Cinema, Politics and Society*, edited by Philip Davies and Brian Neve. New York: St. Martin's Press, 1981. 221–49.

Mulvey, Laura. "Visual Pleasure and Narrative Cinema." *Screen* 16, no. 3 (1975): 6–18.

Nabokov, Vladimir. *Lolita*. New York: Berkeley Medallion Books, 1955.

Nash, Roderick. *Wilderness and the American Mind*. New Haven: Yale University Press, 1967.

Nehring, Neil. *Flowers in the Dustbin*. Ann Arbor: University of Michigan Press, 1993.

Orr, John. *Cinema and Modernity*. Cambridge, England: Polity Press, 1993.

Patton, Phil. *Open Road: A Celebration of the American Highway*. New York: Simon and Schuster, 1986.

Penley, Constance. "Time Travel, Primal Scene, and the Critical Dystopia." In *Alien Zone*, edited by Annette Kuhn, 116–27. New York: Verso, 1990.

Phillips, Karl. "We're Virtually There: SF Film on the Road to Ruin." In *Lost Highways*, ed. Sargeant and Watson, 266–74.

Polan, Dana. *Power and Paranoia: History, Narrative, and the American Cinema, 1940-1950*. New York: Columbia University Press, 1986.

Quart, Leonard. "The Politics of Irony: The Frears-Kureishi Films." In *Re-Viewing British Cinema, 1900-1992*, edited by Wheeler Winston Dixon, 241-48. Albany: State University of New York Press, 1994.

Robert Jr., Henry Flood. "Hot Rods and Customs." In *Automobile and Culture*, ed. Silk, 177-208.

Roberts, Shari. "Western Meets Eastwood." In *The Road Movie Book*, ed. Cohan and Hark, 45-69.

Robertson, Pamela. "Home and Away." In *The Road Movie Book*, ed. Cohan and Hark, 271-86.

Roddick, Nick. *A New Deal in Entertainment: Warner Brothers in the 1930s*. London: British Film Institute, 1983.

Russell, Catherine. "Decadence, Violence, and the Decay of History: Notes on the Spectacular Representation of Death in Narrative Film, 1965-1990." In *Crisis Cinema: The Apocalyptic Idea in Postmodern Narrative Film*, edited by Christopher Sharrett, 173-201. Washington, D.C.: Maisonneuve Press, 1993.

Ryan, Michael, and Douglas Kellner. *Camera Politica: The Politics and Ideology of Contemporary Hollywood Cinema*. Bloomington: Indiana University Press, 1988.

Sargeant, Jack. "Killer Couples: From Nebraska to Route 666." In *Lost Highways*, ed. Sargeant and Watson, 148-68.

———. "*Vanishing Point*: Speed Kills." In *Lost Highways*, ed. Sargeant and Watson, 90-98.

Sargeant, Jack, and Stephanie Watson. "Looking for Maps: Notes on the Road Movie as Genre." In *Lost Highways*, 6-20.

Schaber, Bennet. "'Hitler Can't Keep 'em That Long': The Road, the People." In *The Road Movie Book*, ed. Cohan and Hark, 17-44.

Schatz, Thomas. *Hollywood Genres*. New York: McGraw-Hill, 1981.

Seed, David. *Rudolph Wurlitzer: American Novelist and Screenwriter*. Lewiston, N.Y.: The Edwin Mellen Press, 1991.

Silk, Gerald. "The Automobile in Art." In *Automobile and Culture*, 25-176.

Slotkin, Richard. *Gunfighter Nation*. New York: Atheneum, 1992.

Smith, Henry Nash. *Virgin Land*. Cambridge: Harvard University Press, 1950.

Smith, Julian. "A Runaway Match: The Automobile in the American Film, 1900-1920." In *The Automobile and American Culture*, ed. Lewis and Goldstein, 179-92.

Sontag, Susan. "The Aesthetics of Silence." In *Styles of Radical Will*. New York: Dell Publishing Co., Inc., 1969. 3-34.

———. "Notes on 'Camp.'" In *Against Interpretation*. New York: Delta Books, 1966. 275-92.

Stout, Janis P. *The Journey Narrative in American Literature*. Westport, Conn.: Greenwood Press, 1983.

Stringer, Julian. "Exposing Intimacy in Russ Meyer's *Motorpsycho!* and *Faster Pussycat! Kill! Kill!*" In *The Road Movie Book*, ed. Cohan and Hark, 165-78.

Thompson, Jim. *The Getaway*. 1958. Reprint, New York: Vintage, 1994.

Todd, Pamela. *Bloomsbury at Home*. New York: Harry N. Abrams, Inc., 1999.

Törnqvist, Egil. *Between Stage and Screen: Ingmar Bergman Directs*. Amsterdam: Amsterdam University Press, 1995.

Walker, Beverly. "Malick on *Badlands*." *Sight and Sound* 44, no. 2 (April 1975): 81-83.

Watson, Stephanie. "From Riding to Driving: Once upon a Time in the West." In *Lost Highways*, ed. Sargeant and Watson, 22–37.

Webb, Adam. "No Beginning. No End. No Speed Limit: *Two-Lane Blacktop*." In *Lost Highways*, ed. Sargeant and Watson, 82–88.

Willis, Sharon. "Hardware and Hardbodies, What Do Women Want? A Reading of *Thelma and Louise*." In *Film Theory Goes to the Movies*, ed. J. Collins, Radner, and A. P. Collins, 120–28.

———. "Race on the Road: Crossover Dreams." *The Road Movie Book*, ed. Cohan and Hark, 287–306.

———. "Special Effects: Sexual and Social Difference in *Wild at Heart*." *Camera Obscura* 25–26 (1991): 275–95.

Wood, Robin. *Hollywood from Vietnam to Reagan*. New York: Columbia University Press, 1986.

———. "Ideology, Genre, Auteur." In *Film Genre Reader II*, ed. Grant, 59–73.

Zavarzadeh, Mas'ud. *Seeing Films Politically*. Albany: State University of New York, 1991.

INDEX

Night on Earth, 145

Nihilism: and *Detour,* 31, 93; and *Living End, The,* 213, 214; and *Natural Born Killers,* 198; and road movie genre, 81; and *Road Warrior, The,* 137; and *Two-Lane Blacktop,* 93; and *Vagabond,* 266; and *Vanishing Point,* 85, 108, 114, 289n.18

Nixon, Richard, 197

Nomadic narratives, 83, 184, 259

Oates, Warren, 94, 97, *105*, 118

O'Connor, Frances, 177

Odyssey (Homer), 6–7

On the Road (Kerouac): and *Bonnie and Clyde,* 54, 59; and cultural critique, 11–12; and *Easy Rider,* 66, 67; and *Kings of the Road,* 259; as master narrative for road movie, 10; and race issues, 21–22; and *Stranger than Paradise,* 148; and *Thelma and Louise,* 187; and *Two-Lane Blacktop,* 93; and visionary themes, 149; and wandering, 9, 214; and women, 20

Open landscape: and *Detour,* 31; and *Get on the Bus,* 223; and *Kings of the Road,* 260, 261, 262, 264; and *Living End, The,* 216; and *My Own Private Idaho,* 205, 210; and *Natural Born Killers,* 195; and *Paris, Texas,* 142; and road movie genre, 14–15; and *Road Warrior, The,* 136, 138; and *Straight Story, The,* 240; and *Thelma and Louise,* 185; and *Vagabond,* 267

Orr, John, 5, 15, 289n.15

Outlaw narratives, and film noir, 27, 34

Outlaw road movie: and *Badlands,* 83, 84, 106, 129; and *Bandits,* 274, 275, 296n.16; and *Bonnie and Clyde,* 20, 43–44, 52, 55, 57, 82; and *Delusion,* 180; and *Living End, The,* 216; and *My Own Private Idaho,* 204; and outlaw couple, 84, 87, 117–120, 122–124, 126, 197, 198, 201–202, 203, 204; and road movie genre, 82, 83, 86, 87; and *Sugarland Express, The,* 83, 129; and *Thelma and Louise,* 184, 204; and *Vanishing Point,* 106, 108, 117; and women, 21

Outside Ozona, 177

Over the Hill, 237

Paper Moon, 65, 82, 127

Paris, Texas: and drift, 150; and driving, 143–144, 148; and ending of, 150; and journey narrative, 142–143; and nonclosure, 30;

photographs from, *143;* as postmodern road movie, 133; and *Stranger than Paradise,* 142, 144–145

Parsons, Estelle, 54

Pastoralism, 18–19, 258

Patriarchy: and *Bandits,* 271, 273, 274, 278, 279, 280; and gay road movies, 21, 22; and *La Strada,* 249; and *Living End, The,* 213–214; patriarchal action-heroes, 132, 137; and race, 22, 48; and *Thelma and Louise,* 179, 184, 185, 186, 187, 188–192, 193, 194; and *Vagabond,* 268; and women, 21, 33, 48, 79

Patton, Phil, 26

Peckinpah, Sam, 97

Penley, Constance, 137

Penn, Arthur, 47, 50, 58, 62, 64, 78, 127, 255, 286n.6

People of color: and cultural critique, 176; as drivers, 179, 217–218; and *Natural Born Killers,* 201–203; and road movie genre, 217–235. *See also* Mexicans; Native Americans; Race issues

Perfect World, A, 178

Perlich, Max, 153

Phoenix, River, 204, *206*

Picaresque novel, 7, 12, 266

Picasso, Pablo, 5

Pioneers, The (Cooper), 9

Pirsig, Robert, 12

Pitt, Brad, 177, 190, 276

Planes, Trains, and Automobiles, 133

Plot structure: and *Badlands,* 118, 122; and *Bandits,* 273–274; and cultural critique, 2; and individualism, 17; and *Rain People, The,* 87; and *Repo Man,* 139–140; and *Road Warrior, The,* 136, 138, 139; and *Two-Lane Blacktop,* 93, 97, 100, 145. *See also* Narrative structure

Plunder Road, 26, 27, 41

Political issues: and alienation, 86; and American expansionism and imperialism, 22; and *Badlands,* 118, 123; and *Bandits,* 271, 272, 273, 274, 275, 276–277, 280; and *Bonnie and Clyde,* 50–51, 61, 62, 63–66, 81; divisiveness in, 84; and *Drugstore Cowboy,* 153, 157; and *Easy Rider,* 43, 69, 70, 73, 75, 78–81, 210; and European road movies, 247; and *Five Easy Pieces,* 91, 92; and *Get on the Bus,* 218–220, 222, 223, 224, 225, 226; and *Grapes of Wrath, The,* 30, 62; and *I Am a Fugitive*

THE LEARNING CENTRE
TOWER HAMLETS COLLEGE
POPLAR CENTRE
POPLAR HIGH STREET
LONDON E14 0AF